WAR IN
THE AEGEAN

The Stackpole Military History Series

THE AMERICAN CIVIL WAR
Cavalry Raids of the Civil War
Ghost, Thunderbolt, and Wizard
Pickett's Charge
Witness to Gettysburg

WORLD WAR II
Armor Battles of the Waffen-SS, 1943–45
Army of the West
Australian Commandos
The B-24 in China
Backwater War
The Battle of Sicily
Beyond the Beachhead
The Brandenburger Commandos
The Brigade
Bringing the Thunder
Coast Watching in World War II
Colossal Cracks
A Dangerous Assignment
D-Day to Berlin
Dive Bomber!
A Drop Too Many
Eagles of the Third Reich
Eastern Front Combat
Exit Rommel
Fist from the Sky
Flying American Combat Aircraft
 of World War II
Forging the Thunderbolt
Fortress France
The German Defeat in the East, 1944–45
German Order of Battle, Vol. 1
German Order of Battle, Vol. 2
German Order of Battle, Vol. 3
The Germans in Normandy
Germany's Panzer Arm in World War II
GI Ingenuity
The Great Ships
Grenadiers
Infantry Aces
Iron Arm
Iron Knights
Kampfgruppe Peiper at the Battle
 of the Bulge
Kursk
Luftwaffe Aces

Massacre at Tobruk
Mechanized Juggernaut or Military
 Anachronism?
Messerschmitts over Sicily
Michael Wittmann, Vol. 1
Michael Wittmann, Vol. 2
Mountain Warriors
The Nazi Rocketeers
On the Canal
Operation Mercury
Packs On!
Panzer Aces
Panzer Aces II
Panzer Commanders of the Western Front
The Panzer Legions
Panzers in Winter
The Path to Blitzkrieg
Retreat to the Reich
Rommel's Desert Commanders
Rommel's Desert War
The Savage Sky
A Soldier in the Cockpit
Soviet Blitzkrieg
Stalin's Keys to Victory
Surviving Bataan and Beyond
T-34 in Action
Tigers in the Mud
The 12th SS, Vol. 1
The 12th SS, Vol. 2
The War against Rommel's Supply Lines
War in the Aegean

THE COLD WAR / VIETNAM
Cyclops in the Jungle
Flying American Combat Aircraft:
 The Cold War
Here There Are Tigers
Land with No Sun
Street without Joy
Through the Valley

WARS OF THE MIDDLE EAST
Never-Ending Conflict

GENERAL MILITARY HISTORY
Carriers in Combat
Desert Battles
Guerrilla Warfare

WAR IN THE AEGEAN

The Campaign for the Eastern Mediterranean in World War II

Peter C. Smith and Edwin R. Walker

STACKPOLE
BOOKS

Published in paperback in 2008 by
STACKPOLE BOOKS
5067 Ritter Road
Mechanicsburg, PA 17055
www.stackpolebooks.com

For information on all of Peter C. Smith's books, please visit www.dive-bombers.co.uk

Cover design by Tracy Patterson

Printed in the United States of America

10   9   8   7   6   5   4   3   2   1

Library of Congress Cataloging-in-Publication Data

Smith, Peter Charles, 1940–
    War in the Aegean : the campaign for the Eastern Mediterranean in World War II / Peter C. Smith and Edwin R. Walker.
        p. cm. — (Stackpole military history series)
    Includes bibliographical references and index.
    ISBN 978-0-8117-3519-3
    1. World War, 1939–1945—Campaigns—Aegean Islands (Greece and Turkey).
2. Aegean Islands (Greece and Turkey)—History, Military. I. Walker, Edwin R.
II. Title.

D766.S6 2008
940.54'2958—dc22

2008003170

Contents

Introduction to the 1974 Edition

In telling the story of the War in the Aegean, we have endeavored to lay before the reader all the arguments, and the decisions, that resulted before, during, and after the unhappy campaign in the Dodecanese in the autumn of 1943. Each campaign is unique, but the Aegean disaster has puzzled the world in one respect more than most, as indeed it has puzzled those who participated in it at a local level: Why, at a time of undeniable Allied superiority in the Mediterranean, were the Germans, hard-pressed on all fronts and abandoned by their principal ally, allowed to exercise local domination to such an extent that they not only inflicted a grievous defeat on the British forces, but also frustrated attempts to draw in Turkey on the Allied side and were successful in securing their vulnerable southeastern flank for the rest of the war, all at minimal costs?

"After it was all over," one destroyer captain wrote in a letter to us, "I tried to piece it all together to discover the reason for it all. Despite much effort I felt no wiser than before. Perhaps your book will tell me." We can sympathize with him. We hope that he and our other readers will be a little more enlightened by our presentation of the facts.

There are always more lessons to be drawn from defeats than from victories, but much more attention is still paid to Trafalgar than to the Dutch attack on the Medway River; to El Alamein rather than the fall of Tobruk; to the sinking of *Tirpitz* rather than the breakout of *Scharnhorst* and *Gneisenau* through the English Channel.

Perhaps the one warning that comes out of this book is the frailty of any alliance once an individual nation's own aspirations are threatened. The surrender of the French forces in 1940 after many affirmations to the contrary is perhaps the best twentieth-century example, but there are innumerable examples of just how much each country's own strictly national policies can affect any alliance.

Great Britain is perhaps more sinned against than sinning. No nation could have been a more generous and friendly ally to the United States during the last war, and no alliance more firm and deeply felt than that forged between the two countries. Yet even here, once the United States had become the stronger in terms of military might and manpower, it became more and more the arbiter of Britain's course and fate—and this even under such strong, resolute and proudly nationalistic leadership as that of Prime Minister Winston Churchill. Even he could not halt the trend, at a time when Britain was still a major military power.

What about today? A string of postwar governments either blind or indifferent to problems of defense have left Great Britain in an unenviable position and totally reliant on the United States. In recent years, despite our common heritage and common belief in democracy, we differ on an increasing number of points. Yet should another test come, it will be American power that will protect us and dictate our defense policies.

We would like to express our thanks and gratitude to the following individuals and organizations for their unstinted help and cooperation, although we must stress that our views and conclusions are not necessarily theirs: D. C. Allard; the Army Library; Air Historical Branch, M.O.D.; R.Adm. P. N. Buckley, CB, DSO; Adm. Sir John F. D. Bush, GCB, DSC and 2 Bars; Chaz Bowyer; J. D. Bisdee; *Bundesarchiv*, Freiburg/Br; *Bibliothek für Zeitgeschichte*, Stuttgart; L. V. Chandler; Col. Vittorio de Castiglioni; John Dominy; Michael Cooper; Department of the Navy, Washington, DC; Department of the Air Force, Washington, DC; David L. Evans; Edwin R Flatequal; L. F. Francis; Dr. R. J. L. Ferris; *Capitano di Vascello* Franco Gnifetti; Capt. Edward Gibbs, DSO; Greek Embassy, London; Gerald M. Holland; Historical Section, Cabinet Office; Lt. Col. Sir Douglas Iggulden, DSO; Imperial War Museum, London; Italian Embassy, London; Geoff Jones; Capt. C. A. de W. Kitcat, DSO; Capt. S. le H. Lombard-Hobson, CVO, OBE; Cmdr. R. H. Mercer, DSC; Capt. C. W. Malins, DSO, DSC; Herr Mueller Mangeot; Marina Militare, Rome; Col. S. Nardini; Naval Historical Branch, M.O.D.; Naval Home Division, M.O.D; Thomas J. Price; Corrado Ricci; Dr. Jürgen Rohwer; Franz Selinger; Adm. Sir Alan Scott-Moncrieffe; *Stato Maggiore Dell'Esercito*, Rome; Squadron Leader Doug Tidy, MA, ASAIM; U.S. General Services Administration, Washington, DC; Robert Wolfe; Stan Hollet; and A. J. Thorogood.

Thanks are due to the following authors and publishers for quotations taken from the listed works: Edward Packer, *Hard Lesson in the Aegean* (Purnell); Christopher Buckley, *Five Ventures* (HMSO); Trumbell Higgins, *Soft Underbelly* (Macmillan); Field Marshal Sir H. Maitland-Wilson, *Eight Years Overseas* (Hutchinson); Lord Tedder, *With Prejudice* (Cassell); J. M. A. Gwyer, *Grand Strategy*, Vol. 4 (HMSO); Richards and Saunders, *The Flight Avails* (HMSO); Capt. S. W. Roskill, *The War at Sea*, Vol. 3, Pt. 1 (HMSO); Dudley Pope, *Flag 4* (William Kimber); L. Marsland Gander, *The Long Road to Leros* (Macdonald); *Aegean Adventure*, from D. A. Boyd, *The Dragon*; Group Capt. Kent, *One of the Few* (William Kimber); John Lodwick, *The Filibusters*

(Methuen); Winston S. Churchill, *The Second World War* (Cassell); Lord Douglas of Kirtleside, *Years of Command* (Collins); Arthur Bryant, *Triumph in the West* (Collins); King and Whitehall, *Fleet Admiral King* (Norton); S. G. P. Ward, *Faithful* (Nelson); Col. Julia Cowper, WRAC, *The King's Own Royal Regiment*, Vol. 3 (Gale and Polden); M. Cunliffe, *The Royal Irish Fusiliers* (Oxford University Press).

Should the student wish for more detailed studies of these events from the German, Italian, and Greek viewpoints, we recommend turning to the following works: Dr. Günther Brandt, *Der Seekrieig in der Ägäis*; Karl Alman, *Graue Woelfe in Blauer See*; *Ufficio Storico Della Marina Militare, Le Azione Navali in Mediterrano*, Vol. 16, *Pt Attivita Dopo L'armistizio*; Friedrich-August von Metzsch, *Die Geschichte der 22 Infanterie-Division*; Dimitrios Faka, *Ekthesis epi tes Draseos tou B. Nautikou kata tou Polemon 1940–1944 Tomo B*; and Costa de Overdo, *Le Battalion Scare*.

We have *not* ignored German sources, although we have been criticized for so doing. Some German veterans, if not British critics, acknowledge this fact; Jean-Louis Roba told us that *Hauptmann* Kühne, the leader of the *Fallschirmjägern* who jumped on Leros, when lent a copy of our original book, "was so interested that he immediately went out and bought his own copy. Proof that your book was very good!"

Introduction to the Revised American Edition

Since we completed this book more than thirty years ago, much information has been given to us by various participants and historians, especially from the German side. We would like to thank the following for fresh information included in this book: Lt. Kenneth Hallows, RN, *ML-351*; the late Michael Woodbine Parish, author of *Aegean Adventures, 1940–1943*; Flight Lt. J. W. D. Thomas, No. 227 Squadron, RAF; the late Jeffrey Holland, author of *The Aegean Mission*; Joe Hodgson, King's Own Royal Border Association; Herr Müller Mageot, staff officer, Attack Division *Rhodos*; Lt. D. Russell Whiteford, *LCT10*; *Col.a.s.SM* Vittorio de Castiglioni, *Stato Maggiore Dell'Esercito, Ufficio Storico*, Roma; B. Melland, cabinet officer, London; Cesare Gori, Pesaro; Prof. Comm. Amedo Montemaggi, Rimini; Jean-Louis Roba, Charleroi; W. Cole, 625 A.M.E.S.; Rev. R Anwyl, Catholic chaplain with Royal Irish Fusiliers; Arthur T. Blow, No. 603 Squadron; and Ken Shuttleworth, HMS *Faulknor*.

Unfortunately, all attempts at having a revised and updated edition of our book brought out by a British publisher fell on deaf ears. British publishers were *not* interested in defeats! Despite this attitude, other researchers have recently been more successful, some providing good eyewitness viewpoints of great value. Others have followed our main themes (some quite blatantly just copied our original material without the courtesy of requesting permission) but added little or nothing to the history as here related. A few are very inaccurate, two—one Australian and one American—are atrociously so. Thus we are especially glad to be able to present this new edition of our book to a new generation of researchers and, for the first time, to an American readership. If nothing else, we hope it illustrates how even the closest of friends and allies can have differing viewpoints on matters of great import and moment. This seems particularly relevant today, when the British television and press media are almost universally hostile to our American fellow democracy in the face of terrorist and extremist action around the globe.

Our first edition tried to explode many misconceptions. One of the most pernicious and most enduring, despite the true facts having long been known, is the persistent one that, after Crete in 1941, German paratroops never jumped from aircraft into battle again. At Leros in 1943, they did just that and again took the island. One British critic, writing in the *Times* newspaper in 1979, flatly refused to acknowledge this basic truth, so ingrained has the myth become established in certain corners of the military establishment. Even if one can never hope to convince such diehard skeptics, we at least hope that those with more open minds might take a more enlightened view on this and other demolished legends.

Note on the Dodecanese Islands

The island-studded Aegean Sea is an arm of the Mediterranean stretching from the shores of Greece in the west to the coast of Asia Minor in the east and connected with the Sea of Marmora through the Dardanelles.

The islands of the Aegean form three main groups: the northern Sporades, the Cyclades, and the Dodecanese. The last named group is the most easterly, many of these islands being within sight of the Turkish coast. As the name implies, the Dodecanese consist of twelve islands—Nisyros, Cos, Kasos, Patmos, Calchi, Leros, Tilos, Simi, Stampalia, Lipsos, Scarpanto, and Kalymnos—although by common usage, the islands of Rhodes and Casteloriso are generally recognized as being part of this group as well.

From the sixteenth-century onward, the Dodecanese people had been under Turkish rule, although the bulk of the population was of Greek extraction. They remained so until the Italo-Turkish War of 1911–12, which broke out on September 29, 1911, following Italian plans for colonial expansion in North Africa. Italy had originally set its sights on Tunisia, but when that country came under French control, Italy became determined to secure Libya, which was then a Turkish *vilayet* (the term for the chief administrative division of Turkey). Considerable numbers of Italians had already settled in Libya during the nineteenth century, and the numbers increased during the early twentieth century. In the summer of 1911, Italy and the Sublime Porte, the Turkish government, had considerable diplomatic exchanges over the protection of Italian interests in Libya.

The exchanges did not proceed in quite the way the Italians would have liked, and so on the September 28, 1911, they issued a twenty-four-hour ultimatum intimating that Italy's interests in Tripoli made it necessary for the country to undertake, by means of military occupation, a so-called "civilizing mission" in that area. Italy declared war the next day and attacked Tripoli from the sea on October 3. The Turks withdrew and the Italians occupied the city. Italian forces pushed on eastward and occupied Derna and Benghazi without serious opposition. Fighting continued in a desultory manner throughout the winter and flared up again in the spring of 1912, when the

Italians attacked at several points and defeated the Turks and the Arabs who supported them.

It was during this spring offensive of 1912 that Italy made its move against the Turkish Aegean islands. The operations had three main objectives: to secure bases from which to attack the flow of arms and men from the Ottoman Empire to Libya and Cyrenaica; to use the occupation of the islands as a bargaining chip at the peace table; and to have them as a base for any possible future operations against Asia Minor.

The Italian Navy played the prime role in these operations, and between April 15 and 16, 1912, a naval squadron arrived off Stampalia to prepare for a bombardment of the eastern fortifications of the Dardanelles. It was duly carried out on April 18, as was a bombardment of Turkish positions on Samos. The navy made a landing on Stampalia on April 28 from the ships *Pisa* and *L'Amalfi* and occupied the island. On May 4, forces were landed on Rhodes. The ill-equipped Turks did not offer much resistance and retreated inland, where they soon were forced to surrender after being encircled.

During May, Italian forces occupied the islands of Calchi, Scarpanto, Kasos, Nisyros, Tilos, Kalymnos, Patmos, and Leros without much opposition. The only island that remained in Turkish hands was Casteloriso, the most easterly of the group. The Italian commanders promised to secure the islanders autonomy, but when an insular assembly at Patmos proclaimed "the autonomous state of the Dodecanese" and expressed a desire for union with Greece, the Italians paid no attention—except to impose severe penalties on some of the delegates.

Following the occupation of the Dodecanese and Turkey's defeats in Libya and Cyrenaica, the Turks sued for peace. The negotiations that followed were protracted. They opened in July 1912 at Lausanne with a meeting of the European Great Powers. The chief Italian negotiator, Count Giuseppe Volpi, met with a great deal of open hostility, particularly from France and England, which were now very concerned that Italy held command of the approaches to the Dardanelles. The peace treaty was eventually signed on October 18, 1912, under which Turkey ceded Libya, known as Tripolitania, to Italy.

The Italians undertook to withdraw their forces from the Dodecanese when the Turks had fulfilled their obligations in Libya, but they were not able to complete the withdrawal, as the Turkish Empire, whose European territories at this time stretched to the shores of the Adriatic, had started to crumble.

The Balkan War of 1912–13 between Turkey and its neighbors left the fate of the Dodecanese, still occupied by the Italians, undecided. Italy was determined to maintain its position in the Dodecanese as a bargaining chip against Greek aspirations in the Adriatic, for if the islands were returned to Turkey, they would almost inevitably pass to Greece, which, during the First Balkan War, had occupied the Northern Sporades and other Turkish islands in the Aegean. Negotiations continued during 1914 but little progress was made, and the situation was further complicated by the outbreak of the First World War in August of that year. Italy declared its neutrality. Turkey had concluded a secret alliance with Germany on August 2 and, after some slight hesitation, entered the war on the side of the Central Powers on October 29. Greece was divided; some hoped it might be able to stay neutral, but others supported the Greek prime minister, Eleutherio Venizelos, who was for taking the side of the Allies. The country eventually entered the war in 1917, on the overthrow of the king.

It soon became apparent to Italy that it would be in the nation's best interests to join the Allies, and talks to this effect took place. On April 26, 1915, a secret treaty was signed in London in which the Allies accorded Italy full possession of the Dodecanese as one of the inducements to enter World War I on their side; Italy duly entered the war on May 23 of that year. The agreement signed in London became of doubtful validity, however, when the United States entered the war in 1917, on the understanding that no secret treaties should be recognized.

At the conclusion of the First World War, discussions took place between Italy and Greece on the future of the Dodecanese. On July 29, 1919, Venizelos and the Italian foreign minister, Tomaso Tittoni, reached an agreement whereby Italy promised to cede the Dodecanese to Greece, with the exception of Rhodes, which was to have broad local autonomy. By an additional secret accord, Italy undertook to permit the inhabitants of Rhodes to decide their own fate in the event that the British government announced its willingness to cede Cyprus to Greece, although not before five years had elapsed.

On July 22, 1920, Count Carlo Sforza, Tittoni's successor, denounced the agreement, but on August 10 of that year, simultaneously with the abortive Treaty of Sevres between the Allies and Turkey, a new Italo-Greek accord was signed. Its terms were similar to those of the previous agreement, with the main difference being that fifteen years instead of five were to elapse before the Rhodian plebiscite. To enable Italy to transfer to Greece territory that was still *de jure* Turkish, a special article was included in the Treaty of Sevres by which Turkey renounced in favor of Italy all its rights and titles to the Dodecanese and Casteloriso.

In October 1922, the Italian government unilaterally denounced the accord with Greece, despite a protest from Great Britain, and the Treaty of Sevres was never ratified, being overtaken now by the Greco-Turkish War in Anatolia. In the Treaty of Lausanne of July 24, 1923, which ended this war and superseded the Treaty of Sevres, the Turkish renunciation clause of the earlier treaty was finally embodied as Article 13. The Greek government, however, before accepting the Treaty of Lausanne, expressed in writing its views on the "determination of the future lot" of the Dodecanese. The islands nevertheless remained under Italian rule until the end of the Second World War.

CHAPTER ONE

A Lesson Learned?

In the early hours of February 25, 1941, the first Mediterranean combined operation of the Second World War was launched when troops from No. 50 Middle East Commando were landed on the small Italian island of Casteloriso. The island lies just inside the southeastern limits of the Dodecanese, to the south of the Vathi Peninsula on the mainland of Turkey; it is about 80 miles east of Rhodes and some 150 miles west of Cyprus. Although its total area amounts to only 4 square miles, the island has a useful harbor, shaped like an inverted horseshoe.

The operational plan was for the commandos to carry out the initial assault on the island and then be relieved by B Company, 1st Battalion, the Sherwood Foresters, who were to form the permanent garrison. Once this harbor was captured, the Royal Navy would use it as an advance base for motor torpedo boats and motor launches.

The operation actually got under way on February 23 when the destroyers *Hereward* and *Decoy* embarked 200 commandos at Suda Bay in Crete and quickly sailed for Casteloriso. They were accompanied by the cruiser *Gloucester*, wearing the flag of R.Adm. E. de F. Renouf, commander of the 3rd Cruiser Squadron, who was in overall command of the operation. The force proceeded westward through the Kithera Channel, then south of Crete, and made contact with the submarine *Parthian*, which was acting as a navigational beacon, at a point four miles to the southwest of Casteloriso at 0200 on the twenty-fifth. Here the destroyers were detached to land the commandos.

The landings were made without opposition, and the naval force then patrolled south of the island. The troops quickly occupied the wireless station—although unfortunately not before warning of the attack had been broadcast—the barracks, and the commandant's residence. The Italian garrison consisted of two detachments of troops, each of fourteen men under the command of a noncommissioned officer (NCO). One detachment was based at the wireless station and the other at the lookout post on Monte Viglia. In addition, there were ten armed Italian gendarmes and customs officials with two NCOs. The main armament of the garrison consisted of five machine guns: two at the wireless station, two at the lookout post, and

1

the last held by the gendarmes. The survivors of the opening attack withdrew to the post on Monte Viglia.

It was decided that an attack on the post must await the arrival of the gunboat *Ladybird*, which was due to arrive at Casteloriso at first light on the twenty-fifth. She carried a main armament of two 6-inch guns and also had on board twenty-four heavily armed Royal Marines, who were to supplement the commandos.

The *Ladybird*, which had previously been operating with the Inshore Squadron off the Cyrenaica coast, harassing Italian positions with telling effect, had sailed from Port Said on the twenty-second and arrived at Famagusta on the twenty-third. There she was to await the arrival of the armed boarding vessel *Rosaura*, in order to refuel from her. At Famagusta, the *Rosaura* was to embark the Sherwood Foresters and take them to Casteloriso. She was delayed leaving Alexandria for several hours, however, because the army was late in delivering water cans required for the garrison. Consequently, the *Ladybird*, in order to keep her assignment, had to leave Famagusta without refueling.

The gunboat entered the harbor of Casteloriso early on the twenty-fifth and immediately came under rifle fire from the shore, which she quickly silenced with fire from her pom-pom guns. She also fired twelve rounds of 6-inch shell into the post on Monte Viglia, which was soon captured by the commandos, and she then landed her marines.

The enemy reaction to the landing was quick. Between 0800 and 0930 on the twenty-fifth, Italian aircraft carried out heavy raids on the harbor, the *Ladybird* being their principal target. With little room to maneuver within the harbor, she was soon hit, one bomb landing just forward of the bridge and seriously wounding three men. The officer in charge of the commandos now informed *Ladybird* that the marines would not be required, and they were therefore reembarked. The continuing air raids rapidly made the gunboat's position in the harbor untenable, and she slipped her buoy and headed for Famagusta, where she landed her wounded. The commander in chief of the Mediterranean Fleet approved her decision to withdraw. At Famagusta, she took on twenty tons of oil fuel from drums and later sailed to Haifa for repairs.

B Company of the 1st Battalion, Sherwood Foresters, under the command of Maj. L. C. Cooper, embarked on the *Rosaura* at Famagusta late on the twenty-fourth, and the ship sailed at 0420 on the twenty-fifth, escorted by the cruisers *Gloucester* and *Bonaventure* and the destroyers *Hereward* and *Decoy*. The battalion had been in Cyprus since June 10, 1940, on garrison duties. Early in February 1941, B Company had been ordered to prepare for secret operations, the nature of which was not divulged. On February 22, Major

Cooper was given some further details, but he was neither informed of the location of the enterprise nor shown any maps. It was not until after the *Rosaura* had sailed that he was able to open the sealed envelope given to him before embarkation—an excellent example of security being taken too far! He had had no chance to make proper plans, nor even to discuss details with either his superiors or his subordinates, until after embarkation. On the twenty-fifth, the force headed toward Casteloriso in steadily deteriorating weather, which caused the *Rosaura* to roll heavily.

At 1730, the destroyer *Hereward* was sent on ahead to advise the commandos that they would be relieved by the garrison that night instead of by daylight as originally planned. A daylight landing in the face of the heavy air raids that had been experienced was thought to be too risky.

The *Hereward* arrived off Nifti Point, the southeastern extremity of the island, at 2300 on the twenty-fifth. Her task was to arrange for lights to be placed on the headland and for boats to be gotten ready for the transfer of the garrison troops. On arrival, however, she received a signal from the shore stating that enemy surface ships were in the vicinity and there were at least two to the northward. It was also thought probable that the enemy vessels intended to land reinforcements for the garrison. The *Hereward* immediately sent an enemy report, which led Admiral Renouf to believe that she had actually sighted the enemy ships; he therefore ordered her to attack. The *Hereward* was unable to locate the enemy ships and she finally withdrew southward to meet the *Decoy*.

The Italian Navy, like the air force, had indeed reacted with vigor and enterprise. The destroyers *Francesco Crispi* and *Quintino Sella*, as well as the torpedo boats *Lince* and *Lupo*, all sailed from Rhodes on the twenty-fifth, carrying reinforcements for the hard-pressed garrison of Casteloriso. They consisted of an army detachment of fifteen men, under the command of a second lieutenant of artillery; a naval detachment of thirty-six men, whose main task was to recapture the wireless station and the lookout posts; and a detachment of fifty men from the 13th Blackshirt Company. The ships themselves were also to provide sixty-five men to assist the landing. After a delay caused by bad weather, these reinforcements were disembarked from the *Lince* on the morning of the twenty-seventh under the cover of a bombardment from the *Lupo*.

In the face of this attack from the sea, and with the continuing air raids and a shortage of food and ammunition, the commandos were forced to give ground. They retreated to the southeastern corner of the island to await the arrival of the garrison.

The unfortunate position of the British troops on Casteloriso was, however, quite unknown to Admiral Renouf. The *Ladybird*, which was to have acted as a wireless link with the troops onshore, had departed, and with her departure, the commandos were left only with short-range wireless sets and were unable to communicate with the naval forces. The commander in chief in Alexandria was, therefore, unaware of the situation on the island when Admiral Renouf ordered the return of his forces and was not even fully informed as to whether any ships had been left to cover the island. His first reaction was to order the Australian light cruiser *Perth* to raise steam and clear Alexandria during the morning of the twenty-sixth, but she did not sail, as a signal was received from Admiral Renouf saying that he was flying his staff officer to Alexandria with a full report of the situation On arrival of this officer at 1530 on the twenty-sixth, the commander in chief became aware for the first time that no ships had in fact been left off Casteloriso.

Admiral Renouf's force arrived at Alexandria during the night of February 26–27, and the transfer of troops from the *Rosaura* was quickly carried out. Within an hour and ten minutes of their arrival in Egypt, the first shipload of troops was at sea once more. Half of the company under Major Cooper sailed in the *Decoy*, followed fifty-five minutes later by the remainder under the command of Capt. W. H. A. Becke in the destroyer *Hero*. The troop-carrying destroyers were accompanied by the cruisers *Bonaventure* and *Perth* and the destroyers *Hasty* and *Jaguar*. The whole force was under the command of Capt. H. J. Egerton in *Bonaventure*; Admiral Renouf had reported sick on arrival at Alexandria.

The force made for the island at high speed. During the day, plans for the landing were discussed, and it was decided that five whalers would be used for the operation, each carrying a crew of four naval ratings and ten soldiers.

At 2300 on the twenty-seventh, the island was sighted by the *Decoy*, and the men of the landing party stood by at their boat stations. Ahead of them, a dark chunk of land stood out against the night. There was no moon to light the way, and a brisk wind was blowing. It was cold with occasional rain. The engine telegraphs rang the *Decoy* to a standstill, and the boats were lowered. The shore was 800 yards away, and in a choppy sea, the journey took about twenty minutes. The landing place was in a small rocky bay, and it proved difficult to secure the boats and unload the stores. Of the commandos, there was no sign. No sounds of gunfire could be heard, and there was no clue as to the general situation.

A platoon of men was deployed to secure a bridgehead, and the remainder of the party was employed in unloading stores from the whalers. Major Cooper, his orderly, and a naval signaler then set off to find the commanding officer of the commandos. After some minutes, they came across a stone breastwork containing uniform equipment and several boxes of ammunition; a few minutes later, they came upon a dead British soldier. Things did

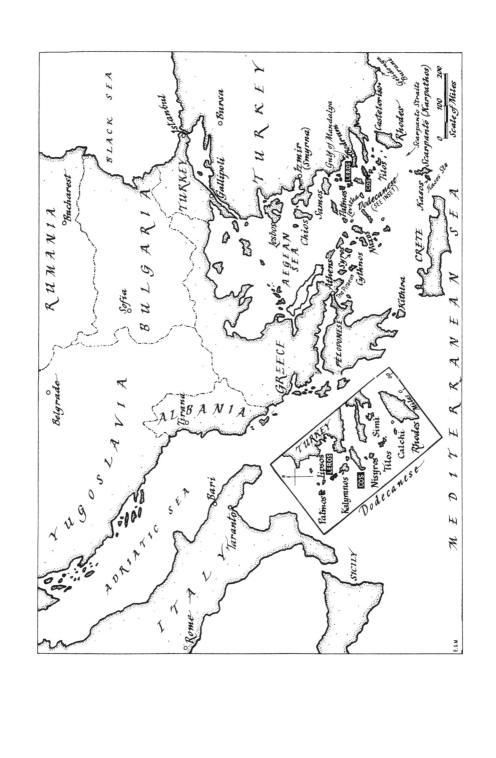

not look promising. Then they came across two sadly demoralized commandos who crawled out from a hole in the ground. They said they had decided to try to swim across to Turkey, as the rest of the force had been wiped out. Major Cooper, however, pressed on and met a commando NCO and a private; the NCO confirmed that the Italians had indeed regained firm control of the island. Cooper therefore returned to the bridgehead and sent out two patrols to try to contact any further survivors of the commandos. He reported the situation to the captain of the *Decoy*, who replied that the commanding officer of the commandos, Colonel Symonds, and nine commando officers were already onboard. Major Cooper then returned to the ship for a conference.

Of the naval forces, the cruisers *Bonaventure* and *Perth* had proceeded to patrol north of the island, and the other destroyers remained off Nifti Point to cover the *Decoy*.

It was evident that things had gone sadly amiss, and Major Cooper decided that the Foresters should land as many stores as possible and prepare to attack the port at dawn. He asked for help from the Royal Navy in dealing with the harbor and for supporting fire for the attack. The naval forces, however, had firm instructions that they must be clear of the island by 0430 the next day because of the risk of air attack. Under these circumstances, Major Cooper reasoned that the tactical situation ruled out any attempt to try to retake the island, and he therefore ordered the withdrawal of his force. In pitch darkness and fighting against a steadily rising sea, the Foresters returned to the destroyer. So ended the operation against Casteloriso. British forces had suffered four men killed, eleven wounded and forty missing; Italian casualties were fourteen killed, forty-two wounded, with twelve men taken prisoner.

The Italian naval force that had brought the reinforcements to the island remained in the area. The *Francesco Crispi, Lince,* and *Lupo* patrolled southward to a distance of thirty miles from Casteloriso until 0330 on the twenty-eighth. The *Quintino Sella* was between Rhodes and Cos. There were also two motor torpedo (MAS) boats, or PT boats, *546* and *561*, patrolling close off the two harbor entrances to Casteloriso, and the submarine *Galatea* was patrolling twenty miles southwest of the island.

The only naval incident during the night of February 27–28 was when the *Jaguar* was nearly hit by two torpedoes, which passed close astern. These had been fired by the *Francesco Crispi*. The *Jaguar* opened fire on her and claimed two hits before its searchlight jammed, causing delay until star shell could be fired. No further contact was made.

The British force was clear of the island by 0300 and arrived at Suda Bay during the afternoon of the twenty-eighth. Here the commandos and the prisoners were disembarked. The Foresters went ashore for a hot meal and sailed again two and a quarter hours later for Alexandria in the *Decoy* and *Hero*, escorted by the *Perth*.

On the passage between Suda Bay and Alexandria, Major Cooper had a very lucky escape. When making his way from the bridge to the wardroom, he was washed overboard by a large wave. Luckily he was spotted by a sailor on the after gun deck, who slung him a rope and raised the alarm. He was safely hauled aboard fifteen minutes later.

The force arrived at Alexandria at 1845 on March 2, and four days later, the Foresters returned to Cyprus somewhat chastened. The affair had been muddled at the highest level from the very start, and it was painfully evident that there was much to be learned about the conduct of this type of operation.

For Britain, this first round, if such it can be called, had ended in a reverse, albeit not perhaps a very serious one. The important question was whether the British had learned from it.

When on September 3, 1939, Britain and France declared war on Germany, Italy remained on the sidelines and declared its neutrality. In the spring of 1940, however, following the massive German victories in France and the Low Countries, Italy had judged that the time was perhaps ripe to enter the war and thus earn itself a seat alongside Germany at the peace table—and qualify also for a share of the spoils of war. So on June 10, 1940, Italy formally declared war on Britain and France.

The Italian naval forces based on the Dodecanese at this time consisted of two destroyers of the 4th Destroyer Division, *Francesco Crispi* and *Quintino Sella*; two torpedo boats of the 15th Torpedo Boat Division, *Solferino* and *San Martino*; eight submarines, *Gondar, Scire, Neghelli, Asciangi, Durbo, Tembien, Beilul*, and *Lafole*; one minelayer, *Legnano*; and about twenty motor torpedo (MAS) boats.

The Royal Navy, although soon to lose the assistance of the French ships, was more than a match for the Italian Fleet and maintained control of both the western and eastern basins of the Mediterranean. The Italian Fleet was not successful in breaking this domination.

With control of the eastern Mediterranean firmly in the hands of the Royal Navy, all maritime communications between Italy and the islands of the Dodecanese came to a standstill, and their supply presented Italy with a serious problem. Although stocks of food and material had been built up on the islands prior to the outbreak of war, the continued maintenance of these supplies was essential; the Italians quickly brought into use some of their minelaying submarines for store-carrying purposes. In all, the submarines made eleven missions to the Dodecanese. The first was undertaken by the *Atropo*, which left Taranto on June 20, 1940, and arrived at Leros two days later; the final mission was made by the *Zoea*, which left for Leros on April 1, 1941.

At the outbreak of war, eight merchant ships—the *Poseidone* (6,613 tons), *Urano* (6,339 tons), *Citta di Palermo* (5,413 tons), *Gartivento* (3,694 tons), *Santa Maria* (3,539 tons), *Egitto* (3,329 tons), *Fenicia* (2,584 tons), and *Alfio* (2,134 tons)—were locked up in the Aegean at Leros. Some of these were suitable for employment as naval auxiliaries, and at the first opportunity they sailed singly for Italy. The first ship, the *Citta di Palermo*, sailed from Leros at 0600 on June 20 and arrived at Brindisi on the twenty-third. The last ship to sail was the *Alfio*, which slipped out of Leros at 0015 on June 23, arriving at Brindisi on the twenty-sixth. All eight ships had uneventful voyages and arrived without mishap—which was a success for the Italians.

Supply by air and submarine for the Dodecanese, however, was insufficient to sustain the garrison and civil populations and the use of merchant shipping had to be considered. It was decided to use small coastal vessels that could be routed across the Ionian Sea and through the Corinth Canal to the Piraeus, where they had to await a favorable opportunity for the more hazardous passage across to Leros.

The British Mediterranean Fleet instituted frequent sweeps of the Aegean by cruisers and destroyers in an effort to intercept and deter traffic to the Dodecanese and they met with their first success on July 28, 1940. The fleet had sailed from Alexandria on the morning of the twenty-seventh, with the object of providing distant cover to northbound and southbound convoys en route between Egypt and the Dardanelles. The following morning, intelligence was received to the effect that the Greek ship *Ermioni* (440 tons), bound for the Dodecanese with an Italian cargo of 500 tons of oil and petrol, would clear the Corinth Canal at about 1100 that morning. The light cruisers *Neptune* and *Sydney* were therefore detached from the fleet, then to the northwest of Crete, to intercept. The cruisers were heavily bombed when in the Thermia Channel, southeast of Athens, but not damaged. Shortly afterward, at 2050, they intercepted the vessel, and she was shelled and sunk. The cruisers then proceeded south through the Kithera Channel and arrived at Alexandria at noon the next day.

During the passage of the north and south Dardanelles convoys, attempts were made to divert enemy air attacks by demonstrations off Casteloriso island, the most easterly of the Dodecanese group. Accordingly, at midnight on July 23, a light cruiser, the *Orion*, and two Australian destroyers, *Vampire* and *Voyager*, sailed from Alexandria. They made a demonstration about ten miles off the island shortly before sunset on the twenty-fourth. The two destroyers then proceeded to Port Said, where they arrived at 1130 on the twenty-fifth.

The destroyers sailed again from Port Said at 1000 on the twenty-sixth, to rendezvous with the cruiser for a further demonstration against Casteloriso. This time they were accompanied by two armed boarding vessels, *Fiona* and *Chakla*, to represent transports. The following evening, the force proceeded as if it was about to carry out landings on the island. Neither demonstration provoked any action from the island's defenses, although the ships fired star shells on the twenty-seventh, and there was no sign of any enemy air activity.

Not daunted by the interception and loss of the *Ermioni*, the small steamer *Tarquinia*, loaded with stores and supplies, successfully completed a voyage to Rhodes and back during September, and so did two sailing vessels. The Italian High Command continued to received repeated requests for reinforcements and stores from the military commander in the Aegean, and plans were therefore made to send two fourteen-knot merchant ships into the Aegean under heavy naval escort. The operation was code-named CV, and some elaborate planning took place before it was considered timely for the convoy to be sailed.

The two merchants ships sailed from Taranto on the evening of October 5, escorted by the 12th Destroyer Division, consisting of the *Lanciere, Carabinieri, Gorazziere,* and *Ascari*. The next morning, the 1st Cruiser Division (*Pola, Fiume, Gorizia,* and *Zara*), escorted by the 9th Destroyer Division (*Alfieri, Oriani, Carducci,* and *Gioberti*), sailed from Taranto and the 3rd Cruiser Division (*Trieste, Trento,* and *Bolzano*), escorted by the 11th Destroyer Division (*Artigliere, Camicia Nera, Aviere,* and *Geniere*), sailed from Messina to overtake the convoy and provide distant cover. The Italians had thus sailed a formidable naval force to back up the operation. That morning, however, Italian aerial reconnaissance reported a British force of two battleships, two cruisers and seven destroyers between Alexandria and the Kasos Straits. The Italians called off the operation forthwith, and all ships returned to the safety of their harbors.

Notwithstanding the failure of Operation CV, the *Tarquinia* made a second voyage to the Aegean via the Corinth Canal. Leaving Italy on October 21, she arrived at Leros on the twenty-eighth and sailed a day later for Rhodes, where she unloaded 482 tons of stores. These, however, were the last supplies brought to the Dodecanese by this route, for on October 28, the Italians invaded Greece from Albania with the hopes of a quick victory that would give them complete control of the Aegean. But the Greeks thwarted the Italian intentions and the invasion ground to a halt.

For Britain, the Greek involvement in the war improved its strategic position in the eastern Mediterranean; with the use of Greek bases at the Piraeus and at Suda Bay in Crete, the task of the Royal Navy in escorting convoys to and from Greece and the Dardanelles was greatly eased. Suda Bay also proved to be a useful fueling base in the sailing of convoys between Alexandria and Malta.

The failure of the Italian offensive had left their Aegean islands dangerously exposed. They could no longer use the route via the Corinth Canal and had to find alternative methods of supply. The route chosen was for merchant ships to sail from Italy direct to Tobruk and then make a dash onward to Rhodes when the opportunity occurred. Four such voyages were completed without incident during December 1940 and January 1941, bringing in more than 4,500 tons of much-needed stores. Supplies by this route were then curtailed by the advance from Egypt of the British Eighth Army, which captured Tobruk on January 21; Benghazi fell on February 6. The Dodecanese Islands were now even more dangerously exposed.

This was surely just the moment the British had been waiting for to launch an attack on the islands—an operation for which the plans had been under consideration for some time, though a lack of suitable landing craft had precluded its earlier execution. On October 30, 1940, the director of combined operations, Admiral of the Fleet Sir Roger Keyes, had first put forward a plan for the capture of the island of Pantelleria, a defended rock about 120 miles west of Malta. The plan, to be known as Operation Workshop, received the active support of British prime minister Winston Churchill. The intention was to sail three assault landing ships from the United Kingdom with the Excess convoy, which was to be passed through the Mediterranean from Gibraltar to the Piraeus. The assault ships were converted Glen liners—*Glenroy* (9,871 tons), *Glenearn* (9,869 tons), and *Glengyle* (9,865 tons)—capable of a speed of 18½ knots and designed to carry 2,000 Special Service commando-type troops who were to capture the island.

It was thought that the island's capture would provide an airfield suitable for use as a staging post for aircraft en route to the Middle East, and that fighters could be based on it for the protection of Britain's ships in the Sicilian Narrows, thus ensuring a direct supply route to the Middle East instead of the long haul around the Cape of Good Hope. After the capture of the island, the highly trained Special Service troops were to be relieved by troops from Malta and then proceed with their special equipment in the assault ships to the Middle East, for operations in that command.

The prime minister's enthusiasm was not shared by the British chiefs of staff, who in November 1940 asked Adm. Andrew Browne Cunningham, the commander in chief of the Mediterranean Fleet, for his opinion of the operation. He replied that he felt the fleet already had very heavy responsibilities in the Mediterranean, and the supply of Malta was not easy; to attempt to supply Pantelleria as well would involve an unjustified diversion of naval forces from the eastern Mediterranean. He therefore proposed that the assault force should be sent directly to the eastern Mediterranean and used to capture some of the Dodecanese Islands, beginning with Stampalia and Scarpanto.

Churchill did not favor this proposal, and despite Admiral Cunningham's views, the Defence Committee in London decided that Operation Workshop should proceed. In the middle of December, however, Britain thought that Germany might be planning a move against Gibraltar through Spain, and the Defence Committee decided to keep the Special Service troops in the United Kingdom, ready for any instant action that might be required. The three assault ships therefore did not sail with the Excess convoy.

At the end of December, the British chiefs of staff proposed to send the force around the Cape of Good Hope to get on with the second half of the plan. The prime minister vetoed this suggestion, preferring that the force carry out the Pantelleria operation on the way. This was now rescheduled for early March.

Up to the end of 1940, the Royal Navy had enjoyed great freedom of movement in the central Mediterranean and almost complete freedom elsewhere. But the situation was soon to change. On November 20 of that year, Hitler had proposed to Mussolini that German bombers operate from Italian bases for a time against the Royal Navy. A directive to this effect was issued on December 10, as Operation Mittelmeer (German for Mediterranean Sea), and in January 1941, *Fliegerkorps X*, many of whose pilots had specialized in operations against shipping, was transferred from Norway to the central Mediterranean. By January 8, 96 bombers were established on Sicilian airfields, followed two days later by 25 twin-engine fighters. By mid-January, the force totaled 186 aircraft of all types. The new formation announced its presence on January 10, when the aircraft carrier *Illustrious*, taking part in one of the complicated operations concerning the passage of convoys through the Mediterranean—including Excess, the convoy with which the original plan was to send the Glen ships—was severely damaged west of Malta and put out of action for several months. On January 12, during the same operations, German dive-bombers hit and sank the 6-inch gun cruiser *Southampton* and damaged her sister ship *Gloucester*. It was now clear that the movement of ships during daylight within range of the dive bombers could be expensive.

It also became apparent to Great Britain that it had to make moves to prevent the spread of the German Air Force to the Dodecanese Islands, from which the Germans would be able to threaten British Aegean convoys and also be able to attack the Suez Canal. The only sure way of preventing this would be for British forces to occupy the islands first to avert this threat. Operations against these islands had always been in the mind of the Middle East Command, but now the situation had become more urgent. In the middle of January, the command asked that the Glen assault ships be sent around the Cape of Good Hope for use in operations against the Dodecanese Islands. Meanwhile a seaborne assault against the small island of Kasos, which lies near Scarpanto just to the east of Crete, had been planned. With Kasos in its hands, Britain would have had complete control of the Kasos Straits, which were the scene of much U-boat and E-boat activity. The British also planned to mount guns on Kasos to command the airfield on Scarpanto.

An agreement to the request for the Glen ships would have meant canceling Operation Workshop, and this the prime minister was reluctant to do. On January 16, the chiefs of staff informed the Middle East Command that the employment of the Glen ships was still undecided, and further, that it was undesirable to stir up the Dodecanese by pinpricking seaborne raids until the program for the whole action against the islands had been settled. Despite a protest from Admiral Cunningham, the operation against Kasos Island was vetoed by the chiefs of staff, the orders for its cancellation arriving a few hours before the assault was due to get under way.

On January 20, the Defence Committee in London agreed that the presence of the *Luftwaffe* in strength in Sicily meant that Operation Workshop was impracticable. It therefore decided that the Glen ships carrying the 2,000 Special Service troops should sail at the end of the month for the Middle East via the Cape as previously intended. In addition, a Mobile Naval Base Defence Organization—specially designed for the rapid defense of captured bases, consisting of more than 5,000 officers and men of the Royal Marines with antiaircraft and coast defense equipment—would be sent a fortnight later. The main objective of these forces was to be the island of Rhodes—with its airfields, undoubtedly the key to the Dodecanese.

The Glen ships were not expected to arrive until March, and the major enterprises in the Aegean were therefore scheduled for early April.

Although the specialized units were coming from the United Kingdom, the main forces had to be supplied from existing Middle East resources. On February 17, the British 6th Infantry Division was formed in Egypt under the command of Major General Evetts and allocated for operations in the Aegean. The division consisted of the 16th Infantry Brigade, 22nd Guards Brigade, Matruh garrison, and various miscellaneous units, all of which now underwent a course of special training at the Combined Operations School, which had been established at Kabrit on the shore of the Great Bitter Lake in the southern part of the Suez Canal.

It was at this point that the Casteloriso fiasco occurred. With all these preparations being made for the impending operations against the Dodecanese, it is small wonder that the vigor of the Italian riposte to the attack caused much consternation in both London and Cairo; recriminations were soon to follow. Winston Churchill was mystified about the outcome of this operation, and on March 9, he addressed a memo to General Ismay, head of the military wing of the War Cabinet Secretariat, saying that he thought it was the duty of the chiefs of staff to have the operation thoroughly probed. He could not understand how the navy had allowed reinforcements to land when, in an operation of this kind, everything depended on the naval forces isolating the island. He therefore considered it necessary that the matter be promptly cleared up on account of the impending and more important landing operations that were due to take place in the Aegean in the near future.

Admiral Cunningham, the commander in chief, also considered the outcome of the operation unsatisfactory, and in his autobiography, he refers to a letter that he wrote to the first sea lord, which contained some caustic comments on the conduct of the operation:

> The taking and abandonment of Casteloriso was a rotten business and reflected little credit on anyone. . . . The Italians were unbelievably enterprising, and not only bombed the island, but bombarded it and landed troops from destroyers. For some reason the Army wireless set did not work, and so we got no information of what was going on. These Commandos we have out here are on a tommy-gun and knuckle-duster basis, and apparently can't defend themselves if seriously attacked. I had sent 25 Marines bristling with Machine guns in the *Ladybird*; but some fool ordered them to re-embark. All we can say is that we have learnt a lot from it and won't repeat the mistakes.

The commanders in chief had anticipated possible recriminations from London, to ascertain the causes of the failure, a Board of Enquiry was convened on March 4 under R.Adm. H. T. Baillie-Grohman, flag officer attached Middle East, and Maj. Gen. J. F. Evetts, general officer commanding the 6th British Infantry Division. The Board's report criticized the action of the *Hereward* on the night of February 25–26 in that she made an enemy report, which led Admiral Renouf to believe that she had sighted the enemy when in fact she had sighted nothing. Also, the *Hereward* should have made a search of the harbor, and around the island, reported the situation accurately to Admiral Renouf, and only then carried out her original orders. Instead of this, she steamed away from the island for some forty miles with the intention of rejoining the *Decoy*—which, incidentally, she failed to do. Because of her actions, a great opportunity for sinking two enemy torpedo boats had been lost. Additionally, the commando troops were not adequately equipped for their task, and the delay of forty hours before the arrival of the garrison, during which the commandos had to cope with enemy reinforcements that landed, was the paramount cause of the failure of the operation.

The mistakes that led to the British failure to capture and hold this small, isolated Italian island some eighty miles from its nearest friendly territory can be summed up as follows: First, a lack of adequate plans and preparations; second, a lack of air cover; and third, the underestimation of the probable reactions of the enemy.

Had the lessons of this particular type of operation been well and truly learned, or would these mistakes be repeated? The pattern of events in the Middle East was soon to undergo a radical change and it was not until the autumn of 1943 that this question was answered.

CHAPTER TWO

Strategy, Plans, and Preparations

The British were not alone in their interest in the Dodecanese Islands. Apart from the Balkan nations themselves, always bickering and casting covetous eyes on any bit of adjacent territory, the major powers all had vested interests in and shifting plans and hopes for this apparent backwater.

First there was the Italian position. In common with all the major European powers at the end of the nineteenth century, Italy had had ambitions to establish itself in the Middle East, and for this the Aegean was a natural stepping-stone. As a basis for its colonial ambitions, Italy had trading and religious ties going back for centuries, evidenced by colonies, churches, and missions in all Arab cities throughout the Middle East. The gains of Libya and the Dodecanese Islands after the war of 1912 had given Italy useful jumping-off points and strategic bases for the continuation of its penetration, as well as permitting the nation to outflank its main opponent and, logically, its next victim, Greece.

By joining in the Great War as a supporter of the ultimately victorious British Alliance, Italy also had hoped to increase its influence, and its hope of a satisfactory deal with the Allies was doubtless a factor in its rejection of the Central Powers, with whom it had been expected to side. Following the dismemberment of the Ottoman Empire and the erosion of the considerable German influence in the area, Italy's stake in the region was expected to increase.

The Pact of London, signed in April 1915, between Italy, Russia, France, and Great Britain had been specific on this point, and this was further emphasized by the agreement of St. Jean-de-Maurienne in 1917, in which the leaders of the last two countries guaranteed to assign to Italy the districts of Izmir, Antalya, and Konya, together with northwest Anatolia. On August 10, 1920, came yet another concession, when France, England, and Italy signed the Treaty of Sevres, again allowing for the Italians to extend their spheres of influence over all these areas.

But just as the Italians were reaching out into the Middle East to grasp the promised fruits of the victory in Europe, these were snatched from them. An upsurge of Turkish nationalism under Kemal Pasha had the effect of nullifying the Sevres Treaty and Italy gained next to nothing. By contrast, England and France extended their influence in the area, especially the former, both through mandates sanctioned by the League of Nations and the use of their unrivaled influence already established through trade and commerce. Great Britain now dominated the area—and Italy felt cheated.

Italy furthermore came into increasing conflict of policy with Britain and France with its subsequent divergent policies in Abyssinia and Spain, and this, coupled with the decline in prestige suffered by both Britain and France with the manifest failure of their appeasement policies, led to yet another shift in power politics, wherein Italy was enabled to make more and more successful overtures toward the Arab countries. In particular, the supply of arms to Saudi Arabia and Iraq, the only two really independent nations in the area, enabled Italy to gain a small footing, which it was eager to enlarge. In all these things, the anchor rock of Italy's bases in the Dodecanese Islands played a remote but significant part, keeping the Greek and Turkish governments alike under threat. Increasing involvement with Arab affairs brought the question of the Anglo-Egyptian agreement into focus, with Italian Libya an obvious jumping-off ground for the conquest of the Suez Canal. In this, the position of the Italian bases in the Aegean was dominant, enabling Italian air and naval forces to strike at the long flank of Egypt's exposed coastline.

It was the planned annexation of Croatia, Greece, and Albania, however, that dominated Italy's immediate prewar planning, and here again its Dodecanese bases came into consideration. On the one hand, they outflanked the Greek mainland, but on the other, they were equally liable to be cut off from the homeland by any vigorous action on the part of the Greek Navy. Although the Italians made great play over the fortification of these islands, it appears from subsequent events that this was largely for propaganda purposes aimed at deterring any Greek assault on them in the event of war. When that war ultimately came, little exploitation was made of the islands, and as the war dragged on, they became more and more of a burden on Italy, although the potential was always there and they were kept fully garrisoned.

It was this potential, coupled with their strategic position in blocking an easy supply route to Russia and their influence on a neutral Turkey, that finally came to interest the British in the Aegean islands. It is also probable that the influence of Winston Churchill, who was always wanting to strike somewhere—even when he lacked sufficient forces—prompted early operational plans. Britain felt that the islands were certainly important enough to risk a small operation to take them, but every attempt to launch such a venture in the early years of World War II was thwarted by the lack of troops or shipping; those attacks that were made came to grief through lack of materiel.

After the tide of war had turned in Britain's favor in early 1943, British feelings were influenced by the need to forestall the Soviets in the Balkans and also to take advantage of the crumbling position of Italy to free Greece. The continuation of Turkish neutrality was always a strong consideration and another lure—one that would justify considerable effort. To persuade Turkey into the war on the Allied side would be a great deal more than an embarrassment to Germany.

Under the prodding of the aggressive prime minister, Britain prepared plan after plan for the occupation of the Dodecanese, right up to the Italian surrender. Then, although the ultimate objectives changed, the lure of the islands remained.

For Germany, the Aegean Islands also proved irresistible. Germany's long-term thinking for the Balkans was not as strongly rooted as that of Italy or Russia, but the security of the oil fields in Romania led to the bailing out of Germany's Axis partner in 1941, and this brought Germany right into the Aegean. Once there, the Germans found that it was a useful base from which to strike at the British convoys trying to relieve Malta, as well as a useful bargaining chip with which to influence Turkey away from the Allies. As the war situation worsened on Germany's main front, in the east, the retention of the Balkans was necessary to protect the country's exposed flanks. With the defeats of the 1943 campaign, they were vital to Hitler as a propaganda point, in the negative sense that Germany must not be seen to be on the retreat on all fronts.

For the Soviet Union, the Aegean Islands had little or no value except insofar as that during the early part of the war, the fact that they were in German hands prevented American arms from reaching their own armies more quickly. The eventual domination of the Balkans had been always a long-term ambition for Russia, but after the Germans invaded Russian territory in 1941, the fight for survival dominated all else. Once the Germans started falling back, however, Stalin was quick to see that the whole area of the Balkans was ripe for the plucking. It was plain to him that Britain soon saw what his game was, but America either did not recognize or would not become involved in "colonial adventures" and turned a blind eye to the actions of its rapacious Russian ally as the Balkan nations fell one by one.

Turkey and Greece were traditional enemies of one another. Neither nation pretended to enjoy the Italian occupation of the Dodecanese, but each regarded the taking over of these islands by the other as an equal—or even more serious—threat. Once Greece had been overwhelmed, Turkey was wooed by both sides, but it was the Axis that was in a position to threaten

Turkish cities—and no Allied promises could make up for this fact. Turkey walked a very successful and wise tightrope right to the end.

The United States never had the slightest interest in either the Balkans or the Aegean area, and it saw any attempts by Britain to take the war into this area as mere stalling for time from an ally that was reluctant to face the cost in the final reckoning, which it knew must be decided in Europe. "On to Berlin" was the only strategy the Americans were interested in. They were not interested in the Dodecanese, except for a strong inclination to try to keep Britain out.

On March 9, 1941, the three Glen ships, carrying the 2,000 Special Service troops who were to spearhead the assault on Rhodes, arrived at the southern end of the Suez Canal. By this time, however, operations in the Aegean had to be set aside once again, owing to the march of events in Greece.

The Greek government had initially declined the offer of British ground forces in its struggle against the Italian invaders, fearing that the arrival of British troops might precipitate a German invasion of Greece through Bulgaria, drawing on German troops already stationed in Romania.

On February 22, 1941, British Foreign Secretary Eden arrived in Athens with a high-level delegation. He told the Greek government that the British War Cabinet believed it was Germany's intention to subdue Greece and immobilize Turkey. In the light of this latest British assessment of the situation, the Greek government, which was determined to fight any aggressor, readily acquiesced to the dispatch of a British military force. Hitler had in fact issued a directive on December 13, 1940, for Operation Marita, a move through Bulgaria for the occupation of Greek Macedonia, with a further possibility of the occupation of the entire mainland of Greece.

The movement of the British Army and Air Force to Greece began on March 4. The continuous convoys of men, stores, and vehicles added further responsibilities to the Royal Navy, whose resources were now stretched to the limit. Admiral Cunningham advised that in view of these added commitments, all offensive plans, including the combined operation against Rhodes, must be postponed. This was a serious disappointment, but it was recognized that the policy of supporting the Greeks had priority. Rhodes and Scarpanto, both with their invaluable airfields so near Crete, were key points. Many times in the years that followed, the British made plans to assault Rhodes, but they could never fit them into the main course of events.

From start to finish, the British campaign on the mainland of Greece was a withdrawal and a disaster. The German invasion opened on April 6, and by the end of the month, they had overrun the country. Worse was to follow, for in May, the Germans launched an airborne assault on Crete and quickly captured the island. North Africa was another story of reverses, for an opportunistic thrust by the newly arrived German *Afrika Korps* under the command of Gen. Erwin Rommel retook Cyrenaica from the British forces, which were in a weakened state because of the siphoning off of troops for Greece.

Thus in two short months, the whole strategic situation in the eastern Mediterranean had completely changed. The Axis powers now had control of Greece, the Greek Aegean Islands, and also Cyrenaica, with the exception of the beleaguered fortress of Tobruk. British forces were everywhere on the defensive, and all plans for offensive operations in the Aegean and elsewhere in the Middle East were dropped once again.

These defeats in Greece and Crete, coupled with the reverse in Cyrenaica, left the British War Cabinet even more resolved to defend the Middle East, and also to use it as a base for offensive operations when its strength had been built up, although sending reinforcements on a large scale was not possible while the threat of a German invasion still hung over the United Kingdom.

Even at this stage, though, the Americans, who became Britain's major ally on their entry into the war on December 7, 1941, found little favor with British strategy in the Middle East. The dim outline of future controversies on strategy in this area first began to take shape at informal meetings between the British and American chiefs of staff, which took place side by side with the political conversations at the historic Atlantic Charter meeting between Winston Churchill and President Franklin D. Roosevelt in August 1941 at Placentia Bay, Newfoundland. The American military experts had little confidence in the British policy at that time, which was one of "holding the ring" around Germany and attempting to wear it down by operations on the periphery combined with intensive air bombardment. The Americans regarded this as a time-wasting and negative policy. They expressed the opinion that the correct way to finish any war was by a direct thrust to the centre, and that operations in the Middle East, or elsewhere, that did not contribute to this aim should be dismissed as merely diversionary.

The remarks made by Harry Hopkins, the president's personal representative, when in London in July 1941 illustrate the American case in its extreme form:

> The men in the United States who held the principal positions, and took the big decisions on defense matters, were of the opinion that in the Middle East the British Empire had an indefensible position, in attempting to defend which great sacrifices were being made.

They felt that at any moment the Western Mediterranean might be closed by the Germans, the Canal might be blocked and the positions of the Mediterranean Fleet made untenable; at the same time Germany might concentrate a great superiority of air and armored forces, which would overwhelm the armies in the Middle East. In their view, the Battle of the Atlantic would be the final decisive battle of the war and everything should be concentrated on winning it.

No one in Britain appreciated the feeling that existed throughout the U.S. military command that the Middle East was a liability from which the British should withdraw. Everyone in authority in Great Britain had made up their minds conclusively on the subject and found it hard to understand how there could be any doubt. At this time, the problems of the Middle East, the interests of the Islamic world, and the interrelationship of Egypt and India were not well understood in the United States.

These and similar arguments were raised once more at the Atlantic meeting. The British Chiefs of Staff pointed out that for practical reasons and for reasons of prestige, they could hardly abandon a theater where some 600,000 men were committed; that the protection of Britain's Persian oil supplies was vital; and that furthermore, Britain wished to retain and develop the only base available to it from which pressure could be brought to bear against Italy.

The British Chiefs of Staff thought at the time that the strong case they put forward had succeeded in convincing the Americans of the soundness of their policy. This was not so, however, for both then and later, the United States regarded all British actions in the Middle East with some distrust, perhaps because the outline of a future conflict of interests was already discernible.

After Germany invaded Russia on June 22, 1941, the major part of its army and air force was committed in the east. Thus the threat of a German invasion of England from across the Channel decreased, and the way was now open for Britain to send reinforcements to the Middle East as fast as shipping resources would allow. The main objective of the reinforced Middle East Command was the destruction of the Axis forces in Cyrenaica and Tripolitania. Until this objective had been achieved, operations against the Aegean Islands, or elsewhere in the Mediterranean, could not be contemplated.

The first British offensive, to accomplish the objective set by the command, was launched on November 18, 1941, and at first made good headway. Benghazi was captured on December 25, but it had to be evacuated on January 28, 1942, following a sharp riposte by German colonel general

Erwin Rommel. The general's forces pushed on to Gazala, where the Germans counterattacked in early February. From the Gazala position, Rommel launched an attack on May 26, 1942. The Germans swept the British forces back to within forty miles of Alexandria, where the line was eventually stabilized at El Alamein.

It was during this period, when the British fortunes in the Middle East had reached their nadir, that the prime minister, President Roosevelt, and their advisers were hammering out decisions that were to shape the future course of the war. In their plans for operations in 1942, the Americans had envisaged a joint British-American cross-Channel invasion of France, and planning for this operation, known as Sledgehammer, was going ahead. Britain, however, favored a move against French North Africa, partly to forestall a possible German occupation, and also with the ultimate objective of opening up the Mediterranean for the through passage of Allied shipping.

The British Chiefs of Staff, however, became increasingly aware of the impracticalities of launching Sledgehammer during 1942. The prime minister informed the president of this, and as a result, the president sent Harry Hopkins, U.S. Army chief of staff Gen. George Marshall, and Adm. Ernest King, commander in chief of the U.S. fleet and chief of naval operations, to London in July 1942 with orders to reach an immediate agreement on plans for joint operations for that year. The American delegation pressed for Sledgehammer, but this the British were unwilling to undertake. To break the impasse, the president instructed his representatives to reach agreement on some operation that would involve American land forces being brought into action against the enemy during 1942. The outcome of these discussions was that on July 25, an agreement was reached for a joint British-American landing in French North Africa, to take place not later than October 30. The operation was given the code name Torch. The U.S. secretary of war, Henry L. Stimson, made a straightforward summary of the situation:

> The "Torch" decision was the result of two absolutely definite and final rulings, one by the British and the other by the President. Mr. Churchill and his advisers categorically refused to accept the notion of a cross-Channel invasion in 1942. Mr. Roosevelt categorically insisted that there must be some operation in 1942. The only operation that satisfied both of these conditions was "Torch."

Following this agreement, Churchill flew to Cairo, where he arrived on August 4. The morale of the troops in the Western Desert, following their long retreat to El Alamein, was low, and the prime minister was convinced that to restore their confidence, it was necessary for changes to be made in the top command. Following his recommendations, the British War Cabinet approved the appointment of Gen. Sir Harold Alexander as commander in chief in the Middle East and of Lt. Gen. Bernard Law Montgomery as the new commander of the British Eighth Army.

The change of command soon brought with it the desired change of atmosphere, and morale was quickly raised. Preparations went ahead for the mounting of an offensive designed to defeat the Axis forces in the Western Desert once and for all. The attack was launched on October 23, 1942, and after twelve days of hard fighting the Axis troops were forced to retreat. The Eighth Army set off on its long road to final victory. Benghazi was captured on November 20, and on January 23, 1943, British forces entered Tripoli. The Eighth Army then pushed westwards and crossed the frontier into Tunisia on February 4. They made a linkup on April 7 with the Torch forces who had landed in Morocco and Algeria on November 8, 1942, under the overall command of Gen. Dwight D. Eisenhower, U.S. Army, and had pushed eastward toward Tunisia against increasing German resistance. The scene was thus set for the destruction of the Axis forces. This duly took place, with the Allies taking nearly 250,000 prisoners. General Alexander was able to signal the prime minister on May 13, 1943, that the campaign was over and the Allies were masters of the North African shore.

With the end of the campaign in North Africa, the Allies were now poised to exploit their success with an invasion of Sicily. The operation was given the code name Husky.

The decision to invade Sicily had been made at the Casablanca Conference, held some months earlier in January 1943. There, Prime Minister Churchill, President Roosevelt, and their top military advisers discussed and agreed upon Allied strategy for 1943. The main lines of offensive action in the Mediterranean were to occupy Sicily, with the objects of making the Mediterranean line of communication more secure, diverting German pressure from the Russian front, and intensifying the pressure on Italy; and to create a situation in which Turkey could be enlisted as an active ally.

Following the Casablanca Conference, the prime minister flew to Cairo and thence on to Adana in Turkey for a meeting with the Turkish leaders. It was hoped that this meeting would prepare the way for a Turkish entry into the war in the summer of 1943. The talks concluded with an agreement that Britain should send equipment for the Turkish forces, and that plans should be prepared for the reinforcement of Turkish forces by British units if Turkey entered the war.

One of the results of the Casablanca Conference was the redesignation of the sphere of operations controlled by the Middle East Command. With the emphasis moving toward Northwest Africa and the central Mediterranean area, the western limits of the command as of February 20, 1943, were to be from a line that ran from the Tunisian-Libyan frontier, through a position 35 degrees north and 16 degrees east to Cape Spartivento in Calabria. With these boundary changes came a change in command. General Alexander became Allied deputy commander in chief in the North African theater under General Eisenhower. Gen. Maitland Wilson, who had been commander in chief of the Persia and Iraq Command, took Alexander's place as commander in chief of the Levant on February 16. Working alongside General Wilson were Air Chief Marshal Sir William Sholto Douglas, the air officer commanding the Middle East Air Command, and Adm. Sir Henry Harwood, who was responsible for the waters of the eastern Mediterranean, with the title of commander in chief of the Levant.

On his appointment as commander in chief, General Wilson was charged with the following four tasks in order: to maintain the Eighth Army, to train and mount the Middle Eastern portion of Operation Husky, to prepare to support Turkey, and to plan amphibious operations in the eastern Mediterranean. Regarding the final directive, Wilson found that plans for the seizure of some of the smaller Aegean Islands, for use as bases by raiding forces against enemy lines of communication in that area, had been under consideration for some time. In furtherance of these minor plans already prepared, a joint planning staff, known as No. 2 Planning Staff and composed mainly of officers from the III Corps headquarters, was set up in Cairo in February 1943 to consider seriously the possibility of a major assault on the Dodecanese—in particular, on the strategically placed islands of Rhodes and Scarpanto.

The initial planning for these operations was complicated by the fact that it was known that both the Greeks and Turks had aspirations for the ultimate possession of the Dodecanese Islands. It was therefore decided that the actual operations should be carried out by British forces only, and that the future of the islands should not be discussed with either of the interested parties.

A detailed plan for a full-scale attack on Rhodes and Scarpanto, and the subsequent occupation of other islands, was produced by May 2. The plan called for a minimum troop requirement for the whole Aegean operation—including the garrison for Rhodes, Scarpanto and the other islands—of three infantry divisions, one armored brigade, two independent infantry battalions, two parachute battalions, and corps troops. The main problem confronting the planners was the provision of adequate air cover for the landing of these forces some 250 miles from British air bases in Cyprus and even farther from those in Cyrenaica. The planners believed, however, that operations in the central Mediterranean would probably be in progress at the time of the assault on the Dodecanese, and that this would deter the enemy from sending reinforcements to the Aegean. As events were to prove, this was a forlorn hope.

The forces required for the Aegean operations were not available from Middle Eastern resources, as the bulk of their fighting troops had been transferred to General Eisenhower's command for the campaign in Tunisia, which was the first commitment. When the question of the withdrawal of some British troops from North Africa to the Middle East was raised, General Eisenhower replied that the ability to furnish British troops after the completion of the Tunisian campaign depended on the decisions of the Combined Chiefs of Staff on the course of the operations in the Mediterranean following the planned invasion of Sicily. He therefore declared that movement of troops from North Africa to the Middle East would follow and not precede these decisions. The decisions of the Combined Chiefs of Staff, however, were not readily forthcoming.

On May 5, 1943, Churchill and his team of advisers sailed from the Clyde onboard the liner *Queen Mary*, en route for Washington for further, and what were to be crucial, talks with the Americans. The main items requiring urgent decisions were first Sicily, and the exploitation thereof, and second the Burma campaign. While on the voyage across the Atlantic, the British Chiefs of Staff drew up a paper setting out their views on the Mediterranean strategy, which they thought should be followed. They were of the opinion that the natural follow-up to the capture of Sicily would be an invasion of the Italian mainland. The paper proposed the seizure of a bridgehead on the toe of Italy, to be followed by a further assault on the heel as a prelude to an advance on Bari and Naples. The British document ended with the conclusion that the Mediterranean offered the opportunities for action in the coming autumn and winter that could be decisive, and at least would do far more to prepare the way for a cross-Channel operation in 1944 than would be achieved by attempting to transfer back to the United Kingdom any of the forces now in the Mediterranean theater. If these opportunities could be taken, the Allies should have every chance of breaking the Axis and bringing the war to a successful conclusion in 1944.

At the conference, which was known as Trident, the prime minister therefore propounded the view that the great prize in 1943 was to get Italy out of the war. He thought that the collapse of Italy, which would leave Germany standing alone, could cause a lowering of the German morale, and this might be the beginning of their defeat. He also visualized that the time would come when a joint American-Russian-British request could be made to Turkey for permission to use bases in its territory from which the Ploesti oil fields in Romania could be bombed and also from which operations could be mounted in the Aegean. Turkey could hardly refuse such a request with Italy out of the way. A further effect of Italy's defeat would be felt in the Balkans where she employed upward of twenty-five divisions in holding down and garrisoning the area. If the Italian Army were withdrawn, Germany would either have to give up the Balkans or withdraw large numbers of troops from the Russian front to fill the gap.

The Americans, however, did not take the same view. They were beginning to feel that the Mediterranean operations were having a "suction-pump" effect and were continually drawing in more and more men and materiel, to such an extent that they feared that even if operations were continued on their existing scale, it would prove impossible to mount an invasion of northwest Europe, which was the linchpin of their strategic thinking. In fact, General Marshall declared that if, as a result of the adoption of a Mediterranean strategy, there was to be only a limited cross-Channel attack, a readjustment of landing craft and troop shipping should be made in favor of the Pacific. This statement was music to the ears of the Anglophobic Admiral King, who was finding it difficult to provide the central and southwest Pacific theaters with sufficient landing craft and who favored that emphasis should be on the Pacific rather than Europe.

The position of the U.S. Joint Chiefs of Staff was that while they admitted that there might be certain merits to operations in the western Mediterranean immediately after the Sicilian campaign, so long as these involved the reduction rather than increase of Allied forces in the theater, they ruled out operations in the Eastern Mediterranean entirely. If the British wished to mount any, they would have to do so alone. Finally, they declared that in any event, if the British insisted on Mediterranean commitments that in American opinion would jeopardize the early defeat of Germany and the ultimate defeat of Japan, the U.S. representatives were to inform the British that the United States might be compelled to revise its basic strategy and extend its operations and commitments in the Pacific.

The bargaining between the two sides was hard and protracted, and despite the prime minister's powerful advocacy for his grandiose Mediterranean plans, he was unable to carry the day. The British did, however, manage to persuade the Americans that operations in the Mediterranean should continue, albeit with a touch of the brakes applied. But the actual course of operations to follow the conquest of Sicily had still not been decided.

The Combined Chiefs of Staff's directives on the major issues at the end of Trident were as follows:

(a) That forces and equipment shall be established in the United Kingdom with the object of mounting an operation with target date the 1st May 1944, to secure a lodgment on the Continent from which further offensive operations can be carried out. . . .

(b) That the Allied Commander-in-Chief, North Africa, should be instructed to mount such operations in exploitation of "Husky" as are best calculated to eliminate Italy from the war and to contain the maximum number of German forces. Each specific operation will be subject to the approval of the Combined Chiefs of Staff. The Allied Commander-in-Chief, North Africa, may use for his operations all those forces available in the Mediterranean area except for four American and three British divisions which will be held in readiness from the 1st November onwards for withdrawal to take part in operations from the United Kingdom, provided that the naval vessels required will be approved by the Combined Chiefs of Staff when the plans are submitted. The additional air forces provided on a temporary basis for "Husky" will not be considered available.

With regard to the eastern Mediterranean, the final summary of the Combined Chiefs of Staff merely stated: "The Combined Chiefs of Staff have taken note of the action, which the Commander-in-Chief, Middle East, is taking in respect of Rhodes and other islands in the Dodecanese. They approve this action, and are considering what further can be done."

A further decision taken at this conference, which eventually was to have a considerable effect on the course of operations in the Mediterranean, was the agreement that in order to keep up the maximum possible pressure on the Japanese, a combined operation against the Arakan in Burma should be staged later in the year, and that this operation was to be given priority of resources after the main operations against Italy.

The prime minister expressed his disappointment at the overall outcome of the talks, and it was then agreed that General Marshall should accompany him to North Africa for on-the-spot talks with the Allied commanders. The party left Washington on May 26 and arrived in Algiers two days later. These talks, however, made little further progress. In the face of the wait-and-see policy adopted by the Americans no clear-cut decision could be reached on post-Husky operations. The decision would have to await the outcome of the invasion of Sicily. General Eisenhower was instructed to send a report to the Combined Chiefs of Staff on the early stages of the invasion, and in the light of this report, a decision would be taken on the follow-up operations. With this the prime minister, for the time being anyway, had to be content.

The invasion of Sicily was launched on July 10, and although the Axis garrison consisted of thirteen divisions, nine Italian and four German, its capture was completed by August 17 in a whirlwind campaign that lasted only thirty-eight days. With the first initial successes of the landings, General Eisenhower was able to recommend to the Combined Chiefs of Staff that an invasion of Italy should follow immediately after the capture of the island. This course of action they approved.

On August 10, General Eisenhower held a meeting of his principal commanders to thrash out the plans for the attack on Italy. It was decided that an assault should be launched across the Straits of Messina early in September, followed by a seaborne landing in the Gulf of Salerno with the object of the early capture of the great seaport of Naples.

In the meantime, the political situation in Italy was in a state of turmoil. The defeats in North Africa, followed by the invasion of Sicily and the threat of invasion of the Italian mainland, had undermined Mussolini's position, and on July 25, he was toppled from power. Marshal Pietro Badoglio was nominated by the king of Italy to take over the reins of government. With the overthrow of *Il Duce*, the possibility of an Italian collapse became very real, with potentially enormous advantages accruing to the Allied cause.

The British Chiefs of Staff, aware of these advantages, decided it was important that no resources at present in the Mediterranean, including landing craft earmarked for other operations, should be dispersed until the situation clarified. In London this action seemed only to be common sense, but in Washington it was felt that Britain had unilaterally abrogated the agreement on grand strategy reached at the Trident Conference. It was against this background of both rising Allied fortunes and rising American irritation that the prime minister and his top military advisers set sail once again, this time for Quebec, where they arrived on August 10 for the important Quadrant Conference.

The Americans came to the conference table at Quebec with views that verged on outright distrust of British Mediterranean policy. They saw behind this policy subtle motivations of a political nature rather than military ideals; they considered that moves in the Mediterranean were concerned more with postwar calculations of the balance of power in Europe rather than with the defeat of Germany in the shortest possible time; and they were convinced that Overlord, the cross-Channel invasion, was an aggressive offensive action that would accomplish military results by itself from its inception.

The Americans had been forewarned by U.S. Secretary of War Henry L. Stimson, who had been in London during the summer and reported to the president just before the conference opened:

> We cannot now rationally hope to be able to cross the Channel and come to grips with our German enemy under a British commander. His Prime Minister and his Chief of Staff are frankly at variance with such a proposal. The shadows of Passchendaele and Dunkirk still hang too heavily over the imagination of the leaders of his government. [The Americans, with no Somme or Passchendaele casualty list in their recent history, although they did have a Gettysburg, and with infinitely greater manpower, did not find it difficult to dismiss the fears of their British allies. After Kasserine, Anzio and the Ardennes, their attitude became a little more understanding.] Though they have rendered lip-service to the Operation, their heart is not in it and it will require more independence, more faith, and more vigor than it is reasonable to expect we can find in any British commander to overcome the natural difficulties of such an operation carried on in such an atmosphere of his government.

The British, too, had been forewarned of the difficulties they were likely to face on their Mediterranean policies. Their Joint Staff Mission in Washington briefed the Chiefs of Staff in the following terms on the American attitude to operations in this area:

> There is apparent in all the U.S. Chiefs of Staff a feeling that the British are not standing firm enough to considered decisions of "Trident," and are tending too readily to depart from these decisions and to set aside the operations agreed upon. They realise the importance of putting Italy out of war, but are not prepared to see "Bullfrog" [the Arakan Operation], the Pacific or "Overlord" suffer unduly in consequence of new commitments in the Mediterranean. They seem particularly to take exception to British "standstill" order in the Mediterranean, to which they refer as a unilateral decision.

That the negotiations were going to be tough for the British there could be no doubt for the Americans were now beginning to flex their newfound muscles and starting to take on the role of senior partner in the Western Alliance after a two-year period of waiting in the wings while their strength built up. At such a moment, the whole long, vexed story of Anglo-American relations, particularly those regarding the Mediterranean, came to a head.

Because of Churchill's enthusiastic plea for operations against Rhodes, the American Chiefs of Staff were now more than ever convinced that the British leader was trying to evade the commitment for a cross-Channel landing in favor of adventures in the eastern Mediterranean. As far as the prime minister was concerned, there was an element of truth in the suspicions voiced by Stimson, for he did in fact fear a repetition of the senseless slaughter of the Western Front offensives of the First World War, with its loss of a whole generation of young British lives. He believed that a cross-Channel assault was not the only way of winning the war, and that our cause might prosper just as well by a more subtle and economical attack against the enemy's back door in southeastern Europe, which now appeared to be almost wide open.

If the prime minister's motives for pressing on in the Mediterranean were somewhat romantic, those of the British Chiefs of Staff were coldly professional. It was their considered opinion that continued Allied pressure in the Mediterranean was a prerequisite to a successful cross-Channel invasion in 1944. Unless sufficient German forces could be contained in the South immediately before and during the crucial first three-month period of Overlord—and a successful campaign in the Italian peninsula with its simultaneous threat to Austria, Southern France, and the Balkans was now the only way this could be achieved—the enemy's concentration against the Normandy landings would be faster than the Allied buildup in the bridgehead, and the very enterprise to which the Americans wished to sacrifice everything, the cross-Channel invasion, would be rendered impossible by a failure of the preliminary operations essential to its success.

The American Chiefs of Staff, however, took the view that the British Mediterranean strategy involved a gamble that the United States should not be prepared to underwrite. As General Marshall explained to the president on July 25, "It was based on the speculation that a political and economic collapse could be brought about in the occupied countries, especially in the Balkans. If that speculation proved to be faulty the Allies would be committed to a long drawn-out struggle of blockade and attrition in Europe." He feared that rather than endure that, the American people might lose patience and turn their attention entirely to the Pacific. With the threat again raised of shifting the emphasis from Europe to the Pacific, which had been broached earlier at the Trident Conference, the British had no alternative but to bow to American pressure. Overlord was to become the primary U.S.-British ground and air effort against the Axis in Europe.

As for the Mediterranean, the Americans agreed that operations should continue with the forces allotted at Trident except insofar as these might be varied by decision of the Combined Chiefs of Staff. Where there was a shortage of resources, those available would be distributed and employed with the main object of ensuring the success of Overlord as a priority over operations in the Mediterranean.

The British had succeeded in getting the principle of flexibility and the recognition of the interdependence of the two operations written into the strategic concept, but only by abandoning their attempt to leave the seven battle-hardened divisions in the Mediterranean. One further result of the discussions was the cancellation of the standstill order on shipping and landing craft in the Mediterranean, which had caused so much concern to the Americans.

With this state of affairs, the British had to be content. The Americans were now firmly in the saddle, and Britain would just have to learn to live with it.

CHAPTER THREE

The Commitment Made

While the weighty discussions on strategy were taking place in Quebec, the Italian surrender daily became more imminent. Badoglio's government had in fact wasted no time in putting out peace feelers to the Allies. The first tentative overture was made on August 3, and discussions continued until September 3, when the terms of Italy's military surrender were signed in an olive grove near Syracuse in Sicily; on the same day, the Eighth Army crossed the Straits of Messina and invaded Calabria. Italy's unconditional surrender was announced on the afternoon of September 8 and thus the Rome-Berlin Axis finally disintegrated.

The Aegean plums were now ripe for the picking, but which side was to enjoy the fruits?

In examining the final assessments of the value of the Aegean Sea area to the future prosecution of the war, one is struck by the clarity and similarity of foresight expressed by both Churchill for Britain and Hitler for Germany, as well as the almost naive truculence of the American Chiefs of Staff and the shortsightedness of their policy. For whereas Hitler and Churchill could both see what might lie beyond the immediate military proceedings in the Balkans, the United States either could not or would not face the truth about German vulnerability in that area—and the all-consuming interest Soviet Russia had shown in it long before World War II broke out.

So with regard to the strategic value of the Balkans, there was a remarkable harmony in the thinking of both Germany and Britain, which contrasted most markedly with the almost complete indifference shown by the United States. To the Americans, their long-cherished cross-Channel invasion plan was the paramount objective in Europe.

For Churchill, the immediate military objective was the island of Rhodes, with its airfields the key to the Aegean. The strategic prizes that could result from its capture were immense. With British forces in air and sea control of the Aegean it was thought that Turkey could at last be persuaded into the war; such a prospect was not to be ignored. It would at once place at the Allies' disposal a group of air bases from which to bomb Greece,

Romania, and Bulgaria. It would also bring an estimated forty-six Turkish divisions into the reckoning, although these would have to depend on the Allies for much of their equipment. The Allies would also gain control of the Dardanelles and Bosporus, whose neutrality so far, governed by the terms of the Montreux Convention, inevitably favored the Germans; the Germans in Greece would at the same time be deprived of supplies from Romania and the Danube Valley. In addition, if the Russian campaign prospered, it would provide a direct sea route to Russia, thus obviating the need for the dangerous Arctic convoys to North Russia, which took up so much of the Royal Navy's strength and resources. Finally, a Turkish alliance would further upset the Germans' delicate balance of forces throughout Europe, threatening them with a new and formidable campaign on their most sensitive flank. The capture of the Dodecanese might indeed appear to them as the prelude to a second Gallipoli.

Hitler, too, had clear ideas of the overall importance of the area. As early as May 19, 1943, faced with the prospect that Italy might soon be unable to carry on the war, he had declared that the Italian peninsula "could be sealed off somehow," but it would be "of decisive importance for us to hold the Balkans. Copper, bauxite, chrome and, above all, security, so that there is not a complete smash there if the Italian matter develops."

The full import of the loss of North Africa in May 1943 had in fact been immediately recognized by the German Supreme Command, the OKW, who realized that probable future developments in the Mediterranean area would threaten the very core of the Axis alliance. Immediately after the end of the Tunisian campaign, the Operations Staff of the OKW prepared a survey of the situation that would arise should Italy withdraw from the war. Plans were drawn up for the reinforcement of German troops in Italy and the Balkans. The orders for the protective measures in Italy under the code name Alaric were issued on May 22, together with those for the Balkans, which was code-named Constantine. Following the downfall of Mussolini and the Allied success in Sicily, both plans were adapted to take into account these developments, and by the end of July, they had been brought up to date and combined into a single plan applicable to Italy and the Balkans, known as Operation Axis.

The first orders for Operation Axis went out on July 28; they were continually revised and updated to meet the changing situation, the final directive being issued on August 30. The German commanders thus had little more than a week to study their final orders, for on September 8 at 1945 hours, they heard Marshal Badoglio announce over the radio the surrender of Italy to the Allied forces. Thirty-five minutes later, Operation Axis began.

The orders decreed that all Italian troops were to be disarmed and given the alternative of disbanding or fighting on with the Germans. The Apennine passes, and the railway installations and main ports in northern Italy were to be seized, as were Italian warships, merchant vessels, aircraft and airfields, and all military installations and equipment. The entire south-eastern theater was to be taken over, including the Aegean Islands.

To implement these orders, the strength of the German Army in the Mediterranean area, including the Balkans, had been built up to just over thirty-eight divisions. The new Army Group F, with headquarters in Belgrade under a new commander in chief, Field Marshal von Weichs, had been set up. The former commander in chief, General Loehr, retained command of Army Group E in Greece and the Aegean but was now subordinate to Weichs in Belgrade.

In the area that had formerly been the provenance of Middle East planning, there were nine divisions, deployed as follows: one mountain division in the Janina area, one line of communications division at Salonika, one infantry division at Larissa, the 104th Infantry Division at Agrenion, the 11th Infantry Division at the Piraeus, the 117th Infantry Division and one armored division in the Peloponnese, the 22nd Infantry Division on Crete, and one division in Rhodes. It was the division based on Rhodes, the key to the Dodecanese Islands, that could thwart any British initiative in this area arising from the Italian surrender.

German troops had first arrived on Rhodes in January 1943, when, by agreement between the German and Italian Air Commands in the Aegean, two batteries of 88-millimeter guns were brought to the island to strengthen the defenses of the airfields. The plan was that the German forces should withdraw when Italian personnel had been trained to man the guns. In fact, the Germans remained and three more batteries were brought to the island. These were followed by German gunnery experts, technicians, and personnel who inspected the coastal defense batteries and set to work constructing ferro-concrete gun emplacements to improve the defenses. Despite Italian protests, the German forces remained on the island.

In April, the Germans strengthened their foothold there when the Axis authorities agreed that a German assault battalion of grenadiers, fully motorized, should come to the island "for maneuvers." As a result of the decisions to safeguard the German position in Italy and the Balkans, three additional battalions arrived in the island in May, by sea and air. Many high-ranking German officers also visited the island during May, including Admiral Fricke, the German naval commander of Group South, and Field Marshal Kesselring, the commander in chief in the south. Toward the end of June, General Kleemann arrived on the island unannounced to the Italians and took over command of the German troops: the general was senior in rank to General Scaroina, the commander of the Italian Regina Division. On July 25, Field Marshal von Weichs himself visited the island, and directives and instructions were given to General Kleemann on the course of action to be adopted should Italians sue for peace. The Germans held numerous exercises both day and night, and General Kleemann's forces were welded into a competent and well-armed mobile division. About two-thirds of the division were spread around in coastal defense positions, and the other third was concentrated inland.

The Rhodes Division, which was known as *Sturm Division Rhodos*, numbered between 6,000 and 7,000 men and was extremely well armed and mobile. The Italians recorded the strength of the German force at the time of the armistice as follows:

- Divisional headquarters at Campochiaro, with divisional services.
- Four battalions of motorized grenadiers, comprising approximately 4,000 men, equipped with 75-millimeter guns, as well as guns of 50- and 28-millimeter caliber, mortars, and antitank guns.
- A reconnaissance group of about 1,500 men, equipped with motorcycles and sidecars with machine guns, about forty armored cars and twenty jeeps.
- A tank battalion equipped with forty-one tanks.
- An artillery group with two batteries of 105-millimeter guns and one of 150-millimeter guns. Many of the guns were self-propelled.
- Divisional artillery consisting of two batteries of 105-millimeter guns and one of 150-millimeter guns.
- A pioneer (engineer) group of approximately 1,000 men, equipped with light armored vehicles.
- Five batteries of 88-millimeter guns for use as either antitank or anti-aircraft guns, half of which were mobile.
- A detachment of 300 Greeks in German uniforms.
- Many minor detachments.

In addition, there were approximately 1,500 German troops on Scarpanto, including a fortress battalion that arrived there on September 6.

Thus the Germans had prepared for every eventuality. What of the British countermeasures?

The prime minister, ever alive to the advantages that could accrue from quick action in the Aegean, sent the following memo on August 3 to General Ismay, chief staff officer to the minister of defence, for the consideration of the Chiefs of Staff Committee:

1. Here is a business of great consequence, to be thrust forward by every means. Should the Italian troops in Crete and Rhodes resist the Germans and a deadlock ensue, we must help the Italians at the earliest moment, engaging thereby also the support of the populations.

2. The Middle East should be informed today that all supplies to Turkey may be stopped for the emergency; and that they should prepare expeditionary forces, not necessarily in divisional formations, to profit by the chances that may offer.

3. This is no time for conventional establishments, but rather for using whatever fighting elements there are. Can anything be done to find at least a modicum of assault shipping without compromising the main operation against Italy? It does not follow that troops can only be landed from armored landing-craft. Provided they are to be helped by friends on shore, a different situation arises. Surely caiques and ships' boats can be used between ship and shore?

I hope the Staffs will be able to stimulate action, which may gain immense prizes at little cost, though not at little risk.

In conventional planning, the Middle East Command staff had been far from inactive. Operations in the Aegean were subordinate to the momentous events taking place in the central Mediterranean, and the plans made were subject to constant change and alteration. In June, it seemed that offensive operations in the Aegean would, in fact, take place, and No. 2 Planning Staff was therefore redesignated Force 292, so as to be ready to act as force headquarters for the conduct of operations in the field. By the middle of the month, however, it became apparent that the assault craft, shipping, and the necessary air forces, would not immediately be available, and the naval force commander and his staff were sent to Algiers to plan post-Husky operations in the central Mediterranean. In fact, no less than seven plans were produced between May and September 1943 for the capture of Rhodes, Crete, and other islands in the Dodecanese and the Aegean. The scope of each plan varied in relation to the object to be obtained, the degree of opposition likely to be encountered, and the scale of cooperation from the Turkish Government.

The early plans envisaged not only the capture of the Dodecanese and Aegean Islands, but also follow-up operations on the mainland of Greece and for overcoming both German and Italian resistance. Later plans after the collapse of Italy, however, dealt only with the capture of Rhodes and

Crete, held by the Germans and supported by Fascist elements of the former Italian garrisons. In some cases, plans had to be made in the absence of the naval planning section and consequently were never fully completed. On four occasions a force was assembled and partially prepared to undertake the capture of Rhodes.

Following the successful landings in Sicily, with unexpectedly small losses of assault craft and shipping, there was sufficient lifting capacity available to the Middle East Command for a seaborne assault on Rhodes. The shipping available at that time for the assault included eight landing ships, tank (LSTs), but of these, five were only being held in the Middle East temporarily and were destined for the Indian Ocean. The 8th Indian Division was allocated for the capture of Rhodes, and therefore underwent combined operations training at Kabrit. A landing rehearsal took place on August 24–26, and the division was ready to sail on September 1. It seemed that the months of careful planning by the command were at last going to bear fruit. However, this was not to be.

The way in which Operation Accolade was prepared in the long months leading up to the Italian surrender throws a revealing light on the conduct of British operations at this stage of the war. Between March 20 and April 27, an outline draft plan was prepared, even though there was little or no current intelligence to base it on. This plan was revised the following month. Between May 29 and June 14, draft plans were drawn up for an alternative operation, Quick Accolade, but as no proper agenda was ever provided for the planners, their meetings were conducted under very unsatisfactory circumstances. The planning staff then attended a course on planning instructions in June before resuming work. When they did embark on detailed planning, it was found that no Royal Naval staff was available. Nevertheless, plans were drawn up without them. These proved to be out-of-date before they were completed. By July the basic plan was ready, but general headquarters then turned down the idea of setting up an advance base and also stated that twice the time allocated, twenty-eight days, would be required to carry out Accolade. New plans were therefore drawn up on this basis, but general headquarters then reverted to the original allocation of fourteen days!

On September 25, the final operation instructions were duly issued to Force 292, which was to take Rhodes with target date fixed for October 20. The shipping available was listed as three landing ships, infantry (LSIs); one headquarters ship; thirteen landing craft, tank (LCTs), each of which was capable of lifting nine Sherman tanks at ten knots; eighteen landing craft, mechanized (LCMs); and eight Z-craft.

The LSIs were to embark their troops at Alexandria and the others were to load at Haifa and Beirut. Paratroops were to capture Maritza airfield and petrol and ammunition would be flow in. By September 10, some 120 paratroopers and their ten transport aircraft were ready and trained for this task. An assault brigade group including one armored unit was to be landed at Lardo to seize Calato airfield, and an infantry company was to land at Castro Ferado to prevent enemy interference from the north. Two infantry companies were to he landed at Cattavia to take that airfield, with follow-up brigades landing at Lardo.

The Warwickshire Yeomanry began to reequip in August when their old Crusader tanks were withdrawn and replaced by Shermans. By the eighth of that month, they had attained their full number of fifty-two tanks, and the Shermans were waterproofed ready for the lift. The 26th Indian Infantry Brigade was actually embarked and rehearsed a landing operation at Suez between August 24 and 26.

On the twenty-sixth, much to everybody's chagrin, an order was received from the Combined Chiefs of Staff that the five LSTs held in the Middle East Command, together with a headquarters ship and three cargo vessels, were to be sent forthwith to India for the operation against the Arakan in Burma. This operation had been given priority of resources after the main operations in Italy at the Washington Conference in May 1943. In view of the possible developments in the Mediterranean part of the shipping destined for the Arakan had been held for a time, but following the decision reached at Quadrant, these ships had to be released. And so once again, British plans for an attack on Rhodes had been nipped in the bud. It was considered at the time that the Arakan operations would be a greater benefit to the war as a whole than the capture of Rhodes. Ironically, as it later turned out, the Arakan operations were canceled.

Shortly after the receipt of this order from the Combined Chiefs of Staff, the 8th Indian Division was put under orders for the central Mediterranean, although, in fact, it did not sail from Egypt until September 20.

Following the transfer of its last fully operational division, the Middle East Command informed the British Chiefs of Staff on August 31 that the only operations that could now be mounted from its resources were small-scale raids, sabotage and guerrilla operations by resistance groups, and unopposed "walk-ins" to areas evacuated by the enemy. Thus at a time when an Italian collapse seemed imminent, the Middle East Command had few resources with which it would be able to exploit the opportunities that would arise in the Aegean following an Italian surrender. This fact seemed to be acknowledged by Churchill:

The trained assault shipping recently taken from him [Wilson] was not beyond superior control, but the American pressure to disperse our shipping from the Mediterranean, either westward for the preparation for a still remote "Overlord" or to the Indian theatre, was very strong. Agreements made before the Italian collapse and appropriate to a totally different situation were rigorously invoked, at least at the secondary level. Thus Wilson's well-conceived plans for rapid action in the Dodecanese were harshly upset.

This state of affairs continued, and although, as one American historian has said, "Wilson was to undertake the long-planned capture of Rhodes largely by bluff," this would not have been necessary had even one-tenth of the materiel, fighter aircraft, and shipping been diverted from the Italian front to the Middle East Command and thrown against the thinly held German line. But the British could not persuade Roosevelt to do any more than to agree, on September 9, that operations in this area should remain a matter of opportunity that could be exploited as the occasion arose. This turned out to be meaningless, because the occasions were happening then and there, throughout the whole of the Aegean Sea, but the sole response by the U.S. Chiefs of Staff was the issuing of a solemn summary that they would consider what further could be done.

Abandoned by the Americans, Churchill now turned to his unfortunate subordinate commanders and attempted to make bricks from straw. He dispatched a typical "Action This Day" type of telegram to Wilson on September 13, when Rhodes had already fallen to the Germans and Wilson had just been informed that he was getting little or nothing from Eisenhower. "The capture of Rhodes by you at this time with Italian aid would be a fine contribution to the general war," the prime minister said. "Let me know what are your plans for this. Can you not improvise the necessary garrison out of the forces in the Middle East? What is your total ration strength? This is a time to think of Clive and Peterborough and of Rooke's men taking Gibraltar."

Unfortunately, the much-tried "Jumbo" Wilson had neither the men nor the shipping to storm into Rhodes. "If today, with full knowledge of the heavy losses we finally suffered, it seems that abandonment would have been preferable," Captain Roskill summed up, "it should be remembered that failure to take any action in the Aegean would probably have been regarded by posterity as a serious reflection on the enterprise of the commanders concerned."

With the prime minister baying at his back but his resources having been spirited away from him, General Wilson made the decision, with the full support of the British Chiefs of Staff and his two fellow commanders in the theater, to go ahead with a less ambitious occupation of some of the lesser islands, including Leros, Cos, and Samos.

Up to this point, all the plans made had involved the use of large numbers of men. Now all this had to be forgotten and speed and improvisation were the order of the day. Even on this reduced scale, however, the vital factor of air support was required and General Eisenhower was again asked to provide, if only for a limited period, the necessary long-range fighters and transport aircraft.

But Eisenhower made clear to Wilson that very little material support of any kind, especially in the air, could be given by North Africa for such an enterprise and he emphasized that the Italian campaign must not be weakened by any other operation in the Mediterranean. Middle East Command must therefore make do with what it had.

At this point, it was seen that the Middle East Command structure suffered from inherent weaknesses, for while General Wilson was answerable to London, the others were not. Air Chief Marshal Douglas was under the operational control of Air Chief Marshal Tedder, the air commander in chief of the Mediterranean Air Command, who in turn was responsible to General Eisenhower. Admiral Harwood also was responsible to Admiral Cunningham, the commander in chief of the Mediterranean Fleet, who had control of the distribution of the naval forces and was responsible for the coordination of all movements throughout the Mediterranean.

On the German side, any hesitancy had come from the general staff, but whereas the British prime minister was not able to overcome objections to his farsighted Aegean aspirations, the German leader suffered from no such inhibitions, sweeping over the objections of his staff and giving his personal decision that the islands were to be held. Up to the time when Hitler made this decision the local German commanders also had been faced with a shortage of men and materiel. It was not until later, following the pacification of Rhodes, that the Germans turned their thoughts to the other major Italian Dodecanese islands of Cos, Leros, and Samos, but at that time forces were not immediately available to occupy these islands, particularly as Italian cooperation was not forthcoming.

The subsequent landing of British troops on these islands further aggravated the German planning in the Dodecanese. In fact, a report by Admiral Lange, admiral commanding in the Aegean, to his superior officer Admiral Fricke, naval commander of Group South, as late as September 18 stated that he considered the Dodecanese, with the exception of Rhodes, completely lost and advised immediate occupation of the Cyclades to establish a defense line of the inner chain of islands and to prevent their being occupied by the British. Admiral Fricke, however, did not consider the position to be that serious, as he was of the opinion that the British had not landed in any great strength. He furthermore thought that it was still possible for the Germans to remain in the Dodecanese. He therefore proposed that Admiral Lange. should assemble all available shipping and arrange with Army Group E to provide the necessary troops to occupy Cos, Leros, and the Cyclades. Admiral Fricke's proposal was later completely justified, when the captain of the former Italian *MAS 522* arrived at the Piraeus from Samos in the early hours of September 19 and was able to give details on the weakness of the British forces. To thrash out the Aegean strategy Hitler called a conference at his headquarters on the twenty-fourth. At the conference, Field Marshal Maximilian von Weichs and Grand Admiral Dönitz, as well as the OKW, presented the Fuehrer with a bleak picture of the situation as it affected the German forces stationed in the Aegean.

Dönitz stated that the situation was precarious. German forces on the Greek mainland were being kept busy with the suppression of partisans and were hardly in a position to prevent a landing in force, he informed the Fuehrer. The naval forces assigned to coastal defense in the region were also of insufficient strength to prevent such a landing. In the Aegean itself, the Germans did not possess any fighting strength worth mentioning. Such light naval units as were available, a few destroyers and minesweepers, would be crushed any time the Royal Navy cared to bring in part of its overwhelming strength. In the vital sector of aerial defense, Dönitz went on—and one can almost picture the Fuehrer's frown—the enemy's superiority was undisputed. This was certainly true; as Portal similarly recorded, there were more fighters and bombers available in the Mediterranean at this time than in the whole of the *Luftwaffe*, but what the Germans apparently were unaware of was the rigid control being exercised to ensure that the bulk of these aircraft stayed west of a line drawn midway between Italy and Greece. The grand admiral continued in a similar vein:

> The bases in the islands, in particular Crete, were established at a time when we were still planning offensive operations in the Eastern Mediterranean area; meanwhile the situation has changed. The Italian armed forces no longer exist and the position on the Balkan Peninsula is in danger for lack of sufficient forces. Maintenance of security in Balkan rear areas has become a difficult task. Advance island bases are of no value in a defensive situation such as this, since the enemy will by-pass them and force their surrender sooner or later by cutting their supplies. Thus we shall lose, without a comparable strategic advantage, irreplaceable troops and material, which would be of decisive importance for the defence of the continent.

He wound up his argument by urging the Fuehrer to make a quick decision and gave him two reasons: First, the evacuation must be undertaken in time. This was before the enemy attacked their sea routes and before he inflicted irreparable losses on their shipping or expanded his bases to the point where he could completely disrupt their seaborne traffic. Second, the scarcity of shipping space and the weakness of the protecting forces at the disposal of the Germans would make this a relatively slow affair.

Hitler listened patiently to all this pessimism and talk of withdrawal and said that though he agreed with the line of argument of Weichs and Dönitz, he could not order the proposed evacuations of the islands, especially the Dodecanese and Crete, on account of the political repercussions that would necessarily follow. The attitude of German allies in the southeast, he declared, was determined exclusively by their confidence in German strength—which was certainly true—and the Turkish attitude was also determined on the same lines: "Abandonment of the islands would create the most unfavorable impression. To avoid such a blow to our prestige we may even have to accept the loss of our troops and material. The supply of the islands must be assured by the Air Force."

Thus the die was cast. While Churchill pleaded with Roosevelt to no avail and Wilson cast around for enough ships to mount an offensive, the Germans acted swiftly. Hitler decreed that the so-called Iron Ring of outer islands was to be reinforced and held. This was the barrier formed by the chain of islands reaching out from the Peloponnese: Kithera-Crete-Scarpanto-Rhodes. He called for the elimination of such weak British garrison forces as had been established by that time on Cos, Leros, and Samos, in that priority. Extra shipping was to be made available from the Adriatic, and aircraft were to be withdrawn from France and Russia. As the OKW Diary mentions, the proposed evacuation of Rhodes and some of the lesser islands, plans for which had already been drawn up by OB *Süd-Ost*, was tactfully not mentioned.

Thus by keeping his nerve at a critical juncture, the Fuehrer ultimately managed to catch the British off-balance; instead of adopting a strictly defensive posture the Germans were soon able to go on the offensive. And Turkey was duly impressed.

Under intense diplomatic pressure from both sides, Turkey initially allowed both Germany and Britain to infringe her neutrality, so long as they kept within reasonable bounds. For the British, this was demonstrated by Turkey's compliance with British requests for the use of Turkish territorial waters and permission for military aircraft to fly over its coast. At Bodrum, an entire base was set up by raiding forces, and the Turks turned a blind eye to it. Hitler was suspicious of the Anglo-Turkish flirtation, but despite intense provocation provided by such bases and the combined use of Turkish territorial waters and airspace, he gave strict orders that the *Luftwaffe* was not to bomb British shipping making illegal use of Turkish waters. Save for two minor incidents, these orders were obeyed.

In fact, the Turks were terrified at the thought of the German bombers based in Greece and the islands smashing their cities in retaliation if they stepped too far over the line; they were equally uneasy about the intentions of a victorious Soviet Army as opposed to a victorious German one. All through the campaign, the British kept up the diplomatic pressure, but as it became more obvious from week to week just who was mistress of the Aegean, so Turkey's attitude became more and more distant toward the Allied cause.

And therefore the Germans were equally granted some advantages. The SD (*Sicherheitsdienst*, the German security service), with the cooperation of the Turkish Secret Service, was allowed to train agents recruited from the Russian minorities, such as the Caucasians and Georgians, and infiltrate them across the Turkish frontier. Meanwhile, when Dönitz complained about the British ships availing themselves of sanctuary daily, Hitler told him this matter would be dealt with at a more appropriate time.

Meanwhile, the British commanders of the Middle East set about examining the slender resources at their disposal. Gen. Maitland Wilson now had at his disposal the 234th Infantry Brigade, which was busily retraining after its long spell of garrison duty in Malta, plus some smaller specialized units.

The Germans at this time had only a limited number of aircraft based on Crete and in Greece, and Wilson reasoned that if the British could establish their own fighters on Cos, they could hope to hold their own, for it was not thought that the Germans had sufficient resources, either seaborne or airborne, to mount an operation to evict them right away. The aid and assistance of the substantial Italian garrisons on Cos and Leros were expected to be forthcoming, and it was further assumed that these units were reasonably equipped for ground and air defense; this last supposition subsequently proved illusory.

Owing to the shortage of shipping, sea transport was almost completely restricted to destroyers or caiques, and therefore the troops earmarked could take with them only their personal weapons, rifles, Bren guns, and mortars. Even such such as jeeps and light antiaircraft guns proved difficult to break down for transportation, and no field guns or heavy vehicles could be sent. Instead, the British forces hoped to utilize the equivalent Italian equipment, especially on Leros, which the Italians had continually boasted was an up-to-date fortress.

On the naval side, Adm. Sir John Cunningham had at his disposal on September 8 equally limited forces for operations in the Aegean. There were the six fleet destroyers of the 8th Flotilla and two Hunt-class destroyers. The 1st Submarine Flotilla had only six boats operational. The 24th and 42nd Squadrons had sixteen motor launches, and these were to prove invaluable; indeed, for the small raiding parties, these light craft were indispensable. They were led by Cmdr. R. E. Courage. The Greek caiques that were requisitioned into the Royal Navy to supplement the motor launches (MLs), were given the grand title of the Levant Schooner Flotilla (LSF) and were led with dash and enterprise by Lt. Cmdr. A. C. C. Seligman. In addition, the RAF had eight high-speed launches (HSLs) for air-sea rescue work, and these were also used for any number of other tasks. The biggest headache for the navy was the absence of air cover for the larger ships during their passage of more than 300 miles in open waters from Alexandria to the battle area and also for the light craft operating from Cyprus.

It was a problem that was never surmounted.

The RAF faced similar problems. It was recognized that any attempted seizure of the Aegean Islands would depend on the quick establishment of suitable airfields in the area to provide for continuous single-engine fighter cover for the occupying garrisons and the supply ships and naval forces. Rhodes contained several suitable airstrips. Although Crete did lie just within extreme range of single-engine fighters operating from Cyrenaica, the majority of the islands lay well over 300 miles from the RAF's bases in North Africa and Cyprus. Long-range fighters could help redress the lack of such bases, but they would always be at a disadvantage against high-performance interceptors like the Messerschmitt Me 109G, and in addition, the RAF had very few long-range Beaufighter squadrons immediately available. True, the USAAF had a large Lightning establishment in Tunisia, but the decisions reached at a high level ensured that these were withheld from the Aegean save for a period too brief to affect the issue.

Shortage of shipping for the supply of the occupation forces played an additional part in the assessment of the burden of the RAF's responsibilities for the campaign. It was decided that parachute troops would supplement the seaborne landings, and fortunately eight Dakotas of No. 216 Squadron were immediately available in Palestine, where they had been sent in August to train with airborne troops.

Preparation for the assault by the RAF took the form of complete photographic cover of the Aegean by Photo Reconnaissance Unit (PRU) Spitfires of No. 680 Squadron, led by Wing Commander Cole. Their initial coverage was completed by the end of August, but the unit was permanently employed throughout September, and during October it flew no less than

196 sorties. So accurate and important was the squadron's work, and so grave a view of this permanent "eye in the sky" was taken by the Germans, that they placed great stress on trying to prevent it. By mid-October, the *Luftwaffe* had installed flak units, which were firing with great accuracy at heights reportedly up to 29,000 feet.

An advanced air headquarters ADEM was set up in Cyprus in order to coordinate all the RAF operations in the Aegean, and a special wing, No. 237, was also established there to control the long-range Beaufighter squadrons. Once Cos was operational, the immediate tasks were to be the provision of short-range fighter cover for Cos Island and over Leros Harbor by Spitfires based at Antimachia, and for long-range cover to be laid on from Cyprus. On-the-ground RAF regiment personnel were to be allocated from No. 500 (Temporary) Wing to defend Cos airfield. Units already training in Palestine were earmarked for this duty. In addition, special signals sections for fighter direction and immediate control were to be set up on Cos, Leros, Casteloriso, and other islands as considered necessary.

More generally, the RAF was allocated several tasks at the opening of the campaign. It was to make strategic bombing and intruder sorties over German airfields in Greece, Crete, and later Rhodes in order to restrict the operations of the *Luftwaffe*. No. 201 Naval Co-Operation Group, with its specialized squadrons, was to attack German shipping plying between Greece and the German-held islands. The duties of the RAF and all the established fighter forces would include the setting up of an air umbrella over the naval forces and supply ships on which the holding of the islands ultimately depended. Should the ships be unable to operate for any long period, the islands would soon become untenable, and the garrisons would be starved into impotence or be taken more readily in any attack. Reconnaissance parties were to be landed to report on the possibility of constructing additional single-engine fighter airfields on Leros, Samos, and Stampalia, but for obvious reasons, this last island was quickly scratched from the list. Before the Allies realized just how much the Germans were in control in the Aegean, a special Wellington flight based in the Delta was employed in leaflet dropping. The leaflet emphasized the armistice, and it was hoped that this would induce the numerically stronger Italian garrisons to rise up against the German troops—a somewhat naive hope at this stage of the war. There is no indication that the British leaflets influenced any Italian troops facing German bayonets.

Initially, No. 7 Squadron South African Air Force (SAAF), with Spitfires, was allocated to operate from the airfield at Antimachia on Cos once the island had been occupied, and two (later six) RAF regiment squadrons were to be moved into the islands. The bulk of the aircraft employed were to be drawn from AHQ, ADEM, or 201 Group. Later, two heavy bomber squadrons of RAF No. 240 Wing were made available. Although operationally controlled by the U.S. 9th Bomber Wing, they were under the administrative control of ADEM. U.S. forces were, much later, made available from time to time. From mid-September onward, two Liberator squadrons, one Mitchell medium-bomber squadron, and thirteen cannon-firing Mitchells operated for a time; for five days in October, six Lightning squadrons were lent—until the U.S. Chiefs of Staff heard about it!

Thus in the air, as well as by land and sea, the Germans were by no means in such an overpowering position, as was so often claimed later. The difference was that the German effort was a concerted one, with set objectives and close cooperation, in conjunction with easier supply routes and closer bases to the operational zone, and thus it proved superior to the somewhat vague and dispersed Allied effort.

Operation Accolade, the Allied occupation of Rhodes, had not yet been abandoned, and General Wilson was still making his plans with a view to the eventual occupation of Rhodes as previously agreed. What were later described as General Wilson's "minimum and modest" needs for such an attack, scheduled for October 20, were submitted by him on September 22. Based on the assumption that he could use the 10th Indian Division and part of an armored brigade, he required only naval escorts and bombarding forces, three LCTs, and a few transports, one hospital ship and enough transport aircraft to lift one parachute battalion. On September 25, Churchill sent a cable to General Eisenhower in yet another effort to open his eyes to what lay within reach and to the consequences if the Allies failed to take heed:

> You will have seen the telegrams from the Commander-in-Chief Middle East about Rhodes. Rhodes is the key both to the Eastern Mediterranean and the Aegean. It will be a great disaster if the Germans are able to consolidate there. The requirements which the Middle East ask for are small. I should be most grateful if you would let me know how the matter stands. I have not yet raised it with Washington.

As the prime minister later recalled, British needs seemed very little to ask from the Americans in order to gain the prize of Rhodes, especially when Britain had earlier, without reservation, placed almost the entire Middle East forces at General Eisenhower's disposal. Although all that was required was sufficient landing craft for a single division, plus a few days' assistance from the main Allied Air Force in order to complete the task, this plea was again unproductive.

Eisenhower replied to the prime minister on September 26, saying that he would "examine the resources carefully to give the Middle East the necessary support." He felt sure, he said, that he could meet their minimum requirements. This was a step in the right direction. The next day brought a complete about-face from the previous negative attitude, and the supreme commander granted the authorization for an armored brigade and some landing craft.

During a study of reports on the German air buildup in Greece, however, Churchill was again forced to comment that things now looked serious for our troops out in the islands. On September 29, the Chiefs of Staff reviewed the matter again. The opinion of Sir Charles Portal was that it would be quite wrong to pull out of the islands, because the German air threat had increased. The correct policy, he added, should be to fight the enemy wherever the opportunity was offered. As Churchill had said, there was only one German Air Force, and the sooner it was ground down the better. But still there remained the unmovable Eisenhower, in whose power the vast Allied air fleets lay.

Cos had by this date fallen to the Germans, and with this British humiliation as a spur, Eisenhower also released six squadrons of long-range fighters. But on October 5, he apparently regretted these two concessions and sent a cable protesting to the Combined Chiefs of Staff that such small diversions of his massive strength were "highly prejudicial to his chances of success in Italy."

In an agony of spirit, Churchill again strove to open the president's eyes. In a long and detailed telegram dispatch on October 7, he again reiterated the many points in favor of moving into the Aegean now. Stressing to his American ally, "I have never wished to send an army into the Balkans, but only by agents, supplies, and Commandos to stimulate the intense guerrilla movement prevailing there," the prime minister begged Roosevelt not to throw away an immense but fleeting opportunity.

But other voices had the president's ear. What Churchill called the "negative forces" held sway in Washington. The president had, at Churchill's request, called in General Marshall to discuss the telegram contents, but in vain. The general was already in receipt of a letter from Eisenhower in which the supreme commander had expressed in vigorous terms that an autumn and winter campaign in Italy would be of greater benefit to the cross-Channel scheme than a Balkan adventure. Such an argument struck a responsive chord in Marshall's heart. As Professor Trumbull Higgins recorded later:

Under the impact of arguments so well calculated to appeal to him, General Marshall hardly required pressure from his own planners, not to mention the outraged naval members of the U.S. Joint Chiefs, Admirals William Leahy and Ernest King, to advise President Roosevelt on 7th October that Eisenhower should send to the Middle East only what he believed he could spare from his Italian offensive.

Roosevelt's reply was to that effect: "It is my opinion that no division of forces or equipment should prejudice 'Overlord' as planned. The American Chiefs of Staff agree."

Such was the hard line as laid down by the Americans, in the face of which Churchill could only point out with clear logic—likewise ignored—that for them to maintain that a delay of some six weeks in the return of 9 landing craft for the Normandy landings, out of a force of more than 500 such vessels, would compromise the landings, still nine months away, was "to reject all sense of proportion."

The now frantic prime minister sent two more long cables as October 8 drew to a close, offering to meet at Eisenhower's headquarters. The president again replied at length with a negative. With his complete rejection came an admonishment: "Strategically, if we get the Aegean Islands, I ask myself where do we go from there? and, *vice versa*, where would the Germans go if for some time they retained possession of the islands?"

With the Soviet thrusts toward Eastern Europe now gathering speed—Smolensk fell on September 25—it was still not apparent to the trusting president just what the stakes were in being first into the Balkans.

The reply received on October 9 quenched, in Churchill's own words, his last hopes. He signaled Gen. Henry Maitland-Wilson that he should keep the occupation of Rhodes firmly in his mind as his number-one priority, but that he should not attempt to do it on the cheap—though one might ask what, if not this, British forces were already doing in the Aegean. He concluded with an assurance: "I am doing all I can." But in truth, against the stonewalling of the Americans, this was now too little to affect the issue. He did, however, manage to wring one tiny concession from Roosevelt, in that the question of Rhodes was stated as not being finally closed, but left open for discussion at the conference in Tunis that same day.

The conference was attended by Adm. Andrew Browne Cunningham, the newly appointed first sea lord, and all the service commanders concerned with operations in the Mediterranean theater except Sholto Douglas, who was in London trying to press for adequate airpower. At this meeting, the Allies received the first news of Hitler's decision to stand and fight south of Rome, and this caused the Rhodes operation to be postponed indefinitely and the recapture of Cos to be ruled out completely. It was felt that in this case, Leros must also be abandoned, but—surprisingly enough—the decision taken at Eisenhower's conference was that Britain should try to hold what islands it still had in its possession. This extraordinary decision was adhered to even at the later meeting held in Cairo; implementing it clearly entailed sending out more reinforcements for the islands.

Although they had urged the holding of Leros, both the British naval commanders in chief present at the meeting came away with the impression that aircraft were to be provided; this was not to be the case, however. Captain Roskill summarized the impasse: "On the one hand stood General Eisenhower, with the authority of the President behind him, and supported by Air Chief Marshal Tedder; while on the other hand stood the Middle East triumvirate, supported by the British Chiefs of Staff and fully cognizant of the Prime Minister's views and purpose."

Sir Charles Portal, chief of the air staff, argued that the Allied air forces in the Mediterranean were more than sufficient to give the islands all the air support they needed. Air Marshal Tedder protested strongly that the operations should not have been launched at all without consultation with him and Eisenhower. This was hardly the point; nor was his later charge that the navy and army were trying to claim the lack of air support as a "false alibi" for the failure of the operations. Air Marshal Sholto Douglas refuted this assertion, but when the smoke cleared away, it could be seen that the Eisenhower-Tedder bloc had ensured that no great diversion of strength had been made from the central Mediterranean to the Middle East apart from a few heavy bomber sorties.

While the Allies thus argued and the British and American armies in Italy commenced what was to prove a two-year slog all the way up the Italian mainland, the Germans, with small but mobile and compact forces such as those first required by the British, had proceeded to take hold of an impossible situation and mold it to their will.

On November 1, General Brooke, chief of the Imperial General Staff, noted in his diary:

> When I look at the Mediterranean, I realize only too well how far I have failed. If only I had had sufficient force of character to swing those American Chiefs of Staff and make them see daylight, how different the war might be. We should have had the whole Balkans ablaze by now, and the war might have been finished in 1943. I blame myself yet doubt whether it was humanly possible to alter the American point of view more than I succeeded in doing.

Twenty times the quantity of shipping that would have helped to take Rhodes in a fortnight was employed throughout the autumn and winter to move the Anglo-American heavy bomber bases from Africa to Italy.

In Churchill's words, "The American Staff had enforced their view; the price had now to be paid by the British."

CHAPTER FOUR

Point and Counterpoint

The commander in chief in the Middle East, Gen. Sir Henry Maitland-Wilson, had found himself at a grave disadvantage when Churchill's stirring call was made, for, with the recently taken decision of the Combined Chiefs of Staff, he and his subordinate commanders had little or nothing with which to "improvise and dare." As he later recalled, the news of the Italian armistice arrived just a few short days after he had been told that the discussions were about to take place. While he admits that he failed to appreciate the speed with which events would follow the armistice, it remains a fact that with his ships, landing craft, and trained assault troops taken away from him, he was placed in an unenviable position.

Rhodes, as always, was the key, and in Rhodes the Italian garrison outnumbered the German forces on the island by 35,000 to 7,000. Hopes were therefore expressed that the Italian governor, Adm. Inigo Campioni, might be willing to seize control of the whole island in his capacity as commander in chief of the Italian troops and sign an alliance with the British who would then move into not only Rhodes but all the islands of the Dodecanese.

Should this be achieved, the Allies believed that the Germans would be faced with many difficulties and supply problems for their garrison on Crete. It was also officially recorded that it would lessen the strategic value of that island as a threat to British North African conquests, the oil pipeline ports and the Levant route to the oil fields in Iraq and Iran. But these were not the only reasons for which Hitler and Churchill were so keen to control the area; their views were somewhat wider.

In any event, and for whatever the reasons put forward, speed was essential—but so was secrecy. General Wilson therefore selected Major the Earl Jellicoe, son of the famous admiral, who was serving with the Special Boat Section (SBS), for the tough job of contacting Admiral Campioni and persuading him to come over with his forces to the Allied cause. If he should prove successful in this task, it was hoped to fly in a stiffening of Allied troops to steel the Italians for the task of disarming the troops of Lt. Gen. Ulrich Kleemann's crack *Sturm Division Rhodos*. It was planned to use the Greek Sacred Regiment, under the command of *Sintagmatarhis* Christodoulos Tsigantes, for this purpose, as these were the troops immediately available, with aid from various smaller units.

Unfortunately, for all the British hopes of a swift, unexpected takeover, the Germans had made ready their detailed plans to forestall just such a defection by their Italian ally, an event they had been expecting for some time. General Kleemann had already strategically concentrated some of his forces in the centre of the island, while the Italians had all been dispersed around the coastline.

So Jellicoe's mission was planned. With "Major Dolby" (the alias of the Polish Count Dobriski, a special operations executive operative), the official Italian interpreter at general headquarters and Sergeant Kesterton, a signaler, it was arranged for his party to be parachuted from a Halifax bomber; they were then to make contact with Campioni and open negotiations with him. It was reported that the old admiral was a somewhat weak and vacillating character, and it was therefore hoped that he could be influenced without too much difficulty. In the event of an initial success by Jellicoe, Brig. D. J. T. Turnbull of the SBS, as officer in charge of the mission, was to follow up in a high-speed launch to continue with detailed talks.

The first piece of bad luck, with which this campaign was to be bedeviled, came when the Halifax carrying the three-man mission arrived over the island of Rhodes on the planned dropping night and found the whole area shrouded in fog and mist. They therefore had no choice but to return to base and try again the following night—thus twenty-four vital hours were lost, and unknown to the mission, with that delay went all hope of their plan working—for on this night, the Italian governor gave a dinner for some of the German garrison commanders at his castle residence.

During the course of the meal, Admiral Campioni learned of the armistice—it is said from the wife of one of the German officers who had heard it on the radio. The wily old admiral did not say anything to his principal guests about this, but allowed them to return to their units. As soon as General Kleemann became aware of the situation, he again sought out the admiral for a discussion of their respective positions. Both sides came to an agreement whereby all troops, German and Italian, undertook to remain in their present positions; this was to prevent bloodshed while a solution was found—or at least this was the line Kleemann apparently put forward. Campioni was quite unwilling to initiate any action against the Germans, even as outnumbered as they were, for he surely was aware of the war weariness and disillusionment of the majority of the Italian garrison. In such a condition, they would stand little chance against the armored and mechanized young storm troopers of Kleemann's command who held the key positions around Rhodes town.

The Germans, on their part, seem merely to have used these talks as a means of gaining time while their own prearranged plan was put into operation. Almost at once, columns of motorized troops were dispatched to take over all the vital airfields—Calato, Cattavia, and Maritza—and before long, the governor was forced to take steps against this breaking of the pledge and tell his troops to resist German infiltration.

Fighting between the Italians and Germans had indeed already taken place in several areas. At sunrise, the Germans started shelling some Italian positions with their 88-millimeter flak guns based around the perimeter of Maritza airfield. This move misfired, however. Although many of the Italians, most of whom were still in complete ignorance of the armistice and the "gentlemen's agreement" that had followed it, gave in, some of the Italian artillery positions around the Maritza perimeter fought back and in a short time had annihilated the German flak guns in their exposed positions. The Italian gunners then turned their attention to the airfield, which was under German control, and started to destroy the aircraft parked there. These consisted of a few Cant Z 1007 bombers and about thirty MC 202 and CR 42 fighters and fighter-bombers of 154 *Gruppo*. Many of these were destroyed by the Italian artillery, and others were blown up by sabotage later. Although a few could be patched up, and the Germans used them for a short while until their own aircraft arrived, a shortage of spares soon grounded them

This was the confused situation on the night of September 9–10, when Jellicoe and his two aides made their drop, all three parachuting down with the intention of landing in the vicinity of Maritza. Almost immediately they ran into more trouble, for a strong breeze was blowing over the dropping zone, and all the men fell widely apart from each other.

The Italians had not been tipped off of their impending arrival, and on spotting the parachutes descending, they quite naturally thought them to be Germans arriving to reinforce the airfield garrison. They opened a heavy, if inaccurate, fire on them, and both Jellicoe and Kesterton were severely shaken, though not actually hit. Count Dobriski, who had never made a parachute drop before in his life, had the added misfortune to land heavily on a metal-surfaced road and broke his leg.

All three men were ultimately discovered, fortunately for them, by Italian troops. Dobriski was the first to be picked up, in great pain, beside the roadway. Despite his condition, he managed to explain to the Italians the reason for his being there to such good effect that they at once dispatched a party to hunt for his two companions while the major was taken to hospital.

Jellicoe, when found, was suffering from acute thirst and nausea; believing himself to have been captured by hostile troops, he had somehow managed to eat the letter that General Maitland Wilson had written to Admiral

Campioni. This worthy performance was unfortunate, as it turned out, for their Italian captors were fully in favor of the mission and did everything they could to help the British party reach the governor without detection. Hospitably entertained by their captors at a nearby officers' mess, both Jellicoe and Kesterton were then transported direct to the governor's palace. Here Campioni was aroused from his slumbers and met them at 0200 hours, with Dobriski translating from a stretcher.

Although he was outwardly sympathetic to Jellicoe and gave him a hearing, Campioni would not commit himself too far. The Germans were treacherous, he assured them; and although fighting was taking place, this was not the same as going the whole way and signing an alliance. After all, the Germans were present, in strength and fully aware of the situation, whereas the British were not. Campioni demanded to know what support would be forthcoming from the British should he take the decisive step. Would they, for example, immediately bomb the German strongpoints at the airfields? (This was later carried out by Wellingtons, Liberators, and Beaufighters, but too late to affect the issue. Leros had no airfields, only seaplane anchorages.)

Jellicoe sought to assure the governor and his aides that help would indeed be forthcoming almost instantly, but only from small parties of paratroops (it may be assumed he did not mention that these would be drawn from the Greek Sacred Regiment!) and men of the Special Boat Squadron and Long Range Desert Group, who had already embarked for the occupation of Casteloriso. The support of larger bodies of British troops could not be promised until at least September 18 because of the shortage of shipping.

Naturally enough, the governor was not greatly cheered by this information. His troops were already engaged in fighting the Germans on a limited scale, but Kleemann was still anxious to put an end to this by negotiation. Indeed, the Germans were constantly sending envoys to talk to Campioni, and Sergeant Kesterton had a narrow escape when he almost dived into the same shelter as a high-ranking German officer when an air-raid warning sounded in the palace.

Admiral Campioni was caught in a cruel dilemma, and he therefore played for time to see how events turned out.

Jellicoe was given permission to set up a radio link with general headquarters in Cairo from the naval wireless station in the castle, and a room, bed, and doctor were made available for Dobriski. Jellicoe was further given permission to remain in the governor's residence, but he was warned not to show himself and to put on civilian clothes if he ventured outside the gates.

The situation thus was far from satisfactory, for while the Italian admiral vacillated and sought the safest way out of his problem, the Germans were systematically consolidating their hold on the island. As one historian later wrote:

It was apparent in fact that while the Admiral and some members of his staff in particular were willing to resist they had hoped to obtain some better guarantee of eventual success than that which Jellicoe was able to offer. These men were after all no heroes. Their lives were at stake and upon their actions in the next few days depended their prospects of survival. They had vegetated very comfortably for three years in a pleasant and moderately secure island. They were neither the first nor the last to be found wanting in decision when the press of great events swept them beyond matters of petty routine.

Jellicoe established radio contact with Cairo and explained the complications. It was arranged, with Campioni's concurrence, that Brigadier Turnbull and his party should be brought in as previously planned, first by seaplane to the island of Simi, and then on to Rhodes in an Italian MAS boat. This done, Jellicoe tried to get a little sleep.

He was awakened at 0500 by the governor himself. Events had escalated alarmingly. It soon became clear that German martial deeds had achieved more than British promises in bringing the admiral to a final decision.

General Kleemann, Campioni told Jellicoe, had presented him with an ultimatum and informed him that the German army was about to attack Rhodes town and the governor's palace. Campioni pointed out that he had risked his life in seeing Major Jellicoe and "Major Dolby" at all and said that he was taking no more chances. As it was, he would probably be shot if news of the interview reached the Gestapo—even though he had refused the British request.

He had therefore sent off urgent instructions that Brigadier Turnbull's party was not to leave Simi, and he now requested that Jellicoe and his men leave Rhodes as soon as possible. He suggested they make for Simi or Casteloriso and await a more suitable moment to renew contact. It was abundantly clear that he had no desire to explain Jellicoe's presence to the Germans should events continue in the present pattern and his castle be occupied by German troops.

Jellicoe realized that there was little point in refusing this request, but he suggested, as an act of good faith and in view of the admiral's somewhat hastily declared intentions to resist the Germans, that the plans of the Rhodes defenses and the Aegean minefields be placed at the disposal of his new "allies." In his haste to be rid of his embarrassing guest, Campioni complied with this request, and as a further act of good faith, he sent his chief of staff, Colonel Fanetza, with Jellicoe to speak with Brigadier Turnbull about the Italian situation firsthand. As it turned out, the Italian plans of their own minefields were so inaccurate as to be valueless. Reliance on them was to cost the Allies several ships before they realized their inaccuracy. This may have been by design, for Campioni was perhaps playing both sides against the middle, or it may have been due to typical Italian inefficiency.

The small party left that night dressed in overcoats several sizes too large for them and armed with a wireless set, a number of bottles of the local wine, and a picnic hamper. An Italian MAS boat, *Ms 12*, then took them to Casteloriso, where they arrived the next morning. Here they found the SBS in control of the island, but Brigadier Turnbull had left for Simi in accordance with the prearranged plan. Jellicoe snatched a hurried breakfast and then, with Fanetza, reboarded the MAS boat to catch up with Turnbull. En route, however, while Jellicoe was sleeping, Fanetza ordered the boat to return to Casteloriso. According to one version, this was out of pique because Jellicoe had laughed when he fell in the water at Casteloriso. But it is much more likely that he was acting on instructions from Admiral Campioni in Rhodes, received on the MAS boat's wireless, when the admiral finally decided to give in. By the time they had again disembarked, news had come in that Campioni had capitulated to General Kleemann.

Count Dobriski had left Rhodes earlier and arrived at Simi on the tenth on board *Ms 15* (*Sottotentente di Vascello* Aracci). He was later taken by Italian seaplane to Casteloriso and thence on to Cyprus.

Before one passes judgment on Admiral Campioni or his men too hastily, it should be remembered that some of the Italian Army units on Rhodes resisted the Germans for five days. The OKW Diary reports that whereas resistance on Crete was overcome by September 9, heavy fighting had been going on in Rhodes since 0800 of that day. This continued throughout the tenth and eleventh, when a German destroyer and some E-boats landed reinforcements for Kleemann's troops. Between September 8 and 11, seventeen Italian officers and other ranks were killed and 300 wounded.

In fact, some artillery units fought on for much longer, and their guns were finally taken by storm troopers with fixed bayonets, only to find most of the Italians dead or dying around their guns. Many Italians were only too eager to surrender to whoever arrived on the scene first, but by no means can all be tarred with the same brush. The governor may seem over cautious, but the fate of many of his compatriots who were later to help the British against the Germans in Cos and Leros shows that his fears were far from groundless.

Some 40,000 Italians laid down their arms, according to German records, and Rhodes with its three vital airfields was firmly in German hands. Messerschmitt Me 109 fighters and Junkers Ju 87 dive-bombers were quickly flown in, followed later by long-range bomber units. It was these, more than any other German move, that proved the decisive factor in the grim weeks ahead. In any case, the chance to take Rhodes by improvisation—if it had ever existed—was certainly gone.

Although Rhodes was for the moment lost to the British, they still believed it desirable to infiltrate the Dodecanese and Cyclades and occupy some of the lesser islands in the rear. To do this with the scanty forces at his disposal entailed a calculated risk by General Maitland Wilson, but it promised to reap dividends at small cost while the mounting of Accolade, the occupation of Rhodes, was reviewed yet again and forces assembled. The British felt that some of the Germans' initiative had to be countered, and so it was arranged.

Even as Jellicoe's mission to Rhodes was coming undone, light forces had been moving into Casteloriso. Three units were involved: Macey's Raiders (No. 8 Special Boat Commando), the Special Boat Section, and the Long Range Desert Group. The Long Range Desert Group had been formed in July 1940 and had established a reputation with its reconnaissance and raiding activities behind the Axis lines in North Africa. The need for this role had ended with the fall of Tunisia, but this group of highly trained men was not disbanded and were now to find equally dangerous work in the islands of the Aegean. The Special Boat Section had originated as the Folbot Section of No. 8 Commando, a Folbot being a type of collapsible and transportable kayak, and Layforce had been formed from the SBS in the Middle East for the assault on Rhodes, which should have taken place in April 1941. With the redundancy of Layforce following the cancellation of the Rhodes operation in 1941, the Folbot Section became known as the Special Boat Section and was attached to the depot ship HMS *Medway* to train with submarines of the 1st Flotilla for sabotage missions on enemy-held coasts. By mid-1943, this unit had grown in size; it consisted of three detachments under the overall command of Major Jellicoe, from the Coldstream Guards.

Like the Long Range Desert Group, the Special Boat Section recruited brains rather than brawn, and its men were experts in gathering and transmitting intelligence. Later these units, together with the Special Air Service (SAS), another little-known unit at that time, were to be combined in the Aegean theater under the title of Raiding Forces, commanded by Brigadier Turnbull. At this period, however, they operated as independent commands, although with common aims and skills. Thus it was in the early hours of September 10 that Turnbull's party of sixty men, with a few antiaircraft gunners and some RAF signalers, having set out from Paphos in Cyprus in naval launches, arrived at Casteloriso. It was reported that "after a few shots the island was ours," in marked contrast to the last British landing on the island, and that the Italian garrison proved "cooperative" and the population was "elated."

While Turnbull had continued on to Simi for the rendezvous with Jellicoe, the Special Boat Section detachment had consolidated its hold on Casteloriso and its Italian garrison of 300. Henceforth known by the code name Trombone, this tiny island off the Turkish coast was to be the main British staging post for units moving up into the Aegean.

The Special Boat Section now moved on to occupy Cos and Leros. The Italian commander on Leros, R.Adm. Luigi Mascherpa, had already been contacted by wireless by General Kleemann on Rhodes and invited to surrender the island, but he had declined to negotiate; he was made of somewhat sterner stuff than Campioni. Therefore, having seen his men ashore on Cos at dawn on September 14, the indefatigable Jellicoe pressed on in his commandeered Italian MAS boat to meet Mascherpa in Leros. The voyage was enlivened by the fact that a rough sea was encountered, and the small boat was soon in difficulties. Notwithstanding the fears of her captain, however, the vessel eventually made landfall at Leros.

Jellicoe went ashore in front of the governor's palace and was taken to meet the admiral, who appeared to be both friendly and willing to help in every way, although Jellicoe was a little perturbed to see that his recent shipmate, Colonel Fanetza, had already arrived. At this stage, he was not quite certain on whose side this man might be, but all went well, and Jellicoe not only was allowed to signal Cairo of the admiral's willingness to cooperate, but also was taken around the island to pick suitable drop zones for parachutists and supplies. Following this tour of inspection, and on top of an exhausting week, he was entertained at a banquet in honor of the new alliance. Finally, almost dropping with exhaustion, he was flown by seaplane back to Casteloriso, where he made a long report on the state of Cos and Leros, and then slept for fourteen hours.

A second party of the Special Boat Section, commanded by Maj. J. M. "Jock" Lapraik, left Haifa on September 12 and was sent to occupy the island of Simi, after first calling in at Casteloriso and Cos. The men were conveyed from Beirut aboard the Royal Navy Motor Launch *ML-351* (Lt. Kenneth Hallows) of the 42nd ML Flotilla, which had aboard four one-gallon tins of ninety-octane fuel on her decks, and arrived off Simi on the evening of the seventeenth. Lt. Anders Lassen was sent ashore by Folbot to make contact with the Italian authorities. He was received by bursts of gunfire but eventually succeeded in landing. The invaders were soon received by the civil and military leaders; in no time at all, Lapraik had assumed command of the island. The Italian garrison consisted of 140 of all ranks, with nine 8-millimeter and two 20-millimeter machine guns, and was commanded by *Tenente di Corvetta* Andrea Occhipinti. They were all placed under British command, and their defensive dispositions were inspected and found to be good. After soothing the local Greek population, Lapraik managed to start turning this tiny island into a major base for raiding and reconnaissance patrols in the area, all under the very noses of the German forces in Rhodes.

The detachment under Maj. David Sutherland that had first occupied Cos had been relieved by this time and had moved on to occupy Samos to the north. They sailed on the night of September 16 and arrived off the island the next morning. Here they were received as liberators by the Greek populace, which, as on Simi, demanded the immediate massacre of the entire Italian garrison. Sutherland eventually was able to dissuade them from carrying this out. An officer from the British Military Mission in Ankara had already arrived and paved the way for them, and Gen. Mario Soldarelli was disposed to be friendly toward them. A detachment of 1,500 Blackshirt Militia was also on the island, and there was no doubt where their sympathies lay. These were counterweighted by the equivalent number of Greek guerrillas, whose fighting spirit was reportly high. Nevertheless the fact that the Blackshirts refused to take orders from Soldarelli inevitably meant that the British would have their hands full here.

On September 21, Lapraik's party carried out its first reconnaissance into Rhodes when two men were landed through a narrow gap in the mine-fields near the New Town. This initial foray was discovered by the Germans, who harried the two men for five days before they could be brought away. But this was only the beginning of operations from Simi.

The men of the Special Boat Section in among the little islands were now joined by the first of the Long Range Desert Group units. Before being sent in, they had fortunately spent the summer among the cedars of Lebanon, where they had received training in mountain warfare. The patrols had to forget all their experiences in the desert and start from scratch. A Squadron was mostly manned by New Zealanders, while B Squadron was made up from both British and Rhodesian volunteers. A Squadron left Haifa on September 21, embarked in the Greek destroyer *Queen Olga*, for one of the 8th Destroyer Flotilla's many runs into Leros and reached Port Laki the next day during an air raid. Almost at once, patrols were sent out into the Cyclades to gather information on German strengths and dispositions: Two patrols of A Squadron under Maj. A. I. Guild were sent out from Leros to watch German shipping and air movements. A party from T1 patrol moved into Kithnos, and the British patrol M1 was sent to Giaros. The Rhodesian patrol S1 went to reinforce Simi and operate from there, while M2 patrol established itself on Stampalia.

By the end of the month, the British had established themselves on Cos, Leros, Samos, Simi, Stampalia, and Icaria; the 2nd Battalion of The Queen's

Royal West Kent Regiment had moved into Casteloriso, already taken, as permanent garrison. Further troops of the 234th Infantry Brigade were being either flown into Cos or taken by destroyer into Leros.

The Germans had not been idle either, and by September 20, British Intelligence at Cairo estimated that they were in control on Lemnos, Mytilene, Chios, the Sporades, the Cyclades except for Icaria, Kasos, Kithera, and Antikithera, as well as Crete and Rhodes. Pasos and Samothrace in the northern Aegean were occupied by the Germans' Bulgarian allies with small detachments.

About their future intentions there was little doubt, and it was anticipated that the neutralization of Cos airfield would be their first priority, which was quite correct, and that it was unlikely that the Germans would attempt any seaborne operations—which proved completely wrong. A further assessment that proved to be optimistic was that the Germans could not release adequate forces from Rhodes, Scarpanto, or Crete in view of their commitments, although it was recognized that the forces available to them in Greece, if they had air support, could furnish the men to clear the area. This proved all too accurate. By the twenty-fifth, it had also become evident that the *Luftwaffe* had received considerable reinforcements.

The Germans not only were able, throughout this period, to maintain their existing seaborne communications—Piraeus-Crete, Piraeus-Rhodes, and Crete-Rhodes—with only small losses, but also considerably stepped up their supply flights from Greece into both Crete and Rhodes, with which the British were unable to interfere at all. In addition to this, the Germans were busy, as indeed were the British, in sending raiding forces into the Cyclades. The Germans set up observation posts and did not garrison the islands in force, except on Syros. Their main concern at this period seemed to be the evacuation of unreliable Italian garrisons and the seizure of as much food and war materiel as they could get their hands on. They had evidently expected a much more aggressive policy from the British than was forthcoming. Only on rare occasions did the raiders and patrols from both sides come into conflict among the myriad of islands, although when they did, there were some hot little actions.

The force under David Sutherland was relieved on Samos by A, C, D, and HQ Companies of the 2nd Battalion of the Royal West Kents, and the detachment moved in to occupy Kalymnos, near Cos, which they hoped to turn into another raiding force base like Simi. It was occupied by a Long Range Desert Group (LRDG) detachment under Capt. R. A. Tinker on September 25.

The Special Boat Section historian recorded the frustration that followed: "For months the SBS had been attacking Germans and could conceive for itself no other role. In the miserable and humiliating weeks which followed the unit was to be employed largely on ferrying forces and expending its energy and the lives of some of its best men on nocturnal trips to Turkey and in the successful defence of islands which it was later ordered to abandon." This is a very one-sided view, but perhaps a natural one for the such attacking units to take.

Five LRDG patrols actually moved into Leros to stiffen the Italian gunners in the island batteries and also make sure they did not have a change of heart when the going got tough and turn their guns onto their new allies. It is said that this task, that of ensuring that the reluctant Italians remained at their posts and manned their guns called for "tact, patience and even force." The Italian communications system was found to be wanting because of the demoralization of the signalmen, and it was later damaged by German bombing. Before the end, links were maintained solely by the LRDG wireless operators.

One of the most notable of the LRDG's successes took place later on the island of Kithnos. Here Capt. Charles K. Saxton and six men of T1 Patrol were taken in a caique of the Levant Schooner Flotilla; the trip was made in three stages at night, and the caique lay up against the shore by daylight at convenient islands along the route. Kithnos was occupied by the Germans with a small force of twenty men who were operating a wireless direction station and a permanent observation post. Because of this, it had originally been intended that T2 should remain on Kithnos for only a fortnight, but the island was found so perfect for keeping watch on the German sea lanes that they stayed there for a month.

The Germans soon became aware of the LRDG patrol but had too few men to make a complete search of the island, small though it was. Captain Tinker and his men kept on the move, changing their hiding places nightly. Sgt. J. L. D. Davis knew a smattering of Greek, and by making contact with friendly islanders, he managed to obtain extra information on German movements.

T2 sighted a large convoy passing between Kithnos and Syros on the afternoon of October 6 and reported its composition, speed and air cover by wireless. This important information resulted in the complete destruction of the convoy on the night of the seventh by a Royal Navy striking force (see chapter 7).

Saxton's little band still remained on Kithnos and sighted and reported several further convoys. Their caique returned with supplies and they took advantage of this to charge their wireless battery on neighboring Seriphos so that the noise did not give their position away. Sergeant Davis was left in charge while this was being done, and he sighted two convoys moving at night.

R1 patrol, commanded by Lieutenant Aitken with six men, was taken into the enemy-held Naxos by motor launch. Here the Germans had a large garrison force of some 650 men, but despite this, Aitken's party remained on Naxos for seventeen days, evading the German patrols by trekking across the island from side to side, aided all the time by friendly islanders. Again they sighted ships moving between the islands and on one occasion reported several ships moored in Naxos Harbor itself; this resulted in an attack by cannon-firing Mitchells and Beaufighters, which sank two ships. Two of the aircraft were shot down and one of them, a Beaufighter, crashed into the sea off the island. Despite the strong German force on Naxos, the pilot and navigator were rescued by the Greek islanders, who hid them in the town and gave them medical attention. The patrol of the LRDG was contacted, and they managed to spirit the two airmen away from the searching Germans and took them back to Leros when the patrol was finally withdrawn on November 6.

Second Lt. M. W. Cross and five men of T2 patrol were sent out to relieve T1 but were landed on Seriphos instead as this was thought to be safer. T1 returned to Leros by caique on October 23. The enemy was now patrolling the area with Arado floatplanes in an effort to stop the transmitting of such vital information by the LRDG, but a Greek shepherd helped them find a suitable hideout—an abandoned goat-hut on top of a 300-foot cliff, smelly and conspicuous, but providing a wonderful view of the channel.

The Germans had a garrison of forty men in the town, some four miles away, but the Greeks organized a warning system to alert the patrol to any likely approach by German troops. Whenever they sortied out, the local postmaster telephoned the monastery, and the priests then dispatched a runner at top speed to the hut.

The New Zealanders remained here for three weeks, during which time their sightings of ships were limited to one 6,000-ton freighter. They did, however, seem to be on the main flight path for *Luftwaffe* transports flying troops and supplies into Cos (see chapter 5 for a detailed account of operations on Cos). After reporting several such flights by four large flying boats, an ambush was laid on by six Beaufighters from Cyprus, which shot all four down when they appeared one day without an escort. T2 was relieved by a British patrol and returned to Leros on November 9.

M2 patrol on Stampalia took charge of the eighty-odd survivors from the German convoy destroyed on October 7 who managed to get ashore there. One of the Levant Schooner Flotilla, the *Hedgehog*, commanded by Sub-Lt. D. N. Harding, was sent from Leros to bring back ten of these for interrogation but developed engine trouble and put in at the island of Levitha, which lay some twenty miles from the western tip of Kalymnos. It was thought that this island was unoccupied, but unknown to the British the Germans had landed a large patrol on it and when a party was sent to *Hedgehog*'s assistance in Motor Launch 359, they found only a smoldering wreck and were fired on from the island.

The navy felt that the reoccupation of this island, only some fifteen miles west of Leros, was further evidence of the Germans' immediate intentions to attack Leros itself. It was considered essential that this island be taken and used as an observation post and warning station; the commander of 234th Infantry Brigade therefore ordered the LRDG to assault and hold it. This order led directly to the so-called battle of Levitha, during which the LRDG received its most severe setback of the whole war.

When they received the order to take Levitha, both Major Gill and Captain Tinker asked, as a matter of urgency, that some prior reconnaissance be made before an assault went in, but because of time pressure, this request was turned down and the troops went in blind. It was thought that the Germans had only a handful of men on the island. David Sutherland's patrol of twenty-two men from A Squadron was withdrawn from its duties with the Italian gun battery on Leros, together with a few men from R1 and T2 Patrols; the remaining twenty-six men from B Squadron, including Y2 and part of S1 Patrols, were added to them, and the whole force was put under the command of Capt. J. R. Olivey.

The attack was made in two prongs, A Squadron landing on the eastern tip of the island and B Squadron to the west. Both were to make their way to the center of the island and take the high ground overlooking the harbor which is on the south coast. The operation had a makeshift air about it before it even started. The men were to be carried to the island in two motor launches and then use Folbots for the actual landing, but it was found that bomb splinters during the many air attacks on the launches off Leros had punctured every boat, and sticking plaster had to be used to patch them up before the invaders could even practice rowing in them. For communication with Leros headquarters, the force relied on the large wireless set, and to keep in contact with each other, four infantry sets were provided. It was not until they were about to leave at dusk on October 23 that it was discovered that the A Squadron set had not been "netted in" with the others. There was nothing they could do at this stage except try to improvise something en route to the island. They were not aided in this by the fact that most of the force suffered from violent seasickness during the journey.

This was merely the beginning. When A Squadron reached their landing point, they had great difficulty in launching their patched-up boats in the choppy sea and were late in going ashore. Some of their equipment was lost in landing on the rugged coast, but what they could salvage they hauled up the cliff face. Sutherland was still unable to contact either B Squadron or the launches.

A bombardment of a house thought to be occupied by the Germans was scheduled by the two MLs, but they mistook a small hut in front of A Squadron for the target, and the LRDG was unable to dissuade them from deluging it with shells. The bombardment merely served to act as a call to arms for the German garrison. Once it had ceased, Sutherland's men moved off to the right and found the burned-out shell of the *Hedgehog*. As they did so, they were assaulted from the rear by heavy machine-gun fire from the vicinity of their landing place.

The detachment was kept pinned down by this for some time, but eventually they put in a counterattack and rushed the enemy positions, taking a German patrol of twelve men prisoner. Trooper H. L. Mallett was severely wounded in this attack and died later. They kept pushing forward toward the ridge and secured it before daylight in the face of further small-arms fire, losing Trooper A. J. Penhall killed and Trooper R. G. Haddow severely wounded in process.

B Squadron was more fortunate, and the men met no resistance as they went ashore. By dawn they had worked their way within 500 yards of the German headquarters. They could hear Sutherland's men fighting on the other side of the island but were still unable to raise them on the wireless. Olivey's men were therefore out on a limb, and the enemy soon began to bring up reinforcements, ultimately cutting them off completely. Encircled and subjected to heavy machine-gun and mortar fire, as well as air attacks from three seaplanes that took off from the harbor, B Squadron was cut to pieces and the majority of the men were taken prisoner.

Meanwhile, Sutherland's force was digging in grimly in its exposed position atop the ridge, overlooking the harbor. The men were machine-gunned by the seaplanes, and return fire from their Brens only bounced off the German machines. Eventually the British were split into three little groups. David Sutherland had with him his wireless operator, the medical officer and the wounded, with three or four others and the German prisoners. In the center was Sgt. E. J. Dobson with the solitary Bren gun, a tommy gun, and the bulk of the men with rifles. On higher ground, farther off, was another small party under Cpl. J. E. Gill.

All were short of food and out of water. Trooper J. T. Bowler volunteered to go get some, together with a runner from Gill to Sutherland. Neither of them was seen again, and they were presumed killed. The troops could not last very long. Soon A squadron joined B in captivity. Gill and three others evaded capture for a time, but after hiding out for four days, they were forced to surrender.

The commanding officer of the LRDG, Lt. Col. J. R. Easonsmith, arrived in a launch during the night of October 24–25 with belated instructions to pull the force out of the island, but the only survivors found were Capt. John Olivey; Captain Lawson, the medical officer; and seven men of B Squadron. Olivey and Major Gill returned the following night, but no one else was found. For such a tiny force the losses were shattering, and on October 28, Easonsmith held a conference with the surviving senior officers of the LRDG to decide their future. It was recommended that with the exception of those patrols still active in the Cyclades, the LRDG should be pulled out of the area—where it felt it was being thrown away on useless missions—and regrouped to train new volunteers in the Middle East to rebuild its strength. Half the men of the LRDG involved were New Zealanders, and the New Zealand government, which had not been consulted about the use of its troops in a new combat area as was customary, was likewise not pleased to see such disastrous misapplication of some of its finest men and made a great deal of noise to that effect.

Although General Wilson pleaded that he could ill afford to let the group go, it was decided to pull out the LRDG as soon as replacements could be found. But before this order could be implemented, it was overtaken by events.

The men of the Long Range Desert Group and Special Boat Section later served on Cos and Leros; in the end, they were to have the distinction of achieving on Simi the only British victory in the islands during the campaign. But although they achieved much, the struggle for the Aegean was not to be decided by small units, however resourceful and daring. It was becoming a war of logistics, one in which, contrary to all expectations on both sides, the Germans were proving superior to the British. As British intelligence had already correctly forecast, the first German target was Cos.

CHAPTER FIVE

Cos Occupied

The island of Cos was a part of the Ottoman Empire until 1912, although the Knights of St. John had occupied it for a long period around the fifteenth century; the remains of the castle constructed by the knights during their tenure still dominate the old town. One of the most fertile of the Aegean Islands, Cos had as its main claim to fame the lettuce named after it. The dominant physical feature is a rugged ridge of limestone, which runs down the full length of the southern part of the island. This ridge dominates the coastline, falling away in steep cliffs, which shelter little bays and good natural harbors. To the north, this escarpment recedes more gently and is more open to cultivation.

The large, flat area around Antimachia provided enough room for the vital airstrip, the only one in the region other than those on the German-dominated island of Rhodes. With Rhodes safely in the hands of the Germans, this was the sole airstrip available to the Allies. Like the solitary Henderson Field on Guadalcanal in the Solomon Islands campaign, it was to be the focal point for both sides, and the fight for its possession would lead to much bloodshed. The sandy beaches on the northern side of the island provided ideal landing spots, but the British did not have much time to construct artificial barriers there. The whole island is little more than twenty-eight miles long by about six miles wide, and the channel between it and the Turkish mainland is a mere mile wide.

Following the earthquake of 1933, which demolished most of the old town of Cos, the Italians had vigorously rebuilt it and constructed a road that snaked from this town, in the northeast of the island, down to Cefalo in the southwest. At the time of the British occupation, the Italian garrison consisted of about 4,000 troops, infantry and artillery, who had been on the island for almost four years. It was found that they were quite prepared to welcome the British forces and even seemed eager to help resist the Germans; the Italian troops, however, were poorly equipped and lacking in adequate means to resist, and their morale had suffered accordingly.

Few defensive measures of a modern nature had been taken to resist a determined assault, and slit trenches had not even been dug. The coastal defense batteries were well sited, but their equipment was obsolete and consisted of old guns placed in open positions with little or no modern fire control. The infantry was widely dispersed about the island and antiaircraft measures were primitive in the extreme. A few German technicians had been on the island trying to overcome these problems, but it appeared that little had actually been done.

The Italian air forces on the island were in an even more pitiful state than the army; they consisted of one section of the 396th Fighter Squadron with eight machines, only four of which were serviceable: two MC 202s, one CR 42, and one G 50. There were only two pilots, *Sottotentente* Giuseppe Morganti and an NCO, but the latter left on the morning of the eighth in a CR 42 for Rhodes and did not return. On the evening of the tenth, Morganti sighted a formation of six He 111s returning to Greece after attacking Italian positions on Rhodes, and he claimed to have shot one down. In retaliation the following morning, two German aircraft attacked Antimachia, destroying two aircraft on the ground and damaging a third.

The Italian garrison had practically no transport, and it was to prove extremely difficult for the British occupiers to make good this deficiency; the only shipping available to ferry in large vehicles was far too slow to risk running the gauntlet of the *Luftwaffe*, whereas high-speed dashes by destroyers, although frequently undertaken, could provide only a limited number of jeeps and trailers because of the limited space on board.

One redeeming feature of the island was the plentiful supply of food, sufficient for both the civilian population of 20,000 and the British and Italian troops. Water was available in the populated regions but scarce in places off the beaten track. Cos town had the only harbor on the island into which supplies could be shipped and unloaded, but although it was well sheltered and used as a base for small Italian warships earlier in the war, its facilities left much to be desired; there was only a single berth alongside the quay, and the shallow water restricted its capacity.

Jellicoe had arrived on Casteloriso after his abortive mission into Rhodes to learn that the German takeover of that island was now completed. In order to gain a quick foothold on the remaining islands, Colonel Turnbull of the Special Forces immediately dispatched Jellicoe with a force under Major Sullivan to seize Cos and Leros.

The Special Boat Squadron had only a single detachment of men, some fifty-five in all, with which to fulfill this assignment, but nothing daunted they sailed from Casteloriso on the night of September 12 in an assortment of small craft including naval motor launches. In order to divert the Germans, attention away from this audacious little armada, the American bombers of the Northwest African Strategic Air Force struck hard at the air-fields on Rhodes.

That strike, carried out by thirty-eight Liberators, may have succeeded in its purpose, but the Germans were probably too busy strengthening their hold on Rhodes to pay much attention to the lesser islands. In any event, no German sea patrols were encountered by the Special Boat Squadron force under David Sutherland, which arrived off Cos Harbor at dawn on September 14.

The Italian commander had expressed his desire to cooperate with the British, and there is little doubt that he reflected the opinion of the major-ity of the islanders, both Greek and Italian. Just about the whole of the pop-ulation of Cos town appeared to have assembled to welcome in the little fleet of "invaders." They greeted Special Boat Section men as saviors as they stepped ashore, throwing flowers and offering them wine. It is doubtful whether the Italians, soon to be placed in an impossible position, would have been so eager to cooperate with the British had they realized how small the follow-up force was to prove or how strongly their former allies just across the water were to react. For the time being, however, the arrival of the little detachment seemed to signal the start of better days for the island, although the Italian commander soon warned Jellicoe that strong reinforcements were needed to hold the island. Unfortunately, neither the reinforcements on the scale required nor the means to protect them once ashore was ever forthcoming.

Jellicoe pressed on to Leros in his Italian MAS boat, while Sutherland's troops moved inland to the vital airstrip at Antimachia, some thirteen miles from Cos town, to ensure its readiness for the arrival of the RAF. The first aircraft into Cos were two Beaufighters of No. 46 Squadron, operating from Nicosia in Cyprus. Squadron Leader Cuddie landed three passengers at dawn on the fourteenth while Flying Officer Atkins orbited to provide top cover. The three men were all from an RAF signal section and were to set up a point-to-point wireless telegraphy station on the island.

Antimachia airfield was found to be suitable for immediate flying opera-tions, and at dusk, six Spitfire Vs of No. 7 (South African Air Force) Squadron flew in, under the command of Capt. H. E. Kirby. The squadron had formerly been on convoy escort and fighter interception duties over the Mediter-ranean from its base at El Gamil near Port Said. On September 11, an advance party of six pilots under Captain Kirby, with a ground staff under command of the squadron's doctor, Captain Rocher, had left for Cyprus on very short notice indeed; all personnel were told to travel light with clothing and rations for two weeks. By the evening of the fifteenth, they were installed at Antimachia. Meanwhile, further reinforcements for the squadron, under

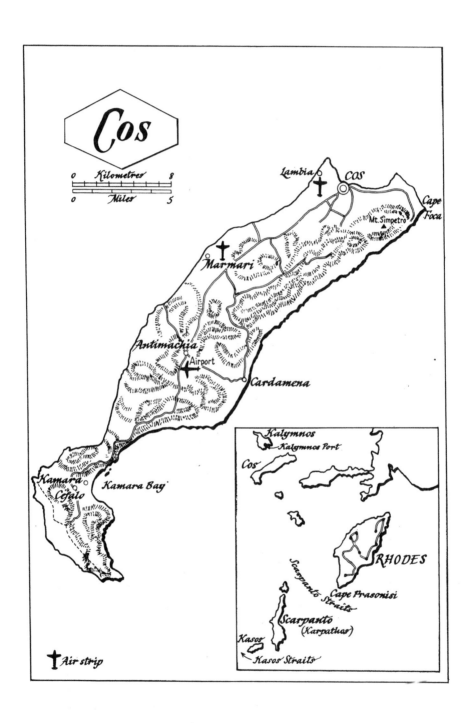

Cos

| Kilometres | 0 | 8 |
| Miles | 0 | 5 |

Lambia
COS
Cape Foca
Mt. Simpetro
Marmari
Antimachia
Airport
Cardamena
Kamara Cefalo
Kamara Bay

Kalymnos
Kalymnos Port
Cos
RHODES
Scarpanto Straits
Cape Prasonisi
Scarpanto (Karpathos)
Kasos
Kasos Straits

✝ Air strip

Maj. Cornelius A. van Vliet, were being hastily organized in Cyprus. The squadron's ground staff was also flown in on the evening of the fourteenth by three Dakota transports of No. 216 Squadron, which were provided with an escort of six Beaufighters from No. 46 Squadron. Italian antiaircraft gunners fired on the Dakotas by mistake but fortunately scored no hits of a serious nature, although one of the Dakota pilots was heard complaining vigorously back at his Cyprus base about a reception committee that left him with half his tail shot away.

Because of the poor state of the defenses and the precarious position of the RAF and Special Boat Squadron personnel on the island, the British decided to stiffen the garrison immediately with a parachute drop of some 120 men of the 11th Parachute Battalion. Commanded by Lt. Col. R. M. C. Thomas, the 11th Battalion allocated its A Company to this initial task. Formed at Kabrit, it was subsequently referred to as the 11th Parachute Brigade in a somewhat amateurish and desperate attempt to impress German intelligence. By the end of August, three of its platoons had reached a sufficiently high standard of training for the brigade to be capable of limited operations. Together with a section of 3-inch mortars and a machine-gun section, this formation was flown out of Mafraq in Jordan in seven of No. 216 Squadron's Dakotas, each of which was overloaded by some 1,500 pounds.

On the night of September 14–15, the faithful transports ferried them from Cyprus, and they made their drop on Cos without incident. The Special Boat Squadron marked the drop zone and the Italians assisted by spreading straw and hay on the ground. The only casualty was one man who sprained an ankle on landing. Like the Special Boat Squadron before them, the paratroops were received with great hospitality by the Italians, who ran up to help them off with their harnesses as soon as they touched down.

The historian Bennett has told how Ultra was almost valueless in warning of German reaction to any of the Aegean invasions the British were to mount, but in the case of Cos, even less information was dispensed than with Leros. The British Official History indeed went so far as to claim that "British intelligence had not detected the Germans' preparations" whatsoever with regard to Cos, other than a "general and long-range" warning issued on the day the first British troops arrived on Cos itself (Playfair, *Mediterranean and the Middle East*, 544).

Together with Sutherland's men, the paratroops now cooperated with the Italian units in organizing defenses in the areas most open to the expected seaborne assault. It soon became apparent that the troops available would have a difficult job patrolling the eighty-mile coastline, let alone defending it completely. The major defense organization was therefore set up in the area surrounding Antimachia, while the men prospected for further

suitable sites for additional airstrips, finding one in the Lambia area. Units of
the RAF Regiment and the 1st Light Anti-Aircraft Regiment were allocated to
augment the poor antiaircraft defenses. Heavy-gun positions were set up in
Cos town, where force headquarters was established, although it was feared
that the open beaches in the Marmari region presented the most serious
threat to the defenders.

The first of these units, No. 2909 Squadron, RAF Regiment, consisting
of two officers and forty men under the command of Flight Lieutenant Wal-
ton, was airlifted by 216's Dakotas straight from Ramat David airfield to Cos.
This unit was equipped with nine Hispano 20-millimeter cannons on univer-
sal ground mountings. The lack of protection afforded the crews of these
weapons soon earned the Hispano the title of the VC (Victoria Cross) Gun
from the army gunners on the island. No. 2909 Squadron arrived at Antimachia at 1000 hours on September 15. The men commandeered two Italian trucks to transport their equipment, and the nine guns were soon set up
on the airfield's perimeter. This was the first time a unit of the RAF Regiment had actually flown into action.

Throughout the day, No. 7 Squadron maintained a standing patrol of
two Spitfires over the airfield and the neighboring islands, with a further two
at instant readiness, but there was no sight of the *Luftwaffe*. The newly
arrived reinforcements took over from the Special Boat Section units, which
left for Samos, while another SBS unit from Casteloriso moved over to the
small island of Simi via Cos. Lt. Gen. Sir Desmond Anderson, commander of
Force 292, arrived on the island the morning of the fifteenth to examine the
situation and left later that day.

The men of the RAF Regiment were faced with the unenviable task of
defending Antimachia airstrip, but they got to it straightaway. The rocky terrain of the country around the airfield made it impossible to dig in without
specialized equipment, which they did not have, and there proved to be
insufficient time to erect even meager blast walls to protect the guns before
the expected German reaction came.

The British were granted a little respite, however, for September 16
remained quiet, and the steady buildup of forces on the island by sea and air
was allowed to continue undisturbed.

On this day, the 1st Battalion of the Durham Light Infantry began to
arrive. This unit, then under the command of Lt. Col. R. F. Kirby, had seen
active service in the Western Desert, in Syria against Vichy French forces,
and in the beleaguered fortress of Tobruk, where the 1st Battalion had
been sent by destroyer from Alexandria to relieve Australian forces. After
the relief of Tobruk, the battalion was hurriedly sent to Malta in January
1942 aboard the destroyer *Kingston* and the naval auxiliary *Breconshire* to

strengthen the garrison. It had remained in Malta until June 1943, when it was transferred to Egypt for rest and retraining. Early in September, it moved, under sealed orders, to Ramat David airfield in Palestine. On the sixteenth, C Company, together with Kirby, boarded Dakotas of No. 216 Squadron. After an easy flight, the Durham Light Infantry reached Antimachia without a hitch, and Maj. J. B. Browne, the company commander, deployed his men around the field.

The 4th Light Anti-Aircraft Battery of the 1st Light Anti-Aircraft Regiment also flew in on the sixteenth, but unfortunately its Bofors guns were following by sea; thus the defense of the strip still lay in the hands of the RAF Regiment with its nine Hispano guns. Other reinforcements arriving by caique, motor launch, and destroyer included the 9th Indian Field Company. The Medical Corps took over a school about eight miles from Cos town and established a fifty-stretcher receiving station there. In another school in town, they set up a dental center, an MI room, and an air evacuation center with twenty stretchers, and they established a dressing station at Antimachia.

The Germans still had not put in an appearance, but by this time, they had settled the question of the larger islands to their immediate satisfaction. The OKW Diary notes that on September 14 *OB-Südost* had reported the final disarming of the Italian garrison on Scarpanto, where there was another important airfield, and that coastal defenses in the "Iron Ring" were all secure. All that remained now was to mop up the Italians who had still not handed in their weapons or openly come over to the German side.

On the seventeenth, the Germans had one division on Rhodes, one more in the Scarpanto-Crete area, a fortress battalion on the Kithira-Antikithira islands, a further three battalions in Velos and Melos, and another on Lemnos. Against this concentration, the small British garrisons on Cos and Leros and the SBS and LRDG units on the lesser islands were gravely outnumbered.

Once Hitler had made the decision to hold the Aegean, the Germans had lost no time in moving in reinforcements, and both the RAF and the Royal Navy were now striving to intercept these convoys—with some considerable success. On the sixteenth, eight long-range Beaufighters of No. 227 Squadron, based at Limassol, caught a small German convoy off the southeast coast of Naxos. The convoy consisted of two freighters and some escort vessels, with a standing patrol of three Arado floatplanes overhead. The Beaus described the ships as one three-island, single-funneled motor vessel of 5,000 tons and another of 2,000 tons with a 700-ton escort. No. 227 Squadron at once attacked the German aircraft, causing them to withdraw after one Arado had been hit and was forced to ditch. The British aircraft then turned their attention to the ships. Both the escort and the larger freighter put up heavy flak, which consisted of 3-inch Oerlikon and tracer, in addition to light machine-gun fire "hosepiped" to form a barrage.

Two bombs were dropped within ten yards of the larger motor vessel, and she received cannon hits on her bow, but these all failed to stop her. There was a near miss on the smaller vessel, and she appeared to sink in three minutes. The Beaufighters suffered no casualties.

The Royal Navy, too, was beginning to make its presence felt. The destroyers *Faulknor, Eclipse,* and *Queen Olga* had left Alexandria at 0800 hours on the seventeenth for an antishipping sweep between Rhodes and Stampalia.

At 1600, an aircraft sighted a convoy consisting of two merchant ships— the 3,830-ton *Pluto* and the 3,754-ton ex-Vichy freighter *Paula*—and a small escort and passed a report to the destroyer striking force at about 1930. Speed and course were adjusted to intercept the enemy between Stampalia and Kandeliusa, just to the east, shortly after midnight. The striking force sighted the convoy at 0017 on the eighteenth, close to land, escorted by *UJ 2104* (a converted whaler, ex-HMS *Kos* captured at Crete, and ex-Norwegian *Darvik*). The three destroyers spent the next twenty-two minutes working around to a down-moon position without being seen by the enemy. At 0039, all three ships opened fire on the enemy from a range of 2,000 yards, achieving complete surprise.

The *Faulknor* and *Eclipse* engaged *Paula*, and *Faulknor* hit her target with the first salvo; when she turned her attention to the escort, after firing three salvos at the tanker, she hit this smaller target with her first rounds. The *Queen Olga* hit the *Pluto* consistently, and by 0050, both merchant ships were well ablaze. *Faulknor* finally dispatched *Paula* with a torpedo, the target sinking at 0115, and the *Pluto* blew up five minutes later. The destroyers then headed for Scarpanto Straits at twenty-nine knots and were clear of enemy waters by dawn, returning to Haifa without further incident.

The enemy escort vessel was subsequently discovered beached on Glino isle off Stampalia, and her crew members were captured and taken to Alexandria; from them, it was learned that the two merchant ships were intended for the evacuation of 6,000 Italians from Rhodes and were carrying specialist personnel and stores to the island when they were sunk.

British, Greek, and Polish submarines were also very active in the Aegean at this time, but targets were scarce and tended to be small, so they were often unsuited to torpedo attack. Typical of the many frustrating patrols made at this time was that of HM Submarine *Trespasser.* On September 3, she attacked an escorted southbound convoy, which consisted of two merchant vessels. All her torpedoes missed. Six days later, she sighted a northbound small motor vessel escorted by a single trawler. She attacked at

0307 and was again unrewarded. The following morning off Rhodes, at 0607 she sighted and attacked with torpedoes a Sauro-class destroyer, again without success. Finally, on the eleventh at 1700, *Trespasser* surfaced to engage two E-boats leaving Rhodes Harbor, but this time heavy fire from shore batteries forced her to leave the scene.

By far the greater part of the Royal Navy's work at this time was running in stores and supplies to Leros and Cos, for which the slim, fast destroyers were used. They were hardly the ideal choice of ship for use as transports, but because of their high speed, they had been pressed into service in this unexpected role on many occasions, such as the evacuations of Dunkirk and Crete. The Fleet destroyers of the 8th Flotilla and the Hunt-class boats of the 22nd Flotilla were engaged on this thankless task nightly throughout September.

From September 17 to 20, the remaining companies of the Durham Light Infantry were flown in to Cos, and the holding troops of the 11th Parachute Battalion were finally pulled out on the twenty-fifth. Also arriving on the island on September 17 was a further detachment of No. 2909 Squadron consisting of two officers and fifty-six men under the command of Flying Officer Hassel, with an additional seven Hispano guns. Two of these were added to the Antimachia defenses, and the remainder were dispersed in the port area to work alongside C Company of the Durham Light Infantry.

The Germans had first become aware of the existence of the RAF on Cos on September 15. An Italian observer post had reported seven Junkers Ju 52 transport aircraft, escorted by two Messerschmitt Me 109 fighters, passing close to Cos, obviously on a supply run to Rhodes. The two patrolling Spitfires were sent out to intercept them, and the German formation was surprised when flying over Stampalia at little more than 300 feet. One Ju 52 was shot down. This little skirmish was to have dire results for No. 7 Squadron, for it quite literally brought the wrath of the *Luftwaffe* down upon their heads.

At dawn the next morning, a single Junkers Ju 88 appeared over the island, obviously on an armed reconnaissance to check out the hitherto undisturbed island. The bomber carried out a single bombing attack on some Italian gun emplacements near the coast and then moved inland to Antimachia airfield. Here it made an initial low-level bombing and strafing attack on the airstrip.

Six of the Hispano guns opened up, and one hit was claimed on the aircraft's starboard engine. The surprised German banked away, turned, and came in again from the west. All the guns now engaged the German bomber with a box barrage—and the enemy flew right through it. One of the RAF gunners was killed at his gun by cannon fire from the bomber, but it had been hit heavily in return and veered out to sea, losing height rapidly.

Before it could get clear, two Spitfires of the standing patrol pounced and quickly dispatched it.

The British now felt that the Germans would know exactly what they were up against at Cos, and they redeployed the Hispano guns in readiness. The Durham Light Infantry helped patch up the bomb craters and keep the strip clear, a task that was to grow increasingly more difficult in the days that followed.

As expected, heavy raids were mounted by the Germans almost at once. At 1100 on September 17, two of No. 7 Squadron's Spitfires intercepted a wave of Junkers Ju 88s heading in toward the island and dispersed them. While they were thus engaged, five Me 109s suddenly appeared over the airfield at "nought feet," taking the gunners by surprise.

They swept in from the south, strafing as they came, and three of the Dakotas parked in the open crumpled and burst into flames. Several soldiers of the Durham Light Infantry were caught out in the open and killed. A second wave of German fighters followed almost immediately. Two Spitfires were destroyed on the ground, and another Dakota was burned and damaged. The pilot of one of the airborne Dakotas, arriving during the raid and seeing Antimachia under attack, was loath to return to Cyprus with his cargo and passengers. After a brief search, he put his plane down on a suitable-looking spot near Lambia on the coast. This proved an inspired move, and work was quickly done to convert the spot into a second emergency landing strip as the scale of attack on Antimachia and Marmari—Salty Flats—was obviously increasing.

The last of the rifle companies to fly in was A Company of the Durham Light Infantry, which found the airfield badly cratered and littered with burning aircraft, but still usable. One of the Dakotas was forced to ditch in the sea off the Turkish mainland during this action. The crew and the Durham Light Infantry platoon aboard were safely rescued by a Turkish fishing vessel. Despite a hasty dash by naval motor launch *ML-351*, which had been provided with a very accurate latitude and longitude of the ditching by one of the other aircraft in company, the soldiers had already been picked up. The Turks refused to hand over the soldiers, despite the fact that Lt. Kenneth Hallows put his command across the rescue ships' bows. According to Hallows, "These Royal Navy motor launches were quite sizable vessels, 110 feet in overall length. They were produced by Fairmile, sometimes in package form to be built elsewhere. In fact, *ML 355* was put together in a small dockyard at Chouba (Cairo) in sight of the pyramids. For these Aegean operations, *ML-351*, my command, was armed with a single 40-millimeter Bofors on the forecastle, two pairs of Vickers .303 machine guns on the bridge, a 20-millimeter Oerlikon abaft the funnel, and two pairs of Breda ex-Italian machine guns on the port and starboard quarters. We were really like a gunboat; you could fire a fairly good broadside with this little lot! We also had an Asdic (sonar) for antisubmarine detection."

The Turks altered course to starboard into even shallower water. Hallows told us: "I had to explain to the Durham Light Infantry major who was on board my ship that we had an Asdic dome sticking out below the keel and couldn't risk knocking it off—adding that I could perhaps put a shot or two across his bows. But as we were in Turkish territorial waters, that might have created something of an incident and appeared on the front of the *Daily Express* the next day!" Thus it came to pass that all the soldiers ended up being interned in Turkey.

With A, B, and D Companies of the Durham Light Infantry deployed around the airfield and C Company in Cos town ready to unload the ships, it was thought best to run in the headquarters section in destroyers, two British and one Greek, via Leros.

The *Luftwaffe* attacks on Antimachia now developed into a daily pattern of gradually increasing tempo. Some of the aircraft were painted white and obviously diverted from Russia. The airstrip was constantly cratered, and the men of the Durham Light Infantry labored continuously to fill in bomb holes and also to prepare the new airstrip at Marmari. Kenneth Hallows told us that the Royal Navy was also roped in: "We were also instrumental in helping the Durham Light Infantry with the construction of a new airstrip, along with the manila rope and gear to which they lashed balks of timber to tow across the ground. They also had the four-gallon tins in which we had carried the ninety-octane fuel. We split them diagonally, filled them with petrol-soaked sand, and used them for flares on the fighter path."

In addition, C Company was employed in unloading stores that were run into the port of Cos. Drainage work was carried out near Marmari, but the Germans soon got wind of this, and all three strips were ultimately subjected to bombing. Considering that the bulk of the defense of the island would fall on the men of the Durham Light Infantry, it was, to say the least, highly unsatisfactory that these combat troops were thus employed instead of installing themselves more securely in their defensive positions and readying themselves for the battle ahead—a battle that was surely coming.

The troops available in September for the attempt on Rhodes were the 234th Infantry Brigade, which had returned from Malta on June 19, 1943. It was entirely composed of regular battalions, but it is no disparagement of them to say that the existence they had led in Malta, a prolonged test of endurance without an opportunity of hitting back, had unfitted them to meet a sudden and unexpected onslaught. A short period of training would have restored them, but under the circumstances, this was impossible. With so many Italian and Greek noncombatants available, it would appear, with hindsight, that it was unwise to further tax these men with laborers' work when they should have been preparing for battle with a highly trained and skilled enemy.

The Germans' attitude was very different—and a great deal more practical. They earmarked the crack Brandenburg Division for the job of clearing the islands with specialized backing units. Their commander, Lt. Gen. Friedrich-Wilhelm Müller, was known as a ruthless and highly competent officer, and his troops were of the same high standard. There was also nothing second-rate or stale about the 22nd *Luftlande* (Air Landing) Division, for example. This unit was strictly an infantry outfit, but it had been well blooded in Belgium and Holland during the campaign of 1940. After service in Russia and the Crimea, the men of the 22nd Infantry Division were transferred to Crete. There they made no bones about crushing the Italian forces, which had sought to desert the Axis. On September 23, for example, the OKW Diary recorded: "Local mopping up continues in Crete. On Kephalonia the local Italian garrison has been annihilated by German forces. The Divisional Staff with General Grandia has been captured. Occupation of Corfu is the next objective, then Cos, Leros and Samos." (While in many ways an inaccurate and very one-sided account of events on Kephalonia, the fictional work *Captain Corelli's Mandolin*, by Louis De Bernières, gives a good insight into events on that island in the autumn of 1943.)

Elements of the 999th Light Afrika Division, the bulk of which served in Tunisia, moved into the area. While on Rhodes, it provided the supporting arms and services for the *Sturm Division Rhodos*, newly formed from the crack 440th Grenadier Regiment of hardened, tough young storm troops. These then were some of the opponents whom the men of the Durham Light Infantry, busy filling in bomb holes and draining marshes, would shortly be facing in hand-to-hand combat.

Luftwaffe strength in the area at the beginning of September consisted of some 235 aircraft, with about 45 Me 109 single-engine fighters, 15 Junkers Ju 88 twin-engine bombers, and 65 Junkers Ju 87 dive-bombers—the Stukas. Reinforcements up to October 3 comprised about 100 additional aircraft: long-range Ju 88s and Heinkel He 111 bomber units flown in from France and the Russian front, single-engine fighters from Austria, and close support units from Russia, which brought the total strength up to some 345 front-line planes. By early October, the *Luftwaffe* could call on 90 Me 109Gs of 3rd and 4th Groups of *Jagdgeschwader* 27, and more than 60 Stukas of *Stukageschwader* 3 and *Stukageschwader* 151, with an average serviceability of 60 percent of all aircraft. As long-range units, there were more than 130 He 111s and Ju 88s belonging to *Kampfgeschwader* 6 and 51, as well as Arado floatplanes and a few Italian Macchi MC 202 fighters.

To answer this buildup in the air, the RAF's total commitment was not overly large. There were two day and two night Beaufighter squadrons, Nos. 46, 89, 227, and 252; a torpedo-bomber Wellington squadron, No. 38; three Baltimore squadrons, Nos. 14, 203, and 454; a Hudson squadron for general reconnaissance, No. 459; three Spitfire squadrons, Nos. 7 SAAF, 74, and 680, a photo reconnaissance unit; and two long-range Hurricane squadrons, Nos. 213 and 237. Most of these units were based in Cyprus or North Africa, whereas the *Luftwaffe* had airfields all around the perimeter of the Aegean, in Rhodes, Scarpanto, Crete, and Greece.

Later, two heavy bomber squadrons of No. 240 Wing, Nos. 178 (Liberator) and 462 (Halifax), took part in the bombing of German airfields. The total number of machines involved amounted in all to 144 fighters of all types and 116 heavy, medium, and torpedo bombers. It quickly became apparent, however, that the long-range Beaufighters could not provide the total air cover necessary for either the British-occupied islands or the supplying ships, and that the few Spitfires on Cos would not be able to operate for long in the midst of such a hornet's nest.

The airfield defenses at Antimachia were again caught flat-footed on September 19 when five Me 109s and five Ju 88s made an attack using butterfly bombs and ground strafing. All the Hispano guns opened fire, but without effect. A Dakota laden with gasoline blew up under tracer fire, and the main ammunition dump, which was being used by No. 2909 Squadron, was also hit and blew up.

During this attack, Leading Aircraftman Martell, manning one of the guns, had his weapon jam up; ignoring an order to take cover, he attempted to free it, assisted by Corporal Higgins and Leading Aircraftman Carter. A bomb exploded near their position and shrapnel cut down all three, killing Martell outright. There was no lack of courage.

In the afternoon came another attack, and No. 2909 claimed a probable Me 109 destroyed. While the commanding officer of No. 7 Squadron was aloft, he shot down another—which made Cornelius van Vliet one of the nine top-scoring South African pilots. The airfield, however, was now again rendered unserviceable. Once more the Durham Light Infantry filled in the holes in time to welcome sorely needed reinforcements in the form of six more Spitfires of No. 7 under the command of Capt. E. A. Rorvik, which arrived on the nineteenth. Unfortunately, increasingly heavy attacks were to write off most of these aircraft within days of their arrival. There were three separate raids on the twentieth between 0500 and 1710. One Heinkel He 111 was shot down by antiaircraft fire, and a second fell to the long-range Beaufighters. On the twenty-first, bombs demolished the military hospital.

Meanwhile, the army gunners had been standing idle because of a lack of weapons, and the army commander sent an urgent signal for the Bofors guns, which were now desperately needed. As General Wilson pointed out, this was easier said than done: "Deficiencies in the Italian AA defences soon became apparent and it was necessary to supplement them with Bofors guns; the designers of these guns had not considered the possibility of loading them into small craft and the greatest difficulty was experienced in embarking them and more so in unloading them on small quays not provided with derricks." While they awaited their guns, the army took over two of the Hispanos, but not with very much enthusiasm, for the men held a poor opinion of it as a weapon. Better weapons were promised but never delivered.

Flight Lt. J. W. D. Thomas of the RAF told us of some of the clandestine missions that No. 227 Squadron was engaged in at this time:

On 24th September, Flight Sergeant Warne and I were told to go to Nicosia to pick up Air Vice Marshal R. E. Saul. When we arrived Group Captain Max Aitken summarily dismissed my pilot and told me *he* would pilot the aircraft to Cos, I was to navigate. After some persuasion by the Group Captain, the Air Vice Marshal agreed to let me occupy the navigator's seat. I anticipated being "jumped" by Me 109s off Rhodes, but the Air Vice Marshal reminded me that he had been an Air Gunner in World War One! We took off at 1658 and arrived at 1858. The flight to Cos, as it happened, proved uneventful, except for the rear hatch flying open; this I was able to close by minor acrobatics while the Group Captain slowed the aircraft down. The Air Vice Marshal sitting forlornly on the cannon ammunition covers offered to help, but I was able to manage.

At Cos we were ushered to a large hall adjacent to the cookhouse. Here No. 7 SAAF chaps were assembled. Air Vice Marshal Saul, with myself as note-taker, asked the No. 7 SAAF chaps what they wanted. They requested candles, shoelaces etc. They were promised 87 AA guns by the weekend and other desirable goodies.

During the night Air Vice Marshal Saul slept in a hut with an armed guard, a corporal armed with a tommy gun. Group Captain Aitken slept on a stretcher in some suitable corner and I in the cookhouse on a glorious Victorian brass-knobbed bed that the cook had "obtained" from somewhere!'

We returned to Nicosia incident-free the following day, taking off at 0710 and arriving at 0910. Events prevented the SAAF from receiving many of the promised articles.

Lambia airstrip was now ready for service, and the reinforcements for No. 7 Squadron were soon to move there. The RAF Regiment was brought up to a strength of 7 officers, 119 men, and 24 guns, and finally, on September 23, the first Bofors guns arrived, were put into position, and manned. Squadron Leader Killallin passed on to the men of No. 2909 that the defense commander had told him that the RAF Regiment up to this time had had the toughest job on Cos and that he was proud of the way they had stood up to their baptism of fire.

It seemed useless to hold down so many of the soldiers once the Antimachia strip had been neutralized and A and B Companies were finally withdrawn and moved east towards Cos town, where they prepared defense works in the orange groves some five miles west of the harbor. C Company was still posted on the outskirts of town, and only D Company, under the command of Capt. J. H. Thorpe, was left with the RAF Regiment gunners to defend Antimachia as best they could. The Durham Light Infantry were still equipped only with their small arms and light mortars.

Meanwhile, a series of large-scale air attacks had been launched against the German bases on Rhodes, Crete, and Greece by the heavy bombers of No. 240 Wing and No. 21 Bombardment Group, in a belated effort to slow down the continuing buildup of German air strength in the theater. On the night of September 22, for instance, some fifty Liberators of the U.S. Ninth Air Force struck at Eleusis in Greece and Maritza on Rhodes. As a direct result of these raids, the *Luftwaffe* was forced into a weeklong lull in its operations against Cos and Leros, but it came too late for Antimachia. It also came too late for the Royal Navy.

The running of patrols and stores had continued despite increased German air activity. Italian naval units based on Leros were also approached to join; these consisted of the destroyer *Euro*, the sloop *Argo*, the minelayer *Legnano*, eight MAS boats, and a few auxiliaries. The MAS boats were roughly the equivalent of the British motor torpedo boats (MTBs). A maintenance base for motor launches was set up at Leros. By September 21, a total of 3,400 personnel had been transported to the area, 2,830 of them by sea, together with more than 1,500 tons of oil fuel and stores and fifteen Bofors guns. The commodore of the Levant Flotillas began a tour of the Dodecanese area to investigate naval requirements for the stepping up of operations still further. On the twenty-second, the first coaster arrived at Leros.

The destroyers *Faulknor, Fury, Eclipse,* and *Queen Olga* landed 1,200 troops and eight Bofors guns at Leros the same night. All four sailed again from Leros after dark on the twenty-second for Alexandria. The *Faulknor* and *Queen Olga* carried out a sweep west of Stampalia and through Kasos

Strait without incident; the *Fury* and *Eclipse* patrolled the north and south ends of the Scarpanto Strait. At 0111 on September 23, the *Eclipse* was rewarded with the sight of a small merchant ship, the 2,428-ton *Donizetti* off Cape Prasonisi, the southwest tip of Rhodes, which she quickly destroyed. Although engaged by shore batteries, the British destroyer was unharmed and suffered no casualties. It was later reported that the vessel she sank had arrived at Rhodes on the nineteenth, with guns and reinforcements for the German garrison and had subsequently sailed on the evening of the twenty-second laden with some 1,576 Italian prisoners of war, loss of life among whom was very heavy. It had all happened very quickly, but for the Italians it was a major tragedy.

The solitary escort escaped inshore, although damaged. This was the destroyer *TA 10*, which had an eventful wartime life. Originally the Vichy-French destroyer *La Pomone*, 610 tons and armed with two 3.9-inch guns, she was given to the Italians, who were short of escorts and renamed her *FR42*. On the Italian surrender, the Germans took her over and gave her her third and last name, *TA 10*.

After the surrender of the Italians on Rhodes, the German commander in chief had started the evacuation of the Italian personnel on September 17, when a group of fifteen officers, both navy and army, was flown to Athens. The mass of the Italians were to be transported to Greece by ship. The German authorities originally planned to embark 2,100 Italians in *Donizetti*, but after embarking 1,576 men, the Italian colonel Arcangioli, in command of the interned Italian military personnel on that transport, informed the German officer in charge that the ship had a capacity for 700 people only; even so, more than 1,500 men were onboard when the ship left the port. She was escorted by just one German destroyer, the *TA 10*, under command of *Oberleutnant* Jobst Hahndorff. Of the passengers, about 600 were air force personnel, 8 were army officers, and the rest, 3 officers, 114 petty officers, and the remainder enlisted men, all belonged to the Italian Navy.

Both ships steered south; their departure was signaled by a clandestine wireless station of the Italians still operating on Rhodes to the Allied Command at Leros asking for the interception of the convoy and the liberation of the Italian personnel on the ship. As Colonel Turnbull, then in command of the Armistice Commission in the Aegean, told an Italian official on the Island of Simi, it was intended to order the SS *Donizetti* to Cyprus after the destruction of the *TA 10*.

Near Cape Prasonisi, the southernmost point of Rhodes, both ships were on intercepted by the British destroyer *Eclipse* on September 23. In the encounter, the *Donizetti* was sunk within a very short time, leaving no survivors. The *TA 10* was damaged by gunfire from the *Eclipse* and beached near Cape Prasonisi. The surviving crews of the *TA 10* sought shelter in the ruins of the former Italian coastal battery on the Cape. No British rescue operations were observed near the sinking of the *Donizetti* and reports do not tell of survivors of that ship reaching the beach by swimming. Colonel Arcangioli searched for dispersed Italian personnel on the island, with the permission of the German command, and hoped to find some survivors; he investigated the beach near Cape Prasonisi but found only the *TA 10* lying in the sea about 100 yards offshore, with her stern awash and her crew on the beach.

After the action, the four British destroyers rendezvoused and arrived together at Alexandria at 1430 on the twenty-third. They brought with them 128 German prisoners.

The Germans reported the *TA 10* as having been salvaged and towed to Rhodes Harbor, where she was scuttled on January 17, 1944, when two British destroyers attacked the harbor. British and Italian sources give another story: The *TA 10* remained beached and was destroyed by aerial attacks from Allied aircraft when, on September 25, four Beaus of No. 227 Squadron from Lakatamia sighted the *TA 10* aground near Cape Prasonisi, lying east to west with her bows facing east. They at once deployed for the attack.

Flying Officer Amos went in first and scored hits amidships with cannon fire, which caused heavy black smoke. Flight Sergeant Shattkey also hit her amidships and on the bridge with cannon fire. The destroyer replied with light flak, which was very accurate. Pilot Officer Gibbard's bomb hung up on him, but he also hit with cannon fire and machine-gun fire above the destroyer's main deck. Last in was Sergeant Swift, and he likewise raked the upper decks with cannon fire, which hit the base of the ship's funnel. His bombs overshot by an estimated five yards. It was enough. Belching black smoke, the *TA 10* rolled over to port, and a Spitfire reconnaissance later confirmed that she had been finished off for good.

The Germans were soon to avenge this vessel; the astonishing immunity enjoyed by the British warships operating within easy range of German airfields was about to come to an abrupt end.

The next day, No. 227 carried out a shipping strike on Syros Harbor. Flight Lt. J. W. D. Thomas described it to us thus:

Because Sergeant Warne was a noncommissioned officer, we were not to lead the strike. However, after passing Cos, the leading navigator became lost in the maze of small islands, and we were requested to take over the lead. This we did.

I realized it was to late to enter Syros Harbor from the eastern side. We were able to turn and conduct our attack in an easterly direction, flying downhill, as it were! We all missed with our bombs but strafed the vessel, a minelayer. I have a photo of this vessel, which was later to cause such damage.

We aimed our two 250-pounds bombs "by guess and by God." We had no sighting device; therefore, what could have been significant successful attacks were limited to such damage as our cannon could effect. This severe limitation applied to *all* the RAF Beaufighter strike squadrons.

On 227, Navigators were rationed to two pans of 100 rounds for our K machine guns for rear defense. We were reluctant to use them in attacks, saving them for defensive purposes. Our real method of defense was to fly very low over the water to deter single-engine fighters with their sight-obscuring noses from getting behind us. Sometimes the rear wheel would touch, and if the drag was sufficient, the aircraft would ditch. I saw this happen on one occasion. Estimating height over the calm, glassy Aegean was a difficulty, with which our pilots coped with admirable skill (most times!).

Pilot Officer Gibbard, with whom I shared a tent, escaped determined attacks by Me 109s by this method; also "skidding," using rudder, was another complementary maneuver. This technique was employed by twin-engine aircraft crews, without specific very low-level training, both in the Middle East and over Norwegian waters. Navigators developed a technique of estimating wind speed and direction by looking at the waves—waves break upwind—and studying the whitecaps gave us the speed.

Interspersed with shipping escort, 227 carried out attacks and sweeps such as that of September 26th.

Meanwhile the navy's destroyers were continuing their hazardous work. *Intrepid* and *Queen Olga* had sailed from Alexandria at 0900 on the twenty-fifth to carry out a sweep through the Straits of Scarpanto and were due to arrive at Leros the following morning. It had been assumed that the Italian antiaircraft defenses for the dockyard would be adequate. The two destroyers, after an uneventful sweep through the Kasos Strait, arrived at Leros Harbor at 0700 on the twenty-sixth. Some two hours later, the harbor was attacked by thirteen Junkers Ju 88s. The Italian naval barracks was demolished in the attack, and the first stick of bombs hit two of the Italian MAS boats some 100 feet astern of *ML-351*; but the bulk of the bombs were aimed at the two destroyers, and *Queen Olga* was sunk straightaway. The two patrolling Spitfires from Cos were out of radio telephone touch and did not sight the bombers. No Italian gun ever opened fire, although the *Intrepid* claimed to have destroyed one of her attackers.

The *Intrepid* took a heavy bomb on the port side of the upper deck at the after end of the after boiler room, which tore a hole about six by three feet in the upper deck and another two by three feet in the bulkhead between the engine room and the boiler room. Further serious damage was caused by splinters, which made holes in the destroyer's hull next to the engine room and after boiler rooms. The port main steam pipe and number three boiler casing were pierced. The after boiler rooms were flooded to a depth of three feet above the floor plates and the danger of a diesel oil fire seemed imminent.

The vessel was towed into shallow water, and temporary repairs were begun at once. Steam was made available in two boilers, giving the ship a capability of twenty knots, but she was never given a chance. The air attacks continued, and during the third attack of the morning, she took another direct hit near her Y mounting, which blew off all the stern structure abaft her X gun. The destroyer settled by the stern with a ten-degree list to port; the forward end of the after superstructure was awash. Flooding continued, and at 0200 on the twenty-seventh, four hours after the last attack, the *Intrepid* capsized and sank. Casualties were five killed, ten missing and presumed killed, and three seriously wounded. The Greek vessel had suffered a total of six officers and sixty-four enlisted men killed.

In all, the *Luftwaffe* made three heavy attacks on Port Laki and other targets in the vicinity, causing much damage in the port area. The *ML-351* was damaged in one of the later attacks and was towed out of Leros by the *ML-354*, under Lt. J. Patterson, RNVR. The *ML-354* towed her all the way to Paphos in Cyprus via Casteloriso, finally reaching Alexandria in Egypt, where she was patched up and eventually returned to the fray for a second tour of operations in the Aegean. On this long journey, they had as a passenger again Andy Lassen, who had sustained a bullet wound in the leg. On arrival, he was admitted to the British General Hospital there. At the same time, other squadrons were making a predawn attack on Cos using flash bombs. This marked the reopening of the air assault on the island—and it was also the final run-up to the intended recapture of the island.

On September 27, the blitz continued in earnest. There was only two minutes' warning of the first attack, and once again the Me 109s drew all the antiaircraft fire while fifteen Ju 88s came in from the north and hit Antimachia. The two patrolling Spitfires were overwhelmed and shot down at once. The Junkers came in three waves, close on the heels of the fighters in their now routine formation, and concentrated on dispersal and takeoff areas while the fighters climbed overhead to provide top cover.

One more Spitfire was destroyed on the ground, and the airfield was again left unserviceable by butterfly bombs with delayed-action fuses. The soldiers at once set to work to fill in the craters, but it was slow, difficult work. Nevertheless, by 1400, Major van Vliet and Lieutenant Basson were airborne and on patrol again.

The Germans were determined this time to give no respite and soon began a second attack. In this attack, the South Africans gave a good account of themselves, and two Me 109s were destroyed before Basson's aircraft was hit. He bailed out and was rescued. Lieutenant Hynd, who was also airborne, survived and managed to land his Spitfire on the airstrip intact, but at the end of the day, only four British aircraft were left serviceable.

The next day, nine Spitfires of No. 74 (Trinidad) Squadron, under Squadron Leader J. C. F. Hayter, were sent to this hot spot. They took off from Cyprus at 1130. While the formation was flying some ten miles east-southeast of Casteloriso, which was in British hands, Flight Lt. Albert Anderson's aircraft developed engine trouble, but they were flying at less than 500 feet, and Anderson had difficulty getting out of his cockpit. His parachute opened late, and although a RAF high-speed launch put out from Casteloriso and other rescue craft and aircraft made searches he was never seen again.

It was a tragic start, but the remaining eight Spitfires reached the island safely and were almost at once thrown into action. Flying Officers H. F. Norman, T. H. Bates, and F. G. De Pass and Flight Sgt. W. J. "Willy" Wilson were sent up on a standing patrol. Later in the afternoon, Flying Off. John Lewis, in Spitfire J-John, ran into five Ju 88s returning to base after a raid on Cos. He made three stern attacks without visible results, but his own aircraft was hit in return.

At 1500, Captain Rorvik and Lieutenants Taylor and De Jager of No. 7 were aloft in three of their remaining Spitfires when they were set upon by a mass of Me 109s and Ju 88s. Both Rorvik and Taylor were shot down, and although De Jager got his aircraft down in one piece, it was the end of the squadron, which was then left with only two serviceable Spitfires.

The German air attacks continued unabated. One Junkers was claimed shot down by the Bofors gunners, but this had only a trifling effect. The Dakotas were still running the gauntlet, and together with the ships, they ferried in a further total of 2,700 men, twenty-one guns, seven jeeps, and 450 tons of stores by the twenty-eighth. The Germans appeared to be able to reinforce their garrisons in the Aegean at a greater rate by air. The invasion attempt was obviously not far off.

September 29 saw No. 74 Squadron fully extended. At 0815, three Spitfires were scrambled away to intercept the first raid of the day, which consisted of three waves of Ju.88s attacking Antimachia. Bates, Mosewell, and Wilson met the first wave, but Wilson became separated and had to work alone. At 22,000 feet, he sighted a single Junkers approaching the airfield. He managed to position himself astern and gave it two good bursts, then continued firing until forced to break away at fifty yards. Wilson last viewed his target diving steeply away, blossoming black smoke. It was later confirmed by an antiaircraft gunner on the ground that this aircraft had crashed.

The other Spitfires were fully engaged with more targets in this first wave, but the controller warned Wilson that a second formation was fast homing in. He soon saw nine Ju.88s dead ahead. Without hesitation, Wilson slammed straight into them in a dive, firing as he went. One went into a shallow dive, obviously damaged, as pieces were seen breaking away from it. This aircraft then crashed and although the hit was claimed by the ack-ack, it seems probable it was Wilson's attack that did the real damage. The remaining bombers of the second wave became disorganized as a result of this audacious action. Wilson saw bits flying off another aircraft as he dived through the formation. As he broke clear again, he observed yet a third wave of nine bombers and proceeded to hand out the same treatment to these.

On his return to land, he was jumped by five Me 109s, but by brilliant flying, he turned the tables on them, causing two to collide with each other; one of these fell in flames. He then flew around the Cos mountains, thus losing the others, and eventually put his aircraft down on Salty Flats—now being used for the first time.

Despite this magnificent solo effort, enough enemy bombers had gotten through to render the Antimachia field completely unserviceable; although some of the Spits managed to land there, another joined Wilson at Salty Flats, where the Durham Light Infantry had by this time made a usable runway some forty yards wide. The whole squadron later shifted over to this strip together with the sector operations tent and took cover in a nearby grove of trees.

Sixty-two ground crew members of No. 74 Squadron were flown by Dakotas from Nicosia to Ramat David in Palestine, and forty of them embarked in a French sloop at Haifa for Casteloriso. The other twenty-two were left behind and at midnight were flown to Cos.

Antimachia was again made operational enough for another day's use. On the thirtieth, however, the surviving pilots sat tight, saving their aircraft for the day of the invasion, which now seemed very close. The Germans contented themselves with reconnaissance flights during the day and were apparently satisfied that all fighter opposition had been neutralized.

Delayed-action bombs were exploding at intervals on Antimachia, and it was out of the question to move there; most of the buildings had been demolished, and the Germans kept a constant watch overhead. The grounded pilots made several expeditions on foot to the mess to collect rations, but this was all. A Beaufighter dropped mail there during the night and also the following night.

Then on October 1, a German convoy—which could well have been an invasion force—was reported at sea. On the second, it was known to be in the area of Naxos, sailing east. Bates, Norman, Lewis, and Harris got four of No. 74's Spitfires airborne after what one of the pilots described as a shaky takeoff and landed on the Salty Flats strip, where two of the aircraft became bogged down. They camped under the trees some 500 yards from the strip, and the Durham Light Infantry camouflaged their aircraft. By the end of this day, only one of No. 7 Squadron's Spitfires was serviceable, and just five of No. 74's.

The RAF Regiment received further reinforcements on October 2, which was a quiet day on Cos. Fifty-five men of No. 2901 Squadron under the command of Flight Lieutenant Fraser, arrived that evening by boat from Casteloriso. As soon as they stepped ashore at Cos Harbor, the air raid warning sounded, but there was no attack. About thirteen men were detailed off for guard duty at the Salty Flats strip, while the remainder slept in the docks. They were to have a rude awakening.

The flare path was lit that evening, and the Dakotas landed the men of No. 74 Field Company plus supplies. The British were receiving ominous reports about the German convoy and were making strenuous moves to intercept it. It was the invasion fleet so long awaited, and it was to determine the fate of the island. But there was still much confusion at this time as to its true destination.

On October 2, the British garrison on Cos stood at 1,600 men, only 1,114 of them combatants—880 of them army and 234 from the RAF Regiment. The Italian troops numbered about 4,000, infantry of the 10th Regiment of the *Regina* Division, commanded by Col. Felice Leggio, and artillery units of the 50th Regiment. These men were ill equipped for the task set before them and now disillusioned about the amount of aid forthcoming. No great numbers of British troops had arrived as they had expected, and the Italians had to face the vengeance of their former ally virtually alone. The five remaining Spitfires were serviced but remained hidden away in the trees to prevent their destruction by surprise attack.

The German invasion convoy was first sighted by aerial reconnaissance on October 1 in the vicinity of Naxos. It actually consisted of seven medium-size transports, three destroyers, and a few E-boats, plus seven landing craft and an assortment of caiques. Because of the *Luftwaffe*'s undisputed domination of the air no ships of the Royal Navy could engage this force by day. The losses of the *Intrepid* and *Queen Olga* off Leros earlier were driven home when on October 1 the Italian destroyer *Euro* was attacked from the air in Partheni Bay, also at Leros. Damaged by near misses, she was abandoned with her hull resting on the bottom of the bay in shallow water. She became a total loss.

A destroyer squadron was nevertheless dispatched to intercept the German force once it was reported. The Hunt-class destroyers *Aldenham*, *Themistocles*, and *Miaoulis*—the last two of the Royal Hellenic Navy—actually sailed from Alexandria at 0830 on the first to carry out a patrol in the Kasos Strait but were unable to trace the German ships at night. They patrolled southeast of Rhodes during daylight on the second to await an opportunity to strike that night, accepting the risks involved. In the meantime the convoy had been resighted from the air, but it was too late in the day to send out a strike force.

When sighted, the convoy was in the Naxos area sailing east, and as planned, the three British destroyers reentered the Kasos Strait that night, but once more they failed to find any trace of the German ships. This was due in part to a faulty prediction of the convoy's destination. It was believed, from all available intelligence, that the ships were bound for Rhodes and not for Cos. General Maitland Wilson later wrote:

> In discussing what might be the enemy's object in despatching this convoy and its destination we did not consider that he had had sufficient time to collect an amphibious assault force to attack any of the islands which we now occupied and as a preliminary to any such operation he would reinforce Rhodes; the course of the convoy, as later reported, heading towards Suda Bay in Crete, tended to confirm this opinion and arrangements were made to lay on an air attack as it passed Scarpanto, while the three destroyers returned to Alexandria to refuel on the night of the 2nd/3rd October.

In coming to this conclusion, the British took into account that the convoy had loaded in the Piraeus with troops from the Greek mainland, whereas their assault troops were already in the islands. They could not have made a more serious error. "The Germans," Maitland Wilson summed up, "by a clever manoeuvre had got us looking in the wrong direction."

Even so, it might have been rectified had the Hunt-class destroyers not been cursed with very limited endurance. Once it was known that the three destroyers were running low on fuel, the *Aldenham*'s force was ordered to withdraw to Alexandria. It was fully appreciated before they had set out that their endurance limitations did not make them the ideal vessels for the job. Indeed, the distance from the scene of operations to the main bases was to be the chief handicap of both the RAF and the Royal Navy during this campaign.

The only destroyers on the Levant Station with sufficient endurance to operate satisfactory were the ships of the 8th Destroyer Flotilla; originally six, they had been reduced to four by the loss of the *Intrepid* and *Queen Olga*. By a stroke of cruel misfortune, the remaining four were not available when the sighting reports came in.

The battleships *King George V* and *Howe* had been lying at Alexandria since September 16, after escorting the surrendered Italian battleships there from Malta. It had already been decided that they should be sailed back to the west on October 1, for they were required at home. When they sailed for Malta at 0806 that day, the four remaining Fleet destroyers, *Faulknor*, *Fury*, *Echo*, and *Eclipse*, sailed as their screen. It was an unfortunate move. As the official naval historian, Capt. S. W. Roskill, later recorded: "In view of the reports of enemy shipping movements in the Aegean received on the 2nd October it certainly now seems that the movement might profitably have been cancelled, and the ships recalled; but the Admiralty had stressed the urgent need for the battleships to return home as soon as possible."

It was just one more incident in what was already looking like a doomed campaign, in which the obvious needs and stresses of the moment escalated through a series of minor miscalculations into tragedy. Without the destroyer strike force, all the Royal Navy could provide to stop the convoy on the night of October 2–3 was two submarines, *Unsparing* and *Trooper*. The former was at once sent to patrol the southern coast to cover the south and west approaches to Cos, and the latter was sent to cover the west and north-west approaches. On the afternoon of the third, another submarine, the *Unruly*, was also sent to operate against the Germans, who were by now land-ing in Kamara Bay. None of these submarines arrived in the area in time to be effective.

The *Unsparing* was the nearest to hand, for she had left Malta on Sep-tember 23 and had sunk a small caique off Cape Malea on the twenty-eighth. On October 2, she sighted a convoy in the distance, but the British vessel was already too far astern to catch up with, let alone attack, the ships; she did attempt to close at her maximum practicable speed but just could not make it. It was later accepted that the ships sighted were indeed part of the invasion force, which was ultimately heading for Cos. On receiving instruc-tions to patrol off Cos on the third, the *Unsparing* complied but saw nothing. She withdrew through the Kasos Straits on the sixth and arrived at Beirut on the ninth.

The *Trooper*, which had sailed from Beirut on September 26, was subsequently sent to patrol east of Leros, where she struck a mine on October 17 and was lost. The *Unruly* arrived on the scene far too late, not sailing from Malta until October 1.

So the destroyers and submarines had all failed to catch the German force. What then remained to the naval commander in chief? In truth, very little. On September 27, the commander in chief in the Mediterranean had signaled to the admiralty that every motor torpedo boat (MTB) would be invaluable in the conditions of island warfare, "which we are fast approaching." He requested that every effort be made to ship more of these vessels to the Mediterranean as soon as possible. And the first three MTBs arrived at Casteloriso from the central Mediterranean on October 6—just three days too late.

There remained the RAF. Once it was established that the Germans had actually landed on Cos, immediate Beaufighter strikes were begun, but again it was all in vain.

On October 3, Beaus operating against the German invasion fleet—which was strongly protected by standing fighter patrols of *Luftwaffe* and Italian single-engine machines—mounted a total of twenty-eight sorties, during which two Ju 87s were claimed and five Beaufighters lost. These strikes were mounted with great gallantry by No. 46 and 89 Squadrons, operating respectively from Idku and Lakatamia airfields in Cyprus.

At 0700 on the third, Wing Cmdr. George Reid of No. 46 with Wright and Foster of No. 89 attacked the convoy, which Reid reported as containing at least four medium-size motor ships. They attacked an escorting corvette with cannon and machine-gun fire in the face of fierce opposition.

Heavy flak damaged all three aircraft, and during their breakaway, they were set on by six Arados. Reid shot one down and Foster claimed another. Reid's navigator, Sergeant Trevett, was wounded in the eye during the battle but managed to navigate his aircraft safely back to base, despite intense pain. For this he was awarded the Distinguished Flying Medal (DFM). Reid's aircraft was badly damaged by flak and crashed into the sea off the Turkish coast. Reid was killed, but Flying Off. W. R. Peasley was only stunned by the impact. He managed to leave the aircraft, which by that time had completely submerged, and gained the surface to be at once picked up by a boat from the mainland.

Four Beaus of No. 46 Squadron from Lakatamia led by Squadron Ldr. W. A. Cuddie, with Warrant Off. E. Ledwidge and Flight Sergeants C. Holmes and Jackson, were airborne against the invasion fleet early in the day in a sortie from which only Jackson returned. Cuddie was last seen low over the water, heading toward the convoy through thick flak. His aircraft was hit and exploded in the air.

Ledwidge attacked the ships and bombed a motor vessel, but his plane was hit in the port wing, causing the inner port fuel tank to ignite. He flew toward the Turkish coast and ditched the aircraft just as the port wing fell off, having been burned completely through. He and Flight Sergeant Rowley paddled ashore near a Turkish lighthouse after eight hours in their dinghy. Holmes was also shot down, but he managed to ditch his aircraft and reach Turkey after several hours afloat.

The Germans lost no major ships in these attacks.

All the last-ditch efforts by these brave pilots could not alter the fact that the Germans were now going ashore on Cos island and operating against a defense that was already looking overstretched.

The ownership of Cos was about to be decided in a single violent day.

CHAPTER SIX

Cos Overrun

The importance of the island of Cos lay in neither its size nor its precise position, but in the fact that it had airfields—the original airstrip at Antimachia, the newly created Salty Flats strip near Marmari, and a third in the making at Lambia. And with Cos, the neighboring island of Kalymnos was also important, because whereas Cos has no port suitable for larger ships, Kalymnos has several; the small but deep harbor of Kalymnos village actually faces the shores of Cos, only a short distance across the water.

The Germans had been quickly preparing plans to strengthen and extend their hold on the Dodecanese as soon as they had secured the key island of Rhodes. The occupation of Cos had been high on their list of objectives, as the Germans regarded it, quite rightly, as second only in importance to Rhodes. The green light for the assault on Cos, to be known as Operation Polar Bear (*Eisbär*), was given on September 24, following Hitler's meeting with Field Marshal Weichs. The detailed naval planning and preparations for the embarking of troops from places as far apart as Crete and the Piraeus, and also the assembly of suitable shipping, were undertaken by the *Seekomandanten Attika*, Captain von Studnitz. The forces the German Navy had available to escort the invasion fleet consisted of two minelayers, the *Bulgaria* and *Drache*; five ships of the 21st *UJ* (*Unterseebootjäger*, or Auxiliary Escort) Flotilla; and six minesweepers, R-boats (*Räumboote*) of the 12th Flotilla, with various assorted landing barges and MFPs (*Marinefährprähme*, or F-lighters). All were under the command of *Korvettenkapitan* Dr. Günther Brandt. According to Italian records, two ex-Italian vessels also took part, the *Crispi* and a Calatafimi-class destroyer.

The plans provided for a main landing on the flat coastline on the north of the island near Marmari, west of Cos town and close to the Salty Flats airfield. A second landing was to be made at Kamara Bay in the southwestern corner of the island. And finally, there was to be a subsidiary landing in the Cape Foca area, to the east of Cos town.

The army units selected for the operation were under the very able command of Lt. Gen. Friedrich-Wilhelm Müller and given the title of *Kampfgruppe Müller*. The group was drawn from the 22nd Air Landing

Division in Crete and consisted of two infantry units, the 2nd Battalion, 16th Panzer Grenadier Regiment, and the 2nd Battalion, 65th Panzer Grenadier Regiment, with fire support from an engineer detachment, the 3rd Battalion, 22nd Artillery Regiment (equipped with self-propelled guns), and the 4th Battalion, 22nd Artillery Regiment (with mountain guns). From these, Maj. Sylvester von Saldern formed the supporting *Kampfgruppe von Saldern*. There was also a part of the 440th Grenadier Regiment, under the command of *Hauptmann* Erwin Dörr, which was part of the 164th Infantry Division. The 164th had stayed on the island of Chios and some smaller islands when the rest had gone to fight at El Alamein and Tunisia in 1942–43. They were also to see combat on Leros later. The follow-up troops were to be paratroops, part of the Brandenburg Regiment from Greece, together with assault pioneers of the 999th Regiment, supported by a battalion of the 11th Field Division, who were to strike inland, capture Marmari, and assault Cos town.

A second group, consisting of the escorts *UJ-2109* and *UJ-2102*, with two MFPs and one steamship carrying the 2nd Battalion, 16th Panzer, was allocated to the southeast coast near Cape Foca. A third group, *UJ-2101*, escorting more assault craft, aimed at landing a company of men in the Kamara Bay area at the southwest corner of the island.

All the landings were made at first light, around 0500, and achieved complete surprise, for the garrison of Cos was still not on the alert, happy in the false interpretation of German capacity and intentions. Despite the increased British air activity on the nights of October 2–3, this interpretation had not yet been corrected.

It was estimated at the time that some 1,200 men had initially been put ashore, and that they were well equipped with light artillery, armored cars, and automatic weapons. A heavy and continuous air bombardment was carried out at the same time over Antimachia, Cos town, Marmari, and any obvious defense works. There was little the RAF could do to counter these attacks, for the *Luftwaffe* provided very comprehensive air cover. Nevertheless, at great risk, Beaufighter strikes were made throughout the day.

On October 3, three crews from No. 227 Squadron—Pilot Off. Percy Glynn, RCAF, and his navigator; Sgt. D. E. Warne, RCAF, and J. W. D. Thomas, navigator; and Sgt. K. Thomas, RAAF, and his navigator—were called to the operations room at around 0430 and briefed to deal with a "possible invasion force somewhere in the vicinity of Naxos." Flight Lt. J. W. D. Thomas told us, "They were very vague. Referring to my Flying Log, which I still have, the preflight briefing was for an armed recce to include Symi, Leros, Nisero, etc." They took off from Lakatamia at 0510, and an hour and a half later, they struck their target, the invasion fleet, attacking with 20-millimeter cannon and machine-gun fire from 4,000 feet down to mast height. The ships were exceptionally well defended with a mass of light flak—the dangerous stuff for low flyers. The Beaus were severely mauled in attacking a much larger and stronger force than had been reported. Flight Lieutenant Thomas described the mission to us thus:

> We passed Castelrosso at 0630, and we then climbed over Cape Marmaris. Crossing the narrow peninsula of Turkish territory to avoid Rhodes, we came upon the invasion fleet in the Cos Channel northeast of the island. We saw a destroyer standing off Cos Harbor but didn't know if it was ours or theirs! We then attacked the main force.
>
> Pilot Off. Percy Glynn, RCAF, did a "crossover turn" over us and was shot down in flames (we nearly collided). We attacked a large merchant vessel, hitting with one bomb, but the other bomb "hung up" on us. They later told us afterward that 2,000 troops had perished. I was shown photographs at 201 Group by an intelligence officer of the ship. Warrant Officer Warne was awarded an immediate DFC for his attack.

Alas, no ship was actually sunk in this strike, although Thomas stated:

> We hit our merchant vessel target with a bomb. This owed more to guess than by God. When we dropped a bomb, my pilot always left the armored doors separating us open. When I felt the moment opportune, I would shout, "Now!" and he would release the bomb. Generally we missed. This was quite an occasion! I observed strikes on the bridge also from my Vickers K gun. I recall the decks being crammed with troops and little boats chugging away toward the shore.

The contrast between such ramshackle antishipping methods employed by the RAF Beaufighters in late 1943—still very much a matter of luck—and the highly precise and accurate dive-bombing employed by the "obsolete" Ju 87 is most marked; it is little wonder that Royal Navy losses were high and German shipping losses negligible, despite equivalent bravery being displayed by the air crew on both sides.

Thomas's narrative continues:

> Sergeant Thomas's navigator was wounded so he flew using us below as his guide. We therefore kept station with him. He had engine trouble and climbed to about 6,000 feet when we were clear of Rhodes. I navigated south to get well clear before altering course

to base. I reported the invasion, "Cos being invaded," at 0715. I recall the time as I had to repeat it on a different frequency—change over time for security reasons.

As we approached Cyprus, we reported the invasion by VHF I was subsequently told the army picked up my transmission at Mersa Matruh and relayed it! On return, we found the airfield a hive of activity. Someone I knew on their way to the briefing room joked with me, saying, "Look what you've started!" The senior air staff officer (a group captain with an Indian ribbon) asked us the form. My concern for the crews taking off led me to approach him and blurt out that attacks by low-flying aircraft (our technique) were impossible. He coldly told me, "I didn't ask you, Navigator," so I retired, suitably abased, to the mess tent! The rest of the debacle is history.

Throughout the day, sorties made up of aircraft from all the squadrons in No. 237 Wing went out, usually four at a time. Few returned.

Unfortunately, Wing Cmdr. Russell Mackenzie, CO of No. 235 Squadron, was away (at group) when the Cos debacle happened. Acting CO was Squadron Leader Ronaldson-Lewis. A few days after the third, on his return, Wing Commander Mackenzie sent for me and asked how many ships had been at the scene. He told me that the Cabinet had wanted to know how many ships were there when Pilot Officer Glynn was killed. I was a bit awed by the original source of the question and replied that I had no clue. Pressed for a number, I said something up to 100, including landing craft, etc., but that it was a wildish guess at best. Wing Commander Mackenzie, his tour of duty as CO being expired, left for 201 Group on October 14, being replaced by Wing Commander Buchanan (a legend in his own right).

Half an hour later, eight Beaufighters under a squadron leader took off to repeat the attack. They too were met with a solid wall of flak, plus single-engine fighters, and six aircraft were lost over the targets. The other two returned safely to Lakatamia, though the squadron leader and one of the navigators were slightly wounded.

This set the pattern for days to follow. Combat reports indicated that the Beaufighter losses were heavy, and these reports were accurate.

Despite these frequent strikes by Beaufighters based in Cyprus against the German fleet, there is no evidence that the landings were in any way delayed by them. The British pilots subsequently claimed hits on two escort ships, two landing craft, and one caique, which were all slightly damaged, but only by cannon fire. One of the covering Arado floatplanes was also shot down, but the Beaus reported that antiaircraft fire over the fleet was intense.

Flight Lieutenant Thomas told us:

> At approximately 4:00 P.M., being the senior officer (flying officer) present, I had to detail two crews of No. 227 Squadron to carry out the last sortie. They returned safely, as the Germans had laid an effective smoke screen over the target area. I was quite relieved. No. 46 Squadron (a night fighter outfit, inexperienced in day strike work) were decimated. We suffered heavy losses. By evening, the wing was virtually noneffective.
>
> I was a few days later made wing liaison officer, with a duty which superseded the squadron commanders' objections, to raise aircraft to provide effective escort for naval units in the area.

Because of their deep draft, the larger steamers lay out in the bay, and their troops and equipment had to be transferred to the MFP for landing. The steamers presented a sitting target for air attack, but despite this, the landing proceeded smoothly. The small motor minesweepers, R-boats, also closed the coast to act as cover and transport for the army. Considerable help was given to the troops ashore by the monitoring of the British signals traffic by German signals units afloat.

On the morning of the third, the Italian lookout post on Kalymnos had given precise reports of the movements of the convoy that had been sighted in the Cos-Kalymnos channel, but the first "official" warning that British Command headquarters received of the landings was a telephone call just before 0500 from the Italian artillery unit holding a position in the hills southeast of Germen. It reported that a large transport and two landing craft were approaching the shore near Marmari and the Salty Flats airstrip. The Italians manning the battery of 75-millimeter guns opened fire too late to have an effect, and the 2nd Battalion of the 65th Panzer Grenadier Regiment was quickly ashore and pushing forward toward the airstrip, where it soon came upon the ten grounded and damaged Spitfires hidden there. The Germans thus rapidly forestalled any hope of even limited air cover for the island by high-performance fighters. They quickly cut the Cos-Antimachia road thus severing all land communications between head-quarters and the airfield. Heavy bombing and strafing by close-support Stuka dive-bombers of all movement along the roads leading to the beaches also facilitated the German advance.

Flight Sgt. David Maxwell, Sgt. Brian Harris, and Flying Off. Guy De Pass, three RAF pilots who escaped, related their experiences. On the night of the invasion, they were encamped by the side of the Salty Flats airfield on the north coast, about 300 yards from the beach and a few miles from Cos town. Maxwell wrote:

> We awoke to hear the noise of landing craft engines and the crackle of machine-gun. We rushed out of our tents and saw red tracers streaking across the beaches and white Very lights soaring into the sky. We could not see the oncoming German troops, but their bullets were whistling over our heads. The advancing enemy met their first opposition from members of the RAF Regiment who were guarding the landing grounds. The Germans advanced across the salt marshes towards high ground where there was a hospital formerly used as a Fascist club. We made for the town of Cos in a jeep with the intention of warning the garrison.

The three men came across a contingent of the RAF Regiment encamped in an olive grove and gave them all the information they could. They were then ordered to leave the island, so they proceeded to the jetty and boarded an Italian motorboat. "As we left the jetty," said De Pass, "a Stuka scored a direct hit and blew it sky high. The German invaders were equipped with all types of light weapons and mortars."

A flight sergeant from Toronto recorded: "I was encamped on the salt flat on the north side of the island when the attack began. The Germans scrambling ashore got between us and our kites and their machine-gun and rifle fire whistled over our heads. We scrambled together a few provisions and made off for the hills, where we hid for six days, sending out scouts to ascertain the position on the rest of the island."

The main strength of the Durham Light Infantry was at this time concentrated five miles west of Cos town, and the men could see the German troops coming ashore over the salt pans. Colonel Kirby had the misfortune to be in the hospital during this opening phase of the landings, but Hugh Vaux, his deputy, had ordered the battalion to take up positions astride the main Cos-Antimachia road, B Company to the north and A to the south. They were spread very thinly on the ground, but they extended their positions almost up to the beach in an effort to bar the way into the town of Cos.

C Company was stationed on the edge of the town, and when a report came in of a landing on the south coast, their carrier platoon, which actually had jeeps instead of carriers, went forward at once to meet this new threat.

They had not gotten far, however, when they clashed with a German patrol moving down the Cos-Antimachia road. Lt. George Sievwright, the commander, and his driver were killed by a burst of fire from point-blank range.

Colonel Kirby meanwhile had seized a motorcycle and joined his men to the west of Cos town. He ordered them to dig in before the Germans had time to organize, but this proved almost impossible, owing to the rocky nature of the ground. The British troops had to rely on the dubious shelter of stone walls and groves to protect them. Before long, the Stukas arrived and circled overhead, seemingly immune to the fire of the pitifully few anti-aircraft weapons available. The Germans thus pounced on any movement or concentrations of British forces instantly, and this constant bombing and strafing did much to harry the Durham Light Infantry. The Italian gun batteries around Gherme also suffered severely.

By this time, reports of further landings in the south had come in and detachments were sent there to forestall the German thrusts. The invaders swung off westward into the hills, however, beating back the Italian battalion guarding this region after heavy fighting. The German objective was to outflank the Antimachia defenses and join up with their paratroops.

Before long, the main German force, well equipped with light artillery and armored cars, had formed up and begun to probe the Durham Light Infantry's defenses. In a short time, the Germans were attacking hard to the front of B Company and also working steadily around its flanks. Despite good work by their supporting mortar section, the forward platoons of B Company were overrun, and their company headquarters lost contact with A Company on its left flank. It soon became clear that the Durham Light Infantry would be forced to give ground, as it was heavily outnumbered.

The men of No. 2901 Squadron, RAF Regiment, were also having their problems. For them, the first alarm had in fact been raised at 0430, when five pilots of No. 74 Squadron, De Pass, Bates, Norman, Maxwell, and Harris, arrived in Cos, having hitched a lift on a jeep. They arrived at the billets of No. 2901 Squadron around 0500 and found most of the airmen were already prepared, having been woken by the initial bombing and strafing. The Spitfire pilots told them that an estimated 400 German troops were ashore near the Salty Flats airstrip.

Fraser, the CO of 2901, then paraded his unit in full battle order, and they marched off to give battle. He led the formation through Cos town until they were held up by a roadblock, which caused them to make a diversion. All this time, intensive bombing and strafing was taking place. Once clear of the town, one section, with two Bren guns and some rifles, was detailed to hold a feature at a point southeast of the main escarpment. The remainder of the men were deployed to the right of the ridge out of sight.

To the front of the first group, to which Cpl. G. Neal was attached, were Italian troops manning heavy guns on the main feature. When first deployed, Neal reported that these guns were in action against German troops in the northwest. Flying Officer Sullivan arrived too late to take command of this party, but in any case, they could do little except to keep cover under the intensive low-level air attack.

Meanwhile, at Antimachia, D Company of the Durham Light Infantry and the men of No. 2909 Squadron, RAF Regiment, guarding the airfield, were also being subjected to heavy attack. After ferocious bombing and strafing, paratroops of the Brandenburg Regiment had dropped on Antimachia. D Company was holding the airfield with less than ninety men, but with the aid of the RAF Regiment and some Italian troops, they held out well until the afternoon despite the ceaseless bombing. The German troops pushing up from Kamara Bay now linked up with those attacking the airfield, and by early afternoon, they made a further strong attack, well supported by mortar fire, against the British defenders.

Men of No. 2909 Squadron kept their guns in action around the airfield perimeter, but with the Germans well established to the north, they were unable to assist with fire from the Hispanos for fear of hitting retreating friendly forces. The guns therefore were pulled back to the south of the airfield. Squadron Leader Killallin ordered the crews to stand by the guns and keep them firing until the enemy got too close; they were then to dismantle them. Killallin went to try to check on the general situation, for they were still cut off from Cos town, but he was not seen again.

German ground activity around the airfield rapidly increased, and by 1700, all the Hispanos were out of action; the only antiaircraft defense left was a few light machine guns. All the troops were ordered to withdraw to Cardamena on the coast. D Company of the Durham Light Infantry had fought until almost its entire strength had been either killed, wounded, or taken prisoner. John Thorpe was severely wounded in the back but managed to escape to the hills; he was later forced to surrender. His companion, Sgt. Maj. Wally Carr, was more fortunate; after a long period of hiding, he managed to get off the island and rejoin his battalion later.

Although the battle for Antimachia had by now been lost, the bloody pitched battle for the approaches to Cos town was still under way in the northeast of the island, with both sides suffering heavily; the Germans were, however, still pressing forward. With No. 2901 still in position, Fraser went forward to visit his men but could tell them little of the confused situation or how the battle was faring. All the British forces were now suffering badly from lack of supplies, food, and water, for nothing much could get past the vigilant Stukas. Fraser left Neal's company with the impression that there was no control over troop movements left at all.

Sullivan was told to hold the position come what may, and Fraser promised to return with food. The men of the RAF Regiment had not eaten for twenty-four hours. Ju 87 sorties were increasing in intensity, though the men witnessed the loss of one of these to antiaircraft fire, the Stuka crashing in flames. It did not make a great deal of difference, however, and soon they saw the Italian gunners cease firing and hastily withdraw toward their position. The Italians informed the RAF men that the Germans were advancing from the hills one and a half miles away.

Soon Sullivan's men could see the Italian guns being remanned by the Germans, and as their crews had left too quickly to immobilize them, these guns were shortly in action, bombarding British positions in Cos town. Sullivan's post was brought under heavy mortar fire, with bursts up to 100 yards to their rear. The detachment held on grimly, and Fraser returned as promised with bully beef and biscuits, but again no information. Taking Sullivan with him, Fraser went back to the squadron headquarters on the outskirts of Cos to try to get clarification.

A little while later, a party of retreating Durham Light Infantry and Royal Artillery gunners passed, and their commander told the RAF men to pull out. Resistance was finally beginning to crumble, for the Germans were again increasing their efforts, using light mountain guns and antitank guns; parties of infantry were constantly filtering through the lightly held British positions.

The German attacks against Cos had been resumed with fresh energy during the afternoon. Once the Italian battery had been overrun, the withdrawal of the British line became inevitable. Sergeant Broome of No. 2901 was unaware of any orders to pull back and told his men to remain, pending the return of either Sullivan or Fraser. But they never came. Within a quarter of an hour, the sniping and machine-gun fire was becoming both intense and accurate. On more than one occasion, it was reported that the magazines of the British Bren guns were shot out of the hands of the defenders as they were being fitted.

At 1900, there was a general withdrawal all along the line except for A Company, which was now completely out of touch with the rest of the battalion. No. 2901 joined in the retreat, pulling back to the outskirts of the town; there they were informed that the Germans had made a pincer movement to the left and right of the town, but that if they kept to the right flank of the German force, they should just get through, and they did.

The town was now being heavily mortared, and Sergeant Broome told his men that he was going back through to try once more to locate his squadron headquarters. The mortar fire grew heavier, and the remaining men were forced to withdraw still further; with the approach of darkness, the unit to which Neal belonged became split up.

Meanwhile, A Company, under the command of Capt. Jim Grey, had been reduced to a strength of a mere forty men and was completely cut off. They had suffered severely earlier in the day when moving forward to deploy on the southern side of the main road, being caught out in the open by eighteen Stukas. Half the company became casualties, and the survivors swung back to maintain contact with two companies of Italian infantry, which were fighting well. At the time of the general withdrawal, Grey had decided to pull his men westward, and in so doing, they joined an Italian battery of 75-millimeter guns, which was still in action although hard-pressed from both the ground and the air. The Germans had launched attacks on this unit from east and west, and Grey offered to assist with his company. Together the Italians and British repulsed both attacks and stayed with the battery until nightfall.

Then the Germans closed in on the positions, lit flares, began their evening meal, and even sang songs.

Grey was organizing a bayonet attack to break up this little assembly when a solitary antiaircraft gunner appeared with the information that the rest of the battalion, now merely 200 strong in all, had pulled back to Cos town. Grey thereupon determined to join them, which they all did without mishap.

The small detachment from No. 2909 that had been ordered the day before to assist the men of 625 AMES—the Air Ministry Experimental Station, a wartime name for a radar station—some twenty miles away on the east coast was meanwhile having adventures of its own. William Cole described to us just how *he* recalled what took place. It differs from official accounts in several details and is interesting in that it shows the lack of knowledge of the man on the ground in a confusing situation of haste and combat, which was typical of the campaign as a whole:

I was a member of 625 AMES. The units assembled at Helwan transit camp with primitive radar equipment—similar to the ASI [air search interrogate] used for submarine and surface vessels in aircraft. With vehicles and a unit of twelve personnel, we journeyed from Helwan-Khantara, through Sinai to Gaza, through Palestine, to Ramat David aerodrome near Haifa. We waited our turn to fly, we knew not where. The unit flew, very low-level, with our equipment to an airfield at night. It is pretty certain that we landed at Marmari, the date would possibly be 28th September. There was a great scramble to unload in the center of the strip so that the plane could take off again immediately. Once dawn broke, everything and everyone was hurriedly taken to the olive groves at the edge of the airfield.

We then started to prepare breakfast, which was quickly interrupted by Stukas who came out of the sun and bombed us. We lost two of the unit—one, Robert Holden, who was killed by my side, and our corporal injured, having been blown up over a well with part of a tree pinning him down. Two of us managed to release him and get him to the shelter of a low stone wall; the Stukas then returned to strafe us with machine-gun fire.

We were ordered to disperse by our unit leader [Flight Sergeant Draper—there were no officers with these small units] to await further instruction. We hid in ditches until we were picked up by a squadron leader in the afternoon and taken in a jeep to our site. My recollection is of a reasonably short journey, certainly nothing like twenty miles, through a town which I now know was Cos town. My further recollection is of standing on a hill, covered with wild thyme, in the evening, which overlooked a large bay.

I would assume that this site was chosen to enable us to pick up aircraft incoming from Rhodes, but bearing in mind the limited range of our equipment, a little over twenty-five miles, and the mountains around us [it was approximately three miles to the Turkish mainland], detection would have been pretty difficult. My guess, and it is only an intelligent one, is that the most easterly we would have been was on the northern slopes of Mount Simpetro, possibly as far east as Cape Foca area, but I think not.

We had only completed setting up our equipment by the night of 2nd October and had not become operational. We were awakened at dawn by the sound of aircraft and saw paratroopers being dropped. Incidentally, no detachment of 2909 had been dispatched to us, even if it had been planned. Communication by land line had been broken. There was a valley at the bottom of which was a dried-up watercourse between our hill and one on which was an Italian gun position. This became the target for the Stukas. Two of us went up to this position, which was under very heavy and sustained bombing attack. From this vantage point, one could see the invading fleet offshore. This tends to focus the location of our site more toward the western slopes of Simpetro, if the fleet was off Marmari.

My recollection of that morning was that the Italians were firing. We quickly realized that we must smash our equipment and burn the secret documents—the latter we did in a cave.

One of our unit, Morgan, had gone on another recce. We did
not see him again. The rest of us, now down to nine, were picked up
by the squadron leader, taken through Cos town, and located in a
shallow watercourse and told to await further orders; two went with
the squadron leader, leaving seven. To our right was a flat expanse,
which I would guess was towards Lambia; occasionally we saw mortar shells exploding in that area. I would guess that we were there
for two or three hours, no contact from anyone, until the Durham
Light Infantry started to come back in dribs and drabs, and as the
firing came closer, told us to get the hell out of it.

Eventually we moved out and back over a short distance to Cos
town; we located the army headquarters who were far too involved
to want to know seven airmen. The town was now under shell fire,
possibly from the captured guns of the Italian position we had visited earlier. I guess it was about midday or one o'clock by then. We
hid up not far from the harbor to the west. Midafternoon, we
decided to try to get more information and returned to the harbor
area. This was now under heavy fire, and we were told that boats
were leaving. A mad dash round the harbor and six of us leaped
onto an already moving air-sea rescue launch; our seventh member,
Cled Williams, a Welsh teacher, would not jump.

The unaccounted members of 625 were the flight sergeant
[Draper] and one who got out six days later, Mathews, Morgan, and
the injured corporal, who was shipped out on the morning of the
third. Cled Mathews, I was reliably informed from another friend of
mine, was taken prisoner on Leros, was a POW, but nothing was
heard of Morgan after.

Our crossing to Turkey was uncanny. The sea was like a millpond
with German aircraft overhead but no attack. We came into
Bodrum harbor and were transshipped to an LCT, where we found
a number of other escapees, mostly army. The story went that the
Turkish authorities gave us twenty-four hours to leave; "trouble"
with the engines extended this period by another twenty-four hours,
further "trouble" with the engines extended this period to forty-
eight hours. By this time, a caique had arrived which was filled by
airmen and soldiery. We sailed at night, close to the Turkish coast,
and hid up on land during day. It took three days to Casteloriso,
then six to seven days spent on that island, which was subjected to
regular bombing, as one would expect being so close to Rhodes.
From there we were taken by a small French passenger boat, accompanied by two destroyers, to Beirut. One of these destroyers was the

Italian *Polo*. A rather interesting experience en route, near Cyprus at night, was a problem with our steering when we started describing circles with the *Polo* fussing around.

The official RAF version of these events differed considerably. It stated that once the AMES men found that they were out of contact with Antimachia early in the day, all their radar equipment was destroyed and the coding documents were burned. Together with four men from No. 2909, they attempted to assist the Italian garrison holding a fort on top of one of the hills nearby, but the Italian commander curtly told them that his orders were not to open fire on the Germans and flatly refused to allow the British into the fort. He could obviously see which way the battle was going to end.

The little party therefore took refuge in the hills, just in time, for the Germans occupied the fort shortly afterward. The British party from Antimachia reached Cardamena later that day and found the village being systematically bombed and strafed. Many of No. 2909 Squadron stayed there and were later taken prisoner when the Germans occupied it on the fourth. Nine men decided to take to the hills and try to join up with other British troops. Another small party of the RAF Regiment that was en route to reinforce the squadron by ship from Casteloriso was warned of the invasion by a British aircraft as it headed for the island; later a British destroyer told the men to return to Cyprus, as there was by then nothing they could do to help.

The five pilots of No. 74 Squadron managed to board an Italian 250-ton naval tanker, *Adda*, under Capt. Domenico Rota, which was sailing for Leros at 1100 that same morning. Soon after leaving the harbor, they ran into the larger part of the German invasion fleet and had to hastily hide up at Kefalcha on the Turkish coast to avoid capture. The Italian crew thereupon sabotaged the ship's engines and refused to obey the captain's orders to continue to Leros, although she did eventually get there.

The CRS post of the Royal Army Medical Corps (RAMC) had been overrun almost at once, but the Germans did not interfere with the workings of the station and brought many of their own wounded in for treatment. The station continued to function in this manner for several days, until the British casualties and RAMC personnel were finally flown out to Greece.

Back at Cos town, the survivors of A Company eventually joined the remnants of B, C, and HQ Companies in a defensive perimeter that was under heavy mortar bombardment. Sustained and vicious fighting continued here until well past nightfall. The Anti-Tank Platoon, under the command of Captain Birchenough, was successful in preventing a flanking movement by the Germans, but by the time this platoon fought its way back to the perimeter, it had been reduced to only a handful of active men. Birchenough had twice brought in badly wounded men under fire and had set on fire one of the undamaged grounded Spitfires before pulling out to prevent the Germans from using it.

Lt. Col. R. F. Kirby now called a conference of all the company commanders to decide the next move. By cruel chance, a mortar bomb fell directly among this group, scything them down. Kirby, Maj. Mark Leather (the commander of HQ Company), Capt. J. E. Stafford, and Captain Bush of the supply party were all wounded, the last fatally. It was a terrible blow coming at a time when the battalion had been fought almost to a standstill without cracking.

Maj. Hugh Vaux assumed command and proceeded to force headquarters for orders where he was told by Col. L. F. R. Kenyon to stand fast for the present but report back again at 2000 hours for further orders. In fact, by that time, Kenyon had decided that with no prospect of reinforcement reaching him that night, resistance of the orthodox kind was useless. His intention, conveyed to the shrunken exhausted garrison that night, was to take the survivors into the hills, covered by a rear guard, and there to continue the fight in guerrilla fashion. The SBS Detachment, on a neighboring island, which had been ordered to counterattack the German forces, although it was less than fifty men strong, had this invitation to suicide countermanded. Cos garrison was still on its own.

Kenyon's signal received at Cairo at 0605 the next day was the last to reach the outside world. It read: "Cos town untenable; intend to continue the fight elsewhere."

This decision taken, the survivors—save for the rear-guard party, which was to hold the town of Cos for as long as possible—were split up into small parties in order to escape observation. They had orders to lie up as soon as morning came. The rendezvous chosen was the village of Cardamena, which contained an Italian food dump and lay some three miles west of the main road between Cos and Antimachia. The survivors dispersed in parties of about twelve men each and moved out of the blazing town during the night:

> In most cases each man had two bandoliers of ammunition and a tin of food, and two blankets were carried by each party. Very naturally all movement had to be made by night, which did not make things easy; the country was rough and rocky, progress was slow, falls frequent and the language unprintable! Each party lay up during the day and kept a wary eye open for German patrols who were beginning to be fairly active in the hills.

The rear guard consisted of a platoon with some mortars, who held out gallantly until 0200 next day. Around Lambia some men of the RAF Regiment and the No. 74 Field Company continued fighting until 0600 on the fourth.

Not all the men trapped on Cos received the order to disperse, which, considering the conditions, was not surprising. Corporal Neal of No. 2901 Squadron found that his unit had been reduced to five men by dusk on the third. From their positions, they watched as boats evacuated soldiers from the harbor area and were either sunk or damaged by heavy mortar fire.

By midnight, it was bedlam in the dock area; the Germans were using powerful searchlights, and although air activity had naturally ceased, they were able to bring heavy mortar and machine-gun fire against any British movement. The only naval loss was *LCT-3*, which had been abandoned because of engine problems and was captured intact by the Germans; two other landing craft, *LCT-114* and *LCT-139*, managed to scramble clear of the final chaos at Cos harbor and escaped. The position was chaotic, and on approaching some Royal Artillery (RA) officers for information, Neal was told that it was now every man for himself. By this time his sole companion was Leading Aircraftman Harris.

Together with three privates from the Durham Light Infantry they explored the shoreline and came across a badly leaking rowboat minus oars. They made four makeshift oars from driftwood, and then, with the two airmen rowing and the soldiers bailing, they set off to try to reach the Turkish mainland.

On the island of Kalymnos, four miles from Cos, a detachment of the Special Boat Squadron had watched the brief battle. During the day, David Sutherland sent in Walter Milner-Barry and his men, who had just come back from a patrol to Chios, with orders to help retard the German advance by demolition. Milner-Barry was also instructed to evacuate as many British troops as he could should the island fall. He at once started carrying out his instructions, and he and his little fleet of caiques spent the next eight nights running into Cos, during which time no less than 105 British combat personnel were rescued. He was also instrumental in organizing an escape plan for collecting strays and directing them to pickup points around the north and south coasts.

A leading aircraftman who escaped from Cos town with a party of RAF ground personnel and infantry as the Germans broke in told of his experiences. A second lieutenant of the infantry took charge of this party of ten, and the men were in Cos for seven days after the first German attack. They were ordered to make for the highest ground, but when they reached the hilltop, they found it was in German hands and had to retire into hiding.

They captured a goat and a sheep and made primitive attempts to cook them. Eventually they were also taken off in a sailing ship.

Through this day and during the night of October 3–4, the situation was as confused in the air over the island and the sea around it as it was on Cos itself.

The RAF continued to strive throughout the day to damage the invasion shipping, but to little avail. On October 3, Beaufighters operating against the German ships off Cos mounted at least twenty-eight sorties, during which two Stukas were shot down. British losses were heavy: Five Beaus were destroyed and seven damaged on one sortie alone, and many more failed to return throughout the day.

Eisenhower, aroused at last, signaled to the Combined Chiefs of Staff and the British Chiefs of Staff on October 3: "This morning Middle East is having some trouble and needs help against increasing hostile air power in Greece. Since this air power is a threat to our necessary use of the Adriatic ports in Italy we are immediately throwing entire Strategic Force in a quick destructive effort against hostile airfields."

The following day, the "heavies" took a hand, and October 4 saw all air units available thrown in, in an effort to turn the tide. Strategic bombing of the German airfields, offensive strikes by long-range and medium bombers, and extensive air coverage missions over the considerable naval forces operating in the Aegean all were vigorously carried out.

The heaviest USAAF contributions were as follows: October 4, forty-four sorties against Tatoi (Athens); October 5, forty-three sorties against Eleusis (Athens); October 9, thirty sorties against Eleusis and thirty-four against Salonika/Sedes; October 10, sixty sorties against Tatoi. No. 240 Wing RAF contributed twelve sorties against Maritza (Rhodes) and Heraklion (Crete) on the nights of October 5–6 and 7–8, respectively.

The Royal Navy was also considerably reinforced. On the evening of the third, it was reported that the situation on Cos was very serious, with the Germans known to be in virtual control of the whole island, except for a small area within a two-mile radius of Cos town. The commander in chief in the Middle East asked for maximum naval assistance. He also requested that six squadrons of Lightnings be made available to cover the naval operations and the immediate dispatch of a transport group in the hope of using paratroops to restore the situation.

But by now, the situation on Cos was already hopeless. Naval response was quick. From Malta, the 12th Cruiser Squadron was placed under the orders of the commander in chief of the Levant, and the cruisers *Aurora* and *Penelope* sailed from Malta at 0830 on the fourth, followed at 1800 by the *Sirius* and *Dido*. A flotilla of Hunts was ordered to Limassol and these four boats, *Aldenham, Rockwood, Miaoulis,* and *Themistocles,* left Alexandria at 0300 on the fourth.

Fleet destroyers had also been dispatched posthaste from Malta to back up these units. The *Faulknor, Fury,* and *Eclipse* sailed with the two cruisers earlier, and two more Fleet destroyers, *Petard* and *Penn,* were to be sailed from Taranto during the afternoon while their sister, the *Panther,* was to leave Malta at 1800 on the fifth. These were all the destroyers immediately available.

Unfortunately, none of these warships arrived off the island before the night of October 4–5. The *Aurora, Dido, Tumult,* and *Pathfinder* made rendezvous sixty miles south of Crete on the morning of the fifth and swept through the Kasos Straits. Apart from a few spasmodic air attacks, this force drew a blank. At 2100, when south of Cos Channel, the two cruisers were in collision. The captain of *Pathfinder,* Lt. Cmdr. C. W. Malins, recalls the incident:

> It was a dark fine night and the cruisers collided with a glancing blow, bow-to-bow, sending up showers of sparks which, from our position on the beam, looked at first like a small firework display. As they drew apart we could clearly see the lights of the mess decks in one of them, I cannot remember which. There was no air attack on at the time and I must presume it was either an error of judgment in taking station or, more likely, when both were zigzagging, a jammed rudder. In any case the damage was not serious.

The ships proceeded in company at nineteen knots to Alexandria, where they arrived on the sixth. Although the damage was not serious, both ships had suffered hull damage above the waterline and the fracture of some plates and frames forward. The *Dido* in fact was not able to take any further part in the operations, but the *Aurora* was again in action within ten days. This mishap at a time when every available warship was needed, and following quickly upon the loss of the destroyers *Intrepid* and *Queen Olga,* was another portent that the Aegean was an unsatisfactory sea for operations by the Royal Navy; the old specter of the Dardanelles, the disastrous 1941 campaigns in Greece and Crete, began to loom large once again.

On Cos, it was virtually all over by the morning of the fourth. The splendid intentions of the garrison commander to fight it out from the hills soon came to nothing. The original plan to rendezvous at the village of Cardamena was thwarted at the outset, for when the first straggling bands of exhausted men reached its outskirts, they found that the Germans were already in control of the region. Several brushes occurred during the night between the small groups of British troops and the newly established German patrols, and many of the garrison were captured while other groups split up and were forced away from the main body.

The bulk of the survivors lay up in the region of Mount Simpetro, where they established a base and posted guards while they reorganized themselves. In all, about sixty men of the Durham Light Infantry were assembled, with various additions from the RAF Regiment and the RA. With their food supplies cut off and water proving to be scarce in the mountains, they were soon in a desperate situation. Many of the men began to go down with malaria and sand-fly fever. Greek shepherds befriended this group at great risk to themselves and gave what food and shelter they could to those worst affected: "A curious dish of mixed margarine and jam was eaten with some relish for want of anything better, and was supplemented, when the opportunity arose, by mountain goat."

It was obvious that this dwindling band of men could offer no resistance of a serious nature to the German occupation forces; it being only a matter of time before they all succumbed to disease or were surprised and killed by the Germans. Plans were therefore made to evacuate as many as possible from the island. The SBS from Kalymnos was already busy doing just this with the smaller pockets of survivors remaining in other areas of the island. It was now decided to get the rest of the men out quickly. They found a Greek carpenter who was willing to help them, and with his aid, a raft was constructed and hidden in a cave near a beach just across the water from the Turkish mainland.

A lighthouse was visible at night on the Turkish coast, and this was chosen as a marker. A small band consisting of nine men from various units, led by Col. "Topper" Browne of the Sappers, was detailed to make the first attempt on the night of October 12–13. On arriving at the cave, they found to their surprise and delight that the SBS was already there waiting for them. Captain Milner-Barry and his men gave Browne the news that a naval caique was due to arrive in the bay the following night to collect him and any survivors he had managed to find. It was doubted that the caique would be able to accommodate the whole party, but all were assembled, and the final decision as to how many could be pulled out was to be left to the commander of the caique *LSF-2*, Lt. A. McLeod, RNVR.

When he arrived at 0200 the following night, he decided to take every one of them, and in all, some eight officers and sixty men were ferried out to the little sailing craft by rubber dinghy. The caique sailed without incident and landed them at Bodrum on the Turkish coast, where a secret SBS base had been set up. From Bodrum, they were sent by other caiques to Casteloriso, where they arrived after a difficult voyage through a violent storm. From Casteloriso, they were subsequently ferried to Cyprus. Lieutenant McLeod made a total of six rendezvous in Cos and Kalymnos and rescued a total of 120 men.

The story of the other small bands of survivors was very much the same. The nine men of No. 2909 who left Cardamena on the fourth reached the temporary safety of the hills the next day, having passed on the way a party of demoralized British troops who were about to surrender. Food was short, but they estimated that they had enough for six days. There followed a long period of hide-and-seek with the German patrols. Local Greeks fed them from time to time and also found an old hut for the exhausted British to lie up in during the day.

It was not until October 22, nineteen days after the German invasion, that this party left the island by boat, finally reaching Casteloriso on the twenty-eighth. On their arrival, the island was subjected to severe bombing, and not surprisingly, after all they had been through, two of the party were badly shocked. This gallant little band left Casteloriso the same day by high-speed launch for Limassol.

Leading Aircraftman Lever, Parker, Young, and Williams, the four men attached to the No. 8 Air Formation Signals Section who took to the mountains on October 4, were accompanied by Sergeant Brand and Corporal Abreau of that unit and more from 625 AMES. They, too, had little food and found water to be scarce off the beaten track, but they somehow managed to escape the attentions of the Germans. For a week they survived alone in the hills, during which time Williams caught dysentery and eight more of the 625 AMES gave themselves up. On the tenth, a shepherd gave them their first decent meal in a week, but eventually both Williams and Parker were stricken with malaria. They traveled from cave to cave, aided by friendly Greeks, for a total of sixteen days, always striving to reach the south coast of Cos and carrying Williams with them as they went. Finally, after many disappointments, they made contact with the Special Boat Squadron and left the island by boat at dawn on October 26, finally reaching Casteloriso on November 4. From here they were flown to Alexandria.

Of their original detachment of 123 officers and men, 98 were taken prisoner, and 8 had been killed, 3 were reported as missing, and only 16 survived to return to their squadron. Much the same fate befell No. 2901 Squadron and the Durham Light Infantry. When the latter finally mustered at Geneifa Infantry Base Depot in Egypt, it amounted to 9 officers and 120 other ranks—all the rest had been lost.

The pilots of No. 74 Squadron who had escaped by sea eventually reached sanctuary at Kefalcha on the Turkish coast, where they joined up with Corporal Neal and Leading Aircraftman Harris of No. 2901 Squadron.

These two men—after sailing their makeshift raft for four hours, during which time they had been illuminated by aircraft dropping flares—reached the neutral coast and joined up with a larger party of the Durham Light Infantry that had come ashore earlier. They stayed with these troops until dawn on the fifth, and then with nine soldiers they boarded another rowboat and proceeded along the coast to a small bay, where they landed. Here Turkish soldiers discovered them and took them to a police station, where they found Norman and Bates of No. 74 Squadron and Alderman and Kelly of No. 2901 Squadron. Their Turkish captors did not interrogate them and seemed puzzled about just what to do with them

Eventually they were sent off in another rowboat to Bodrum, where they boarded the *HSL 1602*, an RAF high-speed rescue launch. At five knots and running on only one engine, it set off for Casteloriso. The voyage took two days, during which time the launch was forced to hide up in a small cove to avoid the unwelcome attention of a force of German landing craft. On arrival at Casteloriso, the launch picked up supplies and then proceeded to Paphos, where the four airmen reported to Pilot Officer Grey of No. 2924 Squadron. They were then sent to Lakatamia, where they finally rejoined the remnants of their units. Norman and Bates were flown to Aboukir in a Cant 506 to report to No. 219 Group headquarters.

De Pass, Maxwell, and Harris of No. 7 Squadron eventually left Casteloriso, where they had arrived in *HSL 2517*, also bound for Paphos. Other members of the squadron, including the commanding officer, continued the fight on Simi until the ninth, when they too were pulled out. The CO and his party left Cape Alepo and sailed down the coast to Marmaris. On October 10, this group called at Antifli and picked up some other men from Simi including thirteen Italians They all eventually reached Cyprus on the thirteenth. Of No. 7 Squadron's pilots and ground staff, all the officers were reported safe by October 7, except the unit's doctor, Captain Rocher, while fifteen other ranks were unaccounted for.

Others had doubly fortunate escapes, such as the Roman Catholic chaplain, Rev. R. Anwyl, who told us: "Just before Cos fell—I think only the day before—I meant to catch a plane [a seaplane] for Cos, where our Durham Light Infantry were. Through wrong information, I missed the plane, which was attacked on the way and, I was later told, crashed, with no survivors. I was believed to be on the plane by those concerned, and I was reported killed, though in fact I had returned to the center of Leros island."

The CO of No. 74 Squadron, "Spud" Hayter, with Squadron Ldr. John Morgan of 33 Sector Ops, Wilson, and John Lewis, took to the hills on the morning of the invasion and spent the whole day trying to find out what was going on. They visited several empty Greek farmhouses for food and water and watched the shelling of Cos town. On the fourth, they made for the south coast and were almost caught by a German patrol. The following day, a shepherd befriended them and led them to water. Hayter also obtained an axe and used it to kill a sheep, which provided them with food for the next two days. With the aid of some youths, they constructed a small raft, but on October 6, they were found by the SBS, which informed them that they could be taken off the following night by caique. They also linked up with two other small parties, five men of the Durham Light Infantry and Blythin, Fox, and Hubble, airmen of their own group. They all went aboard the caique, which arrived at 0200, and then transferred to another small boat. After a three-day-and-night journey hugging the Turkish coast they finally reached Casteloriso. There they met the survivors from Simi, where there had been some hard fighting.

Thus the British came home from Cos.

The OKW Diary reported tersely on October 4: "Cos occupied. 600 English prisoners and 2,500 Italian. Forty guns and twenty-two partly destroyed aircraft captured."

Later these figures were adjusted, and the final tally of prisoners put "in the bag" by the Germans on Cos was 1,338 British and 3,145 Italians. The Germans also captured forty artillery guns, sixteen antiaircraft guns, the abandoned *LCT-3*, a dozen armed fishing boats, and eleven undamaged Allied aircraft. To this booty could be added huge quantities of fuel, ammunition sufficient to equip a fighting force of 5,000 men, and food the like of which the Germans had not seen in months.

But what was not initially revealed was that only 85 men of *Kampfgruppe Müller* had become casualties during the two days of operations, and of this trifling number, just 15 were killed. Cos fell in a day, to be sure, but most of its British defenders have little for which to reproach themselves. They had fought hard and well for as long as was possible. Their efforts were in vain and tarnished by a large number who lamentably failed to do their duty and surrendered without a fight at the first opportunity or headed for the docks. For these latter, their lack of stomach for the fight availed them nothing, as most were captured before they could embark and flee to safety. The truth was that they had never had a chance. Those who had ordered them to "improvise and dare" from afar had not backed up their stirring words with sufficient arms, equipment or anything else; and the commander in chief in the Middle East had perforce to gamble away his best men on a forlorn hope.

The British who survived, either by escape or as prisoners of war, were the more fortunate ones. The trusting Italians, who had thrown in their lot after heady promises of British aid, now found themselves abandoned by all.

Some men of the lookout post at Cape Foca captured by the Germans on the morning of the third did manage to escape to Turkey, but very few others escaped from the island. In the eyes of the British, they were expendable; in the eyes of the Germans, they were traitors to the Axis. The Italian officers who had fought their units with valor against the German invasion forces were summarily executed by firing squads. They were taken in groups on the mornings of the fourth, fifth, and sixth to the beach near Linopoti and shot. In all, Col. Felice Leggio, the garrison commander, and 89 other officers were executed.

A similar fate befell the 350-odd Italians on neighboring Pserimos after X1 patrol of the Long Range Desert Group, commanded by Capt. R. A. Tinker, a New Zealander, was pulled out to Kalymnos on October 4, with the loss of just one man. Three days later, the men of the III/440 landed unopposed and took over the island as a forward base.

The loss of Cos should have been a final warning to those who controlled the destiny of the British venture in the Aegean that the Germans meant business, and with the loss of its last fighter airstrips, little could be done to maintain Britain's position there. But that warning was not taken. "In the Aegean, the Germans—who never expected to win—won because having gained an initial advantage they exploited it with a boldness and sense of purpose which was conspicuously lacking in their opponents."

That lack of purpose and resolve was now to lead to even greater disasters.

Destroyers of the Royal Navy bore the brunt of the sea war in this campaign as in so many others. Here HMS *Pathfinder* is shown closed up at action stations with an air raid pending. CAPTAIN C. W. MALINS

Pilots of 74 Squadron RAF relax briefly in the orange groves between raids on Cos.
SQUADRON LEADER DOUGLAS TIDY

The crew of the German patrol boat *LS-5* on Cos after their vessel had been strafed by the RAF and driven ashore. FRANZ SELINGER

Germans invaders in the Aegean in their makeshift troop carriers. KEYSTONE

The landing barge *F-352* in the Aegean. BIBLIOTHEK FÜR ZEITGESCHICHTE

Drops of supplies and paratroops tipped the scales in favor of the Germans.
The slow, vulnerable Ju52s operated with great success. FRANZ SELINGER

In this water-bound campaign, the Arado 196 floatplane proved invaluable to the Luftwaffe. FRANZ SELINGER

A German Siebel ferry—an MFV—loaded with guns and tractors. BIBLIOTHEK FÜR ZEITGESCHICHTE

British prisoners of war on Cos being marched away. BIBLIOTHEK FÜR ZEITGESCHICHTE

The last British defenders of Cos rounded up. BIBLIOTHEK FÜR ZEITGESCHICHTE

The influence of the Luftwaffe was the deciding factor: Ju88s unload their cargo over Leros. FRANZ SELINGER

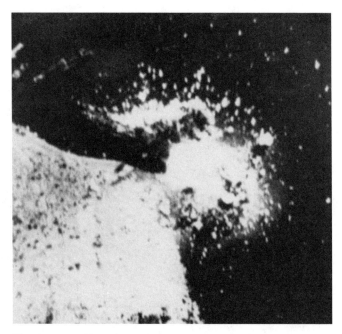

The destroyer HMS *Intrepid*, damaged in an earlier attack on Leros, is hit again and destroyed. FRANZ SELINGER

Paratroop-carrying transports fly over a German caique on the way to Leros.
FRANZ SELINGER

German submarines operated but without much success. This U-boat is returning to
Salamis from an Aegean patrol. FRANZ SELINGER

The ex-Italian destroyer *Calatafimi* serving with the German Navy.

Destroyers of the German invasion force pound the Allied defenses as the invasion of Leros gets under way. FRANZ SELINGER

A German transport loaded with guns, trucks, and material slipping across the Aegean. BIBLIOTHEK FÜR ZEITGESCHICHTE

The German minelayer *Drache* loaded with troops bound for Leros.
BIBLIOTHEK FÜR ZEITGESCHICHTE

The auxiliary UJ-2104. BIBLIOTHEK FÜR ZEITGESCHICHTE

An armed caique and an ex-Italian destroyer supporting the German invasion of Leros. FRANZ SELINGER

UJ-2109, formerly HMS *Widnes*, lying off Santorin. BIBLIOTHEK FÜR ZEITGESCHICHTE

By a combination of skill, luck, and audacity, the German invasion forces crossed the Aegean with little loss. FRANZ SELINGER

The victor surveying the spoils: Lieutenant General Mueller in Leros town,
December 1943. ULLSTEIN

German troops push forward over the difficult terrain of Leros.

British, Indian, and Italian POWs at Port Laki, Leros, with the German destroyer *TA-16* behind. BIBLIOTHEK FÜR ZEITGESCHICHTE

British troops assembling for the surrender of Leros. BIBLIOTHEK FÜR ZEITGESCHICHTE

The Greek destroyer *Adrias,* which succeeded in reaching Alexandria after losing most of her bows. BIBLIOTHEK FÜR ZEITGESCHICHTE

All quiet again: German troops on Samos in December. The Turkish mainland can be seen in the background. BIBLIOTHEK FÜR ZEITGESCHICHTE

A Lockheed P-38 Lightning leaving the runway. U.S. AIR FORCE

CHAPTER SEVEN

Simi Lost; Leros Reprieved

The Germans were surprised at the ease with which Cos had been taken and were now prepared to take immediate steps to mount an offensive against Leros. Some of the surprise at the ease of their victory might have been because the Germans overestimated the British defenses. Churchill disparaged the Durham Light Infantry (DLI) when the island fell, saying, "Cos fell after unsatisfactory resistance," but the late Jeffrey Holland gave us a different viewpoint as one of the men on the spot: "I think Churchill's reference to the DLI on Cos is really disgusting. What could a single battalion do on an island thirty miles long? I am afraid it is also true to say the 234 Brigade was not well trained. It had been rotting away on Malta for three years, yet *Das Signal* for January 1944 stated, 'The British selected for the defence of Leros a Brigade which was expert in fortress defence.' Nice of them to say so, but just not true."

But the Allied setback on Cos had initiated a more realistic policy by the Allies and heralded the arrival of large naval reinforcements, together with the temporary allocations of long-range, twin-engine Lockheed P-38 Lighting fighter squadrons from North Africa; this new development was to make the next stage of the German buildup a much more hazardous operation.

General Müller, GOC 22nd Division on Crete, signaled a report detailing the ease of the victory on Cos early on October 5 (JP6292), and the same day he transmitted a second in which he mentioned landing craft being sent to Syros, midway between Athens and Leros, "in view of future operations" (JP6352). The British read these signals via Ultra, giving them ample notification that the Germans were going to finish the job as soon as they were ready. If any further doubt about their intent remained, the measurable increase in air activity from 100 sorties a day in August to 200 in September to 300 by October should have been a plain enough indication.

With the arrival of the naval reinforcements, the British hoped to maintain a nightly patrol in the Aegean of at least one cruiser and two destroyers. Intensive patrolling by the naval striking forces and RAF and American bombers began almost at once, even though a Photo Reconnaissance Unit flight by Spitfires of No. 80 Squadron had, on October 4, revealed that *Luftwaffe* strength was still being increased. Seventeen Ju 87s and Me 109s had arrived at Maritza on Rhodes. The torpedo-carrying Wellingtons of No. 38 Squadron were engaged on regular nightly sweeps in search of German shipping, backing up the patrols being carried out by the navy's cruisers, destroyers, and submarines. By day, the Germans tended to lie up among the islands, but even so, the numerous sweeps conducted by Allied strike aircraft from North Africa and Cyprus made their hasty scurryings from inlet to inlet a chancy affair.

After the vigilant men of T1 Patrol on the island of Kithnos reported the passing of a German convoy on the night of October 6, it was sighted again at 0415 on the seventh to the southwest of Amorgos by the submarine *Unruly*, under Lt. J. B. Fyfe. The force had sailed from the Piraeus the previous night and consisted of the small merchant ship *Olympus* (852 tons), laden with ammunition and war materiel, and six MFPs, escorted by *UJ-2111*, an armed trawler, under *Oberleuntant zur See* Schunack. The ships were carrying the XI/999 Battalion, bound for Cos. These men were to garrison the island in place of the first line troops who were already there.

First to locate the convoy was the RAF. On the night of October 6–7, six Wellingtons of No. 38 Squadron together with four Hudsons of 459 (RAAF) Squadron were combing the Aegean; at 2236 on the sixth, Flying Off. L. Patterson in Wellington B-Baker sighted a motor vessel of about 3,000 tons in position 37° 08' north 24° 12' east. He telegraphed the sighting for the other aircraft to home in on and commenced his run in at 2300. He launched a single torpedo at his target, but he apparently was sighted, for the ship made a slow turn and the torpedo missed. Patterson then climbed to gain height for a bombing attack, but on doing so lost contact; this he was unable to regain, and the convoy sailed on undisturbed for the rest of the night until sighted by the *Unruly* at dawn.

Now it was Lieutenant Fyfe's turn, and he fired a salvo of torpedoes at 0500. All were misses, but nothing daunted, Fyfe tailed the convoy for another hour, until the bulk of the escorts were unsighted, and then he audaciously surfaced and carried out a brief attack with his 3-inch gun. He reported scoring no less than nine hits on a 1,500-ton merchant ship and three hits on a 500-ton merchant ship. He also scored nine or ten times on three of the Siebel ferries, one or two of which were probably sunk as a result.

Fyfe then took his submarine away from the probes of the escorts by crash-diving, but not before he had sent out a sighting report at 0630. The *Unruly* was hunted later that morning by a force of R-boats, but all their depth charges were a long way off. And by then, the damage had been done: The submarine's signals had been picked up by her big sisters, and the fate of the German ships was sealed.

Several surface striking forces were at sea that night, the largest of which was that comprising the cruisers *Penelope* and *Sirius*, with the destroyers *Faulknor* and *Fury*. These had sailed from Alexandria at 1100 on the sixth, sweeping toward Scarpanto Straits. They now steered toward *Unruly*'s position, and at 0830, they came upon the straggling convoy, which by then was down to some four small transports, several armed trawlers, and six F-lighters. With gun, torpedo, and ram, the British ships soon created havoc among the defenseless ships, and within a short time, they had sunk or set fire to all of them except for one of the F-lighters, which managed to scurry behind an island and evade detection. The massacre left more than 400 German troops dead or drowning in the water, while all the equipment went to the bottom of the sea. Only one damaged barge and one of the little escorts, also heavily on fire, eventually limped away. Both of these could only reach the island of Stampalia where they were captured by one of the British patrols. The eighty sailors and soldiers who stumbled ashore here far outnumbered the British garrison, but they were in no mood to resist and were all taken prisoner. Also captured were two field guns and three trucks.

For the navy, this was a gratifying success after several weeks of fruitless patrolling, and the naval squadron, which had far exceeded the time that was normally considered safe in these waters, now turned its bows south and set course to clear the Scarpanto Straits. It was known that the *Luftwaffe* had been alerted, and in these waters, the old memories of Crete were only too fresh. This time, however, the ships had the resources of the long-range fighters to call upon, and detailed plans had been made to provide them with continuous air cover during their withdrawal. Both Beaufighters from Cyprus and Lightnings from North Africa were on call.

Heavy air attacks developed almost immediately, while the force was still deep in the Scarpanto Straits. Throughout the morning, Junkers Ju 88s and Ju 87s from Crete and Rhodes kept up heavy and sustained attacks.

"We literally screamed for help on the W/T [wireless telegraphy]," recalls Stan Hollet, who was serving aboard the *Faulknor*, and initially that help was forthcoming. Eight Lightnings, P-38Gs, were the first of the promised air cover to be sent out from Gambut to protect the ships, code-named Nostril Force. These aircraft, from No. 71 Squadron, U.S. 12th Fighter Wing, flew a direct route from the base to the Kasos Straits. They sighted the two cruisers and two destroyers at 1030, when they reported their position as being about twenty-five miles northwest of the Scarpanto Straits, steering north by northwest so as to join forces with the destroyers *Rockwood* and the Greek *Miaoulis*. These ships had left Casteloriso on the sixth for a patrol to the north of Rhodes during the night of October 6–7. The old lesson of concentrating the maximum firepower against air attack had not been forgotten, and the two Hunts duly joined up at 1055. The whole squadron now turned south by southeast at high speed, with the eight Lightnings still in contact overhead.

For an hour, from 1030 to 1130, the radar screens remained clear, then *Sirius* picked up the telltale blip of a formation coming in from the southwest, from the direction of Rhodes. The Lightnings were vectored out to intercept. The Americans picked up the German formation heading west at a point some ten miles northwest of Scarpanto Straits, flying at a height of between 6,000 and 7,000 feet. It consisted of five Ju 88s, one Me 109, and one Fw 190. One flight of Lightnings immediately made two attacks on the bomber group, Major Haynes intercepting the Ju 88s some ten miles south of the warships. The second flight of four, led by Lieutenant Taylor, made an attack from above and directly ahead. The Junkers made no evasive turns; they seemed to have been taken by surprise; although one of them opened fire at extreme range. It was ineffective. For a quarter of an hour, the big American fighters tore into the Junkers, and as a result, three of them jettisoned their bombs. One was hit and crashed into the water, its crew bailing out, while another lagged behind the fleeing formation, trailing black smoke from one engine.

It was a highly successful first combat, and the navy signaled its gratitude. After this sharp action, the Lightnings returned to provide cover for the warships, but soon afterward, Lieutenant Taylor reported that his machine was losing fuel, and he was detached to Cyprus with a wingman as escort. The two German fighters now appeared, climbing up from 4,000 feet, and Major Haynes and two wingmen turned to attack them. Discretion being the better part of valor, the Germans withdrew—or in the words of the Mission Report, "They hit the deck and headed for Rhodes!" Meanwhile, another large formation of German aircraft was picked up by radar. The Lightnings were informed, but by this time they were all running short of fuel and had to withdraw to Nicosia. On arrival, Major Haynes found that Lieutenant Taylor had succeeded in getting back but had been forced to crash-land.

A second mission of eight Lightnings had meanwhile left Gambut at 0840, but they were unable to locate the ships. At 1040, the British ships were contacted by wireless and asked for a vector but no reply was received. At this time the ships were not actually under attack, so the reason was probably telegraph failure. The Lightnings flew as far north as Nisyros Island between 1025 and 1105 at 10,000 feet. At 1140, while they were over the east coast of Rhodes, they sighted two German fighters heading northwest but observed no other enemy activity. The Lightnings eventually landed at Nicosia at 1235.

The American Lightnings worked their escort sorties on a rota basis to a timetable and with a series of map references, which allowed the British force to steer only a set course and at a prearranged speed. Thus when the ships turned back, this tight schedule was thrown out—and more drastically so when the existing air escort had to return to base before the relief air group arrived. Radio silence could be broken only in an emergency, by which time it was too late, for the Germans were right on top of the naval squadron's track.

This lack of contact was reported by all the other Lightning sorties flown during the morning, and thus the ships were without air cover during the most critical period. Six Lightnings left Gambut at 0920, one returning with radio failure, and they patrolled between 1045 and 1115 to the south of Rhodes. No contact was made with the warships and the only activity reported was eight Mitchells heading into the area from North Africa. Likewise the fourth mission, eight aircraft, which left Gambut at 1000, arrived south of Rhodes at 1125 and searched until 1330 without result. The final group of Lightnings sent out by the 1st Fighter Group also had an abortive mission, all eight aircraft arriving in the area between 1200 and 1400 hours without seeing or hearing either the ships or the enemy.

During this period, the Lightnings had made contact only with the Ju 88s and these they had easily repelled. It was the arrival of the 1st Group, *Stukageschwader* 3's Stukas over the warships that caused concern. Despite an intensive barrage thrown up by the ships, the dive-bombers broke through time and time again, and all the ships were near-missed. The only brief contact the ships had with the fighter defenses after the departure of Major Haynes's force at 1440 was the appearance at 1130 of two Beaufighters piloted by Miller and Hay of No. 630 Squadron, who located the ships while they were southbound in the Scarpanto Strait. Contact was made and *Sirius* vectored the Beaus out to intercept a raid incoming from Rhodes. The two fighters orbited the ships warily, keeping out of range of their guns, for they had been heavily fired on when they first put in an appearance. While thus searching for the reported bomber formations, they were jumped by German fighters, Me 109s, and Hay's aircraft was hit. He was forced to ditch into the sea.

Under such a scale of attack, it was inevitable that the warships would eventually be hit, and it was the *Penelope* that was finally both hit and near-missed in an attack by eighteen Stukas. The bomb, estimated at 250 kilograms, hit her on the upper deck, port side, abreast of Y turret. It penetrated diagonally forward, piercing the lower and platform decks and breaking up on the port outer shaft. By a stroke of luck, it failed to explode; if it had, the cruiser undoubtedly would have been brought to a standstill, and in these dangerous waters, she then would have been in serious trouble As it was, it left a hole four by two feet in the upper deck, which caused flooding and resulted in a four-degree list to port. This was immediately corrected by counterflooding.

At the same time, two direct-action fused 500-kilogram bombs near-missed the ship. One exploded in the water only twenty-five feet to port of Y turret. The Stukas invariably attacked in a power-dive from astern, and splinters penetrated the hull and superstructure causing severe damage over a wide area and cutting power to the 4-inch main antiaircraft guns, radar warning equipment, and 6-inch barrage director, as well as minor fires. This in effect crippled the *Penelope*'s after antiaircraft defenses. The second bomb detonated seventy-five yards to port abreast the foremast, causing serious splinter damage to the bridge and foremast. The fighting efficiency of the cruiser had been seriously impaired, and owing to fuel contamination, she had to make a temporary reduction of speed, although she was later able to work up to twenty-two knots.

She received a brief respite when at 1400, eight Lightnings from Gambut made contact with the ships, which were then still about 100 miles northwest of their supposed position, but the Lightnings were able to stay overhead for only half an hour. The rendezvous with the two Hunts had cost the squadron dear, for none of the other Lightnings from a further four patrols, each of eight aircraft, that were sent out during the afternoon could locate the warships

At 1800, the *Rockwood* and *Miaoulis* were detached to Limassol, and the *Penelope*, *Sirius*, *Faulknor*, and *Fury* set course for Alexandria, where they arrived on October 8. The *Penelope* was out of action for three weeks while partial repairs were carried out. She was the sole casualty, although all the other ships of the squadron had some close shaves.

Unhappily, the experience of this naval squadron was not to be an isolated one, and the whine and howl of the Stukas again began to assume a significance that many people had hoped was something safely in the past. While the Nostril force was still withdrawing on the seventh, another force sailed from Alexandria that morning on a similar mission. Code-named Credential, the force consisted of the antiaircraft cruiser *Carlisle* and the destroyers *Petard* and *Panther*. They were to rendezvous south of the Scarpanto Straits with the Hunt-class destroyers *Aldenham* and *Themistocles* (Greek), which were coming from Limassol. The combined force had orders to make a sweep through the Scarpanto Straits that night and retire to the southeast of Rhodes during the day. The sweep was carried out as planned but nothing was sighted.

The *Carlisle*, under Capt. H. F. Nalder, and her destroyer force retired as planned during the daylight hours of the eighth. The two Hunts were detached to Alexandria, and two others from Limassol, the *Rockwood* and *Miaoulis*, took ther places. During this time, both of the retiring forces received air support from the Lightnings, but again only a few patrols made contact. Eleven Beaufighters were also assigned by the RAF in Cyprus for this duty.

The first two American missions, each of eight aircraft, took off from Gambut at 0750 and 0820 on the eighth for Operation Credential and carried out a patrol south of Rhodes without success. A third group of eight aircraft took off at 0905 and found the British ships at 1110, covering them until 1145. Their relieving group failed to make contact, and it was not until 1320 that the fifth group managed to locate them, some sixty miles west of their plotted position heading northeast. Cover was provided from 1320 to 1345, when the Beaufighters took over. Fortunately the Germans did not sight Credential on its second inward passage.

Intelligence at Alexandria was full of reports of German shipping movements and the invasion of Leros was seriously expected to take place that night, October 8–9. Maximum effort was made against the German installations on Cos in an attempt to delay the enemy buildup. Included in this effort were several of the Lightning squadrons, which during the day made ground strafing attacks on the Cos airfields. The reason for Credential's immunity during the day became clear when reports were received that upward of forty Ju 88s and thirty Stukas had been carrying out heavy attacks on the Leros defenses.

This seemed to confirm the invasion scare. On this day also came sightings of an enemy convoy at sea. Six Lightnings were up at midday for a sweep over the Leros area. They flew from Gambut to Gaidauronesi island and then on to the Kasos Straits and Kalymnos. From here they patrolled over Leros. During their mission, they reported sighting a large landing craft heading for Kalymnos from the direction of Pserimos island, and a further three small landing barges were seen about 200 yards offshore, west of Scala town. They encountered no German aircraft.

A further sweep was made by eight machines, which arrived over Leros to provide cover at 1545. They orbited at 15,000 feet and at 1600 reported sighting a number of landing craft and then a whole German convoy consisting of four destroyers, a transport, and a cruiser, probably the minelayer *Bulgaria*. A single Ju 88 was in the air over the convoy, and as they watched, it flew over Leros town and carried out a bombing attack. The Lightnings moved to intercept, and two further Ju 88s were seen, as well as a Heinkel

He 111 toward the rear of the German convoy. All the German aircraft were flying at 4,000 to 5,000 feet. One Ju 88 was reported as being brown, the other two dark green. As the Lightnings attacked, the bombers drifted over the convoy for protection. The Lightnings followed them, and the German ships opened fire; the flak was reported to have been too light and inaccurate to bother the American pilots much.

One Ju 88 was hit, with large pieces flying off it, and crash-landed alongside the ships; another was damaged. Forced to break off the action because of a lack of fuel, the returning flight was heavily fired on by flak from Kalymnos island. A third, similar mission also reported five small ships off Leros but no enemy aircraft.

The convoy sighted by the Lightnings included the minelayers *Drache* and *Bulgaria*, which had left the Piraeus on the seventh and were engaged in transporting the troops of X/999 Battalion to reinforce the German garrison on Cos. At 2030 that evening, the *Unruly*, having been instrumental in the destruction the previous day of another battalion of that unfortunate regiment, was now to decimate this one. Lieutenant Fyfe had trailed the convoy for some time, and now he fired a full four-torpedo salvo at it. He was rewarded with one hit, and the 1,108-tons *Bulgaria* blew up and sank in less than a minute off Amorgos Island. She took with her 185 soldiers and many of her crew. The *Unruly* escaped unharmed.

Meanwhile, Credential Force had reentered the Aegean at dusk on the eighth. It was sent farther north than was usually thought safe to patrol off the western coasts of Cos and Leros in an endeavor to intercept the expected German invasion craft. But the Germans were not yet ready to carry out an assault on Leros, and the British ships sighted nothing at all. At 0515 on the ninth, Captain Nalder signaled, "All quiet so far. Am now withdrawing."

Some two hours later, the *Carlisle* reported that she was withdrawing at twenty-three knots, course 174 degrees. Then came a long silence.

In fact, the force had been sighted by the *Luftwaffe* while it was still deep within the danger zone, and the Germans had been shadowing it from 0750. The British laid on strong Lightning cover, and No. 12 Fighter Wing mounted the first sorties. This time the Lightnings all homed in on the naval squadron and provided amost continuous cover throughout the early hours. As a result, no move was made by the Germans, save for constant shadowing.

The Germans had studied reports on the previous operations and were quite sure that if they bided their time, there would come a period when the ships would be left without cover. It was obviously suicidal to sent the slow-moving Stukas out in the face of the powerfully armed Lightnings, so the German commanders on Rhodes plotted the squadron's course south by southeast and waited their chance. For a while it seemed as if it would not come.

The usual eight-plane formation had taken off from Gambut at 0737, but two lost formation and another developed a rough engine and had to return to base early; the remaining five made contact with the *Carlisle* at 0850, when the ships were reported as being some twenty-five miles off the western tip of Kalymnos. They kept watch until 1010, flying at 9,000 feet while the ships maintained a course of 190 degrees. When this group had to leave, the British squadron was near the northern tip of Scarpanto island.

The second formation had taken off from Gambut at 0810, and once again three aircraft were forced to turn back, one with a battery silencer burned out, another with an engine cut out, and the last with only half-filled tanks. The remaining aircraft made contact with the ships while the first formation was still in touch at 0945 and covered them until 1105, when the ships were steering 215 degrees through the strait.

For once everything was working like clockwork. At 1010, the third group slotted into the timetable, patrolling at 6,500 feet until 1100. They reported the weather conditions as ⁹⁄₁₀ overcast with broken clouds at 15,000 feet. Some thirty minutes later came the fourth group of six aircraft, which made contact with the ships at 1040, patrolling at 5,000 feet until 1130, and then leaving. There were still no signs of the Germans. It was the same story with the fifth group, which arrived over the ships at 1100 flying at 10,000 feet. There was complete calm and peace as the aircraft circled the speeding ships, still heading on their southeasterly course to safety. They left at 1155. All these patrols had been made by squadrons from the 1st Fighter Group USAAF, and there was a brief gap of some ten minutes before the next squadron arrived, this time from the 14th Fighter Group.

It was this gap that led the Germans to believe that their moment had at last arrived. Soon the whole 1st Group of *Stukageschwader* 3, which had been patiently waiting in Rhodes, bombed up and ready to go, was ordered to scramble. At noon they struck.

Aboard the ships, the fighter-direction units and radar operators were both experiencing troubles. An insufficient number of cuts were being reported from the radar operators, partly due to the land echoes, which blurred the radar scopes.

In the cramped aircraft plotting room aboard the *Carlisle*, the directing personnel had been closed up at their action stations since dawn and were feeling the effects of fatigue and strain. This had been made worse by two factors. First, the covering Lightnings were only intermittently showing their "identification friend or foe" (IFF) signal beacons, a fault always common, and one on which perhaps they did not appreciate the navy's view. Because of this, every formation that arrived over the ships had to be treated as potentially hostile until it could be visually identified or called up. And second, the patrols were changed frequently and, often being out of sight of the ships, had to be positioned by the ships. This meant an excessive amount of wireless traffic, which made it very easy for the Germans to keep track of the squadron's progress.

This anxious work had continued for some five hours, during which no attack had taken place, although it had been expected at any time. The tension thus built up meant that when the Stukas finally did arrive, there was a natural delay in suspecting and reporting a doubtful target as definitely hostile; there had been too many false alarms.

Thus the Stukas arrived overhead without prior warning and commenced their nerve-racking attacks with great accuracy through a considerable antiaircraft barrage put up by the warships. The *Panther*, under Lieutenant Commander Viscount Jocelyn, was struck almost at once by two direct hits and four near misses. She never had a chance. The first bomb struck her just abaft the funnel and penetrated to her keel before exploding, breaking the ship's back; the second hit came almost simultaneously, and the four near misses close alongside finished her off. She sank, with heavy casualties, in two halves.

The bulk of the Stukas naturally concentrated on the largest target, the *Carlisle*, and she too was soon in trouble. Two bombs close together struck her on or near No. 4 4-inch gun, which was completely wrecked, holing and distorting her afterdeck. They were followed, as each Stuka pulled out over the ship from astern, by two other hits almost in the same place from delayed-action fuse bombs, which both penetrated the ship's vitals and exploded underwater beneath her hull. The old cruiser, a 4,000-tonner built in 1918, had her starboard side plating and framing next to the after oil fuel tanks blown in by these explosions; the stern casing was fractured, and the after magazines, oil fuel tanks, and steering compartments were flooded as a result.

On top of these four direct hits, the *Carlisle* was near-missed by two other bombs that fell on her starboard side next to No. 3 gun and level with her after boiler rooms. The starboard tail shaft and propeller were blown off, the port shaft bracket was buckled out of alignment, and her upper works suffered extensive splinter damage. Her high-altitude directors and telegraph equipment were damaged by the shock of the exploding bombs and by cannon shells. A cordite fire was ignited near the remains of No. 4 gun but was brought under control later. The ship was immobilized as a result of the loss of the starboard propeller and the jamming of her steering gear. Only two guns remained in action and casualties were severe.

It was at this point of high drama that the Stukas, settling like vultures over their prey and intent on finishing off the rest of the battered squadron, received a very unpleasant surprise.

At 1205, the seven Lightnings of Major Leverette's unit, the 39th Fighter Squadron, arrived on the scene. They had sighted the Stukas coming in from the direction of Scarpanto, but by the time they arrived, the attack had commenced and the *Carlisle* had already been hit and set on fire. As they maneuvered into position, the *Panther* was bombed and split in two. At this point, ten or so of the Ju 87s had completed their bombing dives and the remainder were forming up overhead. A Ju 88 was also sighted trailing them; it had a blacked-out nose and was probably taking photographs of the attack.

Major Leverette's flight of four dived into the German formation, while Lieutenant Blue's flight of three stayed topside to cover them. On the approach of the Lightnings, the Stukas jettisoned their remaining bombs and made a run for the lower tip of Rhodes island, but diving from 8,000 feet, the P-38s were soon in among them. There followed a whirling stern chase in which the Americans gave the German pilots a taste of what they had been handing out.

At close range, the big Lightnings had a field day. Major Leverette claimed seven Stukas destroyed, Lieutenant Hanna five, Lieutenant Sprinkle three, and Lieutenant Margison one. Another two were claimed as probably destroyed by Lieutenants Sprinkle and Blue. Nor did the solitary Ju 88 escape, for Lieutenant Blue emerged when it attacked the rear man of Leverette's flight and shot it down. Only lack of fuel and ammunition caused the U.S. pilots to break off the massacre. The Lightnings suffered no casualties; one took a cannon shell through a propeller, and another had a narrow escape when the tip of its propeller hit the wingtip of one of the Stukas during combat. The Americans claimed sixteen Ju 87s destroyed and the ships claimed three, but German records list only seven as having failed to return.

Whatever the failings of the earlier missions, with their decimation of 1st Group, *Stukageschwader* 3, in this brief action, the Lightnings had certainly justified their presence. It was undoubtedly the bloodiest nose the *Luftwaffe* ever received in this campaign. If actions of this sort could have been continued, there is no doubt that the use of Lightning fighters would have been a major factor in deciding the course of the campaign. Unfortunately, this was the last mission undertaken by the P-38s, for on this very day they were withdrawn on Eisenhower's orders.

After this battering, the Germans left Credential Force alone for a while. When the next Lightning flight from the 48th Fighter Squadron arrived overhead at 1235, they reported only three Beaufighters in the air. The *Carlisle* was stationary with the destroyers circling around her. The Beaufighters were from No. 252 Squadron, and they reported that while they were climbing to orbit the ships, they were attacked by three Lightnings from above and behind, one Beau being hit and forced to ditch. There is no mention of this in the U.S. Mission Reports, however.

The final group from the 49th Fighter Squadron had taken off from Gambut at 1130, reaching the ships at 1315, and provided cover for thirty minutes. Again, no enemy aircraft were reported except for a solitary Ju 88 circling at a distance, which made off when the Lightnings arrived. Three ships were reported stationary together, while a fourth was circling searching for survivors. They could see the oil slick from the sunken *Panther*, but that was all that remained of this luckless ship. She had been on her first Aegean patrol having arrived at Alexander from the central Mediterranean as a further reinforcement on the seventh and sailing that same day.

Meanwhile, Cmdr. Richard Egan of the *Petard* and Captain Nalder were assessing the situation. By excellent seamanship, Lt. S. Lombard-Hobson of the *Rockwood* got a line aboard the *Carlisle* for towing, and the squadron limped home at twelve knots, arriving at Alexandria at 1415 on the tenth. *Carlisle*'s casualties amounted to one officer and nineteen men killed and seventeen wounded. She was found too badly damaged to be worth repairing and was written off as a total loss. For the *Carlisle*, it was the end of a long, hard haul; this veteran of the disastrous Greece and Crete operations of 1941 and many convoys to Malta would be seen no more plowing through the waters of the eastern Mediterranean. She remained at Alexandria as an immobile base ship for the remainder of the war.

While their comrades had been defending the warships, another eighteen Lightning aircraft from No. 12 Fighter Wing had been sent out on a bombing and strafing mission against Antimachia airfield on Cos. Three of these aircraft were forced to turn back, but the remainder arrived over the island at 1620. The bomb-carrying aircraft went in to attack from 3,000 feet while the other five aircraft allocated as top cover patrolled at 12,000 feet. They made a direct hit on the main building in the barracks area, with five other bombs dropping among the lesser buildings and two more hitting the runway, one of these was observed to burst among four parked Ju 88s on the north-east corner of the strip. The Germans were caught napping by this attack, as everyone who held Antimachia seemed to be, and no flak was encountered.

All fifteen Lightnings got back to Gambut at 1812, one belly-landing. Not so fortunate were their compatriots who had sortied out earlier. On return to Gambut all these many aircraft had found their base "weathered out" by severe sandstorms. They had flown to the limit of their endurance in covering the ships, and all were very low on fuel. Diverted to alternate strips, these magnificent aircraft were in some trouble and two had to make crash landings. The first flights got down in low visibility, but Flight Officer Mimms crashed on landing and his aircraft was burned out. Another crash-landed in the desert some thirty miles southwest of Sidi Barrani. Five others actually landed at Sidi Barrani, and many more at Mersa Matruh. It was a bad end to a good day for the American pilots. And with their departure from the scene, the *Luftwaffe* was to dominate the sky once again.

⊷ ⚭◊⚮ ⊶

Meanwhile, skirmishes were being hard fought for the possession of the lesser islands. When Hitler had ordered the holding of the "Iron Ring," he had not meant this as a purely defensive strategy and the easy conquest of Cos had led to the German High Command (OKW) to rethink how to throw the British out of the remaining islands. On the sixth, they listed their revised plans and objectives, which included the occupation of Scarpanto, Melos, Leros, Samos, Chios, Mytilene, and Lemnos, with Leros as their main objective. The speed with which all these objectives could be attained depended largely on the amount of shipping that could be made available to transport the combat units forward; the OKW reported at this time that the total amount available to them in the Adriatic and the Aegean was only some 170,000 tons—including some 51,000 tons captured from the Italians. Nevertheless, *OB Süd-Ost* made the following plans for offensive operations after Cos had fallen.

In readiness for the projected operations, radio stations were to be set up on Naxos and Simi. The *Luftwaffe* was to prepare the way for the assault in the usual manner, with systematic bombing of all strong points followed by saturation raids in waves. X/999 was to lead the first wave ashore on Leros itself, and this operation was code-named Leopard. *Kampfgruppe Müller* was not to be allowed to rest on its laurels: once Leros had been won, its next objective would be Samos, and another plan was prepared for this, Operation Poseidon. These operations were now put in hand, but the Germans were to face an unexpected delay in the setting up of the required radio station on Simi.

Lapraik's SBS on Simi had been using its time to build up the island as an offensive base, and he had also organized a patrol flotilla of six caiques to send his men into enemy-held islands. Lieutenant Simpson had taken one such patrol across to Scarpanto and rescued the crew of a British aircraft stranded there, while Lieutenant Lassen had landed on the tiny island of Calchi and so terrorized the twelve unfortunate Italian carabinieri there that they declared themselves ready to die for their country. And indeed this they later did, though with what strategic result is not known; they built

barricades and machine-gun positions, and the SBS landed stores and
equipment for them.

While the fight for Cos was in progress, Lapraik, who had received no
information, went in to see how the fighting was going. As it was obvious
that the Germans were in command, he hastily came out again. En route
back to Simi he ran into a party of No. 74 Squadron ground crew on their
way in to Cos, quite unaware of the state of affairs. These men he brought
back to Simi. Flight Lt. Robert Ferris described the adventures of this party:

> At dusk we embarked on a French destroyer [actually a sloop] from
> Haifa and sailed for Casteloriso. We arrived in the afternoon of the
> following day and found that no arrangements had been made to
> receive us. No means of transport for the next part of our voyage
> was available so we were accommodated for the night in a school,
> which served as a transit camp, but was not equipped as such. Late
> in the afternoon of the following day we embarked on a caique
> manned by a Greek crew of five, taking with us a very small amount
> of maintenance and medical equipment as we had been cut down
> to an absolute minimum. We left Casteloriso at night and our
> course took us along the coast of Turkey, through the Rhodes
> Straits towards the Island of Simi. In conference with the captain of
> the caique we had decided to put in here for four or five hours in
> order to arrive at Cos at dawn the next morning.
>
> As we approached the entrance to the harbour, we were fired on
> by rifles and a 20-mm cannon, fortunately, no one with hit, and we
> made our way to the quayside, accompanied by another caique,
> which had come out to investigate us. On landing, we were met by
> Major Lapraik, a Special Boat Squadron officer who was in com-
> mand of the island. The garrison consisted of approximately 30 Spe-
> cial Boat Squadron men and 100 Italians. Our detachment arrived
> as a welcome reinforcement to this inadequate force, and after a
> quick meal the men were detailed to duty at the various places. Sick
> Quarters was established in a house near General Headquarters.

It was now obvious that the island of Simi was in a dangerously exposed
position and that it was only a matter of time before the Germans moved in.
Force headquarters on Leros therefore instructed Lapraik that should the
enemy land in force, they were to be resisted only sufficiently to inflict casualties upon them; on no account were his highly trained men to be thrown
away in a last-ditch stand for a valueless rock. This order from headquarters
was evidently different from that given in the Levitha fiasco a week later.

Jock Lapraik's garrison now numbered some 220 men: 140-odd Italians, 40 airmen of No. 74 Squadron, and 27 men of the SBS, and a dozen of the LRDG under Capt. Alan Redfern. To the new arrivals, Lapraik issued the following Order of the Day:

> For the benefit of the RAF. As you have recently arrived in this area you are naturally unaware of the military situation in general, and in the island in particular, and consequently your actions seem peculiar under the circumstances. Our situation may be compared with that of Singapore when the Japs were only a short distance away and advancing rapidly, i.e. owing to our great strategic importance there is no doubt whatsoever that we shall be attacked. It is merely a question of whether it is tomorrow, or the next day, or the one after. Let there be no doubt about it, they will come; therefore we must be prepared. Consequently it is essential that everyone be absolutely on their toes 24 hours a day. When a guard is called out it will be in seconds not minutes as was the case last night. When ordered to stand to they will be downstairs and in the bushes like bats out of hell. Everyone must be absolutely on the job all the time no matter what task he is given. We are all doing strange jobs at the moment. We weren't trained as island defenders any more than you were, but we have to carry out the task just the same. When you realize that the next island to this, Cos, has been attacked and almost wound up by the Germans we can understand the gravity of our position so for ——— sake let's get our fingers out and get weaving and we'll show these ———s what we are capable of!

There was much more in the same vein, and it seems to have done the trick. It was issued just in time, for the Germans came at dawn on October 7, but with a party of only forty men. (Some British accounts still claim almost double this number, but German records are quite clear on the matter.) The Germans were from the *Sturmdivision Rhodos*, with Fascist Italian elements, landing from a large caique at first light in Pedi Bay. They had seriously underestimated the number of troops defending the island.

Lapraik had set up a Bren-gun position on School Hill, and Lassen had mounted an old German 20-millimeter gun in the school itself. These all engaged the caique and soon scored hits, but not before the Germans were ashore and making their way up to a ridge overlooking Simi town. Some managed to penetrate to the upper part of the town and started sniping from the houses. Reports were received of landings on other parts of the island, and by 0600 the Italian defenders were falling back before the invaders while their Fascist countrymen called upon them through megaphones to surrender and lay down their arms before they were all killed.

Lassen and the Irish Patrol were therefore dispatched to rectify the situation. Although crippled by a badly burned leg and suffering from internal problems, Lassen stalked and killed at least three Germans and also succeeded in capturing a veteran sergeant who had served in the desert and at Sebastopol, plus a couple of privates. The Italian garrison, aided by Lassen's "advice and backing"—he stood behind them with his gun and refused to let them withdraw any further—soon rallied.

The German invaders were armed only with rifles and automatics, which meant that the few Bren guns the British possessed were invaluable. The guns' smooth working can be attributed in part to Flight Sergeant Schofield, the armorer from No. 74 Squadron on Cos. Lapraik also had sent him for earlier to get a captured Italian Breda into working order. This he did and then adopted it as his own weapon. Positioned above the harbor, Schofield kept his gun firing throughout the attack. He was near-sighted and wore glasses, but even when these were broken by the vibration, the flash eliminator had burned away, and the sights collapsed from the heat of the gun, he still kept it firing.

His gun was in a key position, and when the Germans whistled up a couple of Stukas, Schofield was often the target for their attacks. As well as providing a steady fire, he also risked his life to go down and pull a wounded German soldier to safety. As if this were not enough, he was wounded in the arm but refused to leave his post to have it attended to; it eventually turned septic two days later. A very brave man, making the most of a situation in which he never dreamed he would find himself, Schofield was later awarded the Military Medal, a somewhat unusual decoration for an airman.

In an effort to dislodge the German troops established in the upper town, Lapraik sent in an attack. During the subsequent fighting to establish a Bren gun post on the southern ridge, one man was killed and three others, including Lieutenant Biros, were wounded.

Captain Clynes was now sent to observe and direct frontal fire on the German positions while Stewart Macbeth was sent to Panormiti village with instructions to put in a flanking attack with the Italian troops held in reserve there. By 1300, this was under way. Despite attacks by Stukas, the Germans were forced to continue their withdrawal, and by 1500, they were attempting, in some disorder, to evacuate their wounded and get their men off the beaches.

Eventually the Germans pulled out by boat. By a clever maneuver, one of the Special Boat Squadron caiques forced the schooner carrying the German main party to alter course, bringing the ship into range of the Bren guns on the island. They duly raked it through and through. Apart from the severe casualties aboard the crowded decks of the schooner, the SBS claimed sixteen Germans dead and thirty wounded, with six prisoners. These numbers far exceeded the actual numbers of German troops who landed in the first place and must have included the Italian Fascist elements as well. In addition, a few who had made for the hills were taken by the Greeks, who either shot or decapitated them. The SBS casualties were one killed (Pvt. William Morrison) and three wounded, while the Italians had ten wounded. It was a great little victory for the SBS. Unfortunately, it was to be the only one of its kind.

After this sharp little setback, the Germans decided to form *Küstenschützflotille Dodekanese* and mount guns of the little ships of this flotilla in order to provide covering gunfire for the infantrymen. A second expedition was duly mounted some weeks later, with three times the strength (120 officers and men), but ironically, although this time prepared for death or glory, they found the island deserted.

The SBS and their RAF comrades in arms were not long to enjoy the fruits of victory. Two Stukas came over at two-hour intervals from dawn to dusk and bombed the fortified houses in the village, killing another of the SBS men and twenty Greek civilians. The Bren gunners claimed to have destroyed one of these, but in one of these raids, at midday, Lapraik's headquarters was hit and demolished. Two men were killed and two more trapped beneath the rubble—Cpl. Sydney Greeves with a great weight of debris on his stomach and LRDG Pvt. Langslow Bishop by his foot. Any attempt to extract Bishop intact from this terrible position would have resulted in the bulk of the wreckage falling on Greeves and killing him. It was a ghastly impasse.

The situation was explained to Bishop, and he agreed to the amputation of his foot to save Greeves's life. Flight Lt. R. J. L. "Hank" Ferris, with an American volunteer medic attached to the SBS, Pvt. Porter Jarrell, and then began, in those dreadful conditions, to remove the foot. Ferris had had his medical equipment destroyed and was compelled to work with a pair of scissors and a small wood saw. To get into position, Ferris had to be held upside down by his legs in the dim light of the demolished building. After the foot was amputated successfully, Bishop was removed, but not surprisingly, he died almost at once from the shock and pain.

He died in vain, for his companion, when removed, was also dead. It is difficult to decide who was deserving of the highest praise—Bishop, who had to confront this situation; or Jarrell, who had to explain it to him; or Ferris, who had to operate in impossible conditions—but Jarrell got the George Cross for his work that day.

On the tenth, the Stukas came over again, and orders were received to pull out. The dead and wounded were put on a caique for Casteloriso together with the German prisoners. The RAF men of No. 74 Squadron, who had fought so well in their unexpected role as infantrymen, were also sent back to Casteloriso in another caique on the same day. The withdrawal order given to the Special Boat Squadron was later countermanded, but it was repeated on the twelfth, and Lapraik and his band pulled out.

He was not finished with Simi yet, however. Lapraik was back again within a week to find that the Germans still had not landed there. He made plans, therefore, with Cairo's approval, to set up his raiding base again forthwith.

Meanwhile, the Germans had seized Naxos and other lesser islands from their Italian defenders, and on Kalymnos, the LRDG patrol under Captain Tinker had been pulled out without a fight. They had had a narrow escape earlier. During the Cos invasion, Tinker and twelve others had set off to the island of Pserimos, which lies between Kalymnos and Cos. A mysterious spate of signaling had been seen from this island to the Turkish mainland, and Tinker's men found the man responsible and sent him back to Kalymnos for interrogation. He later turned out to be a Greek agent in British pay!

When the German invasion fleet had arrived unexpectedly off Cos, it had also landed some eighty men on Pserimos to establish wireless telegraphy and dressing stations; this force ran into Tinker's men. The small LRDG force hastily took off into the hills, with the shells of the warships following them, and although they were hunted by patrols, they managed to get back to Kalymnos unharmed. Now they were withdrawn to Leros to await events. The Germans moved in and could now look out over the 2,000 yards of water to Leros, but would they attack?

On October 8, following the annihilation of the convoy by the *Sirius* and *Penelope* and the sinking of the *Bulgaria* by the *Unruly*, the Germans had to defer the planned assault against Leros for twenty-four hours. The continuing nightly presence of British naval forces in the Cos-Leros area threatened the operation with failure, so on the eleventh, General Müller proposed a further adjournment in expectation that the *Luftwaffe* would be able to eliminate the Royal Navy. On the same evening, Gen. August Winter, chief of staff of Army Group E, asked Adm. Werner Lange, the German admiral commanding in the Aegean, whether the German Navy considered it essential that Leros be occupied or whether a further adjournment should be considered. Admiral Lange forwarded this request to Admiral Fricke, naval commander of Group South, who replied that the longer the operation was delayed the more risky it would become. He advocated a short postponement to November 5; by then he would have had time to gather reinforcements and, in particular, crews for the ex-Italian destroyers now in the Piraeus. He did, however, insist that it was necessary to seize Leros in the best interests of the campaign in the Dodecanese.

In a situation report issued on the seventeenth, the OKW revealed that the Germans' heavy shipping losses had led to a serious supply situation that was causing grave concern. In fact, they had seriously considered the complete abandonment of the Leros enterprise.

Two alternatives were put forward as being less costly: an attack on Samos, where the 1,500 Italian Fascists, or Blackshirts, would give them an instantly available reserve of manpower already on the island, or the occupation of the island of Chios to the north. Both the admiral commanding in the Aegean and the *OB Süd-Ost* were for adopting this more cautious plan, but General Loehr was for pressing on with Leopard in its original form, but at a later date. A proposal to deny the use of Turkish territorial waters to British warships was also made, and it was considered essential in order to avoid further serious losses that the British destroyer patrols be stopped.

Hitler soon vetoed this last recommendation; he was all in favor of using strong action against British naval forces, but not at the risk of upsetting the Turks. He had other solutions; the movement of the glider-bomb-carrying Dorniers of *Kampfgruppe 100* was probably what he had in mind on this point. As to abandoning the attack on Leros, he would not hear of it. When the grave shortage of suitable shipping was cited as a reason, he decreed that, following the OKW's request, ferries and lighters from France and F-lighters and their equivalent from the Netherlands should be transported to the Aegean without delay. All small ships now in the Adriatic, he said, were to sail at once for the Aegean. The requirements were for vessels of 1,500 to 2,000 tons, not only for the Aegean, but also in the Black Sea, where the Soviet advance was threatening and which, the Germans were belatedly realizing, constituted their most secure transport route in the area.

So the matter was decided. In furtherance of Hitler's orders, the islands of Calchi and Levitha were occupied on October 18 and 19, and the buildup of forces for the actual assault on Leros was pushed ahead.

CHAPTER EIGHT

"The Wine Dark Sea"

With the decision to abandon the "much-discussed and long-deferred" invasion of Rhodes and the rejection of any move to retake Cos, British strategy was now purely defensive; the wheel had swung full circle. The main preoccupation for the next month was to reinforce the garrisons of Leros and Samos. The long-term hope was to hold on to these two islands throughout the winter and reexamine the possibilities in the spring.

The onus now fell on the Royal Navy, as it had so often before in this war, to carry out a difficult and frustrating task, with limited forces and without satisfactory air cover. The fighting for the next month was mainly the old duel of warships versus aircraft. Vice Adm. Algernon E. U. Willis, who took over from Admiral Cunningham as commander in chief of the Levant on October 15, soon made it clear to the authorities at home what this meant. The naval patrols, he said, could not be continued by day without suffering prohibitive losses.

Unless the *Luftwaffe* could be matched and beaten, the prospects were grim. The RAF was doing all it could, both in maintaining striking forces and in providing the navy with air cover. But as Air Marshal Douglas pointed out, the air strength at his disposal was inferior to that of the Germans, although this was only by a small margin, and what was more vital, the bases from which his aircraft had to operate were too far from the scene for them to be able to make any effective contribution. Douglas concluded that he just could not provide strong enough air cover during the daylight hours to enable the Royal Navy to operate its ships near Rhodes in daylight. This meant, in effect, that the German build up was allowed to proceed by day with a minimum of interference, a situation the Germans duly took full advantage of.

Despite the clear warnings provided by recent events, the navy endeavored for a short while to maintain the pressure of its cruiser and destroyer sorties into the Aegean, while the motor torpedo boats (MTBs) and destroyers operated within Turkish waters. The light forces, destroyers, motor launches, and caiques continued to run in men and supplies to the best of their ability, supplemented by the larger submarines. It was inevitable that

151

such methods would result in only a dribble of the needed reinforcements, and as in the case of Cos, heavy equipment would be sorely lacking.

Adm. "Algy" Willis issued a memorandum on October 17 to the men of the Levant Command to prepare them for the ordeal he knew must lie ahead:

> You are being called upon at the present time to undertake a task that involves a most strenuous routine. The garrisons of Samos and Leros, which include some 2,500 British troops, nearly all of whom are the old defenders of Malta, are dependent very largely on the Navy's efforts. The enemy is collecting a formidable invasion force for use against these islands but this force cannot achieve its object if we maintain in the area a naval force capable of destroying his assault craft and shipping. His own naval forces are insignificant.
>
> The scale of enemy air attack is considerable but by operating at dark, lying up in neutral waters for most of the day, it is hoped that this threat is bearable. Gradually the bombing of enemy airfields is reducing his air potential. His crews are not so well trained or so determined as they used to be and the experiences of the last week have shown that our ships can continue to operate in the Aegean with very little air cover and from time to time damage may have to be accepted.
>
> There is evidence to show that while we are able to maintain naval forces on the present scale in the Aegean the enemy hesitates to launch his invasion. Therefore in the defence of our small garrisons it is essential that we should continue our present operations and endeavor to destroy the enemy's shipping and landing craft until his plans are defeated. The RN has never failed to do its utmost for the British Army in difficult situations and I know it will do it again.

Unfortunately, these sanguine hopes were at that moment being dashed. The previous afternoon a force consisting of the cruiser *Aurora* and the destroyers *Jervis, Penn, Hursley,* and the Greek *Miaoulis* had entered the Aegean, having left Alexandria at 0500. While the Hunts patrolled off the east coast of Kalymnos and Leros, they encountered two E-boats and a sloop off Port Akti, Kalymnos, which they engaged and damaged. Taffrail described this operation:

> It was at 0200 in brilliant moonlight that the two ships moved silently into a narrow cove fringed by steep, tall cliffs. They sighted two E-boats lying close inshore. Opening fire at 600 yards they were

soon hitting and the last they saw of the enemy crews was when they were hurriedly abandoning ship and scrambling ashore. Church [in command of the *Hursley*] next led the way into another small bay, so narrow that there was hardly room to maneuver. It was intensely dark under the shadow of the cliffs, so the *Miaoulis* switched on her searchlight and swept in along the foot of the cliff. There were two more E-boats lying close inshore and they too were fired at and hit. Moving on round the next little promontory they discovered yet another enemy vessel in hiding. Forewarned by the sound of gunfire she was waiting and ready and opened fire as soon as the destroyers appeared too accurately for comfort. The *Hursley* replied hitting with one of her first rounds and then sweeping the enemy's deck with her close range weapons. Before long the enemy's guns were out of action and she was well ablaze. The *Miaoulis* finished her off. German aircraft appeared and made several sharp bombing attacks towards the end of the engagements but both destroyers got away without damage. Some time later as Church said "we heard a colossal explosion in that direction."

The two fleets landed stores at Leros, and so also did the *Aurora* and the Hunts. The force then withdrew through the Kasos Strait and headed toward Casteloriso under constant bombing.

A further naval force consisting of the cruiser *Sirius* with the destroyers *Pathfinder, Eclipse,* and *Beaufort* had been sailed from Alexandria at 0700 on the seventeenth, as reinforcements and the group made a rendezvous with the *Aurora* that forenoon south of Scarpanto Strait. The two cruisers were then to proceed to carry out a bombardment of Cos Harbor. Bombing recommenced and continued throughout the afternoon, and the ships most of the time just had to take it. The sailors had become accustomed to this; Capt. P. W. B. Brooking of the *Sirius* is reported to have heard the following snatch of dialogue between two of his bridge lookouts:

It was the procedure to use two men for this task, one with a pair of binoculars on a gadget, which recorded bearing, and angle of sight while the duty of the second sailor was to report contacts. These lookouts only did twenty minutes on and then changed jobs. On this occasion an old three-badge AB [able-bodied seaman] was on lookout and he had a young ordinary seaman as his mate. The former had been in the Aegean in the days of Crete and was regaling the youngster with gruesome tales of what went on, giving special stress to the punctuality of the Luftwaffe and how they always attacked at the change of watches. After some time the old boy started—with much effect—to inflate his personal life belt. The youngster, by this time thoroughly alarmed asked "Why are you doing that, Jack? Can you see any aircraft?" "No," replied the old hand, "but this is the only bloody air support I'll get in this part of the world."

In fact, when the air attacks started again, the force, code-named Datum, did have the support of four Beaufighters of No. 252 Squadron, which had been vectored out to 8,000 feet to orbit. They sighted six Junkers Ju 88s approaching from the west out of the sun at 13,000 feet in close Vic formation. The time was 1828. The Beaus warned the ships and moved to intercept, but before they could gain sufficient height, the Junkers were already diving onto the squadron; they released their bombs at 6,000 feet and pulled out of their dives at 4,000 to 5,000 feet.

The warships put up a heavy barrage as usual, but this failed to deter the bombers. At 1830, the *Sirius* was hit by a 250-kilogram bomb, which struck the quarterdeck abaft of Y gun. A hole twenty feet in diameter was opened in her upper deck, and the blast and splinters raked the after superstructure. A flash fire was started in the Oerlikon magazines. One 20-millimeter gun was destroyed and the two after 5.25-inch turrets were damaged. In addition, the remaining four bombs of this particular stick all near-missed off the port side of the ship, throwing her over to starboard and putting out of action the torpedo tubes, main aerials, and radar sets, seriously impairing her ability to fight back. Her casualties were fourteen killed and thirty wounded, but her hull was not pierced and she was able to return to Alexandria at twenty knots. Later that month, she sailed for Massawa for repairs.

One of the Beaufighters eventually overtook the retreating German formation and selected the port outside aircraft as his target. He made his approach from the port quarter and opened fire at 300 feet, closing to 200. Hits were observed on the wing and the tail of the Junkers. The Beau then shifted target to the rear starboard aircraft of the Vic, opening fire at 500 feet and closing to 300. The return fire from the powerful bomber was both intense and accurate, and the British fighter was forced to break away. His three companions were also gaining on the enemy when they were recalled by the ships in readiness for the next attack. While the *Sirius* was withdrawing to Alexandria, the destroyers *Eclipse, Pathfinder,* and *Belvoir,* each with forty tons of stores and forty personnel, went on into the Aegean.

Because of the delay caused by the constant bombing, they were unable to land either stores or personnel at Leros that night and proceeded to lie up in Turkish waters during daylight on the eighteenth. Meanwhile, during the night of October 17–18, the *Jervis, Penn, Hursley,* and *Miaoulis* had

Leros

Miles
0   2½

0   1   2   3   4
Kilometres

C.Timari

Partenì Bay

Blefuti Bay

Palma Bay

①

C. Pasta di Sopa

174

M.Viglia
238

②

320

M. Clidi

C. Pasta di Sotto

Grifo Bay

Farinta
256

M.Marcello

284

M.Calagero
199

S.Quirico

×Hospital

Alinda Bay

M.Uplogurna

Conrida

177

64

S.Quaranta

S.Marina

Castello di Bronzi

LEROS

M.Germano ×

105

Kidney

M.Rachi

③ Mt.Appetlci

Gurna Bay

Charing
Cross ×

M.Mera
viglia

Pandeli

⑪

× Windmill

Pandeli Bay

S.Giovanni

145

S.Ncola

M.S.Giovanni

⑤

162

M.Crumidi

▲ 142
PL 248 139

M.Vigla

248

⑧

Gonia
S.Zaccaria

⑥

④

Temenia

M.Patella

⑦

S.Policarpo
228 M.Zuncona

M.Cazzuni

⊚ S.Spirito

Mericcia

Port Laki

S.Giorgio

⑩

M.Tortore
286

PL 250

PL 432

La Madonna

PL 227   P.Cazzuni

⑨ M.Piana
256

M.Scumbarda 327

▪ PL 262

Serraungo Bay

P.Diapori

● ▪ Military strongpoint
● ▲ Batteries & defensive areas
------ Tracks
═══ Roads

E.G.M

emerged from Turkish waters. The two fleets patrolled off the west coast of Kalymnos but sighted nothing. At 2312 on the seventeenth, they carried out a bombardment of Port Kalymnos setting on fire a merchant ship moored alongside the jetty. The two Hunts, after making a recce of Pserimos island proceeded to Cos, where they conducted a ten-minute bombardment of the inner harbor. During the bombardment, the *Hursley* was hit by a 3.9-inch shell, which struck her on the port side just forward of A gun, making a hole four by three feet in her side. They then withdrew north of Rhodes. All four ships together with the *Aurora*, which had been patrolling south of Scarpanto that night, then proceeded to Alexandria, arriving on the eighteenth.

It was at this time that the attitude of the Turks toward this use of their territorial waters by the British became noticeably more difficult, although they never actually took steps to prevent it. In fact, the constant use of neutral waters was to lead to many amusing and complicated situations. On this occasion, as recalled by Lt. Cmdr. C. W. Malins of the *Pathfinder*, they received a signal from the commander in chief telling them to conceal the stores they were carrying while in neutral waters. "A hollow laugh went round the ship. How could you make a jeep look like a boat, or piles of ammunition—on the upper deck!—look like torpedoes? Or, for that matter, forty soldiers look like sailors? I don't think we took this signal very seriously. The weather was hot and we had to let the soldiers come on deck, but the ship's company lent them a cap or two."

As dusk came, the three destroyers left Turkish waters and the two fleets proceeded to Alinda Bay, Leros, where they landed their troops and stores. They then carried out a sweep north of Levitha and Amorgos. Nothing was sighted and the ships then withdrew. While the fleets were thus engaged, the *Belvoir* proceeded to Cos and at 2200 on the eighteenth, she carried out a bombardment of the harbor, setting fire to a petrol dump. The three ships then made a rendezvous and set course for Alexandria.

Also at sea that night were the cruiser *Phoebe* and the destroyers *Fury*, *Hurworth*, and *Beaufort*. This force had left Alexandria at 0630 on the eighteenth. At 0100 on the nineteenth, the Hunts carried out the second bombardment of the night on Cos Harbor. Each ship fired approximately 150 rounds from close range. The *Hurworth* was hit and slightly damaged by return fire from shore. One man was killed and three were injured. At about the same time, the *Phoebe* was carrying out a bombardment of Port Kalymnos and pumped 300 rounds into the harbor with some effect. The *Phoebe* then proceeded to Casteloriso to land stores and then made a rendezvous with the *Hurworth*, and the two ships arrived back in Alexandria on the twentieth. The *Fury* and *Beaufort* lay up in Turkish water to carry out a further patrol on the following night.

After the damage sustained by the *Sirius*, the navy gave up sending the cruisers right into the Aegean, but kept them some distance outside to give the patrolling destroyers what was hopefully termed "radar cover" to direct the Beaufighters during air attacks. As so often before, it was the destroyers that now bore the brunt of these attacks. They eventually adopted a routine that was not to be taken on lightly: "The soldiers would embark in *Pathfinder* during the afternoon," recalls her engineering officer, Cmdr. R. H. Mercer, "and we would steam at fairly high speed throughout the night to arrive in Turkish waters at daybreak."

The pattern was usually for one of the Fleet destroyers—of the *Jervis, Pathfinder,* or *Faulknor* types—to act as leader with a brace of Hunts in company. A cruiser of the 12th Cruiser Squadron would accompany them to the edge of the danger zone and sometimes refuel her smaller sisters at Casteloriso. Just to combat-load these slender vessels, already packed full of fighting equipment and with no space to spare, was a major headache. Between them, Captain Malins and Commander Mercer of the *Pathfinder* provide a very good commentary of what a typical mission was like.

To accommodate the cargo for Leros, we had to train the torpedo tubes on either beam and use the deck space thus provided amidships. When we carried jeeps, trailers, and mountain guns, we landed all the boats, or were supposed to, although I always kept at least a whaler for an emergency. God only knows what we should have done if we had to abandon ship.

Once safely in Turkish waters, the charade would begin with the local guardians. It was on the first trip into Turkish waters that we received the signal to lie up in Turkish waters in order to frustrate the *Luftwaffe* in the daylight. They were then concentrating Stukas in Rhodes. [Of all the aircraft mentioned, this one, regarded as easy meat for fighters, still had an unpleasant surprise for the British with the unsatisfactory antiaircraft weapons they had at the time.] This order came as a complete surprise for us, and we had no idea how we should do this. Entering neutral waters in war was something none of us had ever done before, and a frantic dash was made to find such suitable literature as we had on board to see what the rules were and how we should conduct ourselves in the event. So far as I can recall, we only gleaned the meanest of information and didn't wish to ask Alexandria for more than was necessary. We assumed we should be within the three-mile limit and should, if visited by the Turks, plead a mechanical defect.

This was to become the standard excuse on every occasion, and the Royal Navy obtained quite a reputation for its unreliable machinery at this time. Of course, the Turks knew very well the true situation, but the game still had to be played out.

Under the circumstances, we chose the largest bay we could find with an entrance of three miles width and no inhabitants, since we didn't want to be boarded by the Turks if possible. [On this occasion, the *Pathfinder* lay up in Guvergenik Bay.] We arrived there well after daybreak, with German aircraft shadowing us and watching our every move. On enquiring of the C-in-C how we should conduct ourselves, we were simply and bluntly told that we were not to open fire on enemy aircraft until after they had dropped their bombs. We reckoned it would only take a few hours for the Germans to pass on what we were up to on to Berlin and then knock us off at any time at their leisure. To give ourselves some sporting chance, we did not anchor but steamed slowly round and round the bay, which was a large one, occasionally being sniped at by Turkish soldiers who appeared about midday, in order to have speed available if need be. We had German aircraft constantly in attendance, who flew inland and all around us, all the while keeping at a respectable distance and, of course, flying over Turkish land regardless of its neutrality too!

Here Malins is describing the first sample of Turkish neutral waters; after this, things became more or less routine.

After spending an uncomfortable day in this manner, unable to relax, bathe, or do anything, we fell out of general quarters and hoped for the best and convinced ourselves that the Germans would give us what for, as was their custom, shortly after sunset when we were not strictly within territorial waters. They always preferred to attack in bad light if they could.

Accordingly, at sunset we went to general quarters and prepared for the expected attack from Rhodes, which was only some forty miles away to the southwest.

It was in these tense and expectant circumstances, when they were at full action stations, that a flight of aircraft was reported coming in from the direction of Rhodes. So that there should be no mistake or breaking of the Geneva rules Malins permitted only the director to train on the aircraft and ordered the guns to remain trained fore and aft. The tension was mounting, with everyone without binoculars looking at those who had them, the crew with tin hats and antiflash gear on, holding ammunition in their arms in readiness.

They were all looking at me and wondering just when the old bastard would let them get on with the job in hand, while I attempted to appear calm and collected. I only used my binoculars occasionally; there seemed little point, all was clear to the eye.

After a few minutes of this, I thought I saw the wings of the aircraft, which were adding to the tension by moving damn slowly, fluttering about. It had been a long day and I thought my nerves must be going, so I lit a cigarette. No one spoke and all was absolutely quiet as the ship slowly moved around the bay. After what seemed an age, but was probably only a minute or two, I looked again and for the first time I saw the "enemy" for what they were—a flight of storks, legs and all!

When Captain Malins gave the order, "Relax, relax, relax," he added, "Enemy aircraft are storks." He swears he felt the whole ship lift out of the water as everyone took a deep breath. As was invariably the case at moments like that, someone relieved the tension with a joke. On this occasion, it was the chief bosun's mate, Chief Petty Officer Hughes, the director layer—who, incidentally, had the most powerful binoculars in the ship. The gunnery loudspeaker system was switched on and through the whole ship boomed his observation: "Christ! I knew all my —— sins would come back to me one day."

There was no attack, as Hitler had expressly forbidden any such thing. But on other trips, the *Luftwaffe* adopted the procedure of attempting to provoke the ships into opening fire first, thereby giving them the excuse to bomb at will. They would dive on the ships without releasing their bombs, coming in so low that those on the ships could make out the numbers on their wings, but luckily nobody took a potshot, although it proved a very nerve-racking experience. Later the destroyer anchored rather than continue steaming.

I came to the conclusion that there was no point in steaming slowly around and wearing out my valiant crew, so I anchored. After all, rest is invaluable and the crew might as well enjoy as much of it as they could. The sailors would fish and we may even have slept a bit.

Once the British destroyers took to anchoring, the Turks were always vigilant in coming aboard to check them out—but not for the reasons their commanders might have supposed. Recalls Commander Mercer of the *Pathfinder*:

A boatload of Turkish officers would come on board for breakfast and they were pleased to accept the explanations that we had all entered these waters, yet again, because of mechanical trouble; and I, as the engineering officer, had always previously made certain of this, and the result was conveniently inspected by one of the visitors.

On one occasion, the friendly Turkish officer, who spoke no English, was not in the least bit interested in an open fuel pump the engineer had made ready as in need of repair. All he wanted, he made clear to Captain Malins once the formalities were over, was some tins of marmalade.

After the approach of darkness came the second leg of the journey to Leros itself, usually to Alinda Bay.

At dusk we would weigh anchor and set off for Leros, refueling on the way from *Sirius* or *Dido* or one of the other small cruisers placed strategically en route. At Leros the whole place seemed to be as black as ink, and it was always a sad moment to see our trusting soldiers going over the side to such an inhospitable shore. With one batch of soldiers we landed was a lieutenant RNR. We were amazed to see that included in his baggage was a golf bag and a brand new set of Bobbie Jones steel-shafted clubs. I asked him why on earth was he taking those to Leros and he replied, "Well, you never know, I might get a round." We landed him only a week before the invasion, but he was one of the lucky few to get out, and I met him in Limassol after it was all over, but without his clubs!

In inky blackness, the small ships had to disembark their troops and stores at an island without any real facilities to handle such cargoes.

We used to secure to a small buoy or anchor in Alinda Bay so we could slip quickly if we had to. One always felt a bit naked with lighters alongside—manned by Italians who promptly disappeared when an air raid developed and took hours to find and restart again—and it was no joke trying to fight aircraft one could not see while passing soldiers over the side as fast as possible. No one wanted to hang around very much, and it was amazing how quickly we unloaded in complete darkness. It probably took no more than an hour or so once the Italian lighters had found us in the dark.

We landed all our boats and had a jeep at each davit head with jeep trailers and mountain guns all over the place. I don't remember how we handled the stability problem but seem to remember one was not very keen on using much helm at high speed. We were also very sorry for those soldiers, since we knew in our hearts that they would not be coming home—things looked grim to us and I suppose to them, too. All the same, they went without complaining.

Once the cargo had been disembarked, the ships usually carried out an anti-invasion patrol around the island, then retreated to Turkish waters once more before the trip back to Alexandria or Cyprus. Small wonder that the strain began to tell.

We didn't get much time in harbor in which to relax and get some sleep. This was very evident and as I recall it now, it was only us young COs [aged less than thirty or so] who could actually stand the strain. At least some of our seniors cracked under it.

As losses mounted with little to show for them, even hardier, more aggressive young skippers began, with many of all services, to question the point of it all.

I think it was the morning before we sailed on another of these operations that Algy Willis called a conference of all COs in the Ras-el-Tin canteen, at which he endeavored to explain to us the value and usefulness of all we were so laboriously trying to do. I'm afraid we remained very much unconvinced but overawed by big brass arguments, so didn't put up much objection, though Commodore Agnew of the *Aurora* did make a spirited defense on our behalf. We, having lost Percy Todd, our commander, in the Cos Channel the previous night, did not feel too happy. As the C-in-C left the stage, a voice from the back said loudly, "There you are, chaps; we are now a dwindling company of Cos Channel Steamers." The C-in-C was *not* amused.

Air activity on the British side was constant and not restricted to air cover missions. On the sixteenth, cannon-firing Mitchells shot up an E-boat with their 75-millimeter guns and probably sank a 50-ton caique in the Cos-Kalymnos Channel; the next day, hits were scored on landing craft beached on the north coast of Cos. On the night of October 18, the "heavies" again lent a hand, and Liberators and Halifaxes of Nos. 178 and 462 Squadrons bombed Antimachia airfield, which the Germans were rapidly rehabilitating for their own use.

On the nineteenth, Waters of No. 603 Beaufighter Squadron, together with two Beaus from No. 227, were flying escort for a force of four B-25s. The group was north of Crete and destroyed a Dornier 24 they caught taxiing on the water and also an Arado 195 that was providing fighter cover for a convoy of three landing craft, a trawler, and a caique. They then attacked the ships with cannons and bombs and also scored hits on a 2,000-ton steamer and an F-lighter caught entering Port Kalymnos.

But by far the greatest German loss came on the night of October 18–19, when the ex-Vichy motor ship *Sinfra* (4,470 tons) was caught by a force of torpedo Wellingtons of No. 38 Squadron some forty miles east of the Antikithira Channel. The vessel had left Suda Bay on the evening of the eighteenth for the Piraeus with about 300 Germans and 2,300 Italians on board.

Four Wellingtons were sweeping the area and the first attack was carried out by Sgt. P. R. Bergman's X-X-ray (*MP 640*). He sighted a 4,000-ton motor vessel at 35°54'N, 23°56'E and immediately sent out a sighting report before attacking with a single torpedo which missed astern of his target.

Both Wellington K-King (*MP 655*), piloted by Flight Sergeant Mitchell, and A-Apple (*HZ 378*) homed on to the ship at 2340. Mitchell reporting a 3,000-ton ship and two escort vessels. The ships also sighted him, and he was forced to attack through fierce flak. One torpedo was released, but the result was unobserved because the Wellington was heavily hit and the navigator, Flying Officer Bird, seriously wounded. The *Sinfra* had in fact evaded this second torpedo, but Mitchell had drawn the bulk of her antiaircraft fire away from the second aircraft.

Squadron Leader Milburn was thus able to carry out a classic attack and saw his torpedo hit the freighter slightly aft of amidships, which so damaged the ship that she slowed to a standstill almost at once. A large column of water rose to a height of 100 feet, and she was left burning hard, with the flames visible thirty miles away.

Meanwhile, S-Sugar (*LB 197*), piloted by Flight Sgt. H. F. van der Pol, had received the sighting report from X-X-Ray earlier and came upon the blazing vessel at 0104. He estimated her to be a 4,000-tonner, and she was stopped and on fire at 35°54'N, 23°56'E. He attacked through light flak with a torpedo, which was seen running true toward amidships of the target. The bows lifted clear of the water when it hit, and large clouds of black smoke and two explosions followed. The flak ceased at once.

The ship sank with heavy loss of life. Once more the Germans had their men of the combat battalion put into the water in a few minutes, this time from XI/999. Although Churchill claimed that almost 2,000 Germans were lost with the *Sinfra*, in fact 163 out of 204 of the Germans, along with 390 Italians (from a total of 2,389) and 13 Greeks (out of 71), were later picked up.

The cannon-equipped Mitchells, operating with their Beaufighter escorts, were busy throughout this period, and between October 16 and November 16, they carried out some eighty-six sorties. On the twentieth, the Mitchells damaged two F-lighters off Cos. On the twenty-fourth, No.603's Beaus were again providing the escort with three aircraft—Atkinson, Dalziel, and Eastcott—for three B-25s on an offensive recce in the Cos-Kalymnos area, and they claimed hits and damage on two motor schooners and a caique. One of the Beaus received damage from antiaircraft fire. The same routine was followed on the twenty-fifth and twenty-sixth, but targets by this time were both few and small.

Accordingly, the following day, they varied the strike pattern by making an attack with six Mitchells and Beaus on Antimachia. They attacked at 0915 and caught some Ju 52s disembarking troops. In just this way the Germans had caught the Dakotas and the Durham Light Infantry just a month earlier. Now the roles were exactly reversed. The Mitchells damaged several of the three-engine transports, and the Beaus carried out cannon attacks on groups of troops, a gun park, and also some of the abandoned Spitfires, which were being reassembled by the Germans. The Allied force had no casualties.

A much more ominous sign was the location, by the Photo Reconnaissance Unit Spitfires, of eight Dornier Do.217-K3 bombers at Kalamaki airfield in Greece. These aircraft had been especially adapted to carry the new Hs.293 glider bomb at altitudes that only the Lightning on the Allied side could hope to reach. The Lightnings were by now no more than a memory in the Aegean, which meant that the ships were suddenly faced with a dire new threat.

The Royal Navy had come up against this weapon when the *Luftwaffe* tried it out in the Bay of Biscay; on that occasion, the sloop *Egret* had been annihilated and the Canadian ship *Athabaskan* severely damaged. The weapon was a warhead carried by a small body mounted above it and fitted with jet engines, which started up after it had been released from its parent aircraft. The warhead was packed with 1,100 pounds of explosive and at a speed of 300 to 400 knots was guided onto the target by a simple joystick affair located in the "parent" bomber. The destroyers' antiaircraft fire was useless against them for these bombs were released from heights of up to 18,000 feet.

Had the Germans been able to introduce them earlier in the war, there is no doubt that they would have had a great effect on air-sea warfare, but unfortunately for them, they could only use them in small numbers because of problems of manufacture and a lack of suitable aircraft. So although deadly, they were not decisive. But the eight bombers equipped with them and used in the Aegean were to leave their mark. The Royal Navy was soon to experience this new weapon firsthand, but in the meantime, losses were still being incurred at a mounting rate from more conventional weapons.

On the night of October 20–21, the cruiser *Aurora* together with the *Miaoulis* carried out a night shoot against the port of Rhodes. While this bombardment was being carried out, the destroyers *Fury* and *Beaufort* disembarked stores and troops in Alinda Bay and then carried out a search along the northern coast of Cos; at 2344, they bombarded Cos Roads, where German caiques could usually be found sheltering. Later they made a rendezvous with the *Aurora* in the Scarpanto Straits. This squadron, code-named Nettle, was provided with air cover throughout the day; No. 227 Squadron intercepted some Ju 88s approaching the ships. Pilot Officer Gibbard attacked one at 400 feet and hit it with two accurate bursts; the engine caught fire at once, and bits of the tail and wing flew off. He made another attack, and the bomber, well on fire, crashed into the sea, exploding on impact.

The next night the *Faulknor, Petard,* and *Dulverton* left their hideout in Gurvergenik Bay at 1910, and while the Fleets made a sweep south of Levitha, the *Dulverton* carried out a bombardment of the island. The ships were attacked by aircraft during the night but by skillful use of smoke floats escaped damage. The three destroyers made rendezvous with the *Aurora* the following morning, and the whole force returned to Alexandria.

As they did so, the *Jervis, Pathfinder, Hurworth,* and the Greek *Adrias* sailed for the Aegean. The Fleets were carrying stores for Leros, but when they arrived at Alinda Bay, an air raid was in progress and there were no lighters on hand, so they lay up in the Gulf of Cos on the twenty-second. The Hunts searched Port Vathi and Port Atki for German invasion barges but found none, so they also proceeded to the Gulf of Cos and lay up behind Yedi island. German aircraft did not spot any of the destroyers during the day, and the *Jervis* and *Pathfinder* proceeded once more to Alinda Bay and successfully unloaded their supplies. While the Fleets were thus employed, the *Hurworth* and *Adrias* were dispatched to create a diversion to the south of Leros. On passage there, they ran into a newly laid minefield east of Kalymnos, which the Germans had prepared for the express purpose of catching the British destroyers. The mines were laid by the German-controlled 1,870-ton minelayer *Drache* (the former Yugoslav vessel *Zmaj*) and soon reaped dividends.

First to strike trouble was the *Adrias*, under Cmdr. J. N. Toumbas. She had her bows blown off as far as the bridge, with the loss of twenty-one killed and twenty-one wounded. The *Hurworth*, under Cmdr. R. H. Wright, bravely went to the aid of her sister ship. Commander Wright immediately brought the *Hurworth* up to find out what had happened and prepared to go alongside to take off the crew when the *Adrias* gave warning of a dark shape on the starboard bow, the *Hurworth* then being on her port quarter. The crew of the *Adrias* at that time thought she had been torpedoed, not mined, and suspected the dark shape was an E-boat waiting to catch the *Hurworth*. Commander Wright increased speed and turned across *Adrias*'s bows to engage the suspect when he suddenly realized that the shape was the blown-off section of the *Adrias* still afloat. He stopped the engines, but then there was a blinding flash and the *Hurworth* was enveloped in flames. She too had struck a mine. She was hit on the starboard side, just abaft her bridge and next to the forward boiler room. The force of the explosion broke the ship in half and started a serious oil fire. The fore end sank in three minutes, and the after section remained afloat for only fifteen. Loss of life was heavy, but Commander Wright and eighty-five others were saved.

On board the *Adrias*, Commander Toumbas had to extricate himself from the wreckage on the bridge. He found the 4-inch guns of No. 1 mounting lying right over the bridge. He said afterward that they had had no hope that anyone on the *Hurworth* had survived the terrific explosion they had just witnessed. Fuel from the *Hurworth* caught fire, and he ordered the *Adrias* to go full speed astern to avoid the blazing oil on the surface. After returning to the scene with his crippled, listing ship and finding nothing he decided to make for the Turkish coast. The heel of the ship was so serious that Toumbas ordered the crew to muster on the port side of the quarterdeck to reduce the list as much as possible.

The *Adrias* could still steam, and though all the charts and the compass had been blown away, Toumbas and his navigating officer decided they could make the Turkish mainland in the darkness and beach the ship. Shaping course by the Pole Star and the high mountains, they used the after steering position and, nursing the ship ahead at about five knots, sighted the lights on the mainland at about 0130 on the twenty-third. During this tense journey, Toumbas lost consciousness, but he recovered "under the strong slappings of the quartermaster." A little later the *Adrias* was successfully beached in Gurvergenik Bay.

While the *Adrias* lay crippled, the Beaufighters of No. 252 Squadron maintained a standing air patrol over her during daylight hours, and three motor launches were sent out to her assistance. On the twenty-fourth, two Ju 88s were sighted approaching some five miles to the north, but although three Beaufighters set off in pursuit, they were unable to catch them. On returning to the ships, the fighters passed messages from the destroyers to the commander in chief of the Levant, the *Adrias* signaling by Aldis lamp and the aircraft passing on the message over the air. The *Adrias* was to remain marooned at Gurvergenik for some time, however.

The *Eclipse* and *Petard* planned to land 200 troops at Sandamah Bay in Turkey on the night of October 23–24 for onward passage to Leros. They had sailed from Alexandria on the twenty-third with the destroyers *Exmoor* and *Rockwood* in company, but the *Exmoor* later suffered boiler problems and both the Hunts were sent back. Included among those embarked were A, B, and HQ Companies—including the battalion headquarters—of the 4th Buffs (Royal East Kent) Regiment. Also taking passage was the commodore of the Levant destroyer flotillas, Capt. Percy Todd, who was making the trip in the *Eclipse* to find out what was actually going on, after hearing the many complaints of his destroyer skippers about the futility of it all.

In view of the recent disaster that had overtaken the *Hurworth* and *Adrias*, it appeared to be tempting fate, but the two destroyers passed close by the eastern side of Kalymnos and were proceeding through the Karabakla Channel when at 0050 the *Eclipse* hit a mine laid in forty-eight fathoms of water.

The explosion occurred under the starboard side of the ship near the forward boiler room, and a serious fire started in the bridge structure, from which it rapidly spread, fed by oil fuel from the forward galley tank. Almost at once the forward starboard Oerlikon and the B gun 4.7-inch ammunition exploded, spreading carnage throughout the forepart of the little vessel. The *Eclipse* took on a heavy list to port, which steadily increased until she was over on her beam ends. She then broke in two and sank only five minutes after being hit.

Casualties among the troops on board were ghastly: Captains E. A. Hampton, P. R. T. Daniel (the adjutant), R. S. D. Cudworth (RAMC), R. S. B. White (quartermaster), and D. M. Banker (RAMC), and 2nd Lt. J. L. Collier were all lost together with Regimental Sergeant Major Macdonnell, Regimental Quartermaster Sgt. E. W. Glenn, 6 sergeants, and 128 other ranks all from A and HQ Companies. Those lost included the entire mortar platoon.

The commanding officer of the Buffs, Colonel Iggulden, by sheer determination, kept himself afloat for more than four hours in the pitch-blackness; he and Maj. H. F. Read and some 31 other ranks were finally embarked in the *Petard* and a motor launch. Although her captain, Cmdr. E. Mack, 5 other officers, and 68 men were rescued, loss of life among the naval personnel was equally severe, and Percy Todd was among the 5 officers and 122 sailors who died. The loss of the *Eclipse* coupled with the earlier minings was a hard blow, and according to the commander in chief of the Levant, it came as a severe setback to the Allied effort; naval plans had to be recast.

Naturally, it was wondered how all this could have happened, but it appeared that because of the need for speed in the moving of reinforcements into Leros and the danger of air attack on the island while the troops were disembarking, it had been decided that the plan to offload the troops in Turkish waters was the wisest. It was unfortunate that the two Hunts, which were to act as general-purpose escorts, had to be sent back, but worse still was a signaling error regarding the sinking of the *Hurworth* and damage to the *Adrias*. The position of the minefield was first reported as being in the Karabakla Channel but was, by mistake, "corrected" shortly afterward. This probably led Commander Mack to opt for a course *outside* Karabakla island, with the resulting tragedy. Once again in this unhappy operation, a "minor" error had led to a disaster; nor was this to be the last.

The cruiser *Phoebe* and the *Aldenham* and *Hursley* had also entered the Aegean to create a diversion. The *Petard* was unable to offload her troops and survivors, as only one motor launch was available for transport, because most of the light craft were engaged in rescue work. The troops were therefore transferred to the *Hursley* and *Aldenham* while they lay up in Turkish waters and were landed the next night.

Other reinforcements were continually on their way from Alexandria to the battle zone. The *Faulknor, Beaufort,* and *Belvoir* sailed at 1700 on the twenty-fifth to rendezvous with the *Phoebe*. They were not carrying either stores or troops but were escorted into the Rhodes Channel by the cruiser, which then withdrew while the destroyers proceeded to lie up for the night in the Gulf of Cos. The *Phoebe* patrolled southeast of Rhodes that night, during which time she was shadowed by aircraft that dropped flares. She refueled at Limassol, then sailed to meet *Penn, Dulverton,* and *Miaoulis* north of Alexandria. These three ships were carrying 300 troops and forty tons of stores for Leros. Agents in Turkey reported that E-boats were using the cover of the island of Gurvergenik to lie in wait for targets, so the destroyers were instructed to transfer the troops in Partheni Bay instead.

On October 27, the cruiser *Aurora* left Alexandria with the destroyers *Pathfinder, Exmoor,* and *Blencathra* to relieve the *Phoebe* and her party, which was withdrawing. The destroyers were not carrying troops but were out on an offensive sweep. They were shadowed by German aircraft on their approach until darkness fell, despite making a wide detour east of Rhodes. A strong force of Ju 88s attempted to attack them but was driven off by their Beaufighter escort. While the cruiser lay off to the south, the destroyers pushed into the Aegean and lay up as usual at dawn.

While the destroyers were pushing on into the Aegean, the *Penn*, *Dulverton*, and *Miaoulis* had sallied forth from Turkish waters and carried out an antishipping sweep west of Levitha without success, joining the *Aurora* in the morning, whereupon the whole force returned to Alexandria. After a hasty refueling the cruiser again sailed with the destroyers *Echo*, *Rockwood*, and *Krakowiak*. Again they were bombed fifty miles southeast of Casteloriso but suffered no casualties. This time heavy cloud frustrated their fighter escort, and the German bombers were not intercepted. The destroyers carried on into the Aegean, lying up in the Gulf of Cos. The *Pathfinder*'s force had been unable to find any targets the previous night, and it too returned to its anchorage. Both forces were to make further sweeps on the night of October 29–30. Yet another force of destroyers left Alexandria that afternoon to meet the *Aurora*. These were the *Petard*, loaded with eight jeeps, a trailer, sixty soldiers, and nine naval personnel; the *Belvoir*, with five jeeps, sixty soldiers, and mail; and the *Beaufort*, with one jeep and sixty soldiers. This force met the *Aurora* and headed for Turkish waters. Once more the *Luftwaffe* was waiting for them, and a series of heavy attacks developed during the afternoon of the thirtieth while the ships were in neutral waters.

Beaufighters from No. 252 and 227 Squadrons provided the fighter escort. While on patrol overhead, the four aircraft were warned by the *Aurora*'s plot: "Bandits approaching from the west—get together." They sighted a force of fourteen Junkers Ju 88s, with an escort of six Me 109s, approaching in three Vics. The bombers were at 12,000 feet, with the fighter escort 1,000 feet higher. Before the Beaus could intercept, the ships attacked, and one bomb burst close astern of the *Aurora*, which turned east accompanied by one destroyer.

The Beaus engaged the escorts, and one Me 109 was attacked from ahead and slightly above with the Beau opening fire at 400 feet, then closing to 200 feet. No hits were seen, but the German plane turned over on his back. One of the Junkers was also brought down in this attack, but nevertheless the bombers had gotten through.

Though the Ju 88s carried out their bombing attacks from a great height, they were successful. Tom Price was serving aboard the *Belvoir*, under Cmdr. John Bush. He remembers how this compared with the usual dive-bombing: "This was a wasteful method of bombing but effective when well done and very difficult to avoid, for unless you were on the wings of the group there was nowhere to go for safety. I have a clear memory of the *Petard* on this occasion going full speed outwards, with the apparent intention of scaling the cliffs [of the Turkish coast] on the starboard side of the squadron!"

The ships came through this attack, but it was followed by further waves of both Ju 88s and Stukas, the latter's escort including a few patched-up MC 202s evidently flown by German pilots. During these attacks, in position 36°05'N, 29°47'E, a force of fourteen Ju 87 Stukas, escorted by three MC 202s, broke through, and the 1st Group of *Stukageschwader* 3 demonstrated that their heavy losses earlier had not detracted from their old skills. The *Aurora* was struck by a 500-kilogram direct-action-fused bomb just abaft the after funnel on the after conning position, which was obliterated. Her main battery of 4-inch antiaircraft guns was also severely damaged, her P.1 mounting was wrecked, and three other mountings, both funnels, the port pompom, three Oerlikon mountings, the after director, the port torpedo tubes, and the radar sets and their aerials were all put out of action by this one devastating blow.

The ready-use ammunition on the 4-inch gundeck and the Oerlikon ammunition ignited in one searing blast, and all the heavy antiaircraft guns fell silent, as did the after 6-inch guns. Speed had to be reduced to twenty-two knots to avoid the collapse of the after funnel. Forty-six of the *Aurora*'s crew were killed and twenty wounded, most of her casualties being among her 4-inch guns' crew. As one destroyer captain later recalled: "We destroyers always enjoyed having *Aurora* with us as she always encouraged us to give more than we got from air attacks. She was sadly hit by a Junkers slap between her 4-inch AA battery, which did much damage and killed many of the crew."

Trailing fire and smoke, the *Aurora* put about for Alexandria, escorted by *Beaufort*. This was the last appearance in these waters of this famous ship, her repairs taking more than five months. Meanwhile, the *Petard* and *Belvoir*, with their much-needed troops, attempted to go it alone. They did not make it—although the Beaufighters did their best. Two more German raids found them; sixteen Ju 88s attacked at 1712 and eight more at 1752, when they were forced to turn back to Casteloriso. It was the first raid that caused the damage. Tom Price remembers it vividly:

> John Bush had always maintained that a Hunt Class destroyer, well crewed, with only itself to look after, could beat dive-bombing. For over two hours, we were subjected to every trick they knew, without even a serious near miss. Eventually they resorted to the tactic, which proved our superiority, by coming in from the side and releasing their bomb in a steep bank, thus avoiding having to come directly over the ship and its guns. During this bombardment, a periscope was sighted; fortunately it was friendly—at least, no attack was detected. However, the skill and bravery of the pilots of the Stukas had to be seen to be believed.

Finally, however, one Ju 88 planted a bomb into the *Belvoir*. A direct hit penetrated through her slender hull. "Our bomb," Tom Price continues, "failed to explode and came to rest on a stabilizer—which we didn't use in those days, funnily enough—and was carried to the stern and thrown overboard by about the only man who could lift it. He got the medal he deserved!"

This was in fact the end of the bombing, but the ships put back into Casteloriso until nightfall before renewing the attempt. Their fighter escort had been busy, as their combat report makes clear: "The two destroyers on their own were steering 270 degrees and were seen putting up a heavy barrage. On closing two Vics of eight Ju 88s, each with three MC 202 fighter escorts, were seen attacking from 8,000 feet. All their bombs appeared to have been avoided in the first attack."

One of the Beaus was attacked from dead astern by a Macchi and had her rudder shot away, whereupon a second Beau attacked the MC 202 from 200 feet ahead and slightly above. No hits were observed, but the Italian aircraft went down in a slow spiral dive.

The *Petard* and *Belvoir* lay up in Guvercinlik Bay at 0712 on the thirty-first. Sailing again at 1915, they managed to disembark 120 personnel and stores, including the thirteen jeeps, at Alinda Bay at midnight.

Nor was the *Aurora* the only serious casualty taken from air attacks during this time. Two of the large landing craft, tanks (LCT) had left Haifa for Casteloriso on the twenty-seventh, escorted by two armed trawlers. On the twenty-eighth, these two, *LCT 104*, under Sub-Lt. B. M. Carvill, and *LCT 115*, under Lieutenant Walker, escorted by the British armed trawler HMS *Bream* and the free-French armed trawler *Reine des Flots*. The *LCT 115* carried a cargo of antiaircraft guns for the island, and her sister ship was laden with ammunition for both these and other weapons. South of Cyprus, this little flotilla was picked up and shadowed by the *Luftwaffe*. Later that day they were attacked by German bombers some thirty-five miles from Casteloriso, and at 1800 *LCT 115* was sunk. The first lieutenant of the *LCT 104*, D. Russell Whiteford, later gave us this graphic account of the incident:

> I was taking the afternoon watch as No. 1, when a single aircraft appeared from the direction of the Aegean and circled our small convoy at a height of about 2000 feet. As it presented no immediate threat, I declined to call the CO, who was asleep below. Later when he heard of the incident, he immediately recognized it as a "shutfi" [reconnaissance] plane, closed up the guns' crews, and blasted me all round the bridge for not reporting it to him. At the time, I thought this a little unfair, as I had allowed him a full watch below with his head down!

Towards sunset, unable to hear anything above the noise from the exhausts of our three Napier Lion engines, and with our destination, Casteloriso, just in sight about 40 miles ahead, I saw *Reine des Flots* on our starboard bow blow several warning blasts on her steam whistle. Directly above us was a squadron of Stuka dive-bombers—hovering as though they had been there for some time waiting for us to take notice! Two of these peeled off in a characteristic dive on the French trawler, with near misses, which displaced her boiler. By this time we had our pom-poms in action, and our CO ordered hard a-port to make us a more difficult target.

Our tracers followed two more Stukas down as they dived steeply on to *LCT 115*, making a direct hit in the tank space. Within a few minutes she had turned turtle, and by the time we had completed our emergency turn, only the propellers were visible. We made ready to lower scrambling nets and headed towards the survivors and floating wreckage, but *Reine des Flots*, as senior escort ship, signaled us to head north with *Bream* to the Turkish coast and neutral waters, while she picked up the survivors. By this time the sun was setting, and the Stukas had fortunately headed WNW back to base.

On reaching the harbor of Casteloriso, we unloaded our ammunition and heard that, although the crew of *LCT 115* had all survived, most of the soldiers had been in the tank space among their guns, and a number of these were either killed by the bomb or trapped inside as the ship foundered.

This was a heavy loss, for the shortage of these ships was already crippling. Thirty-five survivors were picked up, but many troops were lost.

It was little wonder then that on October 27, Admiral Willis sent the first sea lord what he described as "rather a gloomy letter about the Aegean situation." He had good reason. "Our light coastal forces were also playing an active part in attacking enemy communications, but their opportunities were limited. Motor launches were based at Leros until the scale of enemy air attacks made this a hazardous undertaking. The MTBs worked from Casteloriso, using Paphos in Cyprus for their rest periods and maintenance."

Motor torpedo boats (MTBs) of the 10th Flotilla had arrived at Casteloriso early in the month, and on the night of October 7–8, they made their debut when three boats left their base and proceeded north of Rhodes to attack shipping off Cos—but none could be found. Instead, they beat up Cos Harbor. When two miles off the harbor, green Very lights were fired from the shore, illuminating the harbor and town. This was an opportunity not to be missed, and the MTBs swept in, shooting up seaplanes and caiques moored in the harbor. Their fire was returned, and one of the MTBs was hit and slightly damaged.

A further striking force left Casteloriso at 1700 on the thirteenth to attack shipping in Port Kalymnos. The attack was postponed until the night of October 14–15 but proved abortive, as no enemy shipping was sighted. Success was not to be achieved until five nights later.

The motor launches were also active, and on the night of October 8, *ML 835* was on patrol east of Leros when a suspicious vessel was sighted off Lipsos island, attacked by gunfire and driven ashore. The vessel turned out to be the 2,737-ton Italian repair ship *Alessandro Volta*, under *Capitano di Corvetta* Stefano Bausani, which was on passage from Leros to Samos. The ship was later attacked by German aircraft and destroyed. *ML 835* became the first Fairmile to be lost in the Aegean when, on October 11, while at Levitha, she was subjected to fifty-seven attacks by Ju 87s, Ju 88s, and Me 109s. Under such a weight of attack, she could not hope to survive, and she eventually caught fire and had to be abandoned. All her crew were saved.

A further motor launch was lost on October 26. *ML 579* was berthed in a small cove in Arki, a small island just north of Lipsos, lying fully camouflaged with one gun cleared away when several aircraft passed overhead, apparently without sighting her. One Ju 88 attacked downsun, however, and dropped a stick of four bombs, one of which smashed through the wardroom while the other three were near misses. The vessel took on a heavy list to port and sank. Two officers and one rating were killed; the remainder of the crew managed to swim ashore.

The efficiency of the MTBs, however, suffered from a lack of a well-equipped advance base. This considerably hampered their activities, and so early in November, the schooner *Ragea* was sailed from Alexandria to Turkish waters to act as a base ship. She carried spare torpedoes, diesel and lubricating oil, and fresh and distilled water. Her presence greatly facilitated the work of the MTBs.

The *LCT 104* carried on despite the loss of her sister, as First Lieutenant Whiteford describes:

> We made several passages between Haifa and Casteloriso about this time. There was virtually no Allied air cover available for this theater of war, and on several occasions we received near misses from bombs in and around the island. Frequently we took refuge in Vathi Creek inside Turkey.
>
> Eventually, when it was recognized that the Dodecanese could not be held, we made a final passage to Casteloriso to evacuate military personnel. We were unsure whether the island had been captured

while we plodded our way there at ten knots from Haifa and, in utter darkness, approached the harbor cautiously west-about. A patrol boat shadowed us as we circled the island but it turned out to be *ML 340*, with my cousin J. H. Robertson as her first lieutenant! She apparently suspected that *we* were the beginning of an enemy landing on Casteloriso!

To supplement the work of the surface ships, submarines also were making vigorous efforts to try to stem the flow of German troops, stores, and supplies to the Aegean Islands. This work was carried out by the submarines of the 1st Flotilla based at Beirut. At the beginning of September, the flotilla had only six boats operational, as several of the T class submarines had been transferred to the Eastern Fleet for operations in the Indian Ocean. Reinforcements, however, were soon on the way from the 10th Flotilla at Malta and 8th Flotilla at Algiers. The reinforcements usually carried out a patrol in the Aegean before proceeding to Beirut. One of the most successful patrols was that carried out by the *Unruly*, whose exploits between the time she left Malta on October 1 and her arrival at Beirut on the twelfth were related earlier.

In the island-studded Aegean, the work of the submarines was not easy, and with the many small antisubmarine vessels available to the Germans, casualties were bound to occur. An early loss was that of the Greek submarine *Katsonis*, which sailed early in September on a special mission to land agents on the coast of Euboea. After completing this special mission, she was to carry out a patrol off Nicaria. Shortly after 2000 hours on September 14, however, she was sighted on the surface in the northern entrance of the Euboea Channel by the German antisubmarine vessel *UJ-2101*, under *Kapitanleutnant* Bollheim. The *UJ-2101* opened fire, and the submarine was heavily damaged. As she lay stopped in the water she was rammed and sunk. The action took place not far from the small harbor of Trikeri. All the crew were Greek, except for the captain and one wireless operator, who were British. The *UJ-2101* picked up fourteen survivors, all wounded, including the British captain and wireless operator.

The first submarine to leave Malta to reinforce the 1st Flotilla was the *Unsparing*, under Lt. A. D. Piper. She sailed from Malta on September 23, carrying out a patrol in the southern Aegean en route for Beirut. On the twenty-eighth, she sank a small caique by gunfire off Cape Malea. She was then ordered to patrol off Cos, where on October 2 she actually sighted part of the invasion convoy heading for Cos but was unable to position herself for an attack. She subsequently withdrew through the Kasos Strait on October 6. The next day, she picked up two German soldiers in a boat some 125 miles from land. They had been adrift for nine days and were certainly pleased to see the *Unsparing*, even though they were to spend the rest of the war in captivity. During the night of the eighth, a suspicious vessel was sighted and star shells were fired to illuminate the target, whereupon the crew of the vessel took to their boats and abandoned ship. But she soon turned out to be a friendly schooner bound from Limassol to Haifa with 1,470 cases of Cyprus brandy for the NAAFI (Navy, Army, Air Force Institution, the British equivalent of the American PX). The *Unsparing* soon persuaded the crew to return to their ship and the submarine then proceeded on her way to Beirut, where she arrived on the ninth.

Submarines were now leaving Beirut at regular intervals for Aegean patrols, and on October 10, the *Torbay* slipped her moorings and headed for the islands.

At 1225 on the fifteenth, a German convoy of two merchant ships and a landing craft was reported east of Naxos in a position 37°00'N, 24°45'E, steering a course of 095° at a speed of eight knots. Naval forces at sea were alerted and the *Torbay* was ordered to adjust her patrol so as to get in position to intercept. The destroyers *Beaufort* and *Belvoir*, which were then lying up in Turkish waters, were also dispatched during the afternoon to intercept the convoy, but although they made a sweep as far north as Amorgos, they sighted nothing. The cruiser *Phoebe* and the destroyers *Faulknor* and *Fury* also made a fruitless search during the night of October 15–16. The German convoy, which included the merchant ships *Kari* (1,925 tons) and *Trapani* (1,855 tons), was carrying about 1,000 troops, motor transport, guns, and motor launches to reinforce the garrison on Cos and sailed from the Piraeus late on the fourteenth. The convoy had turned north during the sweeps by the British naval forces and thus avoided detection. It resumed course for Cos on the sixteenth and at 1230 that day, while east of Levitha, was sighted by the *Torbay*. Viewed through her periscope, it presented a luscious target, sailing in line abreast with two escort vessels and two floatplanes circling overhead.

The *Torbay*, undeterred by the escorts, worked herself into a position to attack and at 1300 fired a salvo of four torpedoes from a range of 1,400 yards. The *Kari* was hit and sank almost immediately, with the loss of 190 of her 510 troop passengers. At the moment the torpedoes were fired, the escort vessel on the port side of the convoy made contact with the *Torbay*, and the expected counterattack began, with one aircraft bomb and seventeen depth charges dropped. The first were fairly close, but after that the accuracy tailed off. On returning to periscope depth, the *Torbay* sighted a UJ-boat four miles away, and this vessel later dropped eleven more depth charges. For the *Torbay*, the remainder of her patrol was uneventful, and she arrived back in Beirut on the twenty-eighth.

While some submarines seemed able to hit their targets on the first attempt, others were not so successful. One such submarine was the *Surf*. She had been en route for the Indian Ocean when on October 5 she was recalled to Suez and then ordered to Beirut to join the 1st Flotilla for operations in the Aegean. She arrived at Beirut on the seventh and left for her first patrol on the twelfth, passing through the Kasos Strait during daylight of the fourteenth. On the sixteenth, when southwest of Leros, she sighted a tempting target—a 3,000-ton escorted merchant ship. While working into a firing position, the escort gained contact and was forced to dive deep to escape the inevitable counter-attack. On surfacing an hour and a half later the target had gotten well away.

At 0714 on the twenty-fifth, the *Surf* carried out a gun attack on a small merchant ship off Amorgos. The merchant ship returned fire accurately enough for the *Surf* to break off the engagement and dive. Her next contact with the enemy was on the twenty-ninth, when she sighted a merchant ship escorted by two antisubmarine craft and two Arado floatplanes north of Mykonos. The attack had to be broken off when the ships entered Port Panormos in Mykonos. Not to be outdone, the *Surf* fired two torpedoes at 1456 from a range of 4,500 yards into the harbor aimed at the merchant ship but no hits were observed. Resourceful as ever, her commander, Lt. D. Lambert, retired to reload his torpedo tubes. He returned at 1825 and fired two further torpedoes at the harbor without success. This second attack was too much for one of the escort vessels, which started to get under way, whereupon the *Surf* withdrew. She arrived back in Beirut on November 3.

On October 24, the *Unsparing* left Beirut for her second Aegean patrol. Her orders were to operate south of Amorgos and attack enemy shipping attempting to reinforce the German garrisons on Cos and Kalymnos. She was to have a short but lively patrol. On the twenty-eighth, the steamship *Ingeborg* (1,160 tons) sailed from Naxos for Cos carrying 375 troops and war materiel. She was escorted by the ex-Italian customs launch *Noio* (60 tons) and the small naval auxiliary *KFK-3*.

At 0230 on the twenty-ninth, when southwest of Anaphi, the convoy was sighted by the *Unsparing*. Some fifteen minutes later, the *Unsparing* fired a salvo of four torpedoes from a range of 3,000 yards. The *Ingeborg* was hit and sank five minutes later. At dawn, the two escort vessels could be seen picking up survivors. Of her total complement of 408 passengers and crew, 319 survived. Two Dorniers also arrived, landed on the sea, and began assisting in the rescue operations. Nothing daunted, Lieutenant Piper decided to attack the escort vessels with torpedoes set to run on the surface. The first vessel to be lined up in his sights was the *Noio*, which was packed with troops. The torpedo ran true and the sixty-ton vessel disintegrated. Lieutenant Piper was unable to line up on the other vessel, and the *KFK-3* responded by dropping depth charges, some uncomfortably close, but the German troops in the water must have suffered more than the submarine. On the thirty-first, the *Unsparing* sighted a caique and surfaced to sink it by gunfire. The caique, however, opened up with a hot and accurate fire, and the submarine was hit by a shell, blowing a hole about a foot square in the bridge casing just abaft the conning tower. The gun trainer was killed, and two ratings and the gunnery officer were wounded. This caused the *Unsparing* to leave her patrol area and head back for Beirut, where she arrived on November 4.

It had been the second attempt by the *Ingeborg* to transport the 999th Division to Cos and had ended in disaster. Although a great many of the soldiers were saved, they were in no condition to fight for a considerable time and had lost all their equipment.

On November 2, the submarine *Simoon* sailed from Port Said, where she had been undergoing a short docking for battery repairs, on what was to be her last patrol. She passed through the Kasos Strait on the fourth to carry out a patrol between Naxos and Mykonos. On the fifth, she was diverted to the Dardanelles approaches and advised by the captain of the 1st Flotilla to operate about five miles west of Tenedos. She should have arrived in this area on the sixth and had been ordered to leave patrol on the fifteenth, but she failed to reply to any signals on the nineteenth. Nothing further was heard of the *Simoon*; it is now thought that she sank the German auxiliary *UJ-2145* (110 tons) and the *Trapanai* (1,855 tons) on her patrol. For many years it was recorded that she had been sunk by a mine, but more careful recent study of German records indicates that she was actually sunk by the German submarine *U-565* around midnight on November 19, southeast of Cos. Although many more submarine patrols were undertaken in this campaign, no further submarines were lost.

On November 3, alarming reports were received by British intelligence concerning the buildup of German forces in readiness for the invasion of Leros. Despite considerable effort and heavy losses, it appeared that the Germans were pressing ahead. Agents told of large-scale landing exercises being practiced from invasion craft in Lavrion Gulf to the north of Athens. Flights by the indefatigable PRU Spitfires brought back photographs showing nine landing craft and two escorts at Lavrion, with a further four landing craft at Zea. They were reported moving eastward on November 5.

The OKW Diary reaffirmed on October 25 that although the period of bad storms in the Aegean was further aggravating their shortages of small ships, the invasion of Leros was to proceed as planned on November 12–13. Plans for the follow up operation against Samos, Operation Interlude, were also proceeding.

The ordnance officer of *Sturmdivision Rhodos* at this time, Herr Müller-Mangeot, throws a most revealing light on the possible failure of attempts to intercept this traffic in a recent letter. He records that the German command on Rhodes was well informed by radio and aerial reconnaissance of every British movement. All the radio frequencies being emitted from Cos, Leros, and Samos were carefully monitored and analyzed. "Every change, even of harbour operations of ships or movement of troop transports was known to us: so, we could establish the defence of the islands in peace."

Every effort was now made to smash this invasion fleet as, in small groups, it slipped across the Aegean Sea, slowly moving from island to island with the inevitability of a flow of lava. It took the Germans from November 5 to 10 to get the bulk of their force across to the jump-off points at Cos and Kalymnos, moving chiefly at night, and if by day under a strong fighter umbrella.

The Beaufighters and cannon-firing Mitchells of No. 201 Naval Co-operation Squadron hunted them by day, and the Wellingtons, submarines, and MTBs by night. Heavy casualties were taken in persistent air strikes against these elusive targets. Also at night, the limited British destroyer patrols, often under air attack, searched the areas where the landing craft were suspected to be lying up and bombarded various harbors. These efforts led to only very limited success. It had been decided by the Chiefs of Staff, after the *Aurora* had been hit, that the use of cruisers was too expensive. Only *Phoebe* was left of the six cruisers sent out in October, and Sir John Cunningham was reluctant to release any more from the central Mediterranean.

On November 3, eight Beaus were dispatched to attack a convoy of thirteen small landing craft and two E-boats reported off Lavrion but failed to locate them. The aircraft involved were seven Beaufighters of No. 603 escorting three Torbeaus—torpedo-carrying Beaufighters—of No. 47 Squadron. The brunt of the costly daylight attacks was to fall on these units in the succeeding days. On the fourth, four Beaus escorted two torpedo bombers on another fruitless search. In the afternoon of the same day, four of No. 603's aircraft made cannon attacks on landing barges secured against the harbor wall at Cos, damaging them all. Four Wellingtons of No. 38 Squadron had carried out a search for the convoy the previous night without locating it; they subsequently bombed Syros Harbor and gun flashes on Seriphos.

On the fifth, when the convoy got under way, four Beaus of No. 603 carried out a sweep around Santorin and then, in pairs, hit Kea and Sefnos. Strikes scored damaging hits on the jetty at Kamara Bay and on two small caiques and a 130-foot barge. Tugs and other barges were damaged at Port St. Nikola on Kea. Later four Beaus escorting three Torbeaus of No. 46 Squadron attacked Lavrion Bay. Three motor vessels, one of 1,500 tons and two of about 600 tons were attacked through intense flak, but the aircraft suffered no losses.

Eight Beaus, four of No. 603 and four of No. 47, were sent in against seventeen barges sighted at Naxos Harbor and located them steaming south of Paros toward Amorgos Bay. The German ships were under a strong aerial umbrella of Me 109s and Arado 196s, which drove the Beaus off and shot down three of them. The Germans had learned their lesson and subsequent Beaufighter strikes took equally heavy losses for little result.

The same party of landing craft had been sighted and suffered an attack in Naussa Bay, Paros, from Beaufighters on the seventh. Wellington aircraft on night ASV patrol sighted them leaving Naussa Bay at 2230, and the destroyers *Pathfinder* and *Penn* moved between Paros and Naxos ready to attack after midnight. They were off Heraklia Inlet, southeast of Naxos, at 0100 on the eighth but failed to make contact. Captain Malins explains why:

A Wellington aircraft was reporting a convoy sighting, presumably the Leros invasion force, crossing the Aegean, and because of high winds it had not yet been able to reach the sanctuary of one of the small islands to hide. We were therefore dispatched to intercept.

We set off as soon as we were able and at full speed sped the odd hundred miles or so in the reported direction, in good and directed W/T contact with the aircraft at all times. As midnight approached and we were still some thirty miles distant, the aircraft, which had been making lack of fuel noises for some time, said he must go and leave us to it, but alas his parting gesture was to discharge a full load of illuminations over his collection of ships.

We saw all this clearly from some twenty-five miles or so. Of course by the time we got to the spot marked X the enemy thus forewarned had taken action, and we found all the honey had run out of the pot. We had neither the fuel nor the time to search the nearby islands to which we presumed they had rushed and only had time to catch and sink one small caique to the south of Paros. It was really difficult to search all the islands with no radar, as all we had was star shell and a searchlight, neither of which was satisfactory for the job.

When we got back to Alexandria after this trip it was touch and go whether we would make it for fuel and got a laconic signal from the C-in-C not to worry for "we will tow you in if necessary." In point of fact, we made it. We were pretty worn out and dispirited. By this time the whole position of Leros looked most precarious, and it was not a happy time to be involved in an obviously ill-conceived operation.

During the forenoon of the eighth, the German landing craft sheltered on the eastern side of Paros and were attacked later, when steaming south of Paros and toward Amorgos, by the Beaufighters. Six aircraft of No. 603 and three of No. 47 Squadron went in against the ships which were heavily escorted by E-boats, armed trawlers and fighters. The British claimed to have shot down one Arado, but they failed to penetrate the screen, although they suffered no losses themselves.

The next day, the ships were seen making their way for Levitha and Stampalia from Amorgos, leaving a damaged F-lighter, two caiques, and a landing craft behind.

Four Beaus and two Torbeaus found two caiques and several barges off the eastern tip of Amorgos but were unable to attack them. Again heavy fighter cover was in evidence—Me 109s, Ar 196s, and Ju 88s—and the Junkers latter chased the Torbeaus off to the south.

On the assumption that the convoy would lie up in Maltezana Harbor, Stampalia, the Wellingtons of No. 38 Squadron bombed this area on the night of November 9–10, but to no avail. A destroyer force consisting of the *Petard*, *Rockwood*, and the Polish *Krakowiak* searched Kineros Island and Levitha and bombarded the southern shore of the latter. Another force consisting of the *Fury*, *Exmoor*, and *Blencathra* left Turkish waters and hunted along Amorgos, searching to within 800 yards of the coastline without success. They were unable to get clear before dawn and lay up in the Gulf of Doris.

On the tenth, the enemy ships were located at 1030 between Amorgos and Leros. Nine Beaus of No. 603 and three Torbeaus of No. 47 were sent in, but one was lost to the fighter escort without result. By the time the invasion fleet was reported to have reached Cos and Kalymnos early the next morning, British intelligence estimated that the enemy had available vessels capable of lifting 2,000 troops.

Leros's turn had come.

CHAPTER NINE

Prelude to Disaster

Samos lies some thirty miles to the north of Leros and is not part of the Dodecanese group, but one of the Greek Aegean Islands. It is separated from the Turkish mainland by only one mile of water, which made clandestine reinforcement and evacuation easier, but it lay so deep in the Aegean waters that its supply, even by the fastest destroyers, was very hazardous. The contours of the island offered little in the way of natural defense, its terrain being flatter and more low-lying than that of Leros or Cos. On the collapse of the Greek homeland in 1941, the Italians had occupied and administered Samos but had attempted little in the way of defense construction, feeling that it lay secure behind the bastions of Crete and Rhodes.

The headquarters of the Italian 6th (*Cuneo*) Division, under the command of Maj. Gen. Mario Soldarelli, had been established on Samos with responsibility for the Cyclades and Sporades, their chief islands being Furmi to the south and the somewhat larger Icaria to the southwest. At the time of the armistice, this division numbered about 9,000 men. Its main units, consisting of the 8th Infantry and the 27th Artillery Regiments, were stationed on Samos, with the 7th Infantry Regiment on Syros. In addition, about 1,000 men of the 24th Blackshirt Regiment had arrived on the island on August 28 as reinforcements for Soldarelli and to assist in putting down the civil disturbances on the island that had followed Mussolini's downfall on July 26.

On the Italian surrender, a small Anglo-Greek mission, headed by an MO4 intelligence officer, Lt. Col. D. Pawson, moved in quickly. It was reinforced shortly afterward by S Patrol of the SBS, commanded by Maj. David Sutherland, which arrived aboard *ML-349*, under Capt. L. F. Ramseyer, on September 13. The commander in chief in Cairo was soon faced with a difficult situation: As Samos was formerly a Greek island, it had technically been liberated and was not occupied enemy territory as the other Italian islands had been. General Maitland Wilson was advised that unless the British troops moving onto the island were accompanied by a representative of the Greek government, there could be a Greek cabinet crisis. Accordingly, a suitable Greek was found and taken into Samos with Maj. Gen. Allan C. Arnold, the British military attaché in Ankara. General Arnold had been briefed by

Maitland Wilson to make an on-the-spot assessment of the situation on the island, and he was soon reporting back that chaos reigned there.

In addition to a large civilian population, which required feeding and was totally dependent on the British forces for its rations, the Italian armistice had brought out into the open the hatred of the Greeks for their Italian masters; with the arrival of British forces, the Greeks were eager to settle old scores. This situation was completely beyond the powers of the Greek government to control, so Maitland Wilson immediately appointed Lt. Gen. L. R. Baird, who had been intelligence officer at Mersa Matruh in 1939–40, to the role of military governor, with two civilian affairs officers to assist him. An agreement was reached whereby they worked in liaison with the local Greek commission headed by a bishop.

It soon became obvious to General Maitland Wilson that the civil affairs side of the operation was threatening to swamp the overriding military significance of the island, and thus a branch organization known as British Liaison HQ Greece was set up with the Greek government under the command of Maj. Gen. L. T. P. Hughes, in order that plans could be made not only for the liberation of Samos, but for the eventual freeing of the whole Greek nation.

Meanwhile, the first regular British army units were moving into the island. The 2nd Battalion of the Queen's Own Royal West Kent Regiment had spent the first four years of the war as garrison troops on Malta, and only in June 1943 did they eventually embark on the troopship *Neuralia* in Grand Harbour and sail to Alexandria. After a brief period at Sidi Bishr transit camp, the battalion moved to Syria while a party of officers and NCOs underwent a mountain warfare course. After various training exercises in Palestine and Egypt, on August 22 the battalion was moved by rail to Lebanon.

On September 11, a detachment under the second in command, Maj. G. V. Shaw, consisting of B Company led by Capt. E. P. Flood, had been sent as a follow-up group for the occupation of Casteloriso. In the meantime, the bulk of the battalion had received something like 100 reinforcements and was under sealed orders to move to an unknown destination. The rifle companies of the battalion had been made up almost to full strength by the disbandment of the Anti-Tank and Carrier Platoons, and it was in this order that the battalion moved on the evening of September 19 to Haifa, where the 8th Destroyer Flotilla was waiting.

The troops labored all night under arc lamps loading gear and equipment onto the destroyers and embarked the following morning, HQ and D Companies in the *Fury* and A and C Companies in the *Faulknor*. Both destroyers were fully laden, their decks crowded with stores, as they slowly edged away from the quayside. The Queen's Own left behind a rear party of some fifty men of all ranks under Captain Plewman, together with the motor transport officer, who was to organize the eventual follow-up of heavy transport vehicles, which could not be carried in the destroyers. Nor was there even time to embark kit bags; the soldiers carried what spare clothing they had in their packs. The battalion's equipment consisted of the normal small arms and 3-inch mortars, with double the usual allowance of ammunition. They also took compo rations for seven days and 1,000 gallons of water in 2-gallon cans. Thus after four years of total war, a typical, almost traditional British expeditionary force was mounted against the Germans in Europe.

The *Faulknor* and *Fury* arrived at Port Laki in Leros early on the twenty-first, and the troops and stores, including Bofors guns, were unloaded using Italian lighters. Ken Shuttleworth, radar operator aboard the destroyer *Faulknor*, provided this snapshot of that frantic operation:

> Some of the loads of equipment were being picked up by a DUKW, and we were throwing boxes down into her. In charge was a red-faced army captain. He shouted at us to hurry and get out before the Stukas came.
>
> Seven years later, I was sitting in the staff room on my first day at Derby College of Art, when in walked the head of ceramics. We both pointed at each other and both said, "I know you!" He had been a prisoner of war shortly after we left Leros.

The disembarked troops then had to be laboriously reembarked in the cargo boat *Eolo* for the second stage of the voyage to Samos. This was not completed until 2000 hours that evening, and then it was found that it was not possible to embark the whole battalion; C Company had to be left on Leros and was to follow three days later. The *Eolo* arrived at Port Vathy, Samos, at 0700 on September 22.

The stores and equipment were then unloaded, and the weary troops eventually marched off through the streets of Port Vathy that day at noon, to be greeted by cheering mobs waving flags from every vantage point. Billets were found in a large tobacco factory on the far side of the bay.

With the arrival the next day of Brigadier Baird, the battalion began to look to its defenses. The Italians were very cooperative and agreed to the loan of two cars and twenty large trucks so that the British battalion could form the island's "mobile reserve." Toward the end of the month, the battalion moved up to Mytilene, which was in a more central position and more suitable for a mobile role. Headquarterse and administration billets were established in the village, and defensive positions were prepared around it.

The supply of the island did indeed prove difficult but was successfully maintained throughout October. Within a few days of the fall of Cos, however, increased air activity was soon apparent overhead. Although the bulk of the air attacks were directed at Leros, a few attacks by Ju 88s were made on Port Vathy and on troop convoys moving farther inland.

On October 30, the Germans bombed and sank the 305-ton fishing vessel *Morrhua* at Samos. The ex-Italian steamer *Taganrog*, which was carrying supplies to Casteloriso, was sunk by *U-565* (Frenker) off the Anatolian coast on the night of October 25–26. The reports of the assembly of a German invasion convoy led the battalion to move into a position in the eastern sector of the island along the Dimitrios Ridge. Here the companies were again living in battle positions but were widely dispersed.

On November 11, the new general officer commanding in the Aegean, Maj. Gen. H. R. Hall, arrived at Samos with his complete staff, and almost simultaneously the Germans made their long-awaited move against Leros. The garrison now could only watch from the wings as the main drama shifted to that island.

One of the best sources on the fighting for Leros is L. Marsland Gander's *Long Road to Leros*, where he has described the island as he found it on his arrival there in early October just before the German invasion:

> The Italians had spent years in fortifying Leros as a naval base and its geographical features lent themselves admirably. It had a most peculiar shape, both in plan and contour. Slightly smaller than Guernsey and so consistently rocky that there is no space for an airfield, the island is also bitten into deeply by half a dozen bays. Two of the main bays, Alinda and Gurna almost cut Leros in two leaving a narrow strip little more than half a mile wide. All these bays are commanded by heights on which the Italians had installed formidable coastal batteries. So impressed were the British military authorities in Cairo with the natural strength of Leros that before I left, although we had been pushed off all the islands except this one and Samos, I was assured by more than one "expert" that we had a reasonable chance of holding it. This despite the fact that owing to the great distance of our nearest fighter bases there never was any chance of putting up a fighter umbrella unless we could persuade the Turks to let us use their airfields. There was also a persistent report which I came across from time to time that Churchill had said Leros must be held at all costs.

Although the Italians had expended much time and energy between the wars in an effort to make this island base into an impregnable fortress, at this stage of the war, its importance had diminished as the tide of battle passed from the eastern to the central Mediterranean. With the threatened invasion of their homeland, and with ultimate defeat staring them in the face, the Italians had had few resources left for the Aegean. According to the Italian Official History, the main function of the island at the time of the armistice was as a submarine base from which to launch attacks on Allied shipping in the eastern Mediterranean, although this had met with scant success. The major submarine successes in this area had been achieved by the German U-boats, which operated from Salamis in Greece. Leros was the home of the Italian 5th Submarine Group, under the command of Capt. Virgilio Spigai and comprising the submarines *Ametista, Beilul, Sirena,* and *Onice.* On September 8, none of these vessels was in the Aegean; the first three were under repair in Italy and the fourth had only just left Taranto.

Also based in Leros was the 4th Destroyer Squadron, which was employed on escort work throughout the Aegean. It consisted of the destroyers *Crispi, Sella, Euro,* and *Turbine,* but only the *Euro* was at Leros; the *Sella* was in Venice under repair, and the *Crispi* and *Turbine* were at the Piraeus. The last two were soon to be taken over by the Germans and used in the Aegean with telling effect.

For local defense, there was the 3rd MAS Flotilla, under the command of Capt. Luigi Borghi. This consisted of four squadrons of MS and MAS boats, sixteen boats in all, of which eight were actually in Leros. The 39th Minesweeping Flotilla, under Cmdr. Carlo Citter, and various naval auxiliaries were also stationed at Leros.

The Italian Air Force was represented on the island by No. 147 Squadron, with ten Cant Z 501 seaplanes for maritime reconnaissance, of which seven were serviceable.

For the defense of the island base, the Italians had installed a formidable array of heavy naval and antiaircraft guns of various calibers. There were twenty-four batteries in all, mounting some forty-three naval and fifty-eight antiaircraft guns. In addition, there were forty-nine heavy machine guns of various calibers for antiaircraft defense, as well as seventeen searchlight positions. The most powerful of these batteries were *Ducca,* situated on Mount Cazzuni and armed with four 152-millimeter and one 120-millimeter guns; *San Giorgio* on Mount Scumbarda with three 152-millimeter and one 102-millimeter; *Ciano* on Mount Clidi, with four 152-millimeter; *Marinata* on Mount Marcello and *Lago* on Mount Appetici, both mounting four 120-millimeter guns. The batteries were officered by the Italian Army, but the actual manning of the guns was carried out by naval personnel. It is not surprising, with this number of guns on such a relatively small island, that in certain quarters in Cairo it was thought that Leros could be held against any scale of attack that the Germans could mount against it. The guns were in very exposed positions, however, and not sited in concrete emplacements but in open mountings; their quality and effectiveness also left much to be desired. General Maitland Wilson later recorded in his *Despatch*: "The defences of Leros were not at all well developed and much of the AA material was out of date and much of the system of fire control was deplorable. Certain natures of ammunition were in short supply."

The Italian garrison in all totaled approximately 8,000 men, of whom 6,000 were navy personnel, but many of these were technicians and administrative staff employed at the naval base. Apart from the batteries, the ground forces available for defense were pretty thin. The army had about 1,200 men, mainly from a battalion of the 10th Regina Infantry Regiment, under the command of Col. Giuseppe Li Volsi. The troops were lightly armed except for one company that had two platoons of 45-millimeter mortars and the 8th Machine Gun Company, which also had an 81-millimeter mortar platoon. In addition, there were the 402nd Blackshirt Company (*Centurione Calise*), though its strength was little more than that of a platoon; two companies of marines guarding naval installations at Gonia and San Giorgio; and 400 air force personnel guarding air installations. All the forces were under the overall command of R.Adm. Luigi Mascherpa, who had been the captain commanding the naval base before the armistice.

This was the state of the Italian defenses when the advance party of the British garrison arrived on the island on September 17. These were men of the 2nd Battalion, Royal Irish Fusiliers, under the command of Lt. Col. Maurice French. Like the 2nd Battalion, Queen's Own Royal West Kent Regiment, they had spent the first four years of the war on Malta, followed by a short spell of retraining in Syria and also at the Combined Operations Centre at Kabrit. The battalion was moved to Haifa transit center on short notice, and shortly afterward, some 300 men embarked on the destroyers *Hurworth* and *Croome*. These destroyers had been part of the escort of Convoy MKS 24 in the eastern Mediterranean when on the fourteenth they had been detached from the convoy with orders to proceed to Haifa with all dispatch. They reached the Haifa boom at 2220 on the fifteenth. Things went smoothly, and there was no delay in berthing, refueling, or embarking the troops of the Royal Irish Fusiliers. The *Hurworth* took aboard eleven officers and 160 other ranks, the *Croome* a few less. Both destroyers slipped at 0115 on the sixteenth. They arrived at Leros at 0800 on the seventeenth, where they reported a friendly welcome. The *Hurworth* disembarked troops alongside, while the *Croome* disembarked her cargo into landing craft without incident. Both destroyers left at dusk the same day for Alexandria. The remainder of the battalion sailed from Haifa at 0700 on the nineteenth on board the destroyers *Intrepid* and *Echo,* arriving at Leros on the twentieth. The destroyers also unloaded four Bofors guns.

Colonel French had, on arrival, decided that the best way of deploying his forces was to hold the highest point in the center of the island. He just did not have sufficient forces to occupy and hold the north and south sections as well. In view of the appalling lack of communications, he decided that his men would best be employed as a strong, flexible reserve behind the static Italian defenses. Plans were laid for the complete battalion to be moved on foot to any part of the island that might be threatened.

Following the fall of Cos, the supply and reinforcement situation became acute. The maintenance of the British garrisons had always been difficult because of the complex lines of communications, which were all vulnerable to interruption and severance. The basic plan had been for direct shipment to Casteloriso, which was used as the main advance staging post between the Aegean and Egypt. Direct shipping to Leros and Cos was also possible initially, while for Samos and the lesser islands, transshipments were to be made in caiques or landing craft from Cos, Leros, or Kusadasi in Turkey. Small store ships were run directly from Egypt and Palestine to Casteloriso, Leros and Cos and there the cargo was transshipped for distribution to the other islands. Much of the escort work between the Levant ports and Casteloriso was carried out by the French escort vessels *Commandant Domine, Commandant Duboc,* and *La Moqueuse* (all of 630 tons); the Greek destroyer *Kondouriotis* (1,350 tons); the Indian sloop *Sutlej* (1,250 tons); and the Australian escort vessel *Ipswich* (650 tons).

The fall of Cos greatly impeded these operations, which had up to that time worked without too much difficulty. Between September 15 and October 3, aircraft of No. 215 Squadron played a great part in maintaining Cos, but with the last base for single-engine fighter cover lost, the navy decided that it could not risk running the store ships into the Aegean directly, and several casualties bore out this view. A number of ships were held loaded in the Middle Eastern ports ready to proceed if a suitable opportunity arose, but in fact they never sailed.

The supply line to Leros and Samos was therefore reduced solely to caiques from Casteloriso or Kusadasi, submarines from Beirut and Haifa, or high-speed dashes by destroyers from Alexandria, although an effort was made to keep air drops going from Cairo. The small island of Casteloriso became the main transshipment point for the whole area, a role for which it soon proved totally inadequate. After the veto on the use of store ships, caiques had to be used, and care was taken to ensure that only those caiques that had refused to sail into the Aegean proper were employed on this run. Supply by warship was used only as an emergency measure, for the navy had

its hands full enough. A number of flying boats and Italian floatplanes operated from Aboukir Bay to carry forward personnel and stores urgently
required. Originally two Sunderlands and four Cants were available, but this
number was reduced by November, when the daily lift did not exceed 3,000
pounds excluding personnel.

These Cants were Italian-manned and came from No. 147 Squadron,
which had soon found itself caught up in the bewildering events following
the announcement of the armistice in September. It was almost the only Italian air unit operational in the Aegean at that time. Once Rhodes fell into
German hands, the officers of this unit had agreed to join the Allied forces
against the Germans. One of the squadron's seaplanes, a Cant Z 506, while
in the area of Stampalia on September 16, was attacked by two Me 110s and
succeeded in shooting one down and damaging the other before being
brought down in the sea in flames. The same month, three more were
destroyed by bomb and machine-gun attacks by Ju 88s while undergoing
repairs and maintenance ashore at Cos. Three Cant Z 606s were employed
for a time in ferrying wounded British troops to Egypt, but the fall of Cos
put a stop to this.

On October 6, the two remaining Italian seaplanes, one a Cant 506 and
the other a Cant Z 501, dispersed to an anchorage on the island of Lipsos to
avoid being destroyed. They eventually succeeded in reaching Limassol in
Cyprus after being damaged both by the Germans in flight and by landing
in rough weather. The Italian 147 *Squadriglie* lost eighty men, including
pilots and ground crew, between September and December while fighting
on the Allied side.

The limiting factor in the use of Casteloriso as a staging base was the fact
that the island had storage facilities for only 4,500 tons, of which just 800
could be gasoline. Towards the end of operations three caiques were used as
floating bunkers holding a further 250 tons of oil and gas. It was also clearly
a logistics officer's nightmare to account for the dispatch and timing of the
arrival of stores and equipment when the caiques could move only intermittently and wherever the chance presented itself.

In view of the extremely critical supply situation, it was made a prime
objective of Middle East Command to secure a suitable overland supply
route through Turkey to Samos. The British used the persuasive argument
that this was needed to supply the civilian population of that island, but
there is no doubt that the ultimate aim was to set up a safe supply organization to bolster Leros and Samos with its military needs—which indeed were
considerable. Up until October 11, a somewhat hodgepodge arrangement
was agreed on, and substantial shipments were made; on the eleventh, General Maitland Wilson recalled:

I formally placed the main responsibility for the island [Samos] with the Military Attaché in Ankara working through Kusadasi and drawing from the dumps which with other objects in view we had established in Turkey. As a result of this decision and of the decision not to evacuate Samos and Leros as an immediate consequence of the loss of Cos, it became necessary to arrange for increased supplies both for civil and military consumption.

These arrangements were duly made with the Turkish government, and until the end of the operation, a regular service of supplies and stores was maintained, moved by both rail and road from dumps and shipped in caiques to the islands. These dumps, however, useful though they were, contained only a limited range of weapons and rations. The Turkish government further compromised its neutrality by supplementing these with gas and oil sent by rail from Syria through their own territory to Kusadasi. The first of these "supply" trains rolled over the Turkish frontier on October 21 and continued until Leros was taken. It is difficult to imagine the island holding as long as it did without Turkey's "benevolent neutrality." Between September 28 and November 16, a total of 3,000 tons were shipped to Samos and 480 tons to Leros. Again in his *Despatch*, General Maitland Wilson made no bones about its usefulness: "From 11th October onwards the supplies from Turkey were intended to be the main source of maintenance for the garrisons of Samos and Leros but they were supplemented to a very considerable extent from other sources."

One such source was the use of submarines to take in essential supplies. The first trip was made by the aging British submarine *Severn*, a vessel completed in 1935 and with a displacement of 1,850 tons. The prime need in Leros was for antiaircraft guns, and the *Severn* was to carry six Bofors guns complete with ammunition. The gun barrels presented no difficulty, as they were stowed forward in the torpedo compartment, but for the carriage of the mountings, it was a different matter. The submarine's hatches were not big enough to accommodate the mountings, and it was therefore decided that they should be carried on the submarine's outer casing fastened by wire hawsers. On October 18, all was ready, and the *Severn* left Beirut for Leros complete with six-gun mountings wired to her casing—a truly remarkable sight. She also carried fifteen tons of ammunition, three tons of gas, miscellaneous stores, and eight military personnel. She entered Port Laki Bay after dark on the twenty-first, and unloading was completed by 0400 on the 22nd. The submarine sailed before daylight, but even so was bombed as she was passing through the boom. Although the bombs missed, they exploded on a nearby cliff, and the *Severn* was showered with rock. She arrived back in Beirut on the 25th. After minor repairs she reloaded and sailed again on the thirty-first, but she developed serious engine defects and had to return to base.

Following this success, another large British submarine, the minelaying *Rorqual*, was similarly employed in bringing in six more Bofors guns and a jeep. Italian and Greek submarines, being somewhat larger than the available British ones, then took over. In total, Allied submarines made seven successful supply trips, including five completed by Italian submarines, carrying in a total of 325½ tons of stores.

Although Turkey adopted a benevolent attitude in helping supply and maintain Samos and Leros from that country, it was not prepared to commit itself further. The constant supply and patrols of the islands were taking a heavy toll of British naval resources, so on October 29, the Chiefs of Staff informed the prime minister that either Leros would have to be reinforced and supplied entirely by submarine, or six squadrons of fighters would have to be based on landing strips in southwest Anatolia to provide the necessary air cover to enable British surface forces to continue operating.

Here indeed was an ironic situation, for whereas the capture of the Dodecanese had originally been touted by the prime minister as a prerequisite for action by Turkey, action from Turkey was now required to secure possession of the islands.

A joint meeting of the foreign ministers of the United Kingdom, United States, and Russia had begun in Moscow on October 19, and they discussed policy toward Turkey. Britain wanted Turkey to enter the war as soon as conditions were suitable and in the meantime to grant the necessary military facilities at once. Russia too was in line with Britain's thinking on this matter but wanted Turkey to enter the war by the end of 1943, calculating that Turkey would contain some ten German divisions. As on previous occasions, however, the Americans did not see eye to eye with their allies on policy in the eastern Mediterranean. They preferred that Turkey remain neutral, concerned about the amount of resources that might have to be diverted to that country should it enter the war. The British and Russian governments, however, signed the following protocol on November 2:

1. The two Foreign Secretaries think it most desirable that Turkey should enter the war on the side of the United Nations before the end of 1943 in order that she may take her part with the United Nations in hastening the defeat of Hitlerism Germany in which Turkey and other freedom-loving states are interested.

2. The two Foreign Secretaries agree that it should be suggested to Turkey on behalf of the United Kingdom and Soviet Governments at the earliest possible date to be agreed upon between them that she should enter the war before the end of 1943.

3. The two Foreign Secretaries agree that Turkey should immediately be asked to give all possible aid to the United Nations by placing facilities at Turkish air bases at the disposal of the Allied Forces and providing such other facilities as the two Governments may be agreed upon are desirable.

The Americans were not involved with making this statement, but they agreed to its terms provided that in the opinion of the Combined Chiefs of Staff, no British or American resources necessary for Overlord or operations in Italy would be committed to the eastern Mediterranean.

Accordingly, British foreign minister Anthony Eden left Moscow on November 4 for Cairo, where he had four meetings with a Turkish delegation headed by their foreign minister, M. Numan, between November 5 and 8. The Turks were sympathetic to the Allied demands but were determined not to join the Allies unless they could be reasonably sure of immunity from German attack. This fear included the Germans' reactions to the immediate as well as future Allied requests. Numan stated that Turkey could not cede air bases in Anatolia without the same guarantees of British protection as would be provided if Turkey declared war. The British, however, were not willing to provide guarantees of protection on such a scale for the use of air bases in Anatolia. Neither side would move from its declared position, and on November 7, the Turks finally stated that their refusal to grant the base facilities was definite, although they would further consider the Allies' larger proposal. Considering the perilous state of the British troops in the Aegean, the Turks could hardly be blamed for their caution.

On Leros, it was unfortunate that a broadcast had been picked up by the garrison to the effect that it was an odds-on certainty that the Turks would allow the use of their airfields. It is not known who dropped this particular brick, but it caused much bitter comment when it became increasingly obvious to the defenders that this was not to be the case at all. Marsland Gander recorded that in the six weeks prior to his arrival the island had suffered 1,000 air raids and some 700 tons of bombs had been dropped.

The principal effect was to tire and demoralize the defenders, with the spectacle of German bomber formations remaining overhead all day long in undisputed possession of the daylight sky, practically unchallenged and rarely harmed by the antiaircraft fire.

The air attacks were mainly concentrated on gun positions and the naval base at Port Laki, which was gradually being reduced to rubble. On October 20, it was reported that the unloading facilities at Leros had been reduced to one fixed crane. Not only were the British faced with the hazardous task of getting stores to the island, but they were now faced with the added difficulty of finding some means to unload them when they did arrive there. And all this had to be organized during the brief hours of darkness, as all vessels had to be well clear of Leros before daylight.

German aircraft had also been taking a heavy toll of Italian vessels using the harbors of Leros. On the same day that the *Intrepid* and *Queen Olga* were lost, the Italian torpedo boat *MAS 534* was also sunk and the *Ms 11* damaged. On October 1, the destroyer *Euro* (1,092 tons) was caught in Partheni Bay and so badly damaged that she had to be written off as a total loss. A particularly heavy raid on October 5 sank the minelayer *Legnano* (615 tons), *Ms 730,* and the steamers *Prode* (1,244 tons) and *Porto di Roma* (470 tons), followed by the sinking of the steamer *Ivorea* (3,274 tons) in Partheni Bay on the seventh. *Ms 15* was sunk and *Ms 11* again damaged in the air attacks on the twenty-fifth. All this provided ample evidence, if any was needed, that the German Air Force ruled the skies over Leros.

Although the navy was handicapped by the size and weight limitations on the stores carried by the submarines and destroyers, they nevertheless shipped the main weight of supplies sent by sea. Dumps of 300 tons were established at Alexandria, Beirut, and Haifa and dumps of 100 tons in Cyprus. In all, and despite its other duties, the navy transported almost 5,000 men, 1,000 tons of stores, more than thirty jeeps and trailers, and forty guns to the islands.

To overcome the difficulties of finding crews for the caiques, who frequently refused to go beyond Casteloriso, crews were made up from naval and army volunteers. In addition, No. 216 Squadron managed to drop some 334,000 pounds of supplies and 200 men between October 5 and November 19, although bad weather frustrated many other attempts.

After the seaplanes could no longer get through, the casualties from the Aegean were evacuated by caique, destroyer, and toward the end, through Turkey. An arrangement was reached whereby the Turkish government agreed to accept up to forty seriously wounded men in the hospital at Bodrum without internment. More serious cases for which operational treatment was required were sent to the Izmir French Hospital.

Despite all these difficulties there was no lack in the final instance of ammunition or supplies on Leros.

On October 3, the Royal Irish Fusiliers were deployed in accordance with Col. Maurice French's plan of a centralized defense in the following manner: A Company was on the north slopes of Mount Meraviglia, from where it could cover both Gurna and Alinda Bays and Rachi Ridge; B Company was in the Windmill Area to cover Gurna Bay, with one platoon from this company detached on the island of Stampalia but later withdrawn; C Company was to the south of Meraviglia, acting as a mobile reserve and covering Pandeli Bay and the southeast; and D Company was on the Rachi Ridge, which overlooked both Alinda and Gurna Bays and the narrow neck of land between the two headquarters was set up in a tunnel on Mount Meraviglia.

All the rifle companies were very weak in numbers and averaged only about sixty other ranks. The Anti-Tank Platoon had been sent to the rifle companies and the Carrier Platoon formed No. 17 Platoon with D Company.

The men of the Long Range Desert Group were sent to the principal batteries in order to stiffen the morale of the Italian gunners and also to maintain wireless links; Y2 patrol was on Mount Marcello and R1 patrol on Mount Zuncona.

The Italian troops were assigned to the defense of the likely landing areas but these positions could only be thinly held. The 8th Machine Gun Company covered Gurna, Alinda and Pandeli Bays with a total of twenty-two machine guns. The Blackshirt Company covered Blefuti Bay with four machine guns, and there were also machine-gun platoons armed with three or four guns at San Spirito, Mericcia, Port Laki, and Serocampo. Backing up these units was the 1st Company headquarters at San Quaranta, with three platoons of infantry in the Gurna sector; the 2nd Company headquarters and another three platoons of infantry were between Mount Meraviglia and Mount Rachi.

Held in reserve was the 3rd Company headquarters, located southeast of Mount Meraviglia, with one platoon dug in on Mount Ancora, a second platoon between Mount Vigla and Temenia, and a third at Serocampo. The 4th Machine Gun Company, with eight guns, was in reserve west of the road junction between Mounts Meraviglia and Rachi. And finally, there was a mortar platoon on Rachi Ridge.

These then were the forces poised to resist the expected German attack following the loss of Cos. The attitudes of the Italian forces varied considerably. There were some outstanding individuals who were to show great bravery and resolution in the days ahead, particularly among the artillerymen, but the majority were indifferent at best, and more concerned of their possible fate should their former German allies prevail than anything else—and with very good reason. The majority of the Italians were stuck with the situation they found themselves in and hoped British promises would somehow outmatch German action. Mascherpa, who had initially been aided and abetted by the increasingly out-of-touch Brig. Ben Brittorous, seemed equally anxious to ingratiate himself with the British (after all, they were *in situ*) while becoming increasingly ambiguous about his position as the German bombing and the obvious lead-up to the invasion became more obvious.

As a final illustration of the difficulties of the British in reinforcing Leros, a typical example was the trials and tribulations of the rear party of the Royal Irish Fusiliers under Captains Slaney, Ambrose, and Mason. At the conference that took place in Syria prior to the battalion's departure for Leros on September 15, Lieutenant Colonel French informed the Motor Transport section that it was to provide the battalion rear party to hand in all the motor transport, antitank guns, carriers, and so on that could not be transported. When the battalion left for Haifa, the rear party organized the handing over of all this equipment, on which they had spent so much time and care, to X Corps when it was finally learned from brigade headquarters in Haifa that only jeeps and motorcycles would be suitable for use on Leros. Assistance was then given in combat loading the destroyers, which took the second party to Leros.

After much administrative work had been completed, during which time they heard of the air attacks on Cos, the party was able to secure space on the TS *Keepong* for the small amount of transport that was to be taken to Leros. In view of the very limited space available on the ship, the jeeps and trailers were packed with as much oil, stores, and camouflage nets as they could carry. In fact, determined efforts had to be made to prevent the loading of a dozen filing cabinets with attendant typists for the staff of one senior officer; the Royal Irish Fusiliers finally won this battle!

In the words of one officer concerned, the *Keepong* turned out to be "a superannuated coal boat from the Malaysian coast . . . in no way equipped to carry personnel." But after Herculean efforts by the party, the vessel was finally stowed aboard and accompanied by Lt. Troy Hanna and Regimental Sgt. Maj. G. Flannagan, who subsequently reached Leros safely. Captain Slaney and Lieutenant Henry were both in Sidon hospital at this time, but Capt. R. Ambrose secured their release, together with Capt. C. R. Mason. The rear party then numbered some sixty-three men of all ranks, and on September 27 they all moved to Beirut with some elation, expecting to sail at once to join their comrades.

But on reaching Beirut and joining forces with Major Scott and a similar party of Queen's Own Royal West Kents bound for Samos, they found that not only was there no ship, but the dock parties concerned knew nothing about their movements. Somewhat dispirited, they all returned to the transit camp and it was not until September 30 that they at last found the steamers *Eolo* and *Koritza* waiting to take them aboard. Half the party was embarked in each ship, but their troubles were not yet over:

> A note on these ships is opportune. The *Eolo* was Italian and a miniature liner running in peacetime between Naples and the volcanic island of Stromboli. She was beautifully fitted and of about 1,000 tons, but had cargo space for baggage only. *Koritza* was a converted flush-deck sailing ship of a type used in the 1890s. She was quite rotten in the decks and had no lifting gear on board, except a short mast forward carrying a boom which could be used as a hoist; she was verminous below.

Escorted by two sloops, the two ships cast off and headed out to sea. But on clearing the harbor mouth and dropping the pilot, when the captain of the *Koritza*, Lieutenant Caller, reached for the lanyard, it came away in his hand and in the same instant it was reported that seawater had entered the boilers. The pilot was recalled, and Captain Ambrose's party returned to harbor and watched sadly as the *Eolo* vanished over the horizon. They returned with the Royal West Kents to Syrian camps overlooking the harbor and waited.

On October 6, they were ordered to drive to Ramat David airfield and later that day were flown by Dakotas to Nicosia, Cyprus. From here they were transferred to a rest camp at Limassol—where, to their amazement, they met Captain Slaney and the men from the *Eolo*.

The *Eolo* finally sailed for Casteloriso with both parties aboard, plus other troops totaling some 200, half of which were men of RAF Regiment Squadron on their way to Cos, and 50 gunners and the Faughs (nickname of the Royal Irish Fusiliers) bound for Leros. When about five miles from Casteloriso, they were intercepted by a destroyer and informed that because of the situation, it was considered unwise for them to carry on; they were to return to Cyprus immediately. The *Eolo* arrived back in Cyprus at dawn on the eighth. Because they had not been expected, they had to spend the following day onboard the ship. A stay of three days at a transit camp was followed by orders to shift immediately to Limassol again. After a wild drive across the island, they reached the docks at 1600 hours and were told that the destroyers that were to transport them had to leave at 1900. That hour came and went and still the ships had not received orders to move. This delay was fortunate, for during it came the arrival of a REME sergeant attached to the battalion with six Piat guns that had been flown in from Palestine for Leros.

After waiting all through the night, the Faughs were joined by other units awaiting shipment and sent off yet again to a transit camp. They twice subsequently prepared to embark in destroyers, only to be told that the orders had been canceled. On one occasion, the Faughs had loaded the antitank guns, stores, and arms which would have been of the utmost value to the defenders of Leros, but alas, these eventually had to be offloaded again, as the destroyers were urgently needed elsewhere. They made contact with some of their wounded comrades being brought back by the destroyers, who told them of the intensive bombing the Germans were carrying out against Leros, but there was still no news as to how they were going to join their battalion.

They also heard an unpleasant rumor from some RAF officers that the Germans had actually landed and were in possession of half the island. It appears that some RAF personnel had escaped from Leros during a heavy raid, under the impression that the Germans had indeed made a landing. The Faughs' officers decided that this was worth investigating and cabled Brigadier Allen at Saratan area headquarters in Palestine. The Faughs volunteered to be dropped by parachute or transported by submarine to join the battalion in the battle—if indeed there were one. On October 13, the order came to assemble at an airstrip outside Limassol but in reduced strength. From here they were flown to Cairo and, after a meal, were transported to Alexandria, where they joined two destroyers that sailed that night for the Aegean. While aboard the destroyer, Captain Slaney was informed by her commanding officer that up to thirty minutes before the Faughs embarked, the ships were standing by to *evacuate* Leros but that these orders had been changed at the last minute. Thus in the early hours of the fifteenth, the rear party finally disembarked during an air raid to join the rifle companies in the defense of the island. The Motor Transport Section was given positions on the south side of Meraviglia under the command of Captain Ambrose.

While the rear party had been wandering around the eastern Mediterranean, Lieutenant Colonel French had been strengthening his defenses. B Company withdrew its platoon from Stampalia just in time to avoid a German attack, which took place on the morning of October 22. It was preceded by a heavy Stuka dive-bombing attack, which knocked out the two wireless stations. This was followed by the dropping of a company of paratroops and a seaborne landing by assault troops. The island was soon in German hands. The fifteen remaining British personnel took to the hills and subsequently managed to return to Leros. The disaster on Levitha followed. The position of Leros was now verging on the critical.

Lt. Col. W. R. Brackett, Royal Artillery, returned to Egypt to place before general headquarters the problems and needs of the island's defenses, while on the island itself the normal routine preparations continued. The principal problem was the increasingly bizarre attitude of Brittorous, who was clearly becoming out touch with the reality of the situation and had lost the respect and trust of many under his (nominal) command. Until the issue could be tactfully resolved, and under nonstop air bombardment, the Faughs improved their defenses, laying out antipersonnel minefields, wire and so on. By night they assisted in the unloading of any destroyers and small vessels that could get through.

It was reported that despite this nonstop work, together with short sleep and short rations, no rest areas or relaxation of any kind, the battalion still was remarkably fit and ready to meet any eventuality.

Meanwhile, a trickle of reinforcements was arriving to aid the Faughs. On the eighteenth, B Company of the Queen's Own Royal West Kents, under Capt. E. P. Flood, which was en route to Samos, was diverted to Leros and positioned on the high ground to the west overlooking Gurna Bay.

Up to the end of October, operations in the Aegean had been controlled by Middle East Command through III Corps HQ (Force 292) and the 234th Brigade under Brig. Ben Brittorous on Leros. The developments in the area, however, led General Maitland Wilson to decide that a separate command should be set up to take over operations on the spot. Maj. Gen. H. R. Hall was therefore appointed general officer commanding in the Aegean, with the specific task of holding both Samos and Leros in order to cause the Germans maximum discomfort. In addition, he was given command of all British, Greek, and Italian forces in the area, as well as naval personnel and shore establishments not under the commander in chief of the Levant or senior British naval officer in the Aegean.

Brig. Robert A. G. "Dolly" Tilney was appointed to the post of fortress commander in Leros and with General Hall arrived on Leros on November 5; from this point in time, HQ Aegean started to control operations. Brittorous relinquished command of the 234th Infantry Brigade, and General Hall decided to make Samos his headquarters. The Reverend Anwyl told us, "By the way, I think Brigadier Brittorous was more responsible than Colonel French for the original defense setup and indeed was politely removed from his post for alleged timidity."

At the same time, further reinforcements began to arrive on Leros. The 4th Battalion, the Buffs, had spent the major part of the war on Malta after coming out of France in 1940, only finally landing at Alexandria on September 20. They spent a few weeks at Sidi Bishr rest camp and were then ordered to embark for Leros. The battalion, 29 officers and 662 men strong, made the move in two sections, and the HQ Section suffered heavily when the destroyer *Eclipse* was mined and sunk on the night of October 23–24. Notwithstanding this tragedy, the remainder of the battalion, 310 officers and men with forty tons of stores, had sailed from Alexandria at 0100 on twenty-sixth aboard the destroyers *Penn, Dulverton,* and *Miaoulis,* disembarking at Patheni Bay from 0300 on the twenty-seventh. They joined Colonel Iggulden and the survivors of the first party. Capt. M. J. W. Smith of the Buffs was also attached to Brigadier Tilney's staff at fortress headquarters.

The other unit to arrive in Leros at the beginning of the month was the 1st Battalion, the King's Own Royal Regiment (Lancaster). In India at the outbreak of war, the battalion had subsequently served in Iraq during the 1941 uprising and North Africa during the desert campaigns of 1942. Withdrawn for rest in July of that year, they had the misfortune to have the ship that was transporting them torpedoed and sunk; one officer and twenty-nine men were lost with the 5,875-ton *Princess Marguerite* on August 17 when she was sunk by the *U-83* off the coast of Egypt. The battalion finally reached Cyprus, where they remained until April 1943. Then they transferred to Syria, rejoining the 10th Indian Division, where they underwent combined operations training.

On concluding this course, the battalion returned to Syria and was stationed some twenty-five miles from Beirut. November 1 found the battalion packed onboard a special train with fifty tons of baggage and equipment following a secret order that gave only twenty-four hours' notice to prepare to move to an unknown destination. No orders were even given as to what equipment and clothing would be required. The train arrived at Alexandria at 1600 hours on November 3, and the troops were quickly hustled aboard the waiting destroyers *Faulknor, Echo, Penn,* and *Pathfinder,* which sailed later that day at 2330 hours, escorted by the cruiser *Phoebe.* All motor transport, antitank guns, and carriers had to be left behind.

Following the loss of the *Eclipse,* a more circuitous and safer route was followed to transport the troops to Leros. The force first proceeded to Limassol, however, where the four destroyers refueled from the cruiser, and then continued unescorted north of Rhodes to the Gulf of Doris.

Here the four ships lay up during daylight on the fourth. After dark that day they were quickly under way, arriving at Leros at 0200 on the fifth. The *Faulknor* and *Pathfinder* unloaded at Porto Lago, while the *Echo* and *Penn* landed their cargo at Patheni Bay, finishing at 0155 and completing by 0400. The troops were quickly disembarked, together with eighty tons of stores, and the destroyers sailed before daylight to lie up once again in Turkish waters, again using Guvercinlik Bay.

In the meantime, requests for a machine-gun battalion could not be met. This meant a further depleting of the ranks of the Royal Irish Fusiliers, for the guns were sent but had to be manned by infantry personnel, something like twenty-four machine guns being so taken over. This reduced the rifle companies and further demands reduced each platoon until the average was only about eighteen strong. A trickle of reinforcements joined them before battle commenced.

Brigadier Tilney now reorganized the augmented defense forces on a completely new plan. Lt. Col. Maurice French's plan for a centralized defense was thrown overboard, and the new policy was characterized by the slogan "No enemy shall set foot on this island unless to be a prisoner of war." French pointed out that it was impossible to cover such a long and intricate coastline; he also felt that it was inadvisable to place too many troops along the coast, since airborne landings were possible. But it was felt in higher circles that the terrain of the island largely ruled this out. Tilney duly reorganized the defenses as instructed. According to the Reverend Anwyl, however, "Before the German landing, I roamed the whole island in my work. In the event, the gunner, Brigadier Tilney, was surely proved wrong."

Major General Hall instructed Brigadier Tilney to organize a defense of all the suitable landing places, and each battalion commander was to see that this was done. After ensuring that his plan was taking shape, General Hall returned to Samos on the night of November 11 to organize his headquarters there.

Leros was now in effect divided into three sectors, all the troops in each sector, including the Italians, coming under the command of the British battalion commander. The three British battalions—the 4th Buffs, 2nd Royal Irish Fusiliers, and 1st King's Own Royal Regiment—were made responsible for the northern, central, and southern sectors, respectively. All were more or less self-contained areas. In the tunnel headquarters on Mount Meraviglia, Brigadier Tilney set up his command post with the Italian commander. A troop of 25-pounders was sited close by; the four 25-pounders had been found in Samos fitted with German sights and ranging aids. The twelve Bofors guns of the 3rd Light Anti-Aircraft Battery constituted the sole effective air defense.

The men of the Long Range Desert Group who had been with the various gun batteries remained with them until they were bombed out, and then joined with Jellicoe's "pirates" of the Special Boat Squadron, who were to act as a small mobile reserve against paratroops.

The other units available were detachments of 9 Field Company, Madras Sappers and Miners; 47 DID of the Royal Indian Army Service Corps; 161 Field Ambulance; and 570 AC-AD, Royal Army Ordnance Corps. A casualty receiving station was established in a private house at Alinda Bay that had been used by the Italians for similar purposes. Other adjoining empty houses were also taken over and accommodation for seventy patients was thus provided: thirty beds and forty stretchers. At Port Laki, a dental center, medical store, and MI room were established in the Italian Naval Hospital.

The Italian batteries were sited on the tops of hills; there were no low-sited antishipping guns. Therefore, six of the invaluable Bofors antiaircraft guns were used in a low-level role and were sited to cover the approaches of possible landing beaches, as were eight of the twelve 2-pounder antitank guns. A further four were still in workshop hands at the time of invasion. In practice, only one of these weapons had a clear shoot during the initial German landings.

Leros has an area of about thirty square miles and is deeply indented with bays. The terrain is rocky and mountainous, with little cover from the air and roads of such poor quality that even jeeps were severely limited in their operations. The coastline is generally steep and rocky; only in the bays are there shelving beaches suitable for seaborne landings. The rocky, scrub-covered slopes are strewn with loose boulders. The mountains that feature so much in the dispositions are nothing more than large prominences and the highest—Meraviglia in the central section—is only about 650 feet high. This height would have been sufficient to observe the entire island, which is only seven and a half miles long, but for other lesser hills screening the view towards many of the inlets along the coast.

Fortress headquarteres consisted of a single twisting tunnel blasted right through the peak of Meraviglia and was entered by cuttings at each end covered with camouflage nets. From one end, gun positions commanded views of the town of Leros in the valley below and of Alinda Bay with its Crusader castle on a 500-foot hill opposite. Close by was a church whose bells were used as an air raid warning. From the opposite entrance, Port Laki and Gurna Bays could be observed, with a rocky peninsula between. Port Laki Bay had been the main Italian naval base; now it was a graveyard for the destroyers *Intrepid* and *Queen Olga* and many small craft. L. Marsland Gander describes the headquarters tunnel on the day of the attack:

> The tunnel was at a guess about five to six hundred feet long and only the central part from which two or three underground chambers opened out was lighted. On entering the tunnel there was complete darkness until turning a corner I came upon the illuminated caves opening out to right and left, where Brigadier Tilney's staff were at work on trestle tables. In another chamber the signalers were busy coding, deciphering and tapping their instruments.

The Buffs were detailed to hold the northern sector of the island, of which the commanding feature was Mount Clidi with Partheni Bay opening to the sea in the northwest corner—where the beaches were most suitable for landings. This area was covered by Maj. E. A. Hole's B Company. On his right was Maj. E. W. Tassell with D Company, whose job was to cover Blefuti and Palma Bays. Facing south to Gurna Bay was Maj. V. C. Bourne's C Company. Mount Clidi, whose "precipitous and apparently almost unscaleable" sides were considered invulnerable, was left lightly held by some Italian troops stiffened by Long Range Desert Group patrols. This was to have unfortunate repercussions for the Buffs.

The Royal Irish Fusiliers were to retain the central portion of the island, but the concentration of forces around the beaches necessitated a considerable reshuffling of dispositions. All types of transport were used to effect the move, including local carts pulled by the men, doors of bombed buildings, and the commanding officer's jeep, but most of the shift was by manpower. Because of the fear of being caught in midmove, the battalion was kept hard at it, with little time between the raids for rest.

By the eve of what was to be the invasion, the battalion was in position. HQ Company was in the "Charing Cross" area with the Pioneer Platoon and HQ Battalion. A Company was on the southern side of Alinda Bay with two 2-pounder antitank guns and six Vickers machine guns. This company was only fifty strong, having had to find crews for the guns and two 3-inch mortars as well. B Company was in position along Pandeli Bay to link up with the King's Own in the south and to support an Italian infantry company in the area. This Italian company deserted en masse during the heavy bombing on the eve of battle, according to the Fusiliers' battalion history. C Company constituted the battalion's mobile reserve and was located on. the southern slopes of Meraviglia overlooking Anchor and Pandeli Bay. D Company was bombed off the Rachi Ridge and was repositioned with its platoons split up as follows: 18 Platoon manned Point 36 overlooking Alinda Bay, 17 Platoon was at Germano on the north side of Gurna Bay; and 16 Platoon was on the opposite side of Gurna Bay linking up with B Company Royal West Kents. D Company was manning nine Bren guns, two Italian machine guns, two 2-inch mortars, and two medium machine guns—defensive equipment in the main.

The dispositions of the Italian forces had also been altered to conform to the new British defense plan, and according to the Italian official history, their ground forces, supplemented by men from the sunken warships *Euro*, *Legnano*, and *Volta*, were deployed in three main groups holding the northern and southern areas of the island and separated by the British headquarters on Meraviglia, where the Italians also had a central sector. In the northern sector, the only army unit was the 402nd Blackshirt Company, with four machine guns at Blefuti Bay. The navy provided groups of seamen from the *Euro* to guard Partheni Bay, the torpedo depot, and battery PL 989 at Cape Timari, while seamen from the *Volta* guarded battery PL 899 on the Blefuti Peninsula.

In the southern sector, the army provided machine-gun platoons at Mericcia, Port Laki, and Serocampo. The 4th Machine Gun Company was on the slopes of Zuncona and Tortora; the 2nd Company with a troop of mortars was on the slopes southwest of Zuncona and on the slopes of Mount Piana; and the 3rd Company, less one platoon, was in the Grotiraccio and Serocampo zone. The navy provided one company of men for the defense of Gonia, and Mericcia had two platoons of men plus a party of seamen from the *Legnano*. There was one company at San Giorgio, one company covering the batteries PL 388 and PL 281, and a platoon of men at battery PL 113. The only air force personnel on the island were located in this sector: six platoons at Serocampo and one at Temenia.

In the center of the island, the army headquarteres was also on Mount Meraviglia with a detachment of Sante Irene. Platoons of infantry were stationed between Meraviglia and Rachi and also between Meraviglia and Mount Patella. A machine-gun platoon was at San Spirito. Two platoons of infantry of the 1st Company were at the head of Gurna Bay; a platoon of the 3rd Company at the Anchor; and machine-gun platoons from the 8th Machine Gun Company at Gurna and Alinda Bays. The navy had a platoon of men guarding Lago Battery and another at the Castello Veneziano. A battery of 47-millimeter guns was manned at Gurna Bay by men from the *Euro*.

In taking up their allocated positions, all the British battalions stressed the lack of transport. The regimental history of the King's Own Royal Regiment provides a good example of the problems they experienced:

Lack of transport made the task of sorting out the battalion, getting stores into position, establishing communications and attempting to dig in very difficult. The ground was so rocky that fire positions had to be dynamited out. All the first week was spent in the various preparations, which, through the complete air superiority of the enemy, was being constantly interrupted. The island was subjected to almost continuous air attack and although comparatively small damage was done or casualties inflicted the effect on morale was considerable. Telephone wires were constantly being cut and this together with the unreliability of the wireless made any sort of control extremely difficult.

The majority of the *Luftwaffe*'s attacks were directed against the Italian antiaircraft defenses, and by November 12, they had succeeded in knocking out thirty of the fifty-eight heavy antiaircraft guns. The batteries on Viglia, Rachi, Cazzuni, and Meraviglia, which mounted the heaviest caliber of anti-aircraft, had not a single gun ready for action by this date. Thus by November 9, with a stream of reports and attacks being made against what was obviously a German invasion convoy, and the resumption on a heavy scale of air attack on the island, which had ceased a few days earlier (from the seventh to the eleventh, the island was pounded by a total of 187 aircraft), the British garrison—hastily assembled, transported piecemeal and without field artillery, armor, heavy equipment, or transport, supported by allies of unknown quality and reliability—prepared to meet General Müller's latest and most audacious thrust across the Aegean.

By November 10, despite all the British could do, some two dozen German landing craft and caiques with escorts had managed to reach Kalymnos and Cos. That night saw the Royal Navy's destroyer striking forces making last-ditch attempts to halt the force before it could reach Leros. The British realized that the German ships would probably have to spend at least one night refueling before making the final hop to Leros. Accordingly, two destroyer forces were dispatched to make bombardments of both Cos and Kalymnos. The first of these forces consisted of the *Petard, Rockwood,* and Polish *Krakowiak,* which sailed at 1730 on the tenth from Gurvergenik Bay. Their orders were to carry out a close inspection of the west coast of Kalymnos Island and then bombard the port itself. The first part of the operation proceeded without incident, and sighting nothing, the destroyers therefore closed the port undetected at 2140.

The *Krakowiak* fired star shells to illuminate the harbor, and the light revealed a medium-sized merchant ship. Although there was a bright moon, star-shell illumination was necessary because the town and harbor were in shadow. Cmdr. Richard Egan of the *Petard* took his three ships in on a course 040 degrees at twelve knots just clear of the known minefield, QB 203, and all ships maintained fire in a sector 340 to 280 degrees at a range of 5,000 to 6,000 yards. Bombardment at a shorter range was not undertaken because of the difficulty in loading the 4-inch high-angled guns, with which all three destroyers were fitted, when depressed because of the resulting height of the breech from the deck and the consequent loss in rate of fire.

Fire was maintained for one and a half hours into the port, and about 1,500 4-inch shells were pumped into the area. There was absolutely no reply from the defenses. During the bombardment, shells ricocheted off the breakwater all over the harbor and town, several bounding up the hill. After one run, the ships reversed course and repeated the operation, but no other shipping could be observed, apart from one solitary merchant ship of about 3,000 tons berthed inside the breakwater; she was on fire.

With the second run completed, the *Petard* signaled *Rockwood* to act independently and finish off the merchant ship. Lt. S. Lombard-Hobson took his ship in as close to the breakwater as the indicated minefield would allow and shelled the freighter at point-blank range. Being on the far side of the breakwater, the ship presented a difficult target to destroy, but one well-aimed salvo augmented a small fire already burning and set the target well ablaze. The *Krakowiak* was also sent to investigate the bay close to the east-ward side of the port but found it empty. The Hunts then withdrew, and the *Petard* closed the harbor for a final inspection. It was disappointingly empty of German landing craft. At 2315, the *Petard* signaled the withdrawal, but by this time they had stirred up a real hornet's nest: The sound of aircraft approaching from the direction of Cos was soon audible.

Unfortunately for the destroyers, conditions were ideal for air attack, with bright moonlight and a clear sky making the aircraft very difficult to spot, while the ships stood out clearly from their wakes. Course for the approach route was set down at twenty knots in line ahead; the ships subsequently adopted a triangular formation. The German planes appeared to work in pairs, and aircraft shadowed the force throughout the night, homing the attacking planes onto it. Several dummy attacks were made, and the only aircraft sighted were Ju 88s. This seemed to be deliberate policy to disguise the fact that glider bombers were operating, for at 0020 the *Rockwood* was hit by just such a bomb in position 36°23'N, 16°55'E.

Fortunately for the destroyer, the bomb failed to explode; it penetrated the bulkhead between the gearing room and the midship seamen's mess deck, leaving the ship just below the waterline in No. 3 oil fuel tank. The steering gear broke down, causing the ship to heel around under full rudder. A fire started in the switch room but was soon brought under control. Lieutenant Lombard-Hobson then attempted to steer the ship by her main engines without reducing speed but as the ship began to list to starboard and settle aft, he realized that the damage must be greater than he expected. He signaled tersely to the *Petard*: "Turkey."

The ship set on a course at twelve knots to pass south of Nisyros Island, but at 0118, the forced lubrication pumps in the *Rockwood*'s gearing room were underwater, and Lombard-Hobson requested a tow. Air attacks were spasmodically occurring, and work in rigging a towline was hampered by the need to keep all guns' crews at action stations. Also, in anticipation of repeating his towing feat with the *Carlisle* earlier, Lombard-Hobson had ordered that "tow aft" be rigged. The gear had to be laboriously unshipped, moved forward, and assembled on the forecastle by cooks, stewards, stokers,

and other members of the supply parties all working close under the guns of
A mounting, which was by this time using full flash propellant.

The *Petard* shackled up and towing began at 0145, while the *Krakowiak*
stationed herself downmoon to ward off further attacks. By steering to pass
south of Nisyros, the ships escaped further attack until the final fifteen-mile
crossing to Cape Palamida, which unfortunately coincided with the bombardment of Cos Harbor by the second destroyer force. This at once
attracted bombers, which sighted the *Petard*'s squadron. They dropped flares
and made two further attacks without hitting the ships. After what the *Rockwood*'s captain described as "five most anxious hours," the ships dropped
anchor in the landlocked bay of Losta in the Gulf of Doris at 0750 on the
eleventh. Oil fuel was transferred to the *Petard*, which brought the hole
above water level. There was only one casualty although when the glider
bomb struck the *Rockwood*, it had bounced twice on the deck and entered
the beef screen, resulting in a gory mess of carcasses all over the deck, which
horrified the captain before the truth was found out.

Various pieces of the bomb were duly recovered and forwarded to
Alexandria via the other two destroyers, but the *Rockwood* had to wait for several days, under the constant scrutiny of the *Luftwaffe* and the Turkish con-
stabulary, until a welder and plating could be ferried in. Eventually she had
to be towed back to Alexandria by the *Blencathra*, finally arriving at 0630 on
November 19.

Meanwhile, the *Faulknor*, *Beaufort*, and *Pindos* of the second strike, under
command of the captain of the 8th Flotilla, Capt. M. S. Thomas, had bombarded Cos Harbor from 0330 to 0335 on the eleventh, but the results were
unobserved. This squadron had been bombed on its approach but not hit.
After the brief bombardment, it withdrew to Port Deremen in the Gulf of
Cos some forty miles from Cos Roads to lie up during daylight. Captain
Thomas's original instructions had been to lie up in the Gulf of Mandalya,
but these had been changed so that he might be in a position to aid the
Petard's squadron if required.

Aerial reconnaissance showed considerable movement of German shipping between Cos and Kalymnos, and as the next force of British destroyers
could not reach the area until late on the night of November 12–13, it was
considered essential that the *Faulknor*'s force conserve its fuel. Captain
Thomas was therefore told to shift berths to be nearer the Cos Channel, and
at 0100 on the twelfth the ships anchored in Alakishli Bay some twenty miles
from Cos Roads. Captain Thomas was instructed to send his two Hunts into
Cos Roads to attack reported shipping. By the light of a full moon, two
groups of eight and seven German landing craft were reported by aircraft to
be on the move at 0120 and 0122, steering northwest from Pserimos Island.

They were well inside the minefields to the east of Kalymnos. These were in fact German invasion barges heading for Leros, but Captain Thomas did not appreciate this. The official naval historian recorded: "Even though the senior officer of the destroyers was troubled by shortage of fuel, and knew that more destroyers could not arrive until the next night, it now seems that he should have taken his ships on patrol earlier. Not until after dark on the 12th did he sweep the waters around Leros; but by that time the enemy had landed."

The captain of the *Faulknor* was not alone that night in being unaware that this was the invasion convoy, however. The commander in chief's operations room, where the reports had already been received, also failed to make an immediate correct assessment of the situation.

> There is no doubt, however, that this was to be the final chance of getting amongst the invasion craft, but still only a chance, for had the destroyers in fact sailed they would undoubtedly have been sighted by enemy aircraft during the full moon period and the landing craft immediately diverted away from any possible danger. There is also no doubt that had Captain D correctly appreciated the situation the destroyers would have sailed to the attack whatever the chances of success and without regard to the retaliatory bombing attacks that would surely follow.

The official historian's closing remarks still hold true, however:

> It thus came to pass that, although we had watched this convoy's passage all the way across the Aegean from the Piraeus to Cos, we failed to intercept it on its final stage. The enemy had boldly discounted any effective threat to the convoy by day, and by night he had concealed his vessels very skillfully; yet it seems undeniable that it should not have reached its destination virtually unscathed.

A recent British account also severely criticizes Thomas's decision, but it was not as clear-cut as some of the armchair warriors make out. You can find the full story, with all the facts, on pages 215–17 of Peter C. Smith's *Destroyer Leader.*

Meanwhile, the coastal forces from Leros had done the best they could. They had not been able to operate on the previous two nights because of severe weather conditions, but on the night of November 10–11, three MTBs made a sweep around Levitha, Stampalia, and Amorgos. Despite good visibility, they made no contacts, and during daylight on the eleventh, they lay up in Turkish waters in the Gulf of Mandalya. Early on the twelfth, *MTB-307*, on passage from Casteloriso to Leros was attacked by two German destroyers off Kalymnos but managed to take avoiding action and arrived at Leros at 0415. The two German destroyers patrolled to the east of the island during the day. At 0445, an MTB force sailed from Alinda Bay at top speed to search for enemy vessels reported four to five miles south of Leros but found nothing. Later it sighted two German destroyers off Pharmako Island but did not attack, as it mistook them for British destroyers heading for Turkish waters. The MTBs lay up in the Gulf of Mandalya at dawn.

The *Faulknor, Beaufort,* and *Pindos* also lay up on the twelfth until darkness fell, as they could not operate without air cover while the *Luftwaffe* was so dominant over the island. Thus it was that during the vital day of the invasion, the only seaborne opposition that the German fleet had to overcome before reaching its objective was a solitary motor launch, *ML 456*, under Lt. Cmdr. F. P. Monckton. She was on patrol to the east of Alinda Bay at 0456 on the morning of the twelfth when she sighted and reported enemy forces twelve miles east of Leros. She proceeded north to engage but ran into two of the destroyers defending some ten landing craft, and after a brief uneven encounter, the gallant little ML was hit by a prolonged burst of fire from some R-boats. The midships Oerlikon was put out of action, the loader being killed and the gunner wounded. The after Oerlikon misfired as a result of a hit on the magazine, and at the same time a shell hit the midship Oerlikon locker and an incendiary cannon shell entered the engine room. Realizing that both guns were out of action and his vessel was on fire, Monckton withdrew to Alinda Bay. After landing her wounded, *ML 456* attempted to run for the safety of Turkish waters. When she was barely two miles from the island, the shore defenses opened fire against the German fleet, and a 6-inch shell from this barrage hit her in the tiller flat, causing severe structural damage. Despite this, she reached Turkish waters at 0745. Her sister ship, *ML 358*, was not so fortunate—caught in the crossfire between the Italian batteries and the German destroyers, she was hit by a heavy shell and sank with the loss of all hands.

ML 456's gallant action was the first warning received by the defenders of Leros that the invasion was at last a fact and no longer a threat. L. Marsland Gander describes the scene as the first German ships nosed into Alinda Bay at dawn on the twelfth: "Five or six miles out to sea in a north-easterly direction moving northwards was a line of tiny craft. Sharp explosions of one Italian gun. It seemed an age before the plume of water and smoke rose far away, much too far away, from the distant landing craft. I glanced at my watch. It was 0510. The Battle of Leros had begun."

CHAPTER TEN

Battle in the Balance

On November 10, Vice Adm. Werner Lange was able to report that the necessary landing craft were now in position, ready and waiting. Accordingly, at 0030 on the eleventh, Army Group E issued the order for Operation Typhoon (*Taifun*) to start at first light on the twelfth. This signal (JP9391) was picked up by Ultra and read by the British as orders for the attack to go in on the eleventh. It was repeated the following day (JP99502 and JP9503) and appeared to indicate that the actual landing had been postponed one day, it was assumed because of British naval activity the night before. The code name of the operation had originally been Leopard, but this had been changed for security reasons.

The seaborne assault groups sailed from Cos town, from Mamari on Cos and from Kalymnos island between 2200 and midnight on the eleventh in two groups. Force West had embarked the II/16 Infantry Battalion in five MFPs, each carrying between 150 and 170 men, a total lift of about 800 troops for the first wave. They had a close escort of two R-boats under the command of *Oberleutnant zur See* Hansjürgen Weissenborn, with two auxiliaries, *UJ-2101* and *UJ-2102*, in support. Force East had about the same number of troops but embarked in smaller landing craft, each containing about 70 men, drawn from the Grenadier Battalion II/65. Again two R-boats provided the close cover under the command of *Oberleutnant zur See* Reserve Kampen, with *UJ-2141* and *UJ-2144* on hand. Command was concentrated in the minelayer *Drache*, with five ships of the 9th Escort Destroyer (T-Boats) Flotilla, the *TA-14*, *TA-15*, *TA-16*, *TA-17*, and *TA-19*, led by *Kommandant* Riede; the E-boat *S-55*; the fourteen small auxiliary warships of the 21st UJ Flotilla, commanded by *Kapitanleutnant* Dr. Brandt; and ten motor minesweeping R-boats, commanded by *Kapitanleutnant* Mallmann and *Leutnant* Weissenborn. All were spread in a covering screen ready to give gun support at sea or ashore.

Lieutenant General Müller's initial landing scheme was audacious and aimed at achieving as much surprise as was possible against an island defense that was in hourly expectation of attack. He had decided to throw his first wave against the eastern side of the northern end of the island, where the assault troops would have to make scramble landings. The main landings would be north of Alinda Bay, where two battalions and one company of assault troops were to go ashore at Grifo Bay and on the headland at Pasta di Sotto; farther north, another battalion was to land at Palma Bay. The main objective of these forces would be Mount Clidi and the coastal *Ciano* Battery located on it. Mount Clidi was the dominant feature in the northern part of the island, and it was here that the British defensive dispositions proved disastrous. As they thought its sides were unscaleable, its defenses were meager in the extreme.

Once they had captured Mount Clidi, the Germans intended to push southward in order to secure Alinda Bay, where they would bring in the second assault wave and also land an antiaircraft battery, field artillery, antitank guns, and heavy infantry equipment. A subsidiary landing was to be made farther down the east coast in company strength at Pandeli Bay, with the object of securing Mount Appetici and with it the *Lago* Battery, which dominated both Leros town and the Castle Hill. Finally, on the west coast, a landing was to be made by one battalion plus a platoon of engineers at Drimona Bay, at the southern end of the larger Gurna Bay.

This was not all, however. In addition to the seaborne landings, a further and most important part of the invasion plan—and one that was to have decisive repercussions on the outcome of the battle—provided for a battalion of paratroops to be dropped in two echelons on the narrow isthmus at the center of the island between Alinda and Gurna Bays; the drop was scheduled for between 0700 and 0900 hours. The paratroops were to be Müller's trump card in securing the centre part of the island. The main objective of his plan was to split the island's defenses in two.

Seaborne opposition to the landings proved to be negligible. The Germans recorded, however, that some detachments of landing craft were bombed during the approach, and although no damage was suffered, it caused the landing craft to arrive off the island later than expected; they were thus not able to land their troops at first light as they had originally planned. In view of this delay, General Müller had to make a quick decision. The paratroops were already on their way to Leros in their lumbering Ju 52 transport aircraft, and they were ordered to return to base. They landed at an airfield near Athens, and the aircraft were refueled in readiness to take off again. As things turned out, this delay did not give any lasting advantage to the British.

The delay in the landing timetable did mean, however, that the invasion forces had to approach the island in full daylight and here was a great chance for the Italian artillery to show its mettle. The larger landing craft of Force West heading for Gurna Bay soon came under accurate and heavy fire from the *Ducci* Battery on Mount Cazzuni and the *San Giorgio* Battery on Mount Scumbarda, which drove them off. These batteries later were given individual attention by the Stuka dive-bombers, but in spite of these attacks and fire from the naval support force, the Germans entirely failed to make a landing on the west coast.

On the northeastern and eastern side of the island, it was a somewhat different story. Here the Germans used smaller landing craft, which were not such easy targets. On their run-in, however, the landing barges were heavily engaged by such Italian batteries as were still in commission following the heavy air attacks of the past month, but with only limited success. The British 25-pounders and Bofors guns that had been installed also opened fire. In some cases, the Italian gunners waited until the landing barges were too close inshore before opening fire, and many of these craft were able to reach the safety of the offshore waters at Pasta di Sotto and in Grifo and Palma Bays. The siting of the Italian batteries did not allow them to reach these areas with gunfire. Casualties were inflicted on the run-in, however, and the British claimed that six landing craft were destroyed in the first wave. The German reaction was predictable and instant. Wrote L. Marsland Gander:

> I scoured the sky and saw four specks resolve themselves into Stukas, our first aerial visitors of the day. The Italian coastal batteries now opened up in earnest, their shells churning up the sea all around the invasion craft. I was standing beside a sturdy, sandy haired sergeant of the Royal Irish Fusiliers who was staring intently through glasses. He turned and remarked that if only we had the Malta gunners on the island they would blow the whole adjectival lot out of the way in no time. Just as the Stukas approached nearer the AA defences of the island began to join the chorus plastering the sky with expanding black and white blobs. The Stukas, in no way inconvenienced by the AA fire, cruised round and round overhead seemingly in no hurry. I conjectured that the Hun intended to use them as flying artillery sending them over in constant relays and waiting for signals from the ground before bombing. It was an infuriating reflection that the Stuka dive-bomber was regarded in the RAF as obsolete. Yet here, because of the lack of fighter opposition, the enemy was preparing to use them again as in the battle of France.

And indeed, this was the case. Although the sortie rate of the *Luftwaffe* has been reported as having been as high as 500 missions a day, in fact German records show that they made a total of only 206 sorties this day, and by far the greatest number of these was by the Ju 87s. The Germans had about 300 combat aircraft on call for this operation, but over the whole five-day period, their total sorties amounted to only 675 to 700, and the weight of bombs dropped in that time did not exceed 600 tons. As in its operations against Cos, the *Luftwaffe* concentrated on Allied artillery and antiaircraft positions while the Me 109s kept the skies mostly clear of British aircraft. The long-established cooperation between Stuka and ground forces worked at its usual brilliant best, with very accurate pinpointing of targets.. At night, the German troops used red flares to guide in the bombers. This accuracy ensured that although the Germans performed with a large degree of economy, the role of the *Luftwaffe* in the capture of the island was paramount.

It was not that the severely stretched RAF did not attempt to bring relief to the British defenders, but despite its efforts, it remained ineffectual all the way through the battle. On the twelfth, the RAF made untiring efforts to attack the German backup convoy and its escorts, and in addition, No. 603 Squadron mounted long-range sweeps to clear the Stukas, but in vain. During these sweeps, the Beaufighters sighted several destroyers off Pega Island and others accompanying barges off Stampalia, which they took to be British, but this was not the case. Such limited destroyer forces as the Royal Navy had on hand would merely have committed suicide by venturing close to Leros in daylight. A strike by six Beaufighters escorting two cannon-firing Mitchells did in fact locate two motor vessels of 3,000 and 2,000 tons, escorted by five small warships and covered by seven Arados. This was probably the floating follow-up support standing offshore. The Allied aircraft scored cannon strikes on the larger merchant vessel and shot up two of the escorts. Two Arados were also destroyed. It made little or no difference to the battle for Leros.

In the north, about 500 troops went ashore in the areas of Palma Bay and Cape Pasta di Sotto. In Palma Bay, all went well for the Germans as the Italian gunners opened fire rather too late. The Germans quickly established some mortar positions, and the troops thrust forward onto higher ground. At the adjoining Blefuti Bay, the Italian batteries covering Porto di Rina reacted more quickly and drove the landing craft away. The Germans made no further attempts to land there.

Back at Palma, the 4th Buffs (Royal East Kent Regiment) launched a prompt counterattack with D Company under Maj. E. W. Tassell. After a fierce struggle, in which Lt. E. J. Ransley earned a Military Cross, they managed to reverse the German thrust. It was a different story on the northern side of Grifo Bay, just a little farther to the south. Here two companies of Germans established a foothold and then started the difficult operation of scaling the precipitous sides of Mount Clidi.

Unfortunately, because of a breakdown in communications, Colonel Iggulden, whose headquarters was inland midway between Partheni and Gurna Bays, was not informed of this threat until 1000 hours, when C Company, 1st King's Own Royal Regiment (the Fortress Reserve Company), under Maj. W. P. T. Tilley, reached him, having been dispatched there by the brigadier. By this time, however, the Germans had stormed through the light defenses and captured the *Ciano* Battery on the summit of Mount Clidi. One platoon now came under Colonel Iggulden's command and he ordered an immediate counterattack, but by the time the platoon went in, the Germans were firmly established. C Company had arrived in jeeps and deployed quickly, but as the men launched their attack, the Germans brought down a heavy mortar fire from their commanding position, effectively smothering the British machine-guns; the King's Own were checked. They soon rallied and attacked again, but the fighting, much of it hand-to-hand, became confused over this difficult terrain, and the British were once again forced back from Mount Clidi.

In the early afternoon, Major Tilley sent a platoon to his right to occupy a small ridge running toward Alinda Bay, thus effectively joining up with the Royal Irish Fusiliers; this left the narrow neck of land between Alinda and Gurna Bays even more dangerously exposed to the next German surprise—the parachute drop.

Major Tilley had not given up his attempts to recapture Mount Clidi, and he launched a final counterattack during the late afternoon with what survived of his company. Further hand-to-hand combat took place, during which C Company forced the Germans down the forward slope. Major Tilley was wounded in the course of this attack. But it was all in vain. The depleted company of the King's Own was immediately counterattacked by German reinforcements that had been landed from barges during the day. The men of C Company no longer had the strength to prevent the Germans from pushing them back a vital thirty yards or so before they dug in and held. L.Cpl. J. Hall now realized that Major Tilley had not reached their new positions so he went back alone under fire to search for him. He succeeded in finding him, although he was within grenade-throwing distance of the Germans' forward positions.

Evening in this sector found the Germans in firm control of Clidi, and the coastal battery on it—a dangerous state of affairs on the first day of battle. Meanwhile the southern landing had gone ashore without opposition and made its way up the awkward slopes of the Appetici promontory. Here, around Pandeli Bay, the Germans were close to Leros town and they thrust quickly across the coastal plain toward the twin objectives of Castle Hill and Mount Appetici. Once established here, they could overlook both the town of Leros and Fortress HQ. By 0900, one gun of the Appetici Lago Battery was in German hands.

To restore the situation, the Royal Irish Fusiliers' mobile reserve, C Company, was ordered to assemble, and by 0845, with 13 Platoon leading, it moved across the outskirts of Leros town and started up the western slope of Appetici. Before the attack, 10 Platoon Royal Irish Fusiliers under Lieutenant West moved to the coastal strip on the southern flank of the mountain to protect and support C Company's flank. They were engaging the Germans with 2-inch mortars and small-arms fire. A Company's 9 Platoon, under 2nd Lt. R. J. Hillman, was positioned in Leros Castle with a Vickers machine gun to cover C Company's left flank.

Fleeing Italian gunners passed through C Company's advancing ranks, and dive-bombing was constant as they moved up the slope; before long they were in contact with the German forces. Bitter fighting ensued when the attack was launched to regain the battery, but despite heavy casualties the Faughs managed to push the Germans from the battery and down the eastern slope. Here the Germans held and made repeated calls on their Stuka protectors. The men of C Company were subjected to heavy bombing, the Ju 87s using ground-strafing tactics and antipersonnel bombs, to which the men on the ground had no reply.

While leading a patrol around the right flank, the company's second in command, Lt. Hugh Gore-Booth, was killed. Fusilier McKeever, himself wounded, attempted to carry the lieutenant back to company headquarters under heavy fire.

Nevertheless, the Germans had been thrown back, and it was reported that they were pinned down, their strength reduced to less than eighty men. It was later realized that this report was more than slightly optimistic. The Faughs had been equally reduced, however, and could not drive the Germans back into the sea. The Brandenburg men held on to their precarious toehold. And for them, help was forthcoming.

In the north, a further brisk action by the Buffs (Royal East Kent Regiment) had resulted in the capture near Grifo Bay of three German officers and forty-five other ranks. Thus the first assaults had received what was thought to have been a bloody nose, but the fact remained that the Germans now had two footholds on Leros.

According to the British, no area of the island was suitable for landing paratroops, so they had not flown any paras into the island to stiffen the defenses. It was therefore all the more dramatic a shock when, at 1630 in the afternoon, the first German transport aircraft appeared over the island. Again L. Marsland Gander described the scene graphically:

An officer emerged from the tunnel mouth, excited and rather pleased because he had just seen 25 aircraft maneuvering low to the westward and it was assumed that they were ours because Jerry does not go in for much wave hopping. I went back through our foxhole and on emerging at the other end had the severest shock so far. Roaring towards me at what seemed eye-level were two twin-engined aircraft spouting fire from their machine-guns in the wings. Afterward I also learnt that they were scattering antipersonnel bombs, but none fell near me. I flattened against the protecting earth while the bullets sang overhead. Then greatly relieved to find myself unhurt bolted back in the tunnel and to the eastern end.

The idea that the Germans would use Paras was so remote from my thoughts that the happenings of the next few minutes had a supremely theatrical and dreamlike quality which almost obliterated the breath-taking surprise. To the east the squadron of five flying destroyer planes [Me 110s] which the Germans had used to make the garrison duck their heads were now bound for home. Twelve or fifteen troop carriers [Ju 52s] were flying at a height of about 300 feet in line astern across the island's narrow waist between Alinda and Gurna Bays. As I watched fascinated something white appeared under the fuselage of the leading machine. It bellied out into a great mushroom beneath which the dark figure of the parachutist looked absurdly small and helpless. Then came another and another, fifteen altogether, mostly with grey parachutes. The first man who was probably the group leader had touched ground before the machine gunners on the sides of Meraviglia had recovered from the paralyzing shock of surprise. Then began a wild outburst of firing from the ground till the air was criss-crossed with red tracer dashes spurting from twenty directions.

These brave men—and none of the British eyewitnesses called them anything else than that—of the 2nd *Einheit Hase* Parachute Division, some 500 strong, dropped in the area encompassed by the triangle of San Nicola, San Quirico, and Alinda. Both they and their transport aircraft presented sitting targets to the men and guns on the hills and slopes all around them, and they were heavily engaged in the air, losing something like 40 percent of their strength before hitting the ground and a further 20 percent from broken limbs on the boulder-strewn slopes and in the deep gullies.

In the northern sector, the paratroops were engaged by the Buffs (Royal East Kent Regiment) from lower Quirico and the northern slopes of Alinda

Bay. Some of the paratroops were shot down by small-arms fire; a Bren gunner of C Company RWKs scored a spectacular hit, his target "falling like a
driven partridge into the sea." Although a stiff breeze was blowing, the
majority of the Germans fell successfully in this area. It was unfortunate that
the King's Own had been redeployed from here a short time before, as the
remaining troops, the Buffs (Royal East Kent Regiment) and the SBS units,
were thin on the ground.

In the central sector troops of B Company of the Queen's Own Royal
West Kents and two platoons of B Company Royal Irish Fusiliers were able to
engage the paratroops with light and medium machine guns. B Company of
the Queen's Own with machine guns on the northwest slopes of Mount San
Giovanni, switched all four weapons to engage the low-flying Ju 52s. In common with all other units engaged, they reported innumerable hits on the
cumbersome machines from point-blank range, but very few fell into the
sea. Of the Faughs, 18 Platoon on Alinda Bay, 17 Platoon on Mount Germano, Gurna Bay and 16 Platoon were all just outside the dropping zone
but within small-arms range, and they were all able to fire at leisure, while D
Company was right underneath the drop.

Once the paratroops were on the ground, however, they soon proved
tough and resilient opponents. The Faughs began to take casualties. Lieutenant Clarke, a South African volunteer who had just joined the battalion,
was killed leading 18 Platoon, which suffered heavy casualties, only Sergeant
McKeown and three men returning to company headquarters after dark,
and 17 Platoon was likewise hard hit, losing Capt. Bill Robinson while leading an attack. The platoon sergeant, Sgt. P. O'Connell, took over 17 Platoon
and led it gallantly. He maintained his position and drove back several
attacks that night and all through the following day, only withdrawing the
remnants on the second night on orders from battalion headquarters.

The Faughs' D Company took the brunt of the drop and also suffered
severe casualties having two of their platoon commanders killed and one
wounded along with many other ranks. Lieutenant Prior of D Company was
wounded and later evacuated. By nightfall, the paratroops had a complete
hold on Rachi Ridge save only for the remains of 17 Platoon; the defenders
had been split as the Germans had planned by the end of the first day's
fighting. At this point, British troops found some important documents on
the body of a senior German officer and forwarded them to fortress headquarters, but events were rapidly escalating.

With the occupation of Rachi Ridge, telephone communication from
fortress headquarters to the Buffs (Royal East Kent Regiment) and the
reserve company in the north was cut. This hampered all efforts at mounting a concerted counterattack to link up the defenders of the island again.

Casualties on both sides had been severe, and in the confused fighting, many of the wounded had been lost. Some were evacuated to the RAP at Charing Cross, others directly to Port Laki Naval Hospital; the No. 161 Field Ambulance was cut off in the northern section of the island. The regimental medical officer, Capt. Jack Barber, did most valuable work. As the situation worsened the wounded were evacuated from the island by any means possible to save them from falling into German hands. The casualty receiving station was soon overrun by the Germans who used it to treat their own and the British casualties alike. This provided the British medics with the opportunity to compare their organization, equipment, and functioning with the German equivalent. The Germans' medical arrangements appeared primitive and were restricted to elementary first aid, but this was probably because they were depending on the early capture and utilization of the existing facilities at the Port Laki base.

No immediate British counterattack was forthcoming. Brigadier Tilney intended to mount one that night to cut a way through the German positions and link up with the Buffs (Royal East Kent Regiment) to the north, using two companies of the Faughs and one from the King's Own. The Fortress Reserve Company had already been committed in the fighting to the north, so now Brigadier Tilney had to decide which of his defended positions to strip to provide the necessary forces—not an easy decision when he was receiving regular warnings from general headquarterse that a further 2,000 Germans would probably be landed on Leros that night or during the following day.

In the end, he took the troops from Mount Appetici, hoping that the Italians could hold this on their own. C Company Royal Irish Fusiliers was pulled out to join HQ Company from the same battalion; to these he added B Company of the King's Own—that battalion's local reserve—to make up his striking force.

They were to rendezvous in the area of Charing Cross, but both of the Royal Irish Fusilier companies had been heavily engaged during the day and their reorganization and concentration in the darkness were not easy. In fact, C Company Royal Irish Fusiliers failed to make the rendezvous at all. Colonel French was ordered to put in the attack as soon after 2000 as possible, and C Company had already started out from Appetici when it received a message directly from the brigadier ordering the company to leave one platoon on Appetici. This was because of representations made by the Italian chief of staff, who had informed Brigadier Tilney that the Italian gunners on Appetici could not possibly hold out on their own without British help. Colonel French and the company commander, who had their orders for the night attack, remained unaware of this change of plans, and a series of misunderstandings resulted. By 2300, it became obvious that C Company would not be at the assembly area in time for the counterattack, which was imperative to restore the situation. It had to be called off.

The Germans took this respite as heaven sent and consolidated their positions, even sending out patrols to probe weaknesses in the British positions, which were many.

Thus the British situation on the island by the late evening of the first day of battle was not entirely happy. In the northern sector, the defenses were holding firm in the area of Blefuti and Palma Bays. The Germans were, however, in command of a stretch of the northeast coast from Cape Pasta di Sotto to Grifo Bay. From here they had pushed inland and captured Mount Clidi and the *Ciano* Battery; they were now pressing toward San Quirico in an effort to join up with the paratroops on this ridge.

In the central and most important sector, German assault troops had gained a foothold on the slopes of Mount Appetici, but the most serious threat came from the paratroops who were in complete control of the neck of land between Gurna and Alinda Bays, including Rachi Ridge and the battery located on it. General Müller had thus achieved his planned prime objective for the first day's fighting: He had succeeded in gaining and maintaining a firm grip on this narrow neck of land, effectively splitting the island's defenses in two. In the southern sector, all was quiet and the British remained in complete control.

Yet in spite of these undoubted German successes, the battle was not yet won or lost. In fact, the German admiral Lange noted in his diary that the situation was very worrying, for the men already landed in particular, but also for the success of the operation as a whole. He was also concerned about the losses suffered by the landing craft during the day and the effect this would have on subsequent attempts to land reinforcements and heavy equipment. What surprised the Germans most, however, was the lack of British naval and air activity against the invasion forces. They had expected these to be on a much greater scale.

With the British failure to launch a counterattack on the night of November 12–13, at a time when an attack was desperately needed to restore a dangerous situation, the outcome of the battle hinged to a large extent upon which side could maintain the flow of reinforcements more effectively. The British sent an urgent appeal for reinforcements from Samos, but none were forthcoming because of a lack of suitable craft to transport them. For the Germans, however, reinforcements were soon to be on hand as Force West, which had earlier failed to effect a landing on the west coast, was now able to land on the northeast coast early on the morning of the thirteenth. This was indeed a timely arrival, for during the day, sea conditions deteriorated and the Germans were unable to use their smaller landing craft.

With the coming of darkness, the first British attempt to intercept any German follow-up convoys got under way. Captain Thomas's 8th Destroyer Flotilla sailed for Leros, sweeping close around the island and, it not for the darkness, in full view of the British troops ashore. L. Marsland Grander wrote:

> Sleep being impossible I abandoned the attempt and was returning from one of my expeditions to stamp out the dying embers of the fire of secret documents when suddenly the Italian searchlight on the Crusaders' Castle opposite tunneled into the night with its roving beam. It roamed hesitantly over the sea for a time drawing an ineffective stream of red tracer from German Spandaus on the beach. Then it illuminated for a brief moment a beautiful sight— two grey streamlined shapes of British destroyers steaming silently in line ahead. There was a spontaneous low cheer from the little group outside the tunnel. Abruptly the general enthusiasm turned to anger for the searchlight was lingering too long as the "Ities" were uncertain of the ships' identity. "Put that bloody light out," yelled somebody across the valley as if there were the faintest chance of the Italians hearing.

The *Faulknor, Beaufort,* and *Pindos* continued their patrol but, not surprisingly after this, found nothing. They were, however, able to comply with a request from the army to bombard German positions on Mount Clidi. But the opposing defensive positions were extremely close and the bombardment had to be checked, as it was endangering British troops. Even so, it did provide a welcome morale booster after a very unhappy day's fighting. An MTB force consisting of *MTB-263, MTB-266,* and *MTB-315* was also at sea, searching along the east coast of Kalymnos, but made no contact with the enemy. Despite these efforts by the navy, the Germans succeeded in landing more troops on the island both that night and early the next morning.

Naval reinforcements were on the way, but the *Luftwaffe* was fully prepared. The 8th Flotilla would have to pull out to refuel, so another force consisting of the cruiser *Phoebe* and the destroyers *Echo, Dulverton,* and *Belvoir* was sent out. After the cruiser had been withdrawn, the three destroyers under the command of Cmdr. Sammy Buss, a famous destroyer skipper, as captain of the 5th Flotilla, entered the Aegean to the north of Rhodes. They were soon picked up and shadowed by German aircraft. At 0310 on the morning of the thirteenth, they were attacked by glider bombers in the Gulf of Cos.

The *Dulverton* was steaming at twenty-two knots when she was struck by a 293-type bomb on the port side abreast the bridge. The explosion tore away the bow section forward of the bridge together with her A mounting, and the small destroyer was soon settling by the head, ablaze from end to end. There was no hope of saving her, and her casualties were heavy. The *Echo* and *Belvoir* managed to rescue 6 officers and 103 men, but Sammy Buss was not among them. They sank the blazing hulk with a torpedo in position 36°50' N, 27°30' E, five miles east of Cos island. The two destroyers then lay up in the Gulf to await the next hours of darkness.

In the morning the weather worsened, and by the afternoon of the thirteenth a full gale was blowing in the area. Meanwhile, *MMS-102*, carrying troops for Leros, had run aground west of Ketapaluka Lighthouse. Plans were in hand to land reinforcements from Samos using motor launches and motor minesweepers on the night of November 13–14.

The Germans, however, were to receive reinforcements well before then.

Despite the weather conditions, the thirteenth saw the highest peak of activity yet achieved by the RAF over the area. Targets were plentiful but heavily defended and the Beaufighters were completely outclassed by the Me 109s of *Jagdgeschwader* 27, which held undisputed control of the air over the island. Four Beaus of No. 603 Squadron escorted five Torbeaus and two Mitchells in a sweep in the Leros-Kalymnos area but made no sightings at all; one Beau was forced to ditch. Later, another sortie, with five Beaufighters, five Torbeaus, and two Mitchells from the same squadrons, returned to the area and strafed German antiaircraft sites on Kalymnos and shot up some Me 109s, but one of the Torbeaus was shot down.

The main feature of the German air operations was again the speed with which their aircraft, mainly Stukas, responded to the demands of their infantry for close support, a result of a direct radio telephone ground-to-air link. The Germans had brought this art of cooperation to a fine pitch following its initiation in Poland and France and its perfection in the Greek, Crete, and Russian campaigns. Their troops took it for granted that the Ju 87s would be on tap instantly. By contrast, the British still lagged behind in this respect.

The German paratroops were as usual highly trained and skilled and their sniper fire was exceptionally accurate. The Ju 52 transport pilots flew their suicidal missions with amazing calm at very low altitudes. A total of ninety-six sorties were mounted against Leros by the *Luftwaffe* this day, the low number being due to the weather.

But not everything went perfectly for the Germans. They suffered from the same confused situation reports as did the British, and this often resulted in equal disasters. At first light on the thirteenth, for example, a landing barge evidently carrying ammunition was seen nosing into Alinda Bay under the impression that the British had been cleared from the area. It was instantly raked from stem to stern by the Italian battery on Castello di Bronzi and by Bofors guns. It was hard hit and blew up with a large explosion. Later a seaplane landed on the waters of the bay seeking shelter and met with the same fate.

The paratroops were further reinforced at 0700 when the Germans made a repeat drop on Rachi Ridge. Preceded by strafing Me 109s, the transports again flew in low over the vital neck of land from the southwest, buffeted by high winds and met with waves of antiaircraft fire. Casualties were again heavy. The Bofors guns had a field day and claimed three Ju 52s shot down in Alinda Bay.

> Again our machine guns chattered away furiously, Bofors guns joined in, and one of the slow troop carriers, hit fair and square, went flaming down into Alinda Bay, a horrifying spectacle, with one solitary parachute visible dragging behind it, the doll-like figure still attached. Another Ju.52 flying lower and lower in distress dropped all its Paras into the water where the silken chutes lingered for a short time like water lilies.

As on the previous day, the patrols of the Special Boat Squadron and Long Range Desert Group went into action against the survivors. On the twelfth, after receiving warnings that German airborne troops were again assembling in Athens, the LRDG concentrated Capt. Charles Saxton's T1 Patrol, 2nd Lt. M. W. Cross's T2 Patrol, and a British patrol into a combined striking force; together with all Jellicoe's SBS men on the island, they went into action thirty-odd strong. During the fighting that day, Maj. Alan Redfern of the LRDG was killed by a German parachutist.

Jellicoe's SBS had concentrated on preventing the Germans from reaching their supply containers with some success, and this they endeavored to do on the thirteenth. It was estimated that no more than a dozen of the 200 paratroops dropped that day ever went into action.

> Some, whose parachutes were evidently damp or packed in a hurry, fell to their death with a roman-candle of silk streaming tautly above them. . . . Some reached the ground alive only to be dragged over rocks and four-foot walls, unable to twist the release catch of their harness. [There was a forty-mile-an-hour wind blowing at the time of this drop.] Some fell in the sea and their drowned bodies floated for hours with the canopy of a parachute for a winding sheet.

The Royal Irish Fusiliers Vickers machine guns and light machine-gun sections had a good shoot at the Ju 52s even before they reached the coast. The Vickers on the slopes of Mount Meraviglia were level with the incoming transports and scored easily. The Fusiliers estimated that two complete loads of paratroops were dropped into the sea from less than seventy feet.

In the southern sector of the island the British spent most of the day preparing for a counterattack to be mounted that night. Not so the Germans, who everywhere advanced. With dive-bomber support, the troops pinned in the narrow coastal plain at the base of the Appetici promontory sent in an attack against the Royal Irish Fusiliers holding the positions.

It was the British intention to hold the enemy in the center at Appetici and stop any movement south along Rachi Ridge. They hoped that this would fully occupy the German troops and enable the Buffs (Royal East Kent Regiment) to counterattack from the north on the fourteenth. C Company, Royal Irish Fusiliers, after a night on the move and missing the rendezvous the previous evening, was in the process of bringing up their 3-inch mortars and small arms to make an attack on the Germans holding the east face of Appetici when they were hit by the German thrust. After a short struggle, C Company was forced to pull back with heavy casualties. Lt. A. Woods, 15 Platoon, was missing and Lieutenant Armstrong, a South African, wounded. The company was now down to a strength of one and a half platoons and was withdrawn to the area of the company headquarters position.

With the loss of Appetici, the Royal Irish Fusiliers' B Company positions were dominated by the Germans, who soon laid down heavy mortar fire in 12 Platoon's area, causing heavy casualties and withdrawal to the houses at the rear of the position. Communications were frequently cut, and the Stukas made all movement hazardous. The Vickers machine-gun section on the south face of Appetici was driven out. From dusk the company was at immediate notice to mount a counterattack against the German position.

A Company still had its 9 Platoon at Leros Castle engaging the Germans on Appetici's northern slopes, while 7 and 8 Platoons faced the enemy on Rachi Ridge and above Alinda Bay. They were to hold this position throughout the battle with antitank 2-pounders, Vickers and light machine guns and 3-inch mortars against anything the Germans could throw at them.

D Company had 17 Platoon still dug in on Germano and had made contact with 11 Platoon of B Company Queen's Own Royal West Kents to their rear. At about 2000, on orders from battalion headquarters, Sergeant O'Connell withdrew those who were left of 17 Platoon back through the Royal West Kents' position but had to leave the wounded behind; 16 Platoon was on the south side of Gurna Bay and was put under the command of the Royal West Kents. During the afternoon, Lieutenant Prior, who was wounded, was replaced by Lieutenant Stokes from HQ Company. Stokes led the platoon into action that day with considerable success when, with a party from 16 Platoon, he took on a larger number of Germans. About twenty were killed and wounded and from the body of a German company commander they took a case, which was found to contain the German plan of attack, including aerial photographs. Private Mills of the Royal West Kents delivered this to the battalion intelligence officer, Captain Rochford.

Captain Barber and Captain Steward-Liberty, the company commander, discussed the possibility of 16 Platoon going in and recovering 17 Platoon's wounded, but it was considered impossible.

By the end of the second day's fighting, the Royal Irish Fusiliers were reduced to the following strengths: A Company had two weak platoons; B Company was still available but weak in numbers; C Company was down to one and a half exhausted platoons; and D Company was almost nonexistent, with 18 Platoon wiped out on day one and the other two much reduced.

In the north, Colonel Iggulden still did not have effective contact with fortress headquarters and decided to make in attacks against the German positions on Mount Quirico, followed up by an assault to recapture the Mount Clidi Battery at dawn on the fourteenth. HQ Company of the Buffs (Royal East Kent Regiment) was allocated the first task, and it occupied Mount Quirico with little difficulty. The Germans rallied, however, and in a fierce attack around 1800, forced HQ Company to give ground. The situation was saved and most of the position retaken by C Company under Lt. F. J. Bell.

Meanwhile, Brigadier Tilney had made his outline plans for action that night, but the Buffs did not receive details of these until late in the afternoon. Tilney's plan included an attack from the north by the Buffs, but such was the importance of the Mount Clidi feature that Iggulden decided to press ahead with his attack, which was well under way. Accordingly, B Company, under Maj. Ernest Hole, went in and cleared the hill with forty prisoners.

The Germans had been pushing down into the built-up area of Alinda Bay, and on completion of the Clidi operation, Major Hole was to have moved down into that area to join forces with C Company in holding them. B Company ran into serious trouble at a feature called Point 242, however, and was held there for most of the day, Major Hole being killed in the fighting. Ultimately the Germans forced the withdrawal of B Company in the evening of the thirteenth to Mount Clidi.

Without B Company's support, C Company, under Maj. Vincent Bourne, was also unable to make any progress. Bourne had no artillery support and met fierce resistance in the house-to-house fighting along the bay. B Company therefore had to withdraw to a defensive position on Mount Quirico.

The remaining company, D, under Major Tassell, was preparing to move south at dawn on the fourteenth to cooperate with the major thrust from the south.

The planned counterattack against Appetici was mounted by the British in the early hours of November 14. Brigadier Tilney's plan was for B and C Companies of the Royal Irish Fusiliers together with HQ and A Companies of the King's Own to put in the attack, the whole force being led by Lieutenant Colonel French. But for the British, almost everything that could go wrong did.

It was discovered that B Company of the Faughs could not easily be extracted from Pandeli Bay, and D Company of the King's Own was therefore substituted. Maurice French was to remain in command of the attack, which now consisted of only one of his own companies and three of the King's Own. Zero hour for the attack was moved back to enable a naval bombardment to be carried out at 0130, followed by the attack at 0200. The bombardment took place between 0045 and 0100 and was carried out by the *Echo* and *Belvoir* using accurate timed firing from close inshore in Alinda Bay against German positions on Mount Appetici. The destroyers fired at point-blank range and shifted targets in response to signals from shore observation posts on Meraviglia. A single German gun opened up, but a full concentration of fire quickly silenced it.

After this bombardment, the *Echo* and *Belvoir* swept the area east of Leros without making any contacts and then proceeded to lie up in the Gulf of Mandalya by dawn. Further destroyer reinforcements, *Penn*, *Aldenham*, and *Blencathra*, reached the Aegean at daylight on the fourteenth.

On the island, an hour before the attack was due to commence, Brigadier Tilney received a report that the Germans were attacking Meraviglia in considerable strength from Rachi Ridge and had already penetrated as far as Charing Cross. Considerable doubt and confusion exist about the origin of this report in all the British records. The historian of the Royal Irish Fusiliers wrote: "Where this report originated from cannot now be traced. Battalion HQ was on the slopes of Meraviglia overlooking Rachi with 'D' Company HQ further still towards Rachi and the writer is satisfied that it did not come from either of these positions."

Whatever the origin, the message had a disastrous result on the planned British assault. Colonel French was ordered to send C Company, Royal Irish Fusiliers, to the Charing Cross position to deal with the situation. About three-quarters of an hour later, because of further alarming reports received of the threat to general headquarters from this German thrust, which was backed by heavy mortar fire, HQ Company of the King's Own was also withdrawn from the attack.

French had originally planned to launch the attack with A and D Companies of the King's Own, which were to clear the position and then hand over to HQ Company to hold and consolidate. A and D Companies were then to withdraw and re-form for further action against Rachi Ridge. French was now left in command of only two companies of the King's Own Royal Regiment. The result was a disaster.

The attack commenced at 0200 on the fourteenth and was led by A Company, King's Own Royal Regiment, commanded by Capt. D. J. P. Thirkwell-White of the Suffolks with Capt. C. J. Bligh as second in command. They were given the searchlight emplacement and gun positions on Appetici as their targets. D Company was to flush out the numerous caves around the hill, each one of which had to be assaulted separately. All platoons therefore had to act independently and soon lost touch. Two platoons of A Company in fact lost direction completely and were not seen again. The rest of A Company managed to reach the first gun position but soon came under heavy fire from its flanks. The company commander and two platoon commanders were killed; Bligh was also wounded and in great pain, but he continued to lead the company until he was again hit in the neck and died on his way back to the CRP.

D Company was raked by heavy machine-gun fire from its left flank but also managed to push its way slowly to the crest of Appetici. The situation was extremely confused, with intense counterfire. Maj. M. R. Lonsdale was wounded and Captains Burke and Mathieson were killed. Sensing the weakness of the British forces, the Germans launched a strong counterattack, which the King's Own Royal Regiment was too weak to repulse; it held on until dawn, when it was driven back by further strong attacks from the 2nd Parachute Division's crack troops. "Every man a tommy-gunner" was how they were later described. Lieutenant Colonel French was killed, and the 1st King's Own was cut to pieces. Only one officer and seventy-five other ranks eventually remustered.

While this massacre was taking place, C Company of the Faughs and HQ Company of the King's Own Royal Regiment had been resting around Charing Cross. The Royal Irish Fusiliers historian continued:

It became clear by this time that the enemy strength from the direction of Rachi Ridge was no greater than a fighting patrol. It is strongly suspected that a number of alarmist reports being spread at this time were being originated by enemy personnel, possibly in British, but most likely in Italian, uniforms; to the writer's knowledge none of these reports ever came from Battalion HQ. Originating in Fortress HQ itself and passing down rather than up which would be the likely course for such reports.

Toward dawn, the Germans did indeed start to infiltrate the slopes of Meraviglia, and at 0700, when it appeared they might be overrun, the naval personnel destroyed all signal books and so on. This made future cooperation with the ships at sea extremely tricky.

Meanwhile, in the northern sector, another gallant but unsuccessful attempt to recapture Mount Quirico was made. But the most successful operation there was a bold thrust south at dawn on the fourteenth by D Company under Major Tassell, which managed to penetrate the narrow neck of land held by the Germans and seized a high prominence known as the Kidney, which was a mile to the west of Rachi Ridge. Although it had thus succeeded in making contact with B Company of the Queen's Own Royal West Kents near Germano, it was unable to push any further southward.

B Company had been established on Mount Germano earlier from its previous dug-in positions on Mount San Giovanni. In their assault, the troops had had to pass right below Rachi Ridge and were subjected to a murderous hail of small-arms fire, and heavy machine guns also opened up on them. Capt. E. P. Flood was wounded but rallied his men. They stormed and took Germano, where they came under the command of the Buffs (Royal East Kent Regiment).

Thus dawn on the fourteenth found the battle for the island still in progress and both sides had taken severe casualties with very little progress. At 0700, Brigadier Tilney reported to Samos that although the situation was critical, there was still a chance. He appealed for every available man and added that he hoped to clear Rachi Ridge.

It is interesting that his assessment of the situation is almost identical to that of his German counterpart. The OKW Diary reported that heavy fighting was continuing but was of the remarkable opinion that the northern part of the island was in German hands. This was far from being the case, and the Buffs were soon to shatter that illusion.

CHAPTER ELEVEN

Typhoon Triumphant

The daylight hours of November 14 were a repetition of the day before, with the *Luftwaffe* flying continuous sorties and the British seeking to reform yet again with a view to finally clearing the dominant feature of Rachi Ridge and joining up with the north.

In the air, sixteen Hurricanes carried out strong fighter sweeps over the air bases on Crete in an effort to reduce the *Luftwaffe*'s sortie rate. The result was a disaster, for the Hurricanes were met with strong defenses, fully alert, and no less than seven were destroyed. A total of nineteen Beaufighters and four Mitchells made offensive sweeps around Leros but had no sightings. Four Baltimores attacked a 4,000-ton motor-ship in Suda Bay without result, and following the German example of aerial supply, two Dakotas successfully dropped canisters of arms and ammunition on Leros.

On land, despite many difficulties, the British managed to hit back with considerable success during the day. In the northern sector of the island, the Buffs were in almost complete control. They had retaken Clidi and recaptured Quirico and were only checked north of Villa Belleni on Alinda Bay by heavy air attacks. They had taken about 130 prisoners. The Germans, however, still held Mount Vedetta.

The LRDG and SBS patrols were operating in the hinterland to prevent infiltration northward from the Rachi Ridge area. Second Lt. R. F. White's R-2 patrol with the Italian guns on Mount Scumbarda in the southern sector directed a shoot landward by the coastal defense guns, a notable achievement. Their targets were to the north of Rachi and Appetici and the jetty at Alinda Bay. The shells were reported to be clearing the ridge on Meraviglia where general headquarters was located by a matter of only ten feet.

Elsewhere, the continuous bombing was gradually taking its toll, and sorties against the positions south of Rachi, Meraviglia, and Windmill Ridge between Meraviglia and Mount San Giovanni, where the 25-pounders and Bofors were located, resulted in most of them being knocked out together with their small supplies of ammunition. By the evening of the fourteenth, British antiaircraft defense consisted of three Bofors guns.

Despite the failure to regain Appetici, Brigadier Tilney was determined to make another effort to clear the center of the island. He held back only such troops as were considered essential to keep the Germans confined. The Buffs were to attack as previously instructed. B and C Companies of the Royal Irish Fusiliers and B and HQ Companies of the King's Own Royal Regiment were to attack and clear Rachi Ridge as far north as Point 100, while B Company of the Queen's Own with D Company of the Buffs were directed against San Nicola.

This latter attack was not able to make progress, and although the fighting was intense, the troops were unable to clear the village in which the Germans seemed to have fortified every house. Both these companies were withdrawn at dusk for food and rest. B and HQ Companies of the King's Own Royal Regiment attacked the German positions from the southwest at about midday on the fourteenth, and the struggle was equally bloody. At a critical juncture, Maj. G. H. Duxbury, commanding B Company, went forward alone and bombed out two machine-gun nests, but he was killed as he approached another. His heroic example led the two companies to renewed efforts and they made a little progress and took prisoners. But their strength was wasting away. With all the other officers in his company dead or dying, Capt. R. L. P. Maxwell received orders to send out yet another patrol. He led it himself and was also killed.

The King's Own Royal Regiment had reached Searchlight Hill, but B and C Companies of the Royal Irish Fusiliers became heavily engaged with the Germans on the southeast slopes of Rachi. The 3-inch mortars under Captain Hoare gave considerable support, and medium machine guns and antitank 2-pounders were all brought into play to break resistance. In the heavy and bitter hand-to-hand fighting that ensued the Germans gave ground very slowly, and the Faughs took severe casualties. Maj. Ben Barrington was among those wounded, by a premature 3-inch mortar shell. Lt. T. West took command of B Company and Lt. E. B. W. Johnson of C, and together they succeeded in working their way around the west slopes of Rachi but were too weak to take Point 100. An attack by the King's Own Royal Regiment was repulsed and it retired to Searchlight Hill, where it remained for the rest of the day. More than fifty German prisoners were taken and escorted back by Company Sergeant Major South of the Royal Irish Fusiliers.

On Mount Germano, B Company, Queen's Own, Royal West Kents, was consolidating its capture of this feature and had made contact with D Company, 4th Buffs. These two companies were then directed against San Nicola. Also, 16 Platoon, Royal Irish Fusiliers, under Lieutenant Stokes, had been under the command of the Queen's Own, Royal West Kents, and was left on

Germano to hold the position and collect the wounded, but nothing further was heard of it.

A Company of the Faughs was originally to join in the attack on Rachi Ridge, but its role was changed to that of providing maximum fire support instead. At Leros Castle, 9 Platoon was out of contact with the rest of the battalion but held out stubbornly until the afternoon of the fifteenth. It was finally taken by two companies of German soldiers who advanced in the face of violent small-arms fire and overran it.

The day's fighting ended with the Buffs, the Fortress Reserve Company, B Company, Queen's Own, Royal West Kents, plus 16 Platoon Royal Irish Fusiliers holding the line Kidney-Point 81-Mount Clidi, and with the King's Own Royal Regiment and the Faughs holding Rachi Ridge as far north as Searchlight Hill and containing the assault troops on the Appetici promontory. The main achievement of the British on the fourteenth had been the reestablishment of communications with the northern half of the island. Confused fighting continued on into the darkness, but when a patrol of the LRDG entered Leros town just before midnight, they found the whole place empty and quiet.

The Germans appeared to be concentrating during the afternoon in the eastern half of the Aiinda-Gurna neck, and a request was made for a naval bombardment. This was carried out by the destroyers *Penn, Aldenham,* and *Blencathra* at 2045. Wrote the Buffs' historian:

> Steaming right up to the boom in Alinda Bay, they opened an intense bombardment with every weapon they possessed. That C Company of the Buffs, on the lower slopes of Mount Quirico, unfortunately suffered casualties from the bombardment detracted little from the great encouragement derived by the troops in consequence of this visible evidence of outside help. Hurried signals succeeded in confining the naval fire to the German area and whatever the results may have been, the heartening effect upon the defenders was incalculable.

The destroyers had entered the Aegean waters late on the thirteenth to lie up off the coast of Turkey on the fourteenth. They had left before dark to carry out the bombardment and attack landing craft, but they found only three caiques in the bay. They also landed some ammunition. After the bombardment, the destroyers carried out a patrol of the area, searching for the landing craft reported from Leros. The destroyers were under constant air attack, including glider bombers, but only the *Aldenham* was near missed— fortunately with no damage or casualties. They saw nothing of the landing

craft, which doubtless had been turned back as a result of air reports of the
destroyers' movements. The destroyers later retired to lie up once again in
Turkish waters.

Meanwhile, plans were still to transport the 2nd Battalion of the West
Kent Regiment, the only fighting troops available as reinforcements, from
Samos to Leros. But the difficulties over the transport of troops that had
plagued the whole campaign continued. The battalion actually received its
orders to move on the twelfth, the day before the invasion of Leros, and it
was planned that HQ, A, and D Companies should embark for Leros that
night at Triganion Harbor. The troops accordingly left their positions at
2000 that evening and completed their embarkation onboard two
minesweepers before midnight. But the naval commander then decided
that because of the adverse weather conditions, it would not be possible for
him to reach Leros in time to disembark the troops and be clear of the
island before daylight. The move was therefore canceled and the troops disembarked and returned to their former positions on Dimitrios Ridge. Late
on the afternoon of the thirteenth, further plans were made to embark the
troops at Vathy, where the harbor was considered to be more sheltered from
the wind. When the same companies arrived at the quay, however, they
found that only one minesweeper had been able to berth because of the
heavy seas. A Company was embarked onboard this vessel, but the remainder of the troops had to wait yet again. The weather then forced the
minesweeper to lie up off the Turkish coast during daylight of the fourteenth, and the troops were not finally landed at Port Laki until 2300 hours.
Maj. Robert Butler, the company commander, made his way immediately to
Brigadier Tilney's tunnel headquarteres at Meraviglia for orders. At 0300, he
rejoined his company at an assembly area west of Port Laki with the news
that it was to carry out an attack on Rachi Ridge. The company duly formed
up at the road junction at Charing Cross.

The *Echo* and *Belvoir*, which had been lying up in Mandalya Gulf, were
now ordered to Samos to pick up the remainder of the Royal West Kents.
Battalion headquarters, C Company, and the Signal Platoon, 187 men in all,
were embarked on the *Echo*, and D Company and the remainder of HQ
Company on the *Belvoir*, during the evening of the fourteenth. The *Echo*
made a high-speed run at thirty knots and landed her troops at Port Laki at
0430 on the fifteenth. Her arrival is described by L. Marsland Gander, who
was there awaiting shipment to Samos along with many of the wounded:

> The destroyer began some delicate maneuvering to squeeze into
> the available space. I could see that the decks were packed with
> steel-helmeted troops. It all seemed crazy. In an hour it would be

first light, the Stukas would come and blow the destroyer and all of us to eternity. Slow astern, slow ahead, stopped; slow astern again. She was sidling alongside with all the skilled use of the engines and steering so natural to the expert seaman and so incomprehensible to the landsman. Now ropes had been flung ashore and willing hands were tying her up. Rapidly methodically wooden chutes were run down over the ship's side on to the wharf. Then heavily burdened soldiers with packs, helmets, rifles and other weapons came sliding down on their rumps. They were so weighed down that many could not stagger to their feet, and the Italian dock laborers waiting had to help them up, to get each man out of the way of the next man slithering behind. In an incredible short time they were all on the quayside shuffling into line and then were marched off into the darkness. The matelots now began to send box after box of ammunition sliding down the chutes.

The troops were met by a liaison officer, and they quickly established battalion headquarters near the Anchor monument, dug slit trenches, and prepared breakfast. Colonel Tarleton went to fortress headquarters, where he was informed that A Company was to cooperate with C Company in the attack, the former from the eastern side and the latter from the south. Maj. M. R. Read then led C Company off to the assembly area south of Leros town.

D Company and the remainder of HQ Company were not to reach Leros until the night of the fifteenth. The slower *Belvoir* had been unable to make the island before daylight and had to lie up in Turkish waters at Pharos Bay during daylight on the fifteenth. Here the troops were transshipped to several vessels to be ferried on to Leros: the motor minesweeper *MMS-103*; three MTBs, the *MTB-266*, *MTB-307*, and *MTB-315*; and the Harbor Defence Motor Launch *HDML-1004*.

The result of this haphazard transport was that the Queen's Own, Royal West Kents, was not able to fight on Leros as a complete unit. B Company, under Captain Flood, was already on the island; the other three rifle companies reached the island at three different times over a period of twenty-four hours. They went into battle in separate actions, and this series of false starts meant that the troops were already tired before they even reached the island.

The Germans, however, also made a further call for reinforcements. Late on the fourteenth, General Müller had asked for a further battalion of the Brandenburg Regiment to be airlifted to Cos. He intended to use it to make a new landing at Pandeli Bay, where he also hoped to land some field artillery. All attempts to get some heavy guns ashore had so far been frustrated. The *Echo*, having taken the wounded onboard, nosed her way out to sea. Although the moon was still shining, dawn, which would bring with it the unwelcome attentions of the *Luftwaffe*, was not far off. Lt. Cmdr. R. H. V. Wyld quickly rang down for full speed for the dash back to safety, but before that he was determined to make one final sweep around the island.

Also at sea that night was a force of three MTBs, which had sailed from Casteloriso the previous night and made an uneventful sweep in the area. They had sighted two destroyers off Pharmako which they had taken to be British but subsequently realized were not, so they swept the area in the hope of finding them again. They swept around the north of the island and up to Lipsos and then swung back down again past Leros toward Kalymnos. At 0215, while between Leros and Kalymnos they were heavily fired on, as usual, by Italian batteries but without any damage. On their return north, they were again fired on by the same batteries despite showing the correct recognition signals.

As the *Echo* was completing her sweep, the three MTBs—*MTB-315* (Newall), *MTB-266* (Broad), and *MTB-307* (Muir)—made a sighting at 0513 north of Alinda Bay. They identified two R-boats proceeding south at speed and laying a smokescreen. *MTB-307* unfortunately had started leaking and had to return to Casteloriso, but the other two boats at once sent out an enemy report and closed the German minesweepers. At that moment, the Italian searchlights ashore were switched on, and their light illuminated about twelve F-lighters and similar landing craft. The Germans were in fact running in yet another large reinforcement convoy of troops and ammunition, and for the first time in this operation, the Royal Navy had caught them. Both MTBs roared in, and at point-blank range, about fifty yards, they opened fire with every gun they could bring to bear. At such a range it was impossible to miss, and the two small boats pumped some 2,000 rounds into the F-lighters as they frantically attempted to gain the protection of the smokescreen or hide inshore. The two German minesweepers engaged the speeding MTBs in a late attempt to shield their charges, but already the nearest barge was well ablaze. The MTBs were about to annihilate the next when a destroyer was sighted in the searchlights, and they swung around to make a torpedo attack on this much more dangerous opponent.

In fact, it was the *Echo*. She too had sighted the F-lighters in the searchlights and the tracer as the German gunners had tried to extinguish them. One was about 4,000 yards away and immediately engaged as she lay motionless.

The F-lighter, which I could see through glasses was crammed with vehicles and guns. She was taken so completely by surprise that she never attempted to return our fire, perhaps her guns were silenced by the first salvoes. Now we were flinging over scores of 4.7-inch shells that erupted all round her in the water till she was lost to sight in smoke and spray. Some of our bricks were plunging into the hull causing great spouts of flame and then after a short sharp action lasting at most only five or ten minutes we left her blazing furiously and drifting helplessly.

The *Echo* sighted the MTBs and challenged just as they did; once contact was established, the three ships continued the carnage. Two other landing craft were destroyed by the MTBs dropping depth charges under their hulls. Then the shore batteries joined in, and the MTBs withdrew while the *Echo* also sped away to join the *Belvoir* in Pharos Bay.

These successes scored by the navy during the early hours of the fifteenth were to have little effect on the battle still continuing on Leros, however.

The plan for the fifteenth was in three phases. The first phase was for an attack northward along the Rachi Ridge up to and including those slopes overlooking the village of San Nicola, still a German fortress. Originally the King's Own from Searchlight Hill was to have carried out this task, but when it was reported that the men were weak in numbers and exhausted, Brigadier Tilney threw in the newly arrived West Kents as recounted. As they were thrown piecemeal into the battle on strange and difficult ground, it was not surprising that they ran into difficulties.

For the second phase, the Buffs would continue their previous good day's work and clear the Germans from Alinda Bay and San Nicola, and then fight their way across the neck and join hands with the thrust from the south. The third phase was for C Company, Queen's Own, Royal West Kents, and a composite company of the Royal Irish Fusiliers, who were now very weak in numbers, to attack north between Rachi and the south side of Alinda Bay under the command of Major Read as described and secure Santa Marina and Point 36.

Only scattered fire support could be expected from the few surviving 25-pounders and coastal guns firing inland.

For the execution of phase one, A Company of the 2nd Queen's Own, Royal West Kents, moved out from Charing Cross once Major Butler had received his final orders from Brigadier Tilney. The *Luftwaffe* was early on the scene, and the West Kents had already taken casualties from bombing at the assembly point, including the intelligence sergeant, Williams, and two other NCOs. The company had to pass north through the positions held by the King's Own at the southern end of Rachi to Point 100, but no covering fire could be expected except for small-arms fire from Searchlight Hill.

A Company moved out at 0830, and its advance was unhindered until it was slightly north of Searchlight Hill. Then all hell broke loose and the leading platoons were swept by sniper fire, mortar bombardment, and attacks from the ubiquitous Stukas, which were quickly on the scene. All the platoon commanders became casualties, and they were halted in front of a strong concrete bunker and swept with automatic fire emanating from their objective, Point 100. Robert Butler managed to take one platoon within fifty yards of the strongpoint but they were unable to assault it. Up to this time the company had suffered twenty-five casualties, including Lieutenant Hewett and Company Sgt. Maj. Frederick Spooner. As all the wireless sets were useless, Butler returned to the other platoons and sent an orderly to request close mortar support and smoke from 25-pounders. A detachment of mortars from the Faughs was sent to their aid and the Bren guns were grouped under Lt. H. D. T. Groom to provide covering fire.

At 1430, the 25-pounders laid down a smoke barrage, and a composite platoon from A Company led off into the inferno. Heavy automatic fire met the troops, coupled with a mortar bomb blanket, but the Queen's Own, Royal West Kents, pushed through it and after slow, steady fighting took and cleared Point 100. The cost to the company was tragic, however, no more than a dozen men held their objective, and casualties included Major Butler, who had been hit in the knee in the last attack. Realizing that twelve exhausted men could not hold the point, he asked for reinforcements but when these were not forthcoming he ordered a withdrawal back to Searchlight Hill.

A Company, when it staggered back into the King's Own Royal Regiment's positions amounted to three sergeants and twenty-five men, who were then organized under command of the King's Own. Most of the company's wounded were later evacuated by destroyer.

The sacrifice of A Company was in vain. When fortress headquarters realized that they would not take their objective by midday, Brigadier Tilney immediately put into operation phase three, while the Buffs were to confine their operations to token demonstrations toward San Nicola and Alinda Hospital.

During the morning and afternoon, C and HQ Companies, Queen's Own, Royal West Kents, moved up to their jumping-off positions south of the village of Santa Marina on the south shore of Alinda Bay. Lt. Col. B. D. Tarleton instructed Major Read to attack the eastern face of Rachi Ridge. It was hoped to take Point 36 and then take the road junction north of it. To follow up this assault was the Royal Irish Fusiliers composite company drawn from B and C Companies.

Of these, B Company, one platoon strong, under Capt. J. W. Salter, proceeded directly to Leros town, while C Company, of about the same strength under Lieutenant Johnson, had withdrawn to the old company area. In addition, 17 Platoon of D Company was ordered to join the rendezvous in the Windmill area. Meanwhile, 7 and 8 Platoons of A Company, Royal Irish Fusiliers, were still holding their defensive positions across the path of any enemy attempt at a linkup of their forces on Rachi and Appetici. Lt. R. A. Ardill was dispatched from battalion headquarters to collect C Company and proceed to the rendezvous. This totally composite company eventually amounted to about forty men in all, but it was late in reaching the rendezvous, which caused the postponement of zero hour.

C Company, Queen's Own, Royal West Kents, went into the attack at 1530 and quickly took a spur that ran out from Rachi Ridge toward the coast. They lost Major Read almost at once, when he was severely wounded, and Capt. E. E. Newbald assumed command. The attack continued, but the platoon leading on the left lost its way. The right lead platoon had lost its commander, Lieutenant Jode, at the start of the attack but kept going forward. Heavy sniping from the houses lining the coast road was the major stumbling block, but following the example of Sergeant Wallington, who worked his way past the snipers, the platoon was able to put in an attack on Point 36, where Wallington was wounded.

The Battalion Reconnaissance Group, which was following up the attack was also held up by fire from the house snipers. Lt. R. A. James and Drummer Brown of the Intelligence Section ran forward under this fire and found a secure position for the section. They made a start in clearing this hornet's nest, and in this task they were joined by the composite company of the Faughs.

The reserve platoon then went forward free from this hindrance, and under Lt. John Browne with some of Wallington's platoon, they stormed Point 36, killing many Germans and taking twenty-five prisoners. The Germans reacted to the loss of this position with a hail of well-directed mortar and machine-gun fire, and the Queen's Own, Royal West Kents, soon took casualties including Lieutenant Browne.

With the lack of reinforcements to consolidate the hard-won ground, the British troops withdrew from both Point 100 and Point 36, which were only about 300 yards apart, almost at the same time, and the hope of a linkup between A and C Companies was gone. By 1900, HQ Battalion of the Queen's Own, Royal West Kents, and about two platoons with the remainder of B, C, and 17 Platoon of the Faughs had withdrawn to the narrow neck between Santa Marina and Meraviglia. The remnants of C Company, Queen's Own, Royal West Kents, had become widely dispersed, but Captain Newbold was able to gather together several small parties after nightfall. Their retreat cut off, they organized the wounded, which included Major Read, at a chapel on the coast road under the padre, Capt. G. M. Young, and the medical officer, Capt. J. C. Seddon. Here they were overrun by advancing German reinforcements and taken prisoner. Captain Newbold managed to withdraw his force to battalion headquarteres after sending a wireless message giving warning of the German movements to general headquarters.

On the northern slopes of Meraviglia, the HQ and D Companies of the Faughs in their holding positions had come under heavy fire and took casualties all through the day. A Company lost Captain Burke at this time.

General headquarters at Cairo suggested that the Buffs be transported by sea to the south of the island to relieve the critical situation there, but even if it had been possible for the Buffs to disengage from a confused and fluid front, only a few rowboats were available to ship them southward. They would have made perfect Stuka bait. Instead the Buffs occupied themselves with demonstrations, but that evening found one of their patrols heavily engaged at Villa Belleni.

A further plan put forward from Egypt at this time was for a parachute drop by 500 men now that the Germans had shown that it could be done. A night drop was suggested, but it was decided that to drop in darkness onto the rocks and gullies of Leros was even more suicidal than to drop in daylight. The area remaining to the British was very small, and the chances of dropping accurately were minimal. This idea was also abandoned. Brigadier Tilney's men had to resign themselves to holding the island with what they had before further German reinforcements arrived.

Meanwhile, in the sector held by HQ Battalion of the Queen's Own, Royal West Kents, the survivors of C Company were being organized in the darkness, with the few Royal Irish Fusiliers men who turned up in the area, to ward off the oncoming Germans. Men were posted in the houses and on a spur of Mount Meraviglia. The first German troops came down the road at 2100. They were in close order and were decimated by the Bren guns of the Fusiliers, the survivors withdrawing hastily up the road. The Germans now began to infiltrate around both flanks while at 2130 they launched a heavy frontal attack. This forced a British withdrawal up the slopes of Meraviglia, where a grenade party under command of Captain Thatcher managed to hold the Germans back.

After heavy and confused fighting, further withdrawals had to be made to the Bren gun pits of the Royal Irish Fusiliers. Here a counterattack was organized under severe mortar fire. The attack ran into showers of grenades, and Capt. D. J. Cropper was among the many casualties. The Germans forced another withdrawal but failed to follow up. Later all the survivors were ordered by Colonel Tarleton to rendezvous at the Anchor.

Just after midnight, Lieutenant Colonel Easonsmith of the Long Range Desert Group with two or three men made a further reconnaissance of Leros town. This time the patrol was greeted not by a dead town, but by automatic small-arms fire and grenades, and Easonsmith was killed. Col. Guy Prendergast again assumed command.

In the air, the fifteenth had been another disappointing day for the British. The previous night, twelve Dakotas supposedly had made a successful drop of ammunition to the defenders of Leros, but the Germans claimed that some of it was actually dropped on Kalymnos. During daylight on the fifteenth, Beaufighters were only rarely seen in the vicinity of the island and were soon chased away by Me 109s. The sole success the RAF achieved that day was when three Beaufighters of No. 603 Squadron who were escorting the Torbeaus and Mitchells over Leros located two German escort destroyers covered by four Arado floatplanes and four Ju 88s southwest of Kalymnos. The escort prevented the Torbeaus from scoring, but the Mitchells claimed to have hit one of the destroyers with 75-millimeter cannon fire.

Thus by the end of the day, the Germans had succeeded in tightening their hold on the whole region south of Rachi and Appetici and were preparing to move south from Leros town. To back up this move, they were planning another landing at Pandeli Bay on the sixteenth. Of the British reinforcements landed on the fifteenth, A and C Companies of the Royal West Kents had been almost wiped out, having been sent in piecemeal in hastily prepared attacks. HQ Battalion and the Signal Platoon had also suffered many casualties, and D Company had still not arrived. What was left of the battalion was widely dispersed, with the largest group of some twenty-five men of A Company under the command of the King's Own on Searchlight Hill. It was clear, however, that the final stages of the battle were approaching, yet in spite of the mauling they had given the British on the fifteenth, the Germans were still not confident of ultimate victory. The OKW Diary was almost hysterically reporting the day's fighting of the fifteenth, when the Germans had taken many casualties despite retaining their hold on the island: "Enemy warships are attacking off Leros. . . . The northern part of the island is reported in our hands . . . [but] it is not so. The fighting is confused and information scarce and changes in control by the enemy results in a continued crisis."

This critical position was soon to be resolved. During the night of November 15–16, the navy attempted yet again to intercept the enemy buildup convoys, but the destroyers *Penn* and *Aldenham*, which made a sweep right around the island, found nothing. The Italian gunners engaged them at dawn and hit the *Penn* above the waterline, though not seriously; there was little damage. The two destroyers then retired to Turkish waters, where they embarked the wounded who had been brought out of Leros by small craft. They then withdrew south to provide the crippled *Rockwood* with protection while she was being towed back to Alexandria by the *Blencathra*.

Further reinforcements had arrived in the Levant Command in the shape of the French destroyers *La Fantasque* and *Le Terrible*. These two big ships, almost light cruisers in size, had a reputed top speed in excess of forty knots and it was hoped that they could use this speed in dashes into the Aegean. The French had lost none of their pride, despite the shattering events of 1940 and 1942, and this was shown when one of these two vessels developed a fault in one of her shafts. When a Royal Navy officer asked whether this meant that she could not take part after all, he was firmly told that a French destroyer on three shafts could always outpace a British destroyer on four! This may well have been true, but unfortunately the ships arrived too late to show their merits. Also too late to affect the issue were the destroyers *Fury, Exmoor*, and the Polish *Krakowiak*, which had arrived at Limassol each carrying ten tons of ammunition for Leros. They sailed for the Aegean but were later recalled.

In the air on the sixteenth, the RAF continued to try. Wing Commander Giles of No. 47 Squadron led attacks on the F-lighters, which had survived the navy's attacks of the previous day and found two such barges escorted by seven Arados, four Ju 88s, and four Me 109s. Despite these enormous odds, the slow Torbeaus went into their attack and caught the German fighters off guard; none of them managed to intercept, and despite intense antiaircraft fire, the Torbeaus managed to hit an MFP, which exploded as Giles passed over it. One Torbeau was lost when it caught fire and ditched, but Giles came through the fighters, the flak, and the explosion.

In the early hours of the sixteenth, from midnight onward, things were looking very dangerous for the British. D Company of the Royal West Kents, under Maj. A. J. M. Flint, had at last arrived on the island and assembled at the Anchor monument, where Capt. B. A. Pond, the quartermaster, prepared them a meal. After consuming this, they took cover in some deep slit trenches in preparation for the usual dawn bombing. The Anti-Aircraft Platoon, under Capt. M. B. Rickord, with four Bren gun carriers, was sent as a fighting platoon to the north. The Mortar Platoon, under Lt. D. A. Cruickshank, was split into three detachments and dug in. All the other units on the island, except a few of the King's Own who were still holding static positions in the south unmolested, had been in action almost continuously for four days. They were exhausted. Water, although plentiful, was not always getting through to the troops and they had taken heavy casualties. They also knew that the Germans still had not been dislodged after three days' fighting, and with additional enemy reinforcements yet to arrive, including some artillery, they would be even harder to push back into the sea. There was, however, no alternative but to try once more to throw the Germans off the island this day, before they had the opportunity to make the further buildup.

Accordingly, the British operational plan for the sixteenth was for the first phase of the previous day's plan to be repeated. The newly arrived D Company of the Queen's Own, Royal West Kents, was to execute this phase. The Buffs were now to carry out the second phase, and depending on the success of these two thrusts, a final attack was to be put in against the paratroops stubbornly holding Rachi Ridge.

Brigadier Tilney was finalizing these plans around midnight when they received reports that the Germans were moving in strength from Alinda Bay towards Leros town, and that HQ Battalion of the Queen's Own, Royal West Kents, had been overrun. Easonsmith's patrol of the LRDG was slaughtered on the northern outskirts of the town around this time, and no word came back from them to fortress headquarters. Soon the Germans pushing south from Leros town came into contact with the forward patrol sent out by the Queen's Own, Royal West Kents, to guard the crossroads leading to Port Laki.

A brisk action followed between the two scouting patrols, and the British withdrew. The Germans did not press further toward Port Laki at this time but consolidated their strength on the southern slopes of Meraviglia and prepared for an assault on Brigadier Tilney's headquarters. D Company of the Queen's Own, Royal West Kents, suffered several casualties from bombing, the Germans directing their Stukas by Very lights. After the withdrawal from the Anchor crossroad position, the remnants of C Company were formed behind D Company's position and reorganized into a composite platoon under command of Captain Newbald. Here they prepared for the execution of phase one.

Meanwhile, in defense of fortress headquarters, the Royal Irish Fusiliers, with a total strength of about two platoons drawn from what remained of B and C Companies and 17 Platoon, attempted to hold the German probes up the mountain. Heavy fighting followed and the Faughs were overrun, losing Capt. John Salter, who was wounded and later died in German hands. Sergeant O'Connell of 17 Platoon was also killed. Despite good work with a Vickers machine gun by Lance Corporal Cunningham of A Company, who broke up one attack and killed ten Germans, the composite platoons were forced back on A Company's positions on the northern slopes.

Dawn found the positions confused and the situation for fortress headquarters desperate. The Germans on Mount Appetici joined up with the main force pushing up from Leros town. At one point Brigadier Tilney and Capt. E. H. B. Baker, the senior naval officer, with all men who could be spared, joined the defense of Meraviglia with what weapons could be found. For a time, they managed to hold the German assault.

Brigadier Tilney felt that Mount Meraviglia and his headquarters were certain to be overrun. The Germans made intense air attacks from dawn onwards, and A Company of the Royal Irish Fusiliers was ordered to withdraw still further. But the company was now almost surrounded and decided to stay where it was and fight to the end. With the decision to abandon fortress headquarters and the sending of a signal to this effect, which also stated that it was unlikely that the island could hold out much longer because of the complete exhaustion of the garrison and the overwhelming air offensive the Germans were making, things were indeed black.

The feeling of hopelessness of the British in that grim and isolated headquarters tunnel at this time was manifested in this signal, which was broadcast uncoded for all to read. Indeed, the German commander Müller read it at 0825 and had it dispersed to his troops on the ground. As he foresaw, it gave them a psychological boost at a critical time to know that the British felt they were done for.

The historian of the Royal Irish Fusiliers concluded that the British position was not as bad as had been estimated, however, and said, "It was unfortunate that this rather depressing signal was sent in clear [e.g., not coded], and immediately intercepted by the enemy." It was later learned that the reason why the signals had been sent out uncoded was because all the secret codes had earlier been prematurely burned by the signals staff to prevent them from falling into enemy hands. Presumably this was done so that the enemy would not be able to read the British signals if the headquarters were overrun. But the fact that all subsequent signals had to be sent uncoded, which ensured that the enemy could read them instantly anyway, showed that some people were not thinking very clearly after three days of nonstop dive-bombing and shelling.

In truth, as headquarters later told Cairo when they were debating whether to emulate the Germans and send in the 11th Battalion of the Parachute Regiment as a last-gasp reinforcement (they eventually decided not to risk it, another marked difference between British and German operational thinking), "It is exhaustion we are fighting not numbers."

D Company of the Queen's Own, Royal West Kents, had started off for its jumping-off line for phase one, taking casualties from air attack as they did so. Just after 0900, Brigadier Tilney arrived at battalion headquarters and ordered the cancellation of this attack. He informed Colonel Tarleton that headquarters on Mount Meraviglia was being evacuated, and that he intended to move out all available men from the battalion along the west coast to reinforce the still-intended attack by the Buffs on Rachi Ridge.

It was at this point that it was learned that the Germans had been held on Meraviglia, and Brigadier Tilney returned to his headquarters. A patrol went northward and made the amazing discovery that Rachi Ridge was clear of friend and foe alike. How had this happened?

Dawn patrols by the B Company of the Queen's Own, Royal West Kents, found that San Nicola village had been abandoned by the Germans. Captain Flood therefore led B Company forward, although he was still suffering from his wounds, and they advanced with a company of the Buffs on their left. Opposition to these two companies was almost nonexistent and prisoners were taken. Point 100 fell, and the British could see the German attacks on Meraviglia. Another company of the Buffs pushed along the shore of Alinda Bay, also against weak opposition and took Villa Belleni, which they found to contain a German hospital with some fifty paratroops with broken limbs inside. With the northern slopes of Rachi cleared, it seemed that the tide had at last turned. But then followed a sequence of mistakes and orders that in a short time turned the advances and marches into utter confusion.

The remainder of the Royal West Kents had begun to disengage before moving north. This proved a very difficult task while under constant bombing and machine-gun fire. There were of course no vehicles to load their stores, and the Mortar Platoon had to disable and leave behind its mortars. Extra ammunition and reserve rations were issued, and at 1030, B Echelon moved out with the survivors of C and HQ Companies and HQ Battalion. The rear guard was provided by D Company. In order to avoid the worst of the air attacks, they split up into small parties under officers or senior NCOs. They were given a general route to follow westward to the south of Mount San Giovanni and then north along the coast to the west of Rachi Ridge. A rendezvous was arranged in the north part of the island. As the Queen's Own, Royal West Kents, marched away, the Germans made no attempt to follow.

On Rachi and the newly taken ground, the men of D Company of the Buffs, B Company of the Queen's Own, Royal West Kents, and the King's Own Royal Regiment were ordered to move off the ridge and fall back to the north. Why such hard-fought ground should be summarily abandoned after its ultimate easy capture was the cause of much amazement. The historian of the Buffs states, "This, it transpired, they had done on the orders of the CO of the King's Own Royal Regiment, who was also out of touch with Brigade, and was under the impression that a general withdrawal to the northwards was planned."

In the north, Colonel Iggulden had received news of the intended arrival of the Queen's Own, Royal West Kents, to join him, but after all communication with the rest of the island ceased, he was left to fight once more on his own initiative with no idea of how the rest of the forces were faring. Once he had received news from Major Tassell that Rachi had been taken, he had gone forward, inspected it, and ordered C Company of the Buffs to accelerate their drive along Alinda Bay and join up with D Company. Then had come the withdrawal from Rachi. All Iggulden could do was position these troops on the Kidney feature and tell them to hold it. He was still not aware of the reasons or indeed who had been responsible for giving the order for this withdrawal.

At this time, Brig. R. A. G. Tilney arrived on the scene near San Nicola, and realizing that the confusion of command must be cleared up quickly, he countermanded Lieutenant Colonel Egerton's withdrawal orders. He then placed all the troops in the north of the island under Colonel Iggulden's orders. A runner was sent to the Queen's Own, Royal West Kents, to countermand their orders to march north and instead direct them to rendezvous at the Anchor once more. But these orders never arrived, and the unit continued its march north throughout the day completely out of touch with headquarters and Iggulden. Finally, Colonel Iggulden was instructed to place on company of his combined and very mixed force in defensive positions on Meraviglia, while the remainder was yet again to occupy Rachi Ridge. It was like the Grand Old Duke of York's orders to the weary men of Iggulden's command; they had taken the ridge that morning, abandoned it in the afternoon, and were now told to retake it. All this and with little signs from the Germans other than unending bombing and hidden machine-gun fire.

After his dashes south and north and his angry efforts to countermand the confused situation, Brigadier Tilney arrived back at his headquarters around 1545. This still held out but was once more threatened. The defenses of Meraviglia at this time consisted of A Company and the pitiful remnants of C Company and 17 Platoon Royal Irish Fusiliers on the northern slopes. Two-pounder guns, mortars, and machine guns in reduced numbers were still putting up individual stands. The Germans now made a concentrated thrust to take fortress headquarters.

Only B Company of the Faughs managed to break out from Meraviglia to Port Laki; the rest of the troops there were overrun in vicious fighting around the cave during the afternoon, in the course of which seven of Brigadier Tilney's staff officers were killed leading futile counterattacks. One by one, all exits from the tunnel were sealed off by advance units of the II/65, II/16, and III/1 of Maj. Sylvester von Saldern's now victorious command, which was almost as exhausted as its captives. Seeing no way out of this impasse, and in order to save further bloodshed, Brigadier Tilney had a white flag shown and, on surrendering himself at his headquarters, told the senior German officer present that he was surrendering not just the tunnel, but the whole island of Leros. By 1730, the German swastika flew over fortress headquarters, and Mount Meraviglia was completely in their hands. Maj. William Sheppard of the Royal Irish Fusiliers was among the prisoners, along with most of his exhausted command.

The Roman Catholic chaplain with the Faughs, Rev. R. Anwyl, told us of his experiences:

> During the actual battle, I was, of necessity, pinned down quite soon to the RAP of the Royal Irish Fusiliers. I see from my own journal that, in fact, I knew almost nothing of the struggle except for what I experienced in the Charing Cross area between Gurna and Alinda Bay. The battalion medical officer, Jack Barber, and Captain Pickering, a medic from, I think, a casualty clearing station, were with me throughout the battle until Barber joined the retreating Irish just before the end. He and Pickering settled the parting between them. There were a number of wounded left with us, and so we stayed till later we were taken POW.

Tilney's decision was known to very few of his own scattered troops, who continued to believe they were to fight on.

The Queen's Own, Royal West Kents, had meanwhile continued its journey northward, all the time under heavy bombing, which caused many delays and some casualties. The unit encountered very heavy sniping while it was passing under Rachi Ridge, and Maj. G. V. Shaw was mortally wounded. The first party to actually reach the rendezvous was that of B Echelon under Captain Pond. To their complete astonishment, Pond and his men found Colonel Iggulden's men forming up for the attack south to Rachi Ridge and the Anchor; they were told to join in. Thus after a long day's march, they were now going into action to take the position they had abandoned that morning without a struggle. Captain Pond's unfortunate men were was not the only ones to find themselves in this almost farcical situation. Many isolated pockets of British soldiers were quite oblivious to all the abandon and retake orders and maneuvers and remained dug in, alone or in small groups, throughout the fighting, convinced that they had held their ground. Word of the capitulation was greeted with disbelief by such parties. (An excellent description of such cut-off units, who remained dug-in at their original post to the end and who felt totally undefeated, see Pauline Bevan's book *Travels with a Leros Veteran.*

For the rest of the Queen's Own, Royal West Kents, together with the stragglers and small parties of lost troops they had picked up on the way, it was a long, tiring journey, and when they reached the rendezvous, as the bulk of them did, they were able to muster about 160 men of all ranks. No other British troops were found at the foot of Mount Germano, and the positions of the Buffs were not known either. Colonel Tarleton therefore decided to make for Mount Conrida after dark, and here they spent the night blissfully unaware of what had happened that evening on Mount Meraviglia. They were later joined by a platoon of the Buffs moving south to join the fray.

Brigadier Tilney had formally announced the surrender of Leros at 1730 that afternoon, but it took a very long time for the news to filter through to all the garrisons. What remained of the British troops were now either marching northward or attacking southward, with no direct contact between the two. Thus throughout the evening and night of the sixteenth and on into the next morning, all was confusion. The Germans appeared to be as surprised about their sudden success as the British troops were at the surrender. Up until that moment, they had been sending back signals, read by Ultra, reporting very tough and dogged British resistance. (The British historian Stephen Roskill dismisses these German reports, however, saying that comments by General Wilson that it had been a "gallant struggle against overwhelming odds" were "excessively flattering to the forces engaged." See p. 222 of Stephen Roskill, *Churchill and the Admirals.*) Not surprisingly, many of the British troops felt cheated and undefeated, but this is always the case, and indeed their cause was hopeless after about 1500.

This was certainly appreciated by general headquarters in Cairo. They had received a final message from Brigadier Tilney around that time saying that the position was desperate, but that the scales might be tilted by a bombardment of German positions in the area of Leros town and Alinda Bay. There was no chance of this before nightfall, however, by which time it was all over. Instead, headquarters readied an evacuation scheme and sailed seventeen caiques to pick up those who could escape. As the news got through to the various units, escape became their main concern, and this was helped by the fact that the dazed Germans made no immediate attempt to round them up.

Major Jellicoe of the Special Boat Squadron had been at the meeting between Tilney and Colonel Iggulden at 1400 when the attack south was ordered. He had returned to his men and taken command of those LRDG units that were out of touch in the north and formed them into a composite force. Later he had taken a jeep and with two aides, Sergeant Workman and Corporal Dryden, had driven to fortress headquarters to get a clearer account of what was happening. On his arrival, he was much chagrined at finding surrender negotiations in progress.

Thinking quickly, Jellicoe told the Germans that his men would not surrender unless he gave them the orders, and because of this he was allowed to drive back north again. His men greeted the news of the surrender with "surprise and horror." The whole party of twenty-five men was rounded up in two jeeps that Capt. H. W. Blyth had found abandoned at Alinda Bay. These men from T-1 and T-2 Patrols of the LRDG and the SBS, then seized an Italian caique in the early hours of the seventeenth and also took control of a small motorboat. They next persuaded the Italians manning the boom in Partheni Bay to open the defenses and sailed to the island of Lipsos to the north of Leros, where they lay up during the day. The following night, they sailed for the Turkish coast, where they joined an old minesweeper and eventually reached Haifa.

Other LRDG units also managed to get away. Colonel Prendergast, Capt. C. H. B. Croucher, and Capt. R. A. Tinker, together with part of R-2 Patrol, hid on Mount Tortore until November 22, when they made contact with an RAF high speed launch, which took them off. The remainder of R-2 Patrol split into two parties. Second Lt. R. E. White and four others found a rowboat sunk at Serocampo Bay and in it reached Turkey. Others were gotten off during the next fortnight; only two of the LRDG were captured on Leros.

B Company of the Queen's Own, Royal West Kents, had taken part in the attack south, and the news of the surrender finally reached them when entrenched near Leros town, having almost completed the full circle. Captain Flood thereupon marched his unit back to Mount San Giovanni, where they destroyed all equipment of value, collected winter clothing, and had a good meal and a sleep. Their comrades encamped at Mount Conrida learnt of the surrender at 0700 on the seventeenth; they destroyed all documents and sent parties to search for boats by which to leave the island. They were unable to find any and so determined to escape once they reached the mainland.

Only two small groups were lucky. Lt. Gordon Huckle, Company Sergeant Major Greenyer, and Privates Crowhurst and Hose of B Company found some friendly Greeks who gave them a small caique in Gurna Bay. It was old and leaked, but they sailed at midnight and lay up in a small inlet during the seventeenth. By constant bailing they kept their craft afloat, and after rounding the northern tip of Leros on the eighteenth, they were picked up by an MTB within a mile of the Turkish coast.

Capt. P. R. H. Turner and Lance Corporal Honey gathered food from the dump at Conrida on the seventeenth and then lay hidden during the hours of daylight. At nightfall they started off for Alinda Bay but were caught by a German patrol. By a feat of improvisation, they managed to convince the German officer that they were Greeks and were released. Reaching Alinda Bay, they again lay low, and on the nineteenth they found some Italian sailors repairing a caique with a view to escape. The Italians agreed to take them along, and they got to Bodrum on the twentieth. They finally arrived at Cairo in a high speed launch on the twenty-third. Sixteen others of the Queen's Own, Royal West Kents, made their way to safety by diverse routes, but this was all.

Of the entire 2nd Battalion, Royal West Kents, eight officers and thirty-five other ranks were evacuated or escaped from Leros, four officers and sixty other ranks got out of Samos via Turkey, and two officers and fifty other ranks who had been with the rear part at Haifa were subsequently concentrated at Fayed Depot in the Suez Canal area and later sailed home. The battalion saw no further active service in World War II.

For the 4th Battalion, Buffs, the picture was much the same. Only Maj. M. R. Read, Lieutenant Tilleard, and six other ranks got off the island. In addition to the men lost when the *Eclipse* was sunk, twenty-four were killed or died of wounds, fifty-nine were wounded and fourteen were reported as missing. The officer casualties were as follows: Maj. E. A Holt, Capt. J. E. O. Roelofsen, and Lt. G. R. Hart killed; 2nd Lt. A. P. Morgan mortally wounded; and Lt. G. R. Hart, Lt. A. C. S. Whaley, Lt. N. P. Reeves, and Lt. F. J. Belle wounded. The rest of them, including Colonel Iggulden, went into captivity. Counting those men drowned at sea, 152 men were killed, 14 missing, and 59 wounded, and this operation saw the end of the battalion that had fought so magnificently for four days and five nights in vain.

The Irish Fusiliers' 2nd Battalion was equally hard hit and very few managed to escape; for the majority, it was the POW pens, and this included Maj. William Shephard. The 2nd Battalion, Royal Irish Fusiliers, was reconstituted from the 6th Battalion at Southampton on May 2, 1944, but also saw no further active service in the war. "It was," records their historian, "the worst blow that had befallen the Regiment since the South African War."

The Roman Catholic chaplain and other prisoners had to wait their fate. "My own ultimate escape, after trying to get away from the island," wrote Anwyl, "was from the *Gradisca* Hospital Ship, a very strange happening especially if you have heard the story of the Anglo-German party which began after the Navy intercepted us. Somewhat riotous it was!" The German hospital ship *Gradisca*, with 1,940 passengers, was stopped off Cape Paluiri on October 28, 1944, by the British submarine *Vampire* (P-72). She was suspected of being used to evacuate fully fit German troops from Salonica. The destroyer *Kimberley* joined them and took over, and *Gradisca* was taken into Khios on the twenty-ninth. The destroyer *Teazer* subsequently joined the escort and took her into Alexandria on November 1. All the British POWs found aboard were freed, and then she was allowed to sail on to Algiers, escorted by the sloop *Stork*, and was finally released on January 20, 1945. The Reverend Anwyl recalled:

> Sad though, to remember the men I tended and buried, quixotic Colonel French, my atheist friend Captain Robinson, whose letter to me was never received. His runner told me of it, but we couldn't collect the wounded from his platoon, and though, when on parole, I found his grave, it was too late. Sergeant O'Neill, Lieutenant Salter, the names come back with hurt. Poor lads from Malta, bombed and unable to fight there, and then, relatively to the space involved, bombed even worse at Leros! The having to fight in platoons, depleted platoons at that! So very sad.

A, B, and D Companies of the King's Own had re-formed and concentrated for a final attack on Mount Appetici on the sixteenth, but before the attack began, they received the news of the surrender and handed in their arms. The battalion had lost fifteen officers killed and eight wounded, and some sixty other ranks were also killed. Five of the wounded officers were evacuated in time, but the last three became POWs. Some sixty other ranks were killed and an unknown number wounded. Eventually just one officer and fifty-seven other ranks reassembled in Palestine. The battalion was made up to strength again by reinforcements, but mainly by disbanding the 8th Battalion. The 1st Battalion subsequently fought with distinction in Italy, as part of the 10th Indian Division.

Their sister battalion, the 8th King's Own, was spared the same fate, for they were under six hours' notice for a destination later found to have been Leros when news came in of its loss; they were sent instead to Palestine.

Finally, sixty men of all ranks from the 1st Battalion Durham Light Infantry managed to slip away from occupied Cos by various routes. Nine officers and 160 other ranks mustered at the Infantry Base Depot at

Geneifa. The battalion was brought up to full strength and saw further war service, landing at Taranto, Italy, on May 4, 1944, also seeing service as part of the 10th Indian Division.

All the fit and "walking wounded" British POWs were finally assembled in the barracks of the Italian seaplane base south of Port Laki. According to the OKW Diary, they amounted to some 200 officers and 3,000 men, and the Germans also took the surrender of 350 officers and 5,000 men of the Italian forces, most of whom had not taken much active part in the struggle. They nevertheless were shown little mercy; reports were later received that the Germans were shooting many Italian officers on Leros. An order from the OKW decided the fate of the others. "All Italian POWs on the island," it commanded, "together with the Jews among the British, are to be transported to Germany."

Most of the British officers and a few men were taken off in the two ex-Italian destroyers on the nineteenth. While at sea, they were invited to drink with the German captain and his officers, who told them that they had fought well against heavy odds. The bulk of the British POWs were later transported to the Piraeus and then marched to Athens. Most of them finished up in prisoner-of-war and work camps in southern Europe.

Even while the British were surrendering to General Müller's men the Royal Navy and the RAF were still active around and over the island. On the night of the sixteenth, MTBs continued to patrol in the hope of intercepting invasion craft but they found nothing. The *Luftwaffe* attacked them with glider bombs, but they escaped damage and joined the destroyer *Fury* in Pharos Bay.

Despite the most determined efforts to embark troops at Port Laki after dusk on the sixteenth, very few could be collected. The *Luftwaffe* was active, and the night was lit by flares and tracers. Many of the soldiers lay so exhausted that they were completely unable to reach the quayside. The last party to get out of Port Laki left only some twenty minutes before the Germans arrived. Thus of the four infantry battalions on Leros, less than 250 men were finally evacuated.

So after a five-day battle, "Fortress Leros" fell.

CHAPTER TWELVE

The End of the Campaign

The fall of Leros left the island of Samos to the north in an unenviable position to say the least. With the island denuded of its British troops, even the arrival of some 350 men of the Greek Sacred Squadron made little difference. Up to then the island had been gradually sorting out its problems and was running smoothly. With Brigadier Baird installed as military governor and with island native M. Sophoulis, a former and subsequent prime minister of Greece, in control of the civil administration, it had functioned well in its premier role as supply center for the neighboring islands, particularly for Leros.

D. A. Boyd, who had been on the island just over a month before the attack, gave a picture of how the battle for Leros affected life on Samos in *Aegean Adventure.* At first the news was good, and great excitement reigned in Samos over the course of the battle. Some 150 German prisoners were evacuated here, being landed at Tigani in the south of the island and sent up to Port Vathy in trucks. They were locked up in Italian headquarters and the Italians were left to guard them. Boyd conversed in broken French and Italian with their chief jailer, an Italian major named Ratti: "I gathered that as far as he was concerned they could rot. Maybe a report received from Leros that the Germans were shooting all Italian officers they took prisoner had something to do with his attitude. However with a little persuasion he provided what he could."

Boyd also made contact with one of the German officers:

One spoke English and used to play tennis at Wimbledon. He had been a company commander in the Leros assault. He had fought in Russia too. He said that he had always been told that the British troops in this war were poor fighters, but he said that he never wanted to meet the British in a fight again. He had a belly full in Leros and would rather fight the Russians any day. He had taken his company into the assault in five landing craft; three of those were sunk by direct hits before they reached the shore, and the remaining two only disgorged a dozen men when they hit the beach. This number was reduced to five before they had advanced more than a few yards, and these surrendered.

As soon as Major General Hall returned to his headquarters at Samos, word came of the assault, and on the night of November 12 came the first appeal for help and reinforcements. None could be sent at that time because of a lack of suitable shipping, but the only British battalion was gradually transferred. At the time Leros fell, the garrison on Samos consisted of only 220 British troops and 380 of the Greek Sacred Squadron, commanded by *Sintagmatarhis* Christodoulos Tzigantes. These Greek troops were actually embarked ready for shipment to Leros when news of the surrender arrived, and they were hurriedly sent ashore again.

General headquarters at Cairo was under no illusions as to the fate of these troops if left where they were and General Maitland Wilson immediately ordered Major General Hall to evacuate from the island, instructing him to leave the conduct of operations in the hands of Brigadier Baird. Later Baird was told that if the Germans should invade Samos, a possibility at any time, and if the Italian resistance crumbled, as it had before, then he and his staff should evacuate as well and leave only the Greek troops and the guerrillas to operate on the island.

These plans were hastened forward when the *Luftwaffe* arrived over the island in force for the first time on the seventeenth. As many as 100 aircraft were reported over the island this day, though this was almost certainly an overestimate. Both the principal towns received damage, but casualties were fortunately light.

On the seventeenth, the day after the fall of Leros, the bombers came. They were Stukas and they confined themselves to dive-bombing the waterfront in the vicinity of the Greek bank, which was hit, and the Italian Divisional HQ. . . . I had hardly finished getting my kit together when the siren wailed again, and this was followed almost immediately by the bursting of bombs, Ju 88s this time. It reminded me of Malta. . . . No air and ground opposition except from small-arms fire, which is practically useless against the armored Ju 88. They flew round in a leisurely manner and got into position and down they dived. Then round they would fly again and repeat the performance.

This demonstration of strength spurred the British into more immediate action than did the recall of the major general. Faced with the prospect of yet a third island being overrun, with the resulting loss of face, they decided at last to cut their losses.

General Maitland Wilson ordered the withdrawal if possible of all British troops and the Greek Sacred Squadron on the night of November 18–19. The air raids had already disrupted communications with his headquarters, and he was determined to get his men out while he could. Brigadier Baird was to stay on the doomed island until the last possible moment "for reasons of prestige and maintenance was to continue as long as possible." The general also ordered that arrangements be prepared for the further evacuation of some Greek civilians if time allowed.

The British military attaché arranged with the Turks for the transportation of these evacuated through Turkey disguised as civilians, and a fleet of caiques left for Samos on the night of the nineteenth. Brigadier Baird and his staff were embarked at Port Vathy along with all the British troops, and Colonel Tzigantes, commander of the Greek Sacred Squadron; Gen. Mario Soldarelli, the Italian commander; the metropolitan archbishop; and 100 Italian civilians. They were undetected by the Germans, although it was thought that E-boats were on patrol. The British later found out that five E-boats had indeed been lurking to the south of Samos to ambush any convoy running for Tigani. Luckily, because of the unwillingness of some of the caique commanders to risk the Samos Channel, the landing point was changed to Kusadasi, averting what might have been a massacre.

Knowing that the Germans still had not landed on the island during the daylight hours of the twentieth, headquarters dispatched a second caique squadron that night and succeeded in embarking all the British and Greek stragglers, 1,000 Greek civilians, and another 100 Italians. A further 2,000 Greeks crossed into Turkey under their own arrangements. The Germans finally sent an occupying force on the November 21, and the Greek Sacred Squadron organized a last-minute lift of still more people, evacuating another 200 Greek and 2,800 Italian civilians during the next two nights. The Turkish authorities organized special trains to transport these south, and the first ran on the twenty-third. The majority of the evacuees were thus transported to Syria, while others were taken slowly down the coast by boat under the protection of RAF launches and similar light naval craft still in the area. The Germans formally announced the surrender of Samos on the twenty-second and later revealed that only 2,500 Italians were taken prisoner there, along with fifty guns, twelve antiaircraft guns, and ten antiaircraft machine guns. They also claimed the capture of the islands of Lipsos, Patmos, Furmi, and Icaria, with a further 350 Italian prisoners.

The slow arrival of stragglers continued all through November, although by this time even the LRDG units operating on Seriphos and

Mykonos had been brought away. Only the island of Casteloriso remained in British hands, and here the garrison was reduced to deceive the Germans into thinking it was abandoned, just a token force being left. The British hoped that these would be able to maintain the island until they were once more able to mount an offensive. They also planned to use it as a base for the Raiding Forces, newly formed from the LRDG and SBS, to operate throughout the winter. For many, it was a weary and frustrating journey. D. A. Boyd described it:

> On the 24th November, we left Kusadasi without regret, and for the next three days and four nights, we lived like sardines in a tin. Thirty-five officers and men with their kit traveled in each railway truck. The first night there was not room for us to lie down, but we improved on this subsequently by hanging up the kits, putting one man in a hammock made out of a blanket, and carefully arranging the remainder each night before the light faded. We did manage to get room to lie down, but it was rather a case of "one move— all move."

They eventually arrived at Medain on the evening of the twenty-seventh. An Italian F-lighter commanded by Lieutenant Stowell of the Royal Naval Reserve, which had left Leros on the fifteenth, eventually arrived at Haifa on the twenty-fifth via Samos with 177 German prisoners, but the last ship to reach safety was the Greek destroyer *Adrias*, which had been badly damaged by a mine and had lain up at Gumusluk ever since.

Since her damage on October 23 and withdrawal to Turkish waters, she had been under constant surveillance by the *Luftwaffe*, which carried out daily reconnaissance of her position but made no attacks. Work continued steadily to make the ship sufficiently seaworthy for her to undertake the 600-mile voyage to Alexandria.

All was ready on December 1, some five weeks after grounding, and at 1815, in the darkness, she backed out of the bay escorted by three MGBs. The weather was thick, and she kept close inshore, hugging the Turkish coast, and slipped passed Cos and Simi. During daylight on December 2, she lay up in Turkish waters camouflaged by nets. After dark the force proceeded on its way, and just after dawn on the third, it made a rendezvous with the destroyers *Jervis* and *Penn* off Casteloriso. The *Adrias* lay up in Kavavia Bay during the third until 1630, when the tug *Brigand* arrived to take her in tow for Limassol, where she arrived at 1915 on the fourth. Here she refueled and then sailed again at 0400 hours.

Under her own power, as towing was proving to be difficult, she headed for Alexandria escorted by the two destroyers, which were later relieved by the *Exmoor* and *Aldenham*. Flight Lieutenant Thomas told us how the RAF gave the crippled ship some measure of air cover on the final leg of her voyage to safety:

> We were sent to give fighter cover to a bowless destroyer near Leros. We found her with some difficulty in the twilight and flashed on our Aldis lamp, "How are you?" Reply (damned hard to read in a Beaufighter), "All right, thank you. How are you?" (typical Navy coolness).
>
> Less happily, there was the chump of a fighter direction officer on an Arethusa-class cruiser who insisted on chatting to us in a crystal blue sky, *sans* cloud cover, just off the tip of Rhodes. Pilot Officer Gibbard, who shared my tent, was nearly shot down on a subsequent sortie by the antics of this chump stirring up the 109s!
>
> Even so, several Ju88s were claimed destroyed or damaged during our escort period. Once we asked the ships we were escorting to pick up survivors from some of our victims; the reply was brief and to the point: "Let the buggers swim!"

The *Adrias* reached Alexandria at 1400 on the sixth and entered the harbor under her own steam at eight knots with, according to one eyewitness, "her blunt bulkhead pushing the Mediterranean in front of her." All the warships in harbor cleared lower decks and cheered ship as the crippled destroyer steamed slowly to her berth. Her Greek captain, Cmdr. J. M. Toumbas, was later awarded the Greek equivalent of the Victoria Cross for his sheer grit and determination in saving his ship.

A message was sent to Messrs. Swan Hunter, the ship's builders, paying tribute to the fine performance of the ship in steaming 600 miles ahead with her bow off to No. 37 bulkhead; this latter bulkhead was damaged, and eventually No. 44 bulkhead took the full pressure of the sea. The ship was not maneuverable astern and made the passage from Cyprus at a speed of eight to ten knots without the aid of a tug—a truly remarkable performance.

Apart from her stout construction, she was saved in some measure by good fortune, for on two occasions she was almost detected by the Germans. While in the Cos Channel, a German hospital ship passed her on the opposite course. The *Wehrmacht* on Cos did not carry out the usual searchlight sweeps, or she certainly would have been discovered. While in the dangerous waters north of Rhodes, she was shielded by blinding rainstorms, and again the *Luftwaffe* was cheated of its prey.

With the arrival of this ship at Alexandria, the final chapter of this sorry campaign reached its conclusion.

Epilogue

That the campaign in the Aegean was a defeat is obvious and, indeed, can hardly be denied. As the last stragglers made their slow way back to safety, Hitler was jubilantly conferring on Lieutenant General Müller the accolade "Conqueror of Leros" and giving his "abundant appreciation" of his success. It must be admitted that this praise had been earned. Edwin Packer, in his summary of the campaign, headed his conclusions "No reward for audacity," and in applying this to the British, he is certainly correct. For the Germans, however, audacity had paid a handsome dividend.

Other historians, although not all, while admitting that the British suffered a grievous setback, have sought to lessen its significance by comparing the British and German losses on a balance sheet that sometimes comes out equal and other times shows a marked advantage to the British. Though all the facts will never be known precisely, it is worth examining a few of these statements in detail in order to get a better picture.

British casualties are well tabulated. The Royal Navy lost heavily in its final duel with the Stukas; indeed, the scale of loss is comparable to the disaster suffered off Crete three years earlier. The cruiser *Carlisle* was damaged beyond repair; six destroyers, two submarines, and ten lesser vessels were sunk. Three cruisers were heavily damaged, as well as four more destroyers. The Germans lost twelve small steamers and twenty minor warships, plus one destroyer wrecked and bombed.

The Royal Air Force lost 115 aircraft, with a further 20 damaged. *Luftwaffe* losses in the same period have not been assessed, but one British historian has stated that "the figures reported at the time, 135 destroyed and 126 damaged, are certainly an over-optimistic calculation." With the example of many other such estimates before us, we can agree that this is probably true. Even now the enormous casualties claimed to have been inflicted on the Germans during the Battle of Britain are still believed by many, although the actual figures were much smaller and have been given in several excellent works. The same will surely be found to apply in the claims and counterclaims of the Aegean air fighting, and it seems doubtful that German aircraft loss exceeded 120 planes.

The army had a casualty list of about 4,800, the size of an extended infantry brigade, but many of these were taken prisoner. The list of officers killed during the fighting on Leros makes it clear, however, that the British suffered particularly heavily in this respect, because of the general bravery and self-sacrifice of these men.

The fighting on Leros was particularly bloody, and the Germans took casualties not far short of the British. In their official communications of the time, they claimed to have taken 200 officers and 3,000 British POWs plus 350 officers and 5,350 Italians. Sixteen antiaircraft guns and 120 cannons were also captured. Their own casualties were appalling. The paratroops in particular were cut to ribbons. As was revealed under a "TOP SECRET" heading in the OKW Diary, the Germans suffered 1,109 casualties in taking Leros, 41 percent of the invading force. These were not all killed, but included the wounded. Some claims by British historians about the casualty ratio are rather misleading. It is on record that the graves on Leros were found to contain 1,000 Germans and 400 British, which conveys, even if unintentionally, the impression that this was the ratio of losses in the battle. If this were so, then it would seem that only 109 of the German casualties were wounded as opposed to killed, which is indeed an impressive figure. Lieutenant General Müller gave his losses for the invasions of Cos and Leros, as 260 dead, 746 wounded, and 162 missing. The British evacuated only 177 captured Germans from Leros before it fell. However historians sympathetic to the British cause add it up, the German number killed is less than a third of the figure claimed at the time.

Why the great difference in calculating? Mainly because German casualties were not separated from Italian at the time, as Churchill adopted his usual "creative accounting." The prime minister was well-known for such exaggeration. Among the many examples, he stated to the House that hundreds of German Stuka dive-bombers had been shot down during the battle of Britain, when the true figure was just fifty-four. Earlier, when at the Admiralty, he claimed that the Royal Navy had sunk fifty German submarines, a totally ridiculous overestimate, when the true, verifiable figure was actually *fifteen*, as proved by postwar studies; spitefully, Churchill even had the director of antisubmarine warfare, Capt. A. G. Talbot, who dared to tell the true figure, removed from his post. (See page 94 of *Churchill and the Admirals*, by Stephen Roskill.)

Churchill's figures on the Aegean casualties were never challenged. For example, Capt. S. W. Roskill in the official history, *The War at Sea*, also states in a footnote that when the *Sinfra* was sunk, nearly 2,000 German and Italian soldiers were lost, which is the exact figure Churchill bragged about to Foreign Minister Anthony Eden. Though this figure is true, a mere fraction of this total were on the opposing side. The *Sinfra* went down with the loss of about 40 German soldiers out of the 500 carried; there were also aboard some 2,000 Italians—loyal to the Badoglio government and the Allies—and 200 Greek partisans, all of whom were being shipped back as POWs. Of these, only about 539 Italians and 13 Greeks were saved. The prime minister's assertion "we drowned 2,000 of them" sounds far more impressive than "we drowned 40 of them." Again, more than 1,200 Italians in transit were lost aboard the *Donizetti*. Clearly the deaths of British allies should *not* be included in the list of German losses, and only a politician grasping at straws would attempt to do so.

The scale of air attacks mounted by the *Luftwaffe* to subdue the Leros garrison has frequently been quoted as being up to 600 missions a day. Yet the official publication *The Rise and Fall of the German Air Force*, compiled by British experts after examination of German records, completely refutes this:

> The major share of the German Air Force in the success of both operations [Cos and Leros] stands out beyond all doubt. Yet this success was achieved, not as has sometimes been suggested by the use of overwhelming air power, but by fully exploiting a favorable situation *with a small force maintaining only a moderate scale of effort* [emphasis added]. Both at Cos and Leros Luftwaffe activity was slighter than had been expected. The total effort in the two days operations for the reduction of Cos amounted to under 300 sorties including 65–75 Me.109 sorties of a defensive character; the main weight of the attack on October 3rd and 4th was born by Ju 87s which flew 140–150 sorties.

Of Leros, it states that operations, although very effective, were only moderate in scale: "during the *five days* [emphasis added] of attack only 676–700 offensive sorties were flown." The *Luftwaffe* had, however, conducted a softening-up campaign during the previous two months (these sorties are listed in Appendix F). Compare this with the Allied effort: From October 1 to 7, the U.S. Army Air Force made a total of 425 daylight sorties against airfields, landing grounds, ports, and bases, and the British made 63 night sorties by heavy bombers alone. From mid-October to mid-November, when the island fell, the U.S. made 317 sorties in seven days and the British 278 sorties on twenty-eight nights by heavy bombers. In daylight attacks against German shipping, American Mitchells made 86 sorties and Wellingtons and Beaufighters 11.

In addition, offensive sweeps were carried out almost daily during the actual period of fighting on Leros. Between November 12 and 17, Beaufighters and Mitchells made 79 sorties. Heavy bombers—American Liberators and Mitchells and British Halifaxes and Liberators—made a total of 212 sorties against airfields in Greece and Rhodes. Wellingtons, Hudsons, and Baltimores made an additional 55 sorties. Spitfires with special long-range tanks and Hurricanes made repeated sweeps over Rhodes and Crete at this time.

Particularly impressive was the record of the faithful Dakotas of No. 216 Squadron, which had operated efficiently and constantly throughout the campaign despite the most difficult and hazardous conditions and some losses. From October 6 to November 19, they flew 87 sorties and dropped a total load of 378,650 pounds. They also flew in the 120 paratroops to Cos, and one of the most outstanding of their efforts was the dropping of 200 officers and men of the Greek Sacred Squadron on Samos on the night of October 31–November 1. None of these troops had ever jumped before, and very few had any experience in flying. Nevertheless, on a pitch-black night, the six Dakotas carried out their mission with complete success. Also, all of the dispatchers they carried were volunteer airmen and soldiers, and flying in slow transports over German airfields packed with high-performance fighters in a round-trip of many hours surely called for a high standard of heroism.

Much has been made of the claim that by this small effort in the Aegean a large concentration of vital forces was drawn into the area from more important zones. This is partially true, but not of quite the significance that many have attached to it. Certainly the small resources of the German maritime fleet in the Mediterranean were called on to the limit, their shortcomings being made up from captured Italian tonnage, and the losses in proportion to the total were large. Certainly, too, the Germans deployed aircraft from Russia and France, but here again only on a small scale, some 150 machines in all. The aircraft used were predominantly of obsolete types anyway, which would have had only a limited value in the main theaters.

For example, the main air weapon, the Ju 87 dive-bomber, although it had a brilliant war record, had been replaced by the Fw 190 fighter-bomber for ground support in the main theater of war, the Russian front, and was mainly used as a night intruder over Western Europe toward the end of the war. The Ju 52s, which gave such sterling service, and the Ar 196 floatplane were both low-performance aircraft and not greatly missed. The bomber groups were soon switched back to the main fronts on termination of the campaign, and their absence was not greatly noticed, even in Italy. Here the Germans were able to hold with ease the Allied ground thrusts; they even counterattacked with telling effect and managed to reinforce as well, despite the massive effort of the heavy and medium bomber forces deployed continually against their communications.

As for the troops employed, with the sole exception of the Parachute Battalion, which was flown in from central Italy via Athens, all were from regiments already in occupation of Greece and the Balkans. Not one soldier of the *Wehrmacht* was otherwise pulled back from Russia or Italy. Some time later, the islands of Cos, Leros, and Samos were handed over by Gen. Friedrich Wilhelm Müller to Assault Division Rhodes, which became the garrison force. Müller survived the war but was tried and sentenced to death by a Greek court for alleged war crimes during his tenure in command on Crete and was executed by them on May 20, 1947.

The Germans were jubilant as well as shocked at the simplicity of their victory. According to the January 1944 issue of *Das Signal* magazine:

> The fighting showed especially, two facets: In the first place, England's sea power, which is engaged throughout the world's seas, was not able to successfully defend important bases in the Eastern Mediterranean from where it had planned to put increasing pressure militarily. In the second place, however, the quick surrender of many enemy island defenders was a surprise. Contrary to the German soldier who, where fate puts him, fights to the last bullet, the soldier of the Western Powers stops fighting the moment he recognizes there is no chance to win the fight.

Failure always brings recrimination, and this campaign was no exception. It is not the aim of this book to censure anyone, but to set out the facts and present the arguments on each side. At the risk of oversimplification, they can be summarized in sections. First is the issue of Churchill versus the Americans, which is intermixed with the arguments involving the Middle East Command and the British Chiefs of Staff. The basic reason for the failure of the campaign was decidedly the question of air power, which can conveniently be summarized as Tedder versus Douglas, while at the level of the actual fighting, it was the soldier and sailor against the "brass hats."

Edwin Packer wrote, "The undoubted strategic advantages which possession of the Dodecanese gave—clearly recognized by Churchill and Hitler, though not by Marshall and Eisenhower—blinded the British into thinking that audacity would be rewarded on this occasion as it had many times before in the history of their country." This is indisputably true; but it is equally true that the Americans, though incredibly blind to the glittering prospects offered, as it seems in retrospect, had a good case for withholding their approval.

Captain Roskill pointed out that "we should take account of the fact that every peripheral operation inevitably grows in size as it progresses, with ever-increasing demands on resources; and the dislike of the American Chiefs of Staff, and of General Eisenhower and his subordinate commanders, for such enterprises, what time the major campaign which they had on their hands still had to be decided, is readily understood."

He added later a further point: "In any theatre of combined operations there is always one position, generally an island, which, because of its geographical position and because it possesses harbors and airfields, is the key to control over a wide area." As everyone realized, this key was Rhodes, and when it was captured by the Germans it was the time for the Allies to abandon the Aegean operation completely or recapture Rhodes first. Neither course was adopted. The Middle East Command instead made the decision to hold the lesser islands, but at first *with the knowledge that the Germans were preparing for the imminent occupation of Rhodes.* This must be stressed. General Maitland Wilson can hardly be blamed for embarking on the occupation of the Dodecanese when he did, even though from the outset the odds were against him. When he made his decision to go in, even Eisenhower was still in favor of Accolade taking place. Following Churchill's telegram to Eisenhower on September 25 and Eisenhower's reply on the twenty-sixth, in which he agreed to spare the asked-for armored brigade and most of the shipping, the assault date was set for October 23 by the Middle East Command. Therefore, the islands would have had to hold out for only one month, and this at a time when the strength and reaction of the Germans were not certain.

Nor can Maitland Wilson be blamed for the loss of Rhodes, for he was given insufficient warning. Had he been given time to organize a demonstration in strength as soon as the Italian capitulation was announced, it is possible that the Germans, unaware of his true strength and expecting the British to have been forewarned—and therefore forearmed—could have been overawed. Certainly there would have been a better chance than that given by withholding this vital information from Wilson until too late. As it was, only the Germans, not the Italians or the British on the spot, were ready when the time came. All else followed.

It was not until the unexpected fall of Cos to the Germans that two points were made clear. First, Hitler had a deep interest in the Aegean, and the German forces there were very much aware of its importance. And second, this reverse had a profound effect on American thinking about the campaign, and they thereafter began to hedge. Eisenhower certainly received more than adequate discouragement from his superiors in Washington.

The new American viewpoint was not made clear until the Tunis Conference, and despite everything that Churchill could do to save the scheme, Accolade was finally abandoned. By this time, the British were fully committed in the islands, but they still could have cut their losses and pulled out without too much difficulty. The arguments that this would have been a difficult operation were later proved to be overly pessimistic; enough stores and troops were run in to more than justify an attempt to get the small garrison out at that time. But it was not so decided.

The outcome of the Tunis Conference and the subsequent decisions taken by the Middle East Command are vital as to why the campaign was pushed on to its ultimate conclusion. Prior to the conference, Portal had telegraphed Tedder on October 7 asking him to keep an open mind on the question of air support for Accolade. Maitland Wilson received a message from Churchill urging him to press strongly for further support for Accolade: "It is clear that the key to the strategic situation in the Mediterranean is expressed in the two words 'Storm Rhodes.'"

The Joint Planners in London were expressing different opinions, however. They felt that the Middle East Command was overestimating the strategic importance of Rhodes; its occupation would not in itself be adequate. They believed, as did the Americans, that further reinforcements would be required. They recommended instead that the islands the British did hold be evacuated.

Nevertheless, two of the principal delegates at the conference had received promptings to the contrary from London. These promptings, however, had little effect on the outcome, for on the evening of October 9, Eisenhower informed Churchill of the result. In this, the prize was agreed to be great, but those present felt that the situation that had just developed in Italy, added to the fall of Cos, did not permit the diversion of the forces promised earlier.

Part two of Eisenhower's telegram is of particular interest: "Every conclusion submitted in our report to the CCS was agreed unanimously by all Commanders-in-Chief from both theaters. It is personally distressing to me to have to advise against a project in which you believe so earnestly but I feel I would not be performing my duty if I should recommend otherwise. All Commanders-in-Chief share this attitude."

The situation in Italy at this time was that the Germans had shown unexpected resilience and were pouring in reinforcements at an enormous rate. Whereas in mid-September, thirteen Allied divisions faced eighteen German ones, by the end of October, there would be only eleven Allied against twenty-five German. There can be little doubt then that the decision reached was the correct one.

Tedder went even further, writing: "There was no doubt in the mind of anyone present at this meeting that 'Accolade' could not now be staged effectively. It was clear to me that the Middle East Commanders had no faith in the project and were relieved at the decision. It was not only a question of German reinforcements in Italy. The weather had changed decisively for the worse."

He cabled Portal that the question of Accolade was considered on its merit and with great impartiality before repercussions on the Italian campaign were examined. Maitland Wilson admitted this in a telegram sent to Churchill. Rhodes could not be taken that year. Why then were the British garrisons in Leros not withdrawn forthwith? Edwin Packer surmised: "They knew the project was dear to the heart of the British Prime Minister. Would he have thought less highly of them if they had cancelled the operation remembering his criticism of Wavell in 1941? No one cared to put it to the test: a reputation for caution was not a characteristic Churchill admired. So the C-in-Cs in the Middle East decided to go on."

Could that have been the reason? Maitland Wilson's cable shows that other things were in their minds. As a substitute for Rhodes, why not Turkey? Again, there was a chance, as when Operation Accolade was still officially on, that if they stuck to Leros and Samos for a little longer, airfields would be made available in that country. Maitland Wilson clearly expressed this thinking: "This morning John Cunningham, Linnel and I reviewed the situation in the Aegean (Sholto Douglas was in London at this time) on the assumption that Rhodes would not take place till a later date. *We came to the conclusion that the holding of Leros and Samos is not impossible, although their maintenance is going to be difficult, and will depend on continued Turkish co-operation* [emphasis added]. I am going to talk to Eden about this when he arrives on Tuesday."

Thus the straw to which they clung, in affirming that the wishes of the prime minister were to be followed as far as possible, was Turkey. There were also other considerations that influenced their decision to a greater degree than the fear of displeasing Churchill. The islands of Leros and Samos had not yet been attacked, and although the fall of Cos had shown that the Germans were determined, it was still not thought that a reinforced Leros could be assaulted successfully for some time. The illusion of "Fortress Leros" still had not been revealed and they felt that it was a bastion that, if garrisoned with good troops, could hold out against an attack. The amount of irritation that they could inflict on the scattered German garrisons on the island—and maintain until either Turkey came in or the long-deferred Accolade could be remounted in the spring—held out the promise of allowing them to hold down large German forces with a limited effort.

The result is succinctly recorded in the official history: "The local commanders did not hesitate; the Chiefs of Staff supported them; and the Prime Minister agreed with both."

Indeed he did. Maitland Wilson received by return an enthusiastic reply: "Cling on if you possibly can. It will be a splendid achievement. Talk it over with Eden and see what help you can get from the Turk. If after everything has been done you are forced to quit I will support you, but victory is the prize."

He was as good as his word. In the event, the pot of gold at the end of the rainbow was not forthcoming. Turkey was more impressed by German victories than by British promises or Soviet threats. There would be no fighter cover from Turkey.

The vital factor of air cover—and the divergence of opinion that resulted between Tedder and Douglas—must be examined together with the rigid command structure, which, in Churchill's words, "drew an imaginary line down the Mediterranean" and relieved General Eisenhower's armies of all responsibility for the Dalmatian coast and the Balkans. "These are assigned to General Wilson, of the Middle East Command, but he does not possess the necessary forces. One command has the forces but not the responsibilities, the other the responsibilities but not the forces. This can hardly be considered an ideal arrangement."

With this command structure, the allocation of air power was also involved. Whereas Wilson was an independent commander and responsible only to London, Douglas and his command in the Middle East were under the operational control of Tedder at Eisenhower's headquarters. This soon led to difficulties. Douglas wrote:

> From the outset I was far from happy about the view of our efforts in the Eastern Mediterranean taken by Eisenhower's HQ. The answers they were giving to our signals to them could never be considered as properly thought out, and I could not understand Tedder's position in all this. He had appeared to approve of our plans to start with, and it was not until some three weeks after we had stated our intentions, and we had actually put them into operation, that he lodged his disturbing complaint about not being consulted.

Tedder's viewpoint was somewhat different:

> So far as I was aware the participation of elements of the Mediterranean Air Command had never been properly considered. The fall of Cos only made such an assessment more urgent. I set out in

detail for Eisenhower's eye the ways in which a determined attack
on Rhodes would diminish our air strength in the Italian campaign.
In particular I anticipated a demand for long range fighters for the
purpose of covering convoys and the assault on Rhodes itself.

Eisenhower's response to Tedder's warning was to send him a reply to
the effect that no specific undertakings should be made for Accolade other
than that of bombing German airfields in Greece, which they had both
already agreed was desirable. Tedder sent a copy of this to Portal and added
that he wholeheartedly endorsed it.

It must also be stressed that even when Accolade was still a possibility,
Tedder, in common with the others, stressed that an essential part of the
revised plan lay in the retention of Cos and Leros, which in his opinion was
as necessary to the capture of Rhodes as its own capture was necessary to
their preservation. Thus when Cos went so quickly, it was to be expected that
he would then have grave reservations about the rest of the plan.

While Cos was being subjected to heavy air attacks, Douglas had made
repeated pleas for the bombing of the Greek and Balkan airfields, but Tedder felt that the bombing of the German supply lines in Northern Italy was
of greater importance. He did in fact signal Douglas before the island fell
that he was very concerned about the way the Aegean operations were
going. He added that commitments were involved that he had had no prior
opportunity of assessing. Tedder felt that events were underlining something he had always thought—that from the air point of view, the Balkans
were strategically one and the same as the rest of the Mediterranean. He
promised that he would do his best to help, but he insisted that he must be
kept informed of future plans.

It was at this time that Portal signaled Tedder that in his opinion, the
Allies should fight the German Air Force wherever it went. He also thought
the Allies could better afford a diversion into the Aegean than could the
Germans and that damage inflicted on the Germans in the Aegean was just
as desirable as damage inflicted in any other theater.

With Cos gone and Accolade abandoned, the question of extra air diversions became even more acute. Tedder felt that they were becoming more
and more wasteful and dangerous; Douglas felt more and more that he was
letting down the other two services. With Portal's message recording his
pleasure at the forward policy being adopted by Middle East Command in
the Aegean and Tedder's signal complaining that he had no prior opportunity of assessing the operations then in progress, Douglas was perplexed. "It
struck me that in some curious way Tedder appeared to be the only one who
was not fully acquainted with what was going on—even London knew and

approved. It confirmed for me my opinion that the time was more than ripe for a fundamental change in the structure of the overall command of the air in the Mediterranean."

From this statement, it can be seen that the two men, although at loggerheads over this particular issue, had both come to the same conclusion, as had Churchill: that the system of command in the Mediterranean at this time was unworkable, unwieldy, and far too inflexible. There can be no denying that in this and in so many similar operations, from the occupation of Norway through the fall of France and on to the desert campaigns, it was the Germans who made unexpected moves and took chances with new and surprising tactics. It has always been the delight of British and American observers and commentators to depict the Germans as dull, methodical plodders who could never adapt. But in fact, time and time again, it was the Allies with their rigid command structures who were caught off-guard by German initiative.

After Leros had suffered the same fate as Cos, both Tedder and Douglas were dispirited. Douglas wrote:

> I prepared a paper in which I summarized all that had happened in the last days of the operation. I was in no mood to pull any punches and I started off with the blunt statement: "I am very dissatisfied with the assistance that I received during the Leros operation." I pointed out that when the deterioration of the weather in Italy had bogged down the battle there—right at the period during which Leros was being attacked—"a wider view should have been taken of the dispositions of heavy and medium bombers and of long-range fighters." I further pointed out that we had asked "not once but many times" for Liberators and Lightnings to be located in Cyrenaica, and that "all we got were a few B-25s at first with disgruntled and later with untrained pilots and armed with semi-experimental 75-mm guns."

He continued much in the same vein; recording that between October 27 and November 14, no attack had been made by Allied heavy bombers from the central Mediterranean on the Greek airfields. On November 14, ninety-one B-25s with forty-nine Lightnings as escorts had bombed Sofia, an attack that, if it had been directed against the Greek airfields instead, might have tipped the scales. Douglas came to the conclusion, in this paper and later, that it was the disregard by the Americans in general, and the indifference of the Mediterranean Air Command in particular, that resulted in the Middle East Command's difficult position during this operation. We can certainly agree with him on the first part of this conclusion. As for the second, Tedder's feelings were also recorded much later, when the campaign was but a memory. They are nevertheless both sincere and, in the context of the U.S. Chiefs of Staffs' attitude, pertinent.

Tedder claimed that he had never ignored the fate of Leros, but that even less could he detach himself from the fate of the Italian campaign. He thought that the whole operation was a gamble that had failed to pay off and added that the assumption that heavy bomber raids could knock out the *Luftwaffe* was quite unrealistic because of the effort they would have required and the weather conditions prevailing at the time. The success of such a scheme was continuity of attack, and this continuity could not have been sustained. He recorded: "One would have thought that some of the bitter lessons of Crete would have been sufficiently fresh in the mind to have prevented a repetition and yet in the sad story of Cos and Leros we had the familiar cries—and justifiable cries—for protection from enemy air attack, complaints of inadequate support from the Air, and heavy casualties in all three Services, because we were compelled once again to attempt the impossible."

Here again we can sympathize with this opinion. One destroyer captain wrote, "We younger destroyer skippers, I think, blamed Churchill." This opinion was strongly endorsed by the late Capt. Stephen Roskill, who asserted, "Most of the responsibility for this failure must surely rest with Churchill," who, Roskill had an "addiction" to capturing islands (for example, his obsession with Pantellaria in 1940 and 1941 and the Azores in the same period) that would have proved difficult to supply. Roskill also stated that the hopes Churchill entertained about Turkey entering the war being the principal plank on which he rested his case "was an illusion." Another study went even further, naming the campaign "Churchill's Folly" and claiming that the full story had "never been told"—which, as *War in the Aegean* was first published in 1974, was patently not so. The author also called the campaign "The Last Great British Defeat of World War II," a dubious statement, with Arnhem at least as a stronger contender.

But all this criticism of the prime minister, though undoubtedly merited, does not seem entirely fair. Despite Churchill's propensity for wild schemes and harebrained interventions, such Operation Catherine, the fiasco of Norway, Operation Workshop, the insistence of the dispatch of *Prince of Wales* and *Repulse* to Singapore against the advice of the Admiralty, and so on, there can be no doubt that on this occasion, he really *did* read Stalin's future intentions for the Balkans far better than the naive Roosevelt and, indeed, the Americans in general.

Certainly the bright vision was Churchill's, and he was extremely reluctant to see it thrown away. "Leros is a bitter blow to me," he told Eden in a telegram sent on November 21. He continued:

One may ask should such an operation ever have been undertaken without the assurance of air superiority? Have we not failed to learn the lessons of Crete, etc.? Have we not restored the Stukas to a fleeting moment of their old triumphs? The answer is that there is none of these arguments that was not foreseen before the occupation of these islands was attempted and if they were disregarded it was because other reasons and other hopes were held to predominate over them. *If we are never going to proceed on anything but certainties we must certainly face the prospect of a prolonged war* [emphasis added].

He also stated that this campaign "constituted, happily on a small scale, the most acute difference I ever had with Eisenhower."

Yet he showed not the slightest hint of remorse for all the sacrifice made for naught, only a politicians' natural desire to gloss over the whole fiasco and quickly forget the part he played in it. Churchill telegraphed Eden: "No attempts should be made to minimize the poignancy of the loss of the Dodecanese. It is, however, just to say that it is our first really grievous reverse since Tobruk 1942. *I hope that there will be no need to make heavy weather over this at all* [emphasis added]."

On the other hand, the Americans adhered to their perfectly valid point that they were fighting against the Germans and the Russians were their allies. However far-sighted Churchill may have been in 1943, he had already hitched his country to the Soviet cause in June 1941, and his policy of reinforcing Stalin at the expense of the British Far East since then somewhat compromised his later "farsightedness" in the Balkans. After all, Churchill had declared, "If Hitler had invaded Hell, I would at least make a favorable reference to the Devil in the House of Commons." If Churchill was dismayed at Roosevelt's belief that he "could do a deal with Joe," it must be admitted that he had given the American leader an early lead in pandering to Stalin's capacious appetite.

Jeffrey Holland, who fought there and returned to the island postwar to ponder the reasons for it all, told us: "The islanders themselves believe that part of the price Churchill would have had to pay (and been prepared to pay) for bringing Turkey into the war would be to accept Turkish sovereignty over the Dodecanese plus Rhodes. Colonel Kenyon thought the whole thing was a bloody shambles."

As before, it was Turkey that saw things more clearly. Said Giuseppe de Peppo, the Italian ambassador to Turkey, "The Turkish ideal is that the last German soldier should fall upon the last Russian corpse."

This fiasco in the eastern Mediterranean had shown that Britain alone could not succeed without American participation or backing. The Americans, with their upsurging strength, had now become the major partner, and as such, they were less ready to accommodate views that did not accord with their own. That this was the turning point in Anglo-American strategy is borne out by General Brooke, the British Chief of the Imperial General Staff, who recorded in his diary on November 1, 1943, that he regretted that he had not had sufficient force of character to swing the American Chiefs of Staff into line with British thinking on the Mediterranean, but although he blamed himself, he doubted whether it was humanly possible to alter the American point of view more than he had succeeded in doing. Henceforth the United States exerted an ever-increasing domination over the conduct of the war, and it took the lion's share in writing the final chapters in the postwar state of Europe. Not only had it surrendered the chance to beat the Soviets into the Balkans, but when the maps were redrawn later, they were to be even more generous to the greedy appetite of Stalin.

An isolated American view was that of Gen. Mark Clark, who wrote that "the weakening of the campaigns in Italy in order to invade Southern France instead of pushing on into the Balkans was one of the outstanding political mistakes of the war." However, Professor Michael Howard dismissed all postwar speculations on the motives of Churchill to thwart the Communist takeover of Eastern Europe as being mainly wrong interpretations of mere wartime expediency on the part of the prime minister. He also added the most pertinent point of all: "The appetites which had been disappointed, especially those for seizing Rhodes and striking across the Aegean at the mainland of Greece, were largely ones which had developed *en mangeant* and which had not received general Allied—or even general British—sanction."

There is one puzzling thing that is hard to understand: When the provision of on-the-spot air cover was so vital to the campaign, and the land-based fighters were not forthcoming, why was it that the navies of the two largest maritime nations the world had ever known could not provide aircraft carriers as a substitute? The British fleet alone had several carriers—two fleet carriers, *Illustrious* and *Formidable*; a light carrier, *Unicorn*; and three escort carriers, *Attacker*, *Hunter*, and *Stalker*—on station at the beginning of September, when the total number of British fighter aircraft were but a drop in the ocean of the Allies' grand total of 4,000 aircraft. To have detached even the escort carriers to operate in the Aegean would have brought the cruisers and destroyers the respite they needed. Indeed, a year later this was done and worked. Instead, they were all withdrawn from the Mediterranean during this period because of heavy losses their aircraft sustained in deck landings supporting the Salerno operation. Perhaps the need for aircraft carriers, even in the landlocked waters of the Mediterranean, is the foremost lesson to be drawn from this campaign. In view of British defense decisions between 1963 and 1997, it seems that nobody in government understood or heeded this lesson, a blindness culminating in the absolute worst of misjudgments—that made by the Thatcher government just before the Falklands War—to sell off the last British carriers and not replace them.

After the Allies had missed their main chance in the Balkans, the Aegean did indeed become a backwater. The German garrisons there were allowed to wither on the vine, and the Allies were satisfied that those troops were locked up away from the fronts in Italy and, later, France. It did not affect the Germans much, for Rome did not fall that easily, nor was Italy quickly conquered. The newly formed Raiding Forces carried out pinprick raids in their usual daring manner, and later escort carriers and cruiser-destroyer strike forces inflicted damage on the German convoy routes, as did strikes by RAF forces. The Soviet steamroller finally plowed through to the north sucking under Romania, Hungary, and Bulgaria, and eventually the Germans withdrew from the Balkans in December 1944. The Allies could take little advantage then; indeed, the British had to make considerable effort in Greece to prevent the establishment of a Communist government, and Yugoslavia and Albania went the same way.

It is, however, futile to wring one's hands over what might have been. There was no guarantee that the mere conquest of the Aegean would have brought Turkey into the war on the Allies' side, nor that the Germans would have abandoned Greece. The Allies were never prepared to follow up with a main assault on the Balkans, no matter what the German reaction to the loss of the Aegean might have been. And even if they had achieved success there, it was at Teheran and Potsdam, and not on the battlefield, that the fruits of battle were decided.

APPENDIX A

Ships under Royal Navy Control

CRUISERS

Aurora, Capt. G. Barnard, CBE, DSO, RN
Carlisle, Capt. H. F. Nalder, RN
Dido, Capt. J. Terry, MVO, RN
Penelope, Capt. G. D. Belben, DSC, AM, RN
Phoebe, Capt. C. P. Frend, RN
Sirius, Capt. P. W. B. Booking, DSO, RN

DESTROYERS

Aldenham, L.Cdr. J. I. Jones, DSO, DSC, RNR
Beaufort, Lt. J. R. L. Moore, RN
Belvoir, Lt. J. F. D. Bush, DSC, RN
Blencathra, Lt. E. G. Warren, RN
Croome, L.Cdr. H. D. M. Slater, RN
Dulverton, Cdr. S. A. Buss, MVO, RN
Echo, L.Cdr. R. H. C. Cyld, DSC, RN
Eclipse, Cdr. E. Mack, DSO, DSC, RN
Exmoor, Cdr. J. Jeffreys, DSC, RN
Faulknor, Capt. A. K. Scott Moncrieff, DSO, RN, and Capt. M. S. Thomas, DSO, RN
Fury, L.Cdr. T. F. Taylor, DSC, RN
Hambledon, L.Cdr. G. W. McKendrick, RN
Haydon, L.Cdr. R. C. Watkins, RN
Hursley, L.Cdr. W. J. P. Church, DSO, DSC, RN
Intrepid, Cdr. C. A. de W. Kitcat, RN
Jervis, Capt. J. S. Crawford, DSO, RN
Lamerton, L.Cdr. G. T. S. Gray, DSC, RN
Panther, L.Cdr. Viscount Jocelyn, RN
Pathfinder, L.Cdr. C. W. Malins, DSO, DSC, RN
Penn, L.Cdr. J. H. Swain, DSO, DSC, RN
Petard, Cdr. R. C. Egan, DSO, DSC, RN
Rockwood, Lt. S. R. Le H. Lombard-Hobson, RN
Tetcott, L.Cdr. A. F. Harkness, OBE, DSC, RD, RNR

Tumult, L.Cdr. N. Lanyon, DSO, DSC, RN
Wilton, Lt. G. G. Marten, RN

Greek
Adrias, Cdr. J. N. Toumbas, RHN
Kanaris, Cdr. Zartas, RHN
Miaoulis, Cdr. C. Nikitiases, RHN, Cdr. E. Boudouris, RHN
Pindos, L.Cdr. D. Fifas, RHN
Queen Olga, L.Cdr. G. Blessas, DSO, RHN
Themistocles, L.Cdr. N. Sarris, RHN

Polish
Krakowiak, Cdr. Naracewisz

SUBMARINES
Rorqual, L.Cdr. L. W. Napier, DSO, DSC, RN
Seraph, Lt. N. L. A. Jewell, MBE, DSC, RN
Severn, L.Cdr. A. N. G. Campbell, RN
Shakespeare, Lt. M. F. R. Ainslie, DSO, DSC, RN
Sibyl, Lt. E. J. D. Turner, DSO, DSC, RN
Sickle, Lt. J. R. Drummond, DSO, DSC, RN
Simoon, Lt. G. D. N. Milner, RN
Sportsman, Lt. R. Gatehouse, DSC, RN
Surf, Lt. D. Lambert, DSC, RN
Torbay, Lt. R. J. Clutterbuck, DSC, RN
Trespasser, Lt. R. M. Favell, DSC, RN
Trooper, Lt. J. S. Wraith, RN
Unrivalled, Lt. H. B. Turner, DSC, RN
Unruly, Lt. J. P. Fyfe, DSC, RN
Unsparing, Lt. A. D. Piper, RN

Greek
Katsonis, Cdr. Lascos, RHN

Polish
Dxik, Cdr. Romanowski
Sokol, L.Cdr. G. C. Koziolkowski

MOTOR TORPEDO BOATS

10th Flotilla
260, T.Lt. H. F. Wadds, DSC, RANVR

263, T.Lt. A. G. Fry, RANVR

266, T.Lt. J. N. Broad, RNZNVR

307, T.Lt, J. G. G. Muir, DSC, RNVR

309, T.Sub-Lt. K. H. Roll, RNVR

313, T.Lt. T. G. Fuller, DSC, RNZNVR

315, T.Sub-Lt. L. E. Newall, DSC, RNZNVR

MOTOR GUN BOATS

Part 60th Flotilla

645, T.Lt. B. L. Bourne, RNVR

646, T.Lt. B. L. Knight-Lacklan, RNVR

647, T.Lt. M. Mount-Stevens, DSC, RNVR

MINESWEEPERS

MMS 102, T.Lt. D. R. Browell, RNVR

MMS103, T.Lt. F. C. V. Murray, RNVR

BYMS72, T.Lt. E. H. Taylor, RNR

BYMS73, T.Lt. C. Thomson, RANVR

MOTOR LAUNCHES

24th and 42nd Flotillas

299, Lt. D. A. P. Smith, RANVR

308, T.Lt. H. Murgatroyd, RNVR

337, T.Lt. L. A. Thurgood, RNVR

340, T.Sub-Lt. J. H. Robertson,

349, T.Lt-Cdr Alan H. Ball, RNVR, SO 42nd Flotilla

351, Lt Kenneth Hallows, RNVR

354, Lt. J. W. "Pat" Patterson, RNVR

355, Lt. Geoffrey W. Searle, DSC. RNVR

356, T.Sub-Lt K. L. Lloyd, DSC. RNVR

357, T.Lt. R. L. "Jonah" Jones, RNVR

358, T.Sub-Lt. K. L. Shute, RNVR

359, Lt. Geoffrey W. Whittam, DSC, RNVR

456, L.Cdr. F. P. Monckton, RNR, SO 24th Flotilla

461, T.Lt. R. M. Argyle, RNVR

579, T.Lt. J. Bain, RNVR

835, Lt. B. M. Close, RANVR

836, T.Lt. A. E. Clarke, DSC, RNVR

British and Allied Ships Sunk and Damaged

CRUISERS DAMAGED
Penelope, bombed October 7, Scarpanto Strait
Carlisle, bombed October 9, Scarpanto Strait
Sirius, bombed October 17, Scarpanto Strait
Aurora, bombed October 30, off Casteloriso

DESTROYERS SUNK
Intrepid, bombed September 26, Leros
Queen Olga, bombed September 26, Leros
Panther, bombed October 9, Scarpanto Strait
Hurworth, mined October 22, off Kalymnos
Eclipse, mined October 24, Karabakla Channel
Dulverton, bombed November 13, Gulf of Cos

DESTROYERS DAMAGED
Hursley, damaged by gunfire October 17, off Kalymnos
Adrias, mined October 22, off Kalymnos
Rockwood, bombed November 11, Gulf of Cos
Penn, damaged by gunfire November 16, off Leros

SUBMARINES SUNK
Katsonis, by *UJ 2101* September 14, Euboea Channel
Trooper, presumed mine October 17, Aegean Sea
Simoon, presumed mine November 15, off the Dardanelles

SUBMARINES DAMAGED
Unrivalled, depth charged October 12
Torbay, depth charged October 16
Unsparing, shell fire October 31
Unseen, depth charged November 16

COASTAL FORCE CRAFT SUNK AND DAMAGED

LCT 3, lost October 3, Cos

ML 835, bombed and sunk October 11, Levitha

Hedgehog, engine trouble October 17, captured at Levitha

MTB 313, bombed and damaged October 17, Casteloriso

ML 1015, lost October 21, foundered in the Aegean

ML 579, bombed and sunk October 26, off Lipso

LCT 115, bombed and sunk October 28, off Casteloriso

LCM 923, November 11, captured at Leros

ML 358, sunk by gunfire November 12, Leros

ML 456, damaged by gunfire November 12, Leros

BYMS 72, November 11–12, captured at Kalymnos

APPENDIX C

Store-Carrying to Leros by Submarines

Severn, October 21–22, 41½ tons
Rorqual, October 23–24, 50 tons
Zoea, October 26–27, 48 tons
Corridoni, October 29–30, 45 tons
Atropo, October 30–31, 43½ tons
Menotti, October 31–November 1, 49 tons
Zoea, November 6–7, 48½ tons

A total of 325½ tons of stores were carried to Leros by submarine. All but the first two were Italian vessels.

APPENDIX D

Allied Air Forces

Squadron	Aircraft	USAAF Type	Air Force
7	Spitfire, Supermarine	Pursuit	SAAF
13	Blenheim, Bristol, Baltimore	Light bomber	RHAF
15	Baltimore (Martin A-30)	Medium	RAF
38	Wellington, Vickers	Heavy bomber	RAF
46	Beaufighter, Bristol	Light bomber	RAF
47	Beaufighter, Bristol	Light bomber	RAF
74	Spitfire, Supermarine	Pursuit	RAF
89	Beaufighter, Bristol	Light bomber	RAF
213	Hurricane, Hawker	Pursuit	RAF
227	Beaufighter, Bristol	Light bomber	RAF
237	Hurricane, Hawker	Pursuit	Rhodesian
252	Beaufighter, Bristol	Light bomber	RAF
454	Baltimore (Martin A-30)	Medium	RAAF
459	Hudson (Lockheed Super)	Medium	RAAF
680	Spitfire, Supermarine (PRU)	PRU	RAF
603	Beaufighter, Bristol	Light bomber	RAF
178	Liberator (B-24)	Heavy bomber	RAF
462	Halifax, Handley-Page	Heavy bomber	RAAF

PRU = Photo Reconnaissance Unit
RAAF = Royal Australian Air Force
RAF = Royal Air Force
RHAF = Royal Hellenic Air Force
Rhodesian = Rhodesian Air Force
SAAF = South African Air Force

Order of Battle of *X Fliegerkorps* on September 30, 1943

BOMBER UNITS

4/KG 6		
5/KG 6	II/KG 6	Ju 88
6/KG 6		
4/KG 51		
5/KG 51	II/KG 51	Ju 88
6/KG 51		
1/KG 100		Do 217K3

DIVE-BOMBER UNITS

1/StG 3		
2/StG 3	I/StG 3	Ju 87
3/StG 3		
4/StG 3	II/StG 3	Ju 87
5/StG 3		
13/StG 151		Ju 87

FIGHTER UNITS

7/JG 27		
8/JG 27	III/JG 27	Me 109
9/JG 27		
10/JG 27		
11/JG 27	IV/JG 27	Me 109
12/JG 27		
II/ZG 26		Me 110

RECONNAISSANCE UNITS

2/AG 2	I/AG 2	Ar 196
3/AG 2		

FLAK UNITS

1/FG 123	I/FG 123
2/FG 123	
1/FG 126	I/FG 126
2/FG 126	
2/FG 125	

TRANSPORT UNITS

1/TG 4	Ju 52
1/TG Go242.2	

APPENDIX F

Air Attacks on Leros, September 26 to October 31

Date	No. Raids	No. Aircraft
September 26	2	25
September 27	1	30
September 29	3	60
September 30	3	60
October 1	6	46
October 4	4	50
October 5	5	79
October 6	5	78
October 7	5	80
October 8	4	18
October 9	6	29
October 10	3	76
October 11	3	24
October 12	8	62
October 14	3	65
October 15	10	34
October 16	11	76
October 17	7	28
October 18	2	28
October 19	6	24
October 20	2	28
October 22	11	44
October 23	5	47
October 24	4	15
October 25	4	16
October 26	11	50
October 27	4	16
October 30	1	5
October 31	1	6

APPENDIX G

Italian Army Units in Place on September 8, 1943

ARMY OF THE AEGEAN (GHQ RHODES)

50th Infantry Division *Regina*, dispersed across all Italian Dodecanse Islands (HQ Rhodes)

6th Infantry Division *Cuneo*, dispersed across occupied islands in the Sporades and Cyclades (HQ Samos)

51st Infantry Division *Siena*, mainly on Crete (HQ Naples) as part of 11th Armata

The breakdown of the Aegean Units

6th Infantry Division *Cuneo*

7th Infantry Regiment, Syros

8th Infantry Regiment, Samos

27th Infantry Regiment, Samos

50th Infantry Division *Regina*

9th Infantry Regiment, Rhodes

10th Infantry Regiment, Cos

309th Infantry Regiment, Rhodes

50th Infantry Regiment, Rhodes

OTHER UNITS ON RHODES

Commando del 56th Anti-Aircraft Artillery Regiment

Commandi del 35th, 36th, and 55th Artillery Regiments

Comando del 331st Infantry Regiment

51st Infantry Division *Siena* (Crete)

31st Infantry Regiment

32nd Infantry Regiment

51st Artillery Regiment

Notes

The authors of this work have been given access to official documents. The authors alone are responsible for the statements made, conclusions drawn, and views expressed in this work.

The page numbers given in the left-hand column indicate where quotations are made from the sources noted; further particulars of publications are found in the Bibliography.

CHAPTER ONE
13   *A Sailor's Odyssey*, Viscount Cunning of Hyndhope

CHAPTER TWO
20   *Grand Strategy*, J. M. A. Gwyer
21   *On Active Service in Peace and War*, Henry L. Stimson and McGeorge Bundy
26   *The Second World War*, W. S. Churchill
26   *The Mediterranean and the Middle East*, I. S. O. Playfair
27   *Grand Strategy*, Michael Howard
28   *The Second World War*, W. S. Churchill
28   *On Active Service in Peace and War*, Henry L. Stimson and McGeorge Bundy
28   *Grand Strategy*, Michael Howard

CHAPTER THREE
32   *Grand Strategy*, Michael Howard
34   Italian Official History
35   *The Second World War*, W. S. Churchill
36   *Naval Operations, Aegean*, Vice Admiral A.U. Willis
38   *The Second World War*, W. S. Churchill
38   *Soft Underbelly*, Trumbell Higgins
39   *The War at Sea*, Capt. S. W. Roskill
40   *Fuehrer's Naval Conferences*, R.Adm. H. G. Thursfield
41   *War Diary of the OKW*, Walther Hubatsch
43   Letter to the author
47   *The Second World War*, W. S. Churchill
47   *Soft Underbelly*, Trumbell Higgins
47   *The Second World War*, W. S. Churchill
48   *The War at Sea*, S. W. Roskill
48   *Triumph in the West*, Arthur Bryant
48   *The Second World War*, W. S. Churchill

CHAPTER ELEVEN

229   *Historical Records of the Buffs*, C. R. B. Knight
230   *Historical Records of the Buffs*, C. R. B. Knight
230   *Long Road to Leros*, L. Marsland Gander
237   *War Diary of the OKW*, Walther Hubatsch
240   *Faugh a Ballagh*
242   *Historical Records of the Buffs*, C. R. B. Knight
244   *Churchill and the Admirals*, Stephen Roskill

CHAPTER TWELVE

249   *Aegean Adventure*, D. A. Boyd

EPILOGUE

257   *The Rise and Fall of German Air Force*
259   *Hard Lesson in the Aegean*, Edwin Packer
260   *The War at Sea*, S. W. Roskill
261   *The Second World War*, W. S. Churchill
261   *History of the Second World War, Grand Strategy*, John Ehrman
262   *With Prejudice*, Lord Tedder
262   *Hard Lesson in the Aegean*, Edwin Packer
263   *The Second World War*, W. S. Churchill
263   *The War at Sea*, S. W. Roskill
263   *The Second World War*, W. S. Churchill
263   *Years of Command*, Lord Douglas of Kirtleside
264   *With Prejudice*, Lord Tedder
266   Letter to the author
266   *Churchill and the Admirals*, Stephen Roskill
266   *Years of Command*, Lord Douglas of Kirtleside
266   *With Prejudice*, Lord Tedder; *The Second World War*, W. S. Churchill
267   *Ciano Diary*
268   *Calculated Risk*, Mark W. Clark
268   *The Mediterranean Strategy in the Second World War*, Michael Howard

Glossary

AA	Antiaircraft
AOC	Air officer commanding
AOK	Army High Command
BYMS	British yard minesweeper
CC RR.	*Carabinieri Riseraare*
CD	Coastal Defence
CO	Commanding Officer
COS	Chiefs of Staff
Cwt	Hundredweight
D	Senior officer, destroyers
DCO	Director control officer
DDMI	Deputy director military intelligence
DFM	Distinguished Flying Medal
DLI	Durham Light Infantry
DMO	Director of military operations
DSC	Distinguished Service Cross
DSO	Distinguished Service Order
D1, D2, etc.	Day one, day two
F-lighter	Self-propelled barge
FDO	Fighter direction officer
Folbot	Folding kayak
HA	High altitude
HAA	Heavy antiaircraft
HDML	Harbor defense motor launch
HE	High explosive
HF	High frequency
HMS	His Majesty's Ship
HSL	High-speed launch
Hunt	Hunt-class destroyer
IFF	Identification friend or foe
I-Boat	*Infantrieboote*, German landing craft, infantry
JPS	Joint Planning Staff
Ju	Junkers
LA	Low angle
KFK	*Kriegsfishkutter* (motor fishing boats)
KORR	King's Own Royal Regiment (Lancaster)
LAA	Light antiaircraft
LG	*Lehrgeschwader* (Training and Development Wing)
LRDG	Long Range Desert Group

MEF	Middle East Forces
MFP	*Marinefährprähme* (F-lighters) (German self-propelled barge)
ML	Motor launch
MO	Medical officer
MMS	Motor minesweeper
MT	Motor transport
MTB	Motor torpedo boat
Me	Messerschmitt
MG	Machine gun
NCO	Noncommissioned officer
OCTU	Operational Commands Training Unit
OKW	*Oberkommando der Wehrmacht* (Wehrmacht High Command)
pdr	Pounder
Pil-Boat	*Pionierlandungsboot* (engineer landing craft)
POW	Prisoner of war
PRU	Photo Reconnaissance Unit
RA	Royal Artillery
RAF	Royal Air Force
RAMC	Royal Army Medical Corps
RASC	Royal Army Service Corps
R-Boat	*Raumboot* (German motor minesweeper)
RCO	Range control officer
RCS	Royal Corps of Signals
RDF	Radio direction finding (radar)
RE	Royal Engineers
RHAF	Royal Hellenic Air Force
RIrF	Royal Irish Fusiliers
RM	Royal Marines
RN	Royal Navy
RNR	Royal Naval Reserve
RNVR	Royal Naval Volunteer Reserve
RSM	Regimental sergeant major
RT	Radio telephone
RWK	Royal West Kent Regiment
SAAF	South African Air Force
SAP	Semi-armor piercing
SAS	Special Air Service
SBS	Special Boat Squadron
SIG	Special Intelligence Group
SS	Special Services
StG	*Stukageschwader* (Stuka Wing)
TA-boat	German ex-French or ex-Italian torpedo boat (light destroyers)
TOO	Time of origin
U-boat	*Unterseeboot* (German submarine)
UJ-Boat	*Unterseebootjagd* (German antisubmarine auxilliary)
USAAF	United States Army Air Force
VHF	Very high frequency

Bibliography

Barclay, C. N. *The History of the Sherwood Foresters (Nottinghamshire and Derbyshire Regiment), 1919–1957.* London: W. Clowes, 1959.

Bennet, Ralph. *Ultra and Mediterranean Strategy, 1941–1945.* London: Hamish Hamilton, 1989.

Benyon-Tinker, W. E. *Dust upon the Sea.* London: Hodder & Stoughton, 1947.

Bevan, Pauline. *Travels with a Leros Veteran.* N.p.: PB Books, 2000.

Brandt, Günther. *Der Seekrieg in der Ägäis.* Saarbrucken: n.p., 1963.

Bryant, Arthur. *Triumph in the West.* London: Collins, 1959.

Buckley, Christopher. *Five Ventures.* London: Her Majesty's Stationery Office, 1954.

Churchill, W. S. *The Second World War.* Vol. 2. *Their Finest Hour.* Vol. 3. *Closing the Ring.* Boston: Houghton Mifflin, 1952.

Clark, Mark W. *Calculated Risk.* New York: Harper, 1950.

Cowper, Julia. *The King's Own: The Story of a Royal Regiment.* Vol. 3. *1914–1950.* London: Oxford University Press, 1957.

Cunliffe, Marcus. *The Royal Irish Fusiliers, 1793–1950.* London: Oxford University Press, 1952.

Cunningham of Hyndhope, Viscount Andrew Browne. *A Sailor's Odyssey.* London: Hutchinson, 1953.

Deichmann, Paul. *Designation of Oberbefehlshaber Sud as Supreme Commander in the Mediterranean Theatre in September 1942 Pursuant to Fuehrer's Order.* Statement made at Garmisch on March 31, 1947. U.S. Archives Document MS D-008.

Denham, H. M. *The Aegean: A Sea-Guide to Its Coasts and Islands.* New York: Scribner, 1970.

Eden, Sir Anthony. *The Reckoning.* London: Cassell, 1965.

Ehrman, John. *History of the Second World War. Grand Strategy.* Vol. 5. London: n.p., 1970.

Gander, L. Marsland. *Long Road to Leros.* London: MacDonald & Co., 1945.

Gwyer, M. A. *History of the Second World War. Grand Strategy.* Vol. 3. London: n.p., 1964.

Higgins, Trumbell. *Soft Underbelly.* New York: Macmillan, 1968.

Holland, Jeffrey. *The Aegean Mission: Allied Operations in the Dodecanese, 1943.* Westport, CT: Greenwood Press, 1988.

Howard, Michael. *The Mediterranean Strategy in the Second World War.* London: Weidenfeld & Nicolson, 1968.

Hubatsch, Walther. *War Diary of the OKW.* Vol. 3. *January–December 1943.* Frankfurt: n.p., 1953.

Kay, R. L. *The Long Range Desert Groups in the Mediterranean. Volume of New Zealand Army in World War II.* New Zealand Department of Internal Affairs, War History Branch, Auckland.

Kent, Johnny. *One of the Few.* London: Kimber, 1971.

King, Ernest J. and Walter, M. Whitehall. *Fleet Admiral King.* New York: Norton, 1952.

Knight, C. R. B. *Historical Records of the Buffs: Royal East Kent Regiment, 1919–1948.* London: Medici Society, 1951.

Levi, Aldo, and Fioravanio Giseppe. *Avvenimenti in Egeo dopo l'armistizio (Rodi, Lero e isole minori)* . Rome, Italy: Ufficio Storico della Marina Militare, 1972.

Logwick, John. *The Filibusters.* London: Methuen, 1947.

Mancione, Gino. *I Martiri dell'Egeo, L'amaro volto di una tragedia Italiana.* Rome, Italy: Casamari, 2001.

Metzsch, Friedrich-August von. *Die Geschichte der 22. Infanterie-Division, 1939–1945.* Kiel: H. H. Podzun, 1952.

Packer, Edwin. *Hard Lesson in the Aegean: Purnell History of the Second World War.* London: n.p., 1968.

Parish, Michael Woodbine. *Aegean Adventures, 1940–43.* Sussex, England: The Book Guild, 1992.

Playfair, I. S.O. *The Mediterranean and the Middle East.* Vols. 1, 2, and 4. London: Her Majesty's Stationery Office, 1967–70.

Pope, Dudley. *Flag 4.* London: Kimber, 1954

Richards, Denis, and George Saunders. *The Royal Air Force, 1939–45.* Vol. 2. *The Flight Avails.* London: Her Majesty's Stationery Office, 1954.

Rintelen Gen. Enno von. *The German-Italian Co-Operation During World War II.* Statement made on April 21, 1947. U.S. Archives Document MS B-495.

Rissik, David. *The Durham Light Infantry at War.* Durham, England: Durham Light Infantry, 1953.

Roskill, S. W. *The War at Sea.* Vol. 3, Part 1. London: Her Majesty's Stationery Office, 1960.

Roskill, Stephen. *Churchill and the Admirals.* London: Collins, 1977.

Schenk, Peter. *Krieg um die Ägäis.* Hamburg, Germany: Verlag E. S. Mittler & Sohn GmbH, 2000.

Seidemann, Hans. *Commitment of the Second Air Force OB SUD, Beginning November 1941until Allied landings in November 1942.* Statement made on May 9, 1947. U.S. Archive Document MS. D-160.

Smith, Peter C. *Destroyer Leader.* Barnsley: Pen & Sword, 2004.

———. *Luftwaffe Colors, Junkers Ju 87 Dive-Bomber.* Vols. 1 & 2. *1939–45.* London: Classic Publications, 2006.

———. *Ship Strike!* Shrewsbury: Airlife, 1998.

Stimson, Henry L., and McGeorge Bundy. *On Active Service in Peace and War.* New York: Harper, 1948.

Sutherland, David. *He Who Dares: Recollections of Service in SAS, SBS, and MI5.* London: Leo Cooper, 1998.

Taprell, Dorling, writing as Taffrail. *Eastern Mediterranean, 1942–45.* London: Hodder & Stoughton, 1947.

Tedder, Lord Arthur. *With Prejudice.* London: Cassell, 1966.

Thursfield, H. G. *Fuehrer's Naval Conferences. Brassey's Naval Annual.* London: Brassey's, 1948.

Tidy, Doug. "Dodecanese Disaster and the Battle of Simi." Talk given by Squadron Leader Tidy on December 14, 1967, to South African Military History Society.

Tinker-Benyon, W. E. *Dust upon the Sea.* London: Hodder & Stoughton, 1947.

Ward, S. G. P. *Faithful: The Story of the D.L.I.* London: Thomas Nelson, 1963.

Wilson, Henry Maitland. *Despatch: Middle East Operation, 16th February 1943 to 8th January 1944.* Published as a supplement to the *London Gazette.*

———. *Eight Years Overseas.* London: Hutchinson, 1948.

Willis, A. U. *Naval Operations, Aegean.* Published as a supplement to the *London Gazette.*

Index

Page numbers in italics indicate illustrations.

Stackpole Military History Series

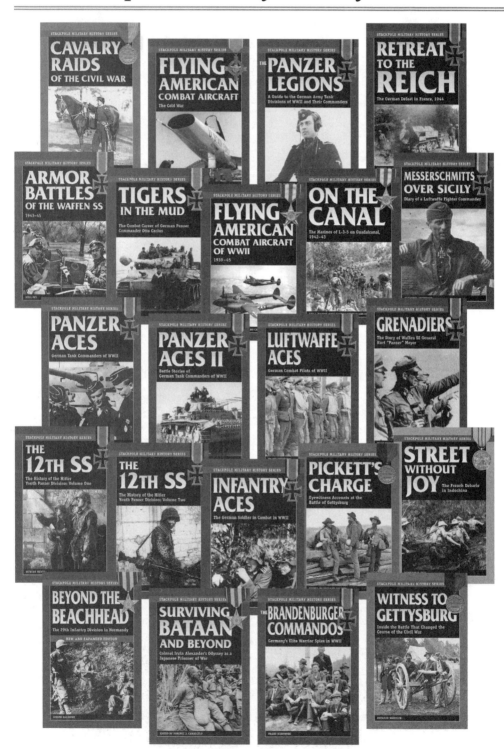

Real battles. Real soldiers. Real stories.

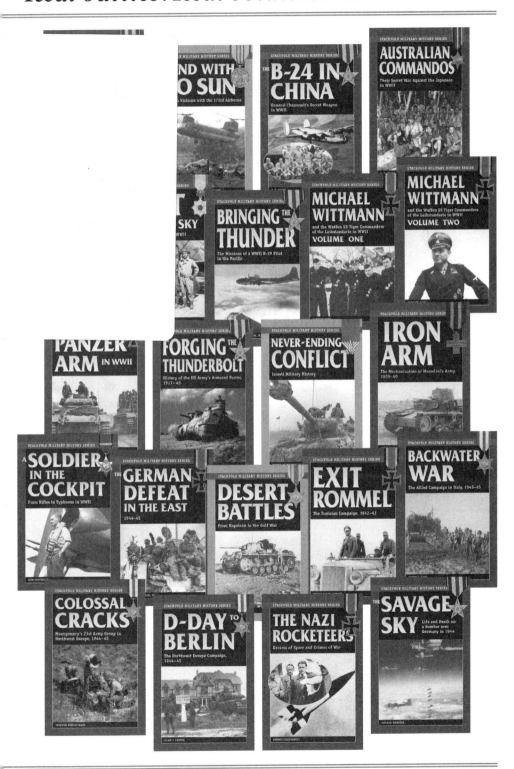

Stackpole Military History Series

Real battles. Real soldiers. Real stories.

Stackpole Military History Series

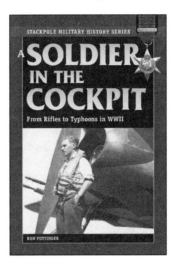

A SOLDIER IN THE COCKPIT
FROM RIFLES TO TYPHOONS IN WORLD WAR II
Ron Pottinger

In October 1939, barely a month after World War II
erupted in Europe, Ron Pottinger was conscripted into the
British Army as a rifleman in the Royal Fusiliers. A year
later, amidst pilot shortages due to losses during the Battle
of Britain, he transferred to the Royal Air Force, where he
began flying the 7.5-ton Hawker Typhoon fighter. He flew
dozens of dangerous ground-attack missions over occupied
Europe through bad weather, heavy flak, and enemy
fighters before being shot down in early 1945 and ending
the war in a German prisoner of war camp.

$16.95 • Paperback • 6 x 9 • 256 pages • 91 photos

WWW.STACKPOLEBOOKS.COM
1-800-732-3669

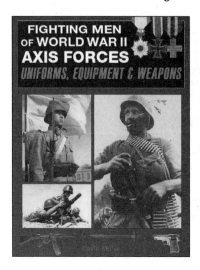
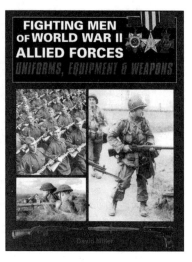